Challenging Trans

and Work

The Knowledge Economy and Education
Volume 2

Scope:

The aim of this series is to provide a focus for writers and readers interested in exploring the relation between the knowledge economy and education or an aspect of that relation, for example, vocational and professional education theorised critically.

It seeks authors who are keen to question conceptually and empirically the causal link that policymakers globally assume exists between education and the knowledge economy by raising: (i) epistemological issues as regards the concepts and types of and the relations between knowledge, the knowledge economy and education; (ii) sociological and political economic issues as regards the changing nature of work, the role of learning in workplaces, the relation between work, formal and informal learning and competing and contending visions of what a knowledge economy/knowledge society might look like; and (iii) pedagogic issues as regards the relationship between knowledge and learning in educational, community and workplace contexts.

The series is particularly aimed at researchers, policymakers, practitioners and students who wish to read texts and engage with researchers who call into question the current conventional wisdom that the knowledge economy is a new global reality to which all individuals and societies must adjust, and that lifelong learning is the strategy to secure such an adjustment. The series hopes to stimulate debate amongst this diverse audience by publishing books that: (i) articulate alternative visions of the relation between education and the knowledge economy; (ii) offer new insights into the extent, modes, and effectiveness of people's acquisition of knowledge and skill in the new circumstances that they face in the developed and developing world, (iii) and suggest how changes in both work conditions and curriculum and pedagogy can led to new relations between work and education.

Challenging Transitions in Learning and Work

Reflections on Policy and Practice

Edited by

Peter Sawchuk
University of Toronto, Canada

Alison Taylor
University of Alberta, Canada

SENSE PUBLISHERS
ROTTERDAM / BOSTON / TAIPEI

A C.I.P. record for this book is available from the Library of Congress.

ISBN: 978-90-8790-887-4 (paperback)
ISBN: 978-90-8790-888-1 (hardback)
ISBN: 978-90-8790-889-8 (e-book)

Published by: Sense Publishers,
P.O. Box 21858, 3001 AW
Rotterdam, The Netherlands
http://www.sensepublishers.com

Printed on acid-free paper

TABLE OF CONTENTS

PETER H. SAWCHUK AND ALISON TAYLOR

1. UNDERSTANDING CHALLENGING TRANSITIONS IN LEARNING AND WORK

INTRODUCTION

The purpose of this volume is to present both a critical and expansive exploration of learning and work transitions. In part, it is a response to contemporary understandings of the relationships between education, lifelong learning and the knowledge economy. Taken as a whole, this volume is aligned with research that has recognized that learning and work transitions are increasingly complex, extended across the life course, differentiated and in turn differentiating across social groups. In this sense, our response can be seen as being critical of the homogenization of diverse experiences. What is the nature of the transitions for different social groups? Are these transitions the same as or different from those presumed by dominant 'school-to-work' notions that continue to inform policy? And, perhaps the most important question of all that we ask: *How?* How do these challenging transitions emerge and how are they navigated? To answer such questions we suggest the need to expand concepts of transitions.

Our collection begins from a set of premises that are different from those of the dominant policy and research traditions. As we make clear in this introduction, the volume presents an expanded *critical vocationalism* approach to learning/work transitions. These transitions we feel are *challenging* for those enmeshed in them and need to be *actively challenged* through critical research we report. We present a range of detailed discussion and analysis across different dimensions of learning/work relations: transitions from education *to* work, from work *to* education, and transitions *within* educational and training systems, occupational and work life. Throughout, we emphasize the need to develop ways of understanding the context, social differences and power relations that define how learning capacities are productive and reproductive of uneven social and economic prosperity.

Beyond an interest in recognizing context, differences and power, the *critical vocationalism* perspective taken up in this volume also provides us with a particular orientation to informal dimensions of transitions, learning and experience. While this volume does not fixate strictly on these informal dimensions, they remain a strong, underlying theme in virtually all contributors' attempts to engage in research into challenging transitions. Indeed, one of the major contributions of a critical vocationalist approach is its interest to recognize learning and experience throughout its full range of variation that in the final instances allows us to better

P. Sawchuk and A. Taylor (eds.), Challenging Transitions in Learning and Work: Reflections on Policy and Practice, 1–24.

understand the complexity of learning/work transitions throughout the life course. We claim that beyond rhetorical flourishes the informal dimensions of learning and experience are rarely recognized in a meaningful way within dominant theoretical or policy-based transitions research.

In our view, there are explanations for this omission of meaningful attention to informal learning and experience in transitions research. We argue this is because informalized dimensions of learning and experience do not fit comfortably with approaches (implicitly or explicitly) committed to individualization and the commodification of learning and experience. Given the socially embedded and, not infrequently, collective nature of informal learning processes and outcomes, they remain difficult to credentialized. Moreover, careful attention to the informalized dimensions of learning and experience admit what most mainstream approaches to transitions, education and work simply cannot: the negative as well as the positive outcomes of learning – the good, the bad and the ugly. A critical vocationalism approach, in this sense, demands attention to the experience of barriers and the individual and group scarring that result as every bit as predictable as positive outcomes of participation in schooling, training, the workplace, and the transitions between them. Given that challenging transitions are rarely formally recognized as anything but aberrant problems, we claim that attention to informal learning and experience tends to illuminate such transitions not as aberrations but as latent institutional functions.

The impetus for this volume, its conceptual framing and much of the research emerges from the team of Canadian researchers who together completed case study and survey projects within the Social Science and Humanities Research Council of Canada's 'Work and Lifelong Learning' (WALL) network (2002–2007) (see *www.wallnetwork.ca*) led by D.W. Livingstone. This network was composed of researchers from seven universities and myriad community groups, unions and associations from across Canada. While all of the research in this volume is Canadian-based, half of the contributions emerge directly from the research, discussion and debate of the WALL network. The 12 case studies of WALL were qualitative in nature and, while not all of these are represented in the volume for those that are the specificities of relevance are noted in individual chapters. In several instances, these case studies also involved small-scale surveying of particular occupational groups and/or workplaces which are, likewise, described in individual chapters. The large WALL Canadian national survey of learning and work practices generated a sample of over 9000 respondents. It is described in Chapter 2 of this volume, and is referenced in several other chapters as well. This survey is the largest of its kind to date and serves as an important counter-balance to the focused, qualitative studies of the volume. With this WALL research as a foundation, the remaining half of the contributions to this volume – Chapters 3–8, 12 and 16 – were selected as dialogic complements that extended and deepened our understanding of challenging learning/work transitions in particular areas.

Finally, we note that while research in this volume is Canadian its significance is not limited to this national context alone. The WALL research network functioned in the context of international debate and reflection. It included a team of international research advisors (from Europe, South America and Australia) whose perspectives constantly informed its findings and interpretation. To further sharpen comparative assessment, the introductory and concluding chapters speak directly to how the research relates to other national situations and research. Moreover, as available comparative transitions research and, not least of all, the global economic events of 2008–2009 that demonstrated trans-national interdependency have shown, it seems clear to us that insights from individual countries can and should be used to shed light on others. In fact it may be the case that the Canadian context encourages comparative insights all the more given its historical admixture of economic, labour market and labour relations legacies. That is, these legacies have clear roots in anglo-European, franco-European as well as American models. And, one final way that this research on transitions may have inherent comparative value lies in the fact that Canada (like, for example, Norway) has achieved particularly high rates of educational attainment. In this sense, given the fixation in so many countries (including in Canada) on educational attainment as a solution to problems of contemporary learning/work transition, this situation suggests Canadian research may serve as a one among a small group of other particularly relevant contexts from which to begin critical re-evaluation. Indeed, the truth of the relationship between educational attainment and learning/ work transitions is a contradictory one, as we hope to show, but our point is that consideration of the Canadian context may encourage further critical appreciation of research and policy issues actively being considered in one's own country. Of course, none of this can erase the differences between national contexts. And, this is why we discuss such differences in our introductory and concluding chapters. As such and with such supports in place, our sense is that readers – aware of the specificities of their own and possibly other national contexts – will be able to see the *forest* of comparable dynamics amidst the *trees* of national differences.

ECONOMIC CONTEXT OF LEARNING/WORK TRANSITIONS

Before proceeding further with our introduction we want to take a moment, however, to briefly present our understanding of the economic context within which different perspectives on learning/work transitions are figured. Significant economic instability around the globe at press time makes any simple contextualization problematic. Uncertainty within virtually all major, international comparative reports on economic and labour market conditions provides us with little choice but to take a medium-term outlook of both the past and future.

In these terms, an important point to begin with derives from observations published by the Organization for Economic Cooperation and Development (OECD). This literature acknowledges that over the last two decades advanced capitalist countries have seen sustained growth in labour market participation along with a growth in the number of jobs workers tend to have in their working lives (OECD 2008). While beginning in 2008 this trend made a reversal – short of major social and economic restructuring – in all likelihood it will return. Over a slightly longer period we also see that not only formal educational attainment but participation in a range of non-compulsory learning/training have likewise grown

(OECD 1998, 2001). Particularly significant for us, however, is that the OECD (2008) has confirmed that a wide variety of forms of labour market discrimination remain a serious issue in virtually all member countries (including G10 countries), and that treatment based on a range of social differences (including gender, age, disability and race/ethnicity) have continued to play a crucial role in the growing disparities in employment participation as well as in disparities in the quality of employment. Reporting on data just prior to accelerated global turmoil, this same 2008 OECD report goes on to provide indications that traditional labour market transitions were already increasingly fragile and exclusionary. Related to this, it was also reported that the number of so-called 'stepping stones' required by youth to solidify a place in the labour market appeared to be multiplying. In fact, for both youth and adults the number of jobs in a working life has continued to rise over the medium-term, and to make matters more complicated still the OECD (2008) also identified that (undeclared) informal employment was likewise expanding.

Informing our concern for challenging transitions, our summary interpretation of these matters suggests a trend of both polarization. In the language of labour market segmentation theorists, primary labour markets (i.e. good jobs) are likely shrinking in relation to overall labour force participation. Workers in primary labour markets retain a capacity to positively cope with and experience forms of (relative) control in the course of their transitions, either laterally or vertically, and in the medium-term past and future have and will see either stable or growing remuneration. Within the growing secondary labour market, however, structural factors appear to have created distinctive forms of complex learning/work transitions, and in so doing bring questions of social difference and non-linearity into even sharper relief.

In relation to this interpretation of global economic context, equally important is how organizations such as the OECD and many member states understand available solutions. While, recognizing a role for state regulation rhetorically, the dominant tendency still appears to presume growth of labour market opportunities in general to be the key technical fix. From a public policy perspective, this continues to translate into an allegiance to viewing educational and vocational training attainment as the only viable mode of public intervention. Obviously, such tendencies set a specific course in policy, practice and understandings of learning/work transitions which continue to marginalize differentiated and differentiating experiences.

In this sense, the economic context and way it is understood by mainstream policy and research perspectives retains, to our minds, a conviction that suitable education, training and informal learning environments associated with work, if further developed, have the capacity to generate relatively transparent, equitable and linear learning/work transitions. Such perspectives comfortably admit that in a knowledge economy these transitions may be more learning-intensive and multi-institutional. But, as we will see below, such perspectives retain a privileged place, implicitly or explicitly, for particular conceptual touch-stones: namely, post-industrialist, human capital and rational choice theories. And, resting on a generalized growth solution, in these formulations education is regarded, unproblematically, as the primary response to satisfying social and economic need vis-à-vis individualized cost-benefit decisions. It is within such approaches that – despite the economic context we summarize here – learning/work transitions will more than likely continue to be subject to a homogenizing and normalizing, rather than critical and differentiated consideration.

ASSAYING THE LITERATURE AND ESTABLISHING OUR FRAMEWORK

As Staff and Mortimer (2003) comment: 'A diverse set of life changes mark the transition from adolescence to adulthood, including school completion, entry into the full-time labor force, and economic self-sufficiency' (p. 361). As a host of researchers have likewise confirmed, transitions to work have become more extended and complex (e.g., Marsden, 1999; Sackmann and Wingens, 2003; Hannan, Raffe and Smyth, 1997; Van Berkel and Hornemann Møller, 2002; López Blasco, McNeish and Walther, 2003; Walther and Pohl, 2005; McVicar and Anyadike-Danes, 2002; Breen, 2005; Anisef, Axelrod, Baichman-Anisef, James and Turrittin, 2000; Evans, 2002; Grubb, 1996). Indeed, amidst this complexity some have gone so far as to suggest the term 'transitions' to have lost its analytic value (e.g., Brooks 2007). However, it seems that many others, like us, have simply begun to recognize the need to expand how we think about transitions in order to examine the concept of learning and work transitions more carefully for their multiple, differentiated and non-linear dimensions. In this section we wish to register some related disciplinary traditions as well as the most pronounced bodies of learning/work transitions research that form, either implicit or explicit, companions to the material in this volume.

In this context it is important from the start for us to note that this collection is rooted in but not confined to educational studies, broadly conceived. It offers, as we have said, a (critical) *vocationalist* perspective. But vocationalist perspectives are hardly alone in their consideration of transitions. This volume contrasts and dialogically engages with a series of other traditions with vitally important points to make of their own. Minimally, these include sociology attending to life transitions and biography, trans-disciplinary studies of the life course, the life history tradition, institutionalist and neo-institutionalist sociology, political science, economics, and so on. Among these many choices of perspective, for us two traditions stand out however. And, although the linkage to them are more implicit than explicit, it is relevant to begin by briefly registering each in order to better situate our own vocationalist approach.

First, life course research (e.g., Mortimer and Shanahan 2003; Sackmann and Wingens 2003) including the many contemporary, multi-disciplinary applications of the 'life course approach' have expanded at an accelerated pace over the last two decades. This includes those drawing on the tradition to inform health and epidemiology, gerontology, studies in marriage, family, drug addiction, obesity, sports, crime, housing and urban studies, immigration, consumer behaviour and social policy to name only a cross-section of applications. Our approach is distinct from this tradition, but to our minds linkages to it retain important potential given our interest in expanding understandings of learning/work transitions that inevitably must incorporate such wide-ranging issues as well. That is, while some of these topics are registered in contributions to this volume many others are beyond its present scope, and thus we see a future for critical perspectives on learning/work transitions as necessarily including these other, sometimes life-defining, matters. Minimally, it is unlikely that health, family-life, participation in the criminal justice system and housing – as assessed in the life course research tradition – can remain separate from full appreciations for the factors that shape the many forms and periods of learning/work transition.

Likewise, given our concern for broadening learning/work transitions research, neo-institutional analysis offers an additional, broad tradition with clear connections to our goals in this volume despite it being beyond our present scope. Having origins in several disciplinary homes (e.g., economics, sociology, political science and more recently organizational studies), neo-institutional approaches over the past two decades have established relevant means of assessing how institutional practices are conditioned by relationships with other, mediating institutions. For example, as we see in this volume, labour market participation is understood in relation to education, apprenticeship programs, the labour processes, the states, and so on. The complex circuits suggested by neo-institutional approaches provide examples of what we refer to in this volume as inter-institutional dynamics. Neo-institutional perspectives also have, as of late, developed an interest beyond simply the reproduction of organizational structures, rules, norms, and so on. They have, for example, provided accounts of inter-institutional isomophorism to generate relevant theories of embedded agency, often connected to the analysis of social position and fields of action. Questions of inter-institutional competition (for legitimacy as well as resources; e.g., DiMaggio and Powell, 1991), the de-coupling of institutional functions to provide flexibility in response to increasingly tight inter-institutional networks (e.g., Scott, 2001) have a family resemblance to the matters which our volume explores.

Both the life course and the neo-institutionalist traditions remain implicit resources for further development of our perspective here. They remain implicit rather than explicit, but retain the potential for fruitful, future research and dialogue. In turning toward learning/work transitions research itself however, there are several important sets of companion works and bodies of work that we wish to brief register as well.

First, we see that the bulk of research confirms a substantial understanding of youth oriented, school-to-work transitions. These include the especially informative work by Shavit and Müller (1998), Stern and Wagner (1999), and contributions to Heinz (1999; see also Heinz, 2002). In Canada specifically, recent scholarship can be found in book form in Gaskell and Rubenson (2004), Scheutze and Sweet (2003) and Krahn (1996). Some of the material above utilizes a life course perspective, but the bulk offers a critical reflection on contemporary relations of transitions including both detailed qualitative analysis as well as structural and policy effects regarding, in particular, educational experiences and occupational outcomes. For example, matters discussed include standardized and occupationally specific curriculum and stratification (e.g., Shavit and Müller, 1998), the restructuring of vocational education and apprenticeships for better transitions (e.g., Stern and Wagner, 1999), biographical orientations to schooling and work (e.g., Heinz, 1999, 2002), and the shifting effects of human capital on school-to-work transitions and its relationship to occupational segregation (e.g.,

Gaskell and Rubenson, 2004). Though our volume is interested in more than simply youth transitions and we are arguably more intensive in our tracing of the effects of social differences and power relations, taken together these sources form a relevant backdrop and recommended companions to the types of questions we raise.

Distinct from these examples of key pieces of research are the largely separate Canadian and European survey analyses of transitions currently available. In this research, again we see the focus tends to be on youth primarily, and that there is less interest in understanding the interlocking mechanisms of difference and power. Nevertheless, we can begin by noting that Canada's best survey data base for understanding youth transitions has been recently compiled. The Youth in Transition Survey (YITS) was developed as a longitudinal means of collecting data beginning with two age groups producing its first cycle in 1999. The first group was aged 15 and the second 18–20 years. In total, almost 52,000 youth from across Canada participated in the first cycle of the survey. The first follow-up survey took place in 2002 and included over 40,000 youth, and the second follow-up survey interviews took place in 2004 including over 37,000 youth respondents. This has produced a range of cohort and sequence analyses to date (e.g., Clark, 2000; Bowlby and McMullen, 2002; Zeman, Knighton and Bussière, 2004; Livingstone, 2004; Shaienks, Eisl-Culkin and Bussiére, 2006; Shaienks and Gluszynski, 2007; Hango and de Broucker, 2007, Krahn and Taylor, 2005). We consider this another important companion to understanding the dynamics of transitions we explore in this volume. Despite its focus on youth, it broadens appreciation for the sticking points at definitive periods of the transition process, and allows the testing of observations emerging from the qualitative studies here and elsewhere. With the existence of similar longitudinal data sets, such as the European Community Household Panel (1994–2001; e.g., Peracchi, 2002; Brzinsky-Fay, 2007), this research, in turn, allows additional capacity to compare Canadian data with those gathered in European countries to add further substance to models of, for example, generalized vocational tracks versus highly structured ones, universalized benefits and supports policies versus highly targeted ones, and so on. Again, like the resources we have already registered, these studies provide a valuable backdrop for understanding the findings reported in this volume.

Having taken a moment to recognize some companion traditions outside of learning/work transitions research, and two separate clusters of research within it, we now turn our attention to properly situating our vocationalist perspective in specific terms in the remainder of this section. Indeed, to begin to analytically grasp the wide variation in transitions research, we draw on a basic continuum for comparing and contrasting approaches either implicit or explicit across available quantitative, qualitative and policy-based research including those already cited. We suggest that this literature can be understood in light of the continuum running between *new vocationalism* and *critical vocationalism* approaches. We use the term 'continuum' here to resist dichotomizing the differences. While maintaining that distinctions do exist, in fact, most of the work we have just registered only rarely falls easily onto one end of the continuum or another.

In its most extreme form *new vocationalism*, as we use the term in this collection, is defined by the argument that narrowly prescribed occupationally-specific knowledge and skill sets are becoming less important within contemporary, fast-paced, global market economy. Replacing them are abilities related to independence, evaluation, conflict resolution and team-work (see discussion by Lehmann, 2000). An important distinction here is that this argument is centred on *adaptation* of workers to the needs of the economy. For this, a touch-stone of new vocationalism is the notion of 'human capital' (cf. Gaskell and Rubenson, 2004). However, the human capital thesis, and the utility-maximization research of Nobel laureate Gary Becker (1964) specifically, did not simply appear from thin air. Rather, it along with the new vocationalism approach developed an educational and training as well as life, occupational and career development perspective standing on the shoulders of a broader thesis on society and economy; one with European but in particular American roots in the post-World War Two era. The 'industrialism/post-industrialism thesis' summarized early in the work of Kerr, Dunlop, Harbinson and Myers (1960; see Sawchuk, 2006 for further explanation) has for almost a half a century articulated and developed extensive research reflected by key, contemporary presumptions of new vocationalism. That is, education and training are the prime means through which individuals develop capacities for an increasingly information/knowledge-centred economy (e.g., Touraine, 1971; Bell, 1973; Zuboff, 1988; Frenkel, Korczynski, Shire and Tam, 1999). These complementary approaches argue that changing skill requirements in the workplace have been caused by new technologies as well as flatter, looser and more 'flexible' organizational structures which emphasize individuality and problem-solving. In later iterations, such approaches promoted the idea that all workers need to be symbolic analysts or knowledge workers (e.g., Reich, 1991; Grubb, 1996). Indeed, the coherence between post-industrialism thinking and new vocationalism is, to our minds, both remarkable and remarkably persistent.

Powerful supports for the new vocationalism perspective are to be found amongst virtually all OECD policy literature and economic outlook material (OECD 1996, 1998; 2001, 2004, 2008). The World Bank and the International Monetary Fund, likewise, now orient to, amongst other matters, the issue of lifelong learning, work and human capital generation as well. Such policy views have taken a lifelong learning perspective on transitions including both youth and adult/continuing forms. As primarily an individual/adaptive perspective however it has inherent difficulties admitting structural contradictions rooted in both institutions of education and economy. Necessarily such perspectives presume that better and more responsive education, continuing education, vocational and workplace training – for youth, employed and unemployed adults, from 'cradle to the grave' (OECD 1996) – can adequately address the types of problems we identified earlier in our summary of economic, labour market and transitions context. Of course, the new vocationalism perspective has begun to register informal learning in the life course. To date, however, this appears both selective and persistently difficult to apply concretely vis-à-vis anything but rhetorical flourishes. What may be particularly relevant to note, however, is that in its individual/adaptive orientation what is – indeed what must be – presumed first and foremost is that neither young nor established workers currently possess the necessary capacities to effectively live and work in the present and future economy. They are in (perhaps a permanent state of) deficit. This is a presumption that we challenge both in this volume and elsewhere (e.g., Taylor, 2005; Lehmann and Taylor 2003; Livingstone and Sawchuk, 2004).

We are not alone in this view (e.g., Kincheloe, 1999; Griffin, 1999; Hunt, 1999; Evans, 2002; Evans, Hodkinson and Unwin, 2002; Coffield, 2007), but the international summary provided by Bynner (2001) brings additional focus in this regard. He offers a critique of the 'economism' inherent in mainstream views of transitions specifically. Our volume shares this view as well. National and international policy continues to construct transitions in a specific way: "the starting point being the immature unemployable child and the end point the independent employable adult" (Bynner, 2001, p. 5), yet it is an end point perpetually receding. Bynner's solution is to instead think in terms of the "interconnectedness of activity across the different domains of life" (p. 7). For him, there is a distinct lack of attention to broader political climate, culture and the effects of other spheres of institutional and non-institutionalized life as dimensions of the transitions process.

Offering an alternative, political/analytic approach *Critical vocationalism* challenges most if not all of the presumptions of post-industrialism, human capital, rational choice theory, new vocationalism and their associated policy expressions. However, just as new vocationalism has important intellectual roots in industrialism/ post-industrialism thinking, so too does critical vocationalism have roots in critical analyses of gender (see review in Griffin, 1985; Sharpe, 1994), race (see review in Galabuzi, 2006), disability (e.g., Oliver, 1996) and social class (e.g., Braverman, 1974). As we have shown elsewhere (e.g., Lehmann and Taylor, 2003), the reality behind the rhetoric of new vocationalism is that it has tended to ignore or at least minimize how education systems – hand-in-glove with labour markets and work systems – are shaped by the tensions and contradictions inherent within processes of control, conflict, accommodation and occasionally resistance. There remains, in Livingstone's (2004) terms, a significant 'education-jobs gap' that continues to be either ignored, under-recognized or mis-interpreted in the new vocationalism tradition (see also Roberts, 2003; Osterman, 1996). Likewise, social divisions are perpetuated and in fact intensified under these conditions vis-à-vis the relationship between biographical agency, social structures and social histories (see contributions to Heinz, 1999 and particularly Heinz, 2002). And in summary, our observations result in the following, initial points of emphasis we wish to note regarding our critical vocationalism perspective on learning/work transitions:

a) vocational education and training, including attention to informal on-the-job learning has intensified as people are staying in school longer and availing themselves more frequently of adult, continuing education as well as training opportunities;
b) vocational training is increasingly important for securing employment in competitive, increasingly internationalized labour markets;
c) skills and knowledge developed in vocational preparation are not effectively utilized in the labour process;

d) labour processes are just as likely to reduce the use of judgment, autonomy and discretion by narrowing the terms of performance as they are to require independence, flexibility and creative problem-solving;
e) experiences and 'biographical agency' are socially differentiated across relations of dis/ability, gender, race and class lines.

In keeping with our recognition that simple dichotomies do little justice to understanding the distinctions between new vocationalism and critical vocationalism perspectives, it is important to not conclude our comments here without registering overlaps. Clearly, we see that 'human capital' approaches over the last decade in particular have expanded to include notions of 'social capital'; a revelation that has expanded the application of the basic capital accumulation metaphor to collective practices, interrelations and social structures which suggests a movement toward a more critical analysis in some cases. Considerations of social capital, while popular, have seemed to remain secondary to transitions-related policy to date however. Likewise, if we associate a narrow labour market orientation with new vocationalism, we might just as well observe that a great deal of transitions studies oriented by critical vocationalism have not consistently dealt with an expansive inter-institutional perspective that takes into account what actually happens at work. Many critical approaches remain fixated on the distribution of education and training generally, often continuing to ignore a variety of specific social groups, and focusing simply job attainment rather than the quality of these experiences.

With these types of caveats in mind, to our minds it remains relevant to position this volume on the critical vocational end of the continuum we have just outlined. And, having outlined our approach in broad strokes, we can now specify with additional details that will be useful in understanding the collection as a whole.

EXISTING LITERATURE AND EXPANDING THINKING ABOUT LEARNING WORK TRANSITIONS

In seeking to expand understandings of transitions from a critical vocationalism perspective, it is important to first ask ourselves what types of variables and mechanisms have been associated with challenging transitions to date in the research. As we mentioned earlier, understood as 'learning and work transitions' specifically, the most detailed research has tended to focus on youth and early adulthood. As such, this is where we begin. At the same time, it may be the case that studies of youth and early adulthood offer some points of general guidance for understanding transitions more broadly.

Beginning with recent Canadian research on youth transitions, we see that there are a variety of social variables that shape the patterns of transition and marginalization in and out-of high school and post-secondary education, and then into and out-of the labour market. Several key social variables are strongly correlated with specific transitional pathways. The detailed Canadian survey research of Hango and de Broucker (2007) for example substantiate this well. These variables include gender where being female strongly correlates with transition interruptions as well as incidences of returning to school. Aboriginal ancestry has shown a strong negative correlation with engaging in continuous education transitions toward labour market participation. People living in urban centers in Canada are much more likely to return to school. And finally, experiencing a disability has shown amongst the strongest negative correlations with both continuous education and disrupted transitions to and within the labour market. Not well covered in the Hango and de Brouker analysis (2007), however, we note some specific figures on transitions for immigrants within Canada. According to Gilmore (2008), we see that for immigrant youth, unemployment was highest among those of African and Eastern European origin, followed by those youth born in Latin American, West Central Asian or the Middle Eastern countries. Youth unemployment for Canadian youth was lowest for those from Southern Asian countries, and virtually all immigrant youth groups show higher levels of unemployment and poorer quality employment than Canadian-born youth.

Looking beyond Canada, analysis of international data, for example, in Breen's assessment of 27 OECD countries (2005), highlights a variety of similar dynamics, and provides some additional explanation. It argues that two key factors explain differential learning and work transitions from youth and into early adulthood: i) the ability of the educational system to effectively signal the suitability of a job seeker for a specific form of employment; and ii) the degree of employment regulation and specifically the degree to which employers are prevented from dismissing workers more or less easily early in their job tenure. Breen goes on to indicate that despite the call for greater flexible and generalized skill sets, in detailed analysis it is specific skill and knowledge sets taught at schools on a consistent basis that appear to result in stronger youth employment. Close partnerships between industry and educational systems are said to be central. In these terms, Germany, Austria and the Netherlands appear to offer the most effective models of such linkages (though there is variation in how this achieved). Despite Sweden's apparent deviation from specific vocational skill and knowledge set teaching, it still seems to generate relatively high youth employment levels however. It would seem to do this on the basis of strong employment regulation which underlines all the more the importance of paying attention not simply to education but the workplace as suggested earlier in our discussion of critical vocationalism. Countries such as Canada (as well as the UK, the US, Australia) appear to offer neither strong linkages with industry through their general education or vocational education and training streams, nor strong employer regulation and thus suffer from higher levels of youth unemployment, often despite very high levels of educational attainment overall.

Taking a different approach altogether, Brzinsky-Fay's (2007) innovative international comparison of transitions within 10 European countries (using sequence analysis software developed for researching human genetics), highlights quantitatively the importance of many of the points we have associated with a critical vocationalism perspective. Like the Canadian-based research we began with, Brzinsky-Fay makes some important in-roads into understanding questions of universality of experiences to develop characterizations of national 'volatility' and 'integration' vis-à-vis learning and work transitions. Such an approach offers a chance to further challenge the myth of linearity linked to public policy goals.

Contributions to our volume may shed further light on the question of how it is that countries like Germany have generated significantly stronger culture of 'bridging' and 'return' sequences in learning/work transitions when compared, for example, with the UK? Or, thinking beyond the traditional 'General Qualifications' versus 'Vocational Specific Qualifications' frameworks, our volume informs the question of how it is that the countries such as the UK have generated much more successful 'express' transition sequences. Brzinsky-Fay (2007) identifies all of these features of transitional event sequences, and others as well, but how these are produced is less clear. In combination, international comparative analyses such as Breen (2005), Brzinsky-Fay (2007), and others (e.g., Pohl and Walther, 2007) likewise pose important research questions that the type of research presented in this volume can address, particularly so in relation to concerns for non-linearity and its relationship with social differences and power.

In sum, existing research – nationally specific research in Canada as well as international comparative literature – highlights the effects of a range of social differences on learning/work transitions. It also broadens a sense of the types of variables associated with challenging transitions. It demonstrates the need to further understand how non-linear transitions come about, and, in so doing, the complexity of transitions and the need to attend to broader institutional arrangements within and across education and training, the labour market and workplace. The contribution of this volume to these types of findings is by way of posing the questions of how educational signaling and labour market regulation function differently for different social groups, how such things function differently at different points in multiple transitions within and between institutional spheres. These questions are best answered, we suggest, through a combination of careful extension of the issues raised through quantitative research and detailed qualitative, exploratory study of the frequently under-studied groups and contexts. Drawing on these exemplar studies simply as cases in point, we see that nationally specific demographic information is essential for understanding transitions, both the more traditionally focused inter-institutional (e.g., school-to-work/work-to-school) but also the intra-institutional transitions (within education and workplaces), for youth as well as adults.

For a proper understanding of the critical vocationalist perspective that orients this book, however, a few more words on this idea of agency and choice may be necessary. Building on some of the themes referenced immediately above we can say that the quantitative research on learning and work transitions limits access to how it is that people make active, even if limited, choices in constructing their own pathways. Sometimes these choices are made in a rational manner in the course of life planning. Indeed, sometimes these choices (amongst both youth and adults) are made out of an orientation of resistance – whether this is a resistance to forms of schooling, parents, peers, communities among youth, or forms of adult resistance opposing employers, work organizations for example. Whatever the case, it is crucial to know what people choose but also the patterns of choices are rooted in biography, identity, situation and emergent life course. The rationality of such choices is wholly dependent on not simply objective conditions but biographical horizons, and indeed the complex, shifting and subjective interpretations of both. Answering these types of questions demands a thick description of context, relations and dynamics.

Our volume provides such analysis, but on this matter we can also register some invaluable Canadian research on youth to make a broader, general point. Lehmann (2005) shows how working-class youth of differing gender and ethno-racial backgrounds become actively involved in their own streaming into particular work and learning pathways. This is not a new observation in itself, however he goes on to identify 'critical junctures' or points of choice-making that can both transform and reproduce patterns of marginalization in the transition processes. Varying in their moment of appearance in individual lives, the emergence of a concrete orientation to, for example, 'job rewards' appears crucial and more elusive to predict than at first glance. Likewise, moments when clear articulation of autonomy brought on by work – almost universally expressed in the way that youth contrast notions of 'real work' with either part-time work or their studies – are equally crucial, highly variable and related primarily to parental as well as peer group orientations. Our point in this regard is this. The meaning and social relations of transitions to employment as well as transitions within employment are always actively constructed. Youth and adults actively generate the horizons of choice unique to the circumstances which are often shared by their social groups. Processes such as these, once initiated, can have a robust, enduring effect on learning efforts, occupational or career advancement choices and transitions.

A variety of international studies confirm this type of appreciation of the learning/work transition process as well. In Australia, for example, Stokes and Wyn (2007) argue subjective achievements of agency as 'investments in identity [that] foreshadow the emergence of new meanings of careers" (p. 495). Heinz (1999) likewise suggests an emphasis on structured agency as a particularly powerful means to understand transitions to labour markets. In the UK similar arguments in the work of Shildrick and MacDonald (2007), and Furlong, Cartmel, Biggart, Sweeting and West (2003) show how 'at-risk' and 'hard-to-reach' youth from impoverished neighbourhoods follow their life transitions from teens and into adulthood in similar ways. They identified enormous variability and 'unpredictability' in their lives following school (whether exit comes from graduation or dropping-out) that were peppered with periods of unemployment. These transitions feature longer periods of unemployment, longer duration of dependency on parents than generations past. Recognition of forms of human agency are central to these Canadian, Australian and UK examples, following the original example set by Paul Willis (1977), where we perhaps first came face-to-face with how youth play an active, decision-making role in selecting transitions that are most available and most commonly portrayed to them: portrayed to them in ways shaped by identity, the social production of roles, possibilities and limits.

COMPONENTS OF A CRITICAL VOCATIONALISM APPROACH TO TRANSITIONS

At this point we have offered some initial definition and background for a critical vocationalism approach which was then followed by a selective review of literature which raised additional traditions, findings and questions which could be taken up from this perspective. As we have outlined it, a critical vocationalism perspective demands we both look beyond and question the default social spheres and social variables that have largely, though not exclusively, defined the literature on learning/work and transitions to date. In other words, in an era of lifelong learning, 'school-to-work' transition needs to be understood as but one inter-institutional dimension of the broader phenomenon of the learning/work transition complex. Equally important are the learning/work transitions of various specific social groups within the aggregate. Consider for a moment, both the complexity and specificity inherent to the manner in which immigrants to virtually every advanced capitalist countries are forced to engage in uneven, byzantine (if not Kafkaesque) circuits of learning/work transitions that are non-linear, fraught with barriers and regularly mediated by non-school-based occupational regulatory bodies. Alternatively, we could just as easily look at the role of voluntary (unpaid) work, the growth of paid work for students, the growth of continuing education amongst working adults, and the various mediations each of these patterns entail for contemporary learning/work transition circuits. None of this is to presume that linearity is undetectable, at least within the sub-set of successful transitions of particular social groups and individuals within what we earlier referenced as primary labour markets (cf. Furlong, Cartmel, Biggart, Sweeting and West, 2003). It does mean that challenging these normalized, homogenized forms of inter-institutional transitions requires attention to biography, social characteristics as well as the ongoing constructions of social differences within the transition process.

Importantly, our approach seeks to understand how *intra-institutional* transitions also shape the barriers and successes of *inter-institutional* learning/work transitions. For example, opportunities for mobility across programs within secondary and post-secondary institutions clearly inform the possibilities and patterns of inter-institutional transitions. Moreover, intra-institutional transitions might also include transitions between schools and related training systems such as union-based apprenticeship, employer-based apprenticeships, or transitions mediated by national vocational qualification systems as in Britain, or as in Canada, systems of 'employability skills' offered by the Conference Board and later Human Resource and Social Development Canada. And likewise, intra-institutional transitions include movements in and across workplaces. Examples here would include cases where employees undertake employer-based training moving to new positions (i.e., transitions within internal or sectoral labour markets), or in some cases where whole groups of workers must make a transition from one labour process to another signifying a learning/work transition which transforms an entire office, shopfloor, and sometimes even an entire occupational group or sector. A critical vocationalism approach encourages such concerns, and specifically these types of considerations have the capacity to expand our appreciation beyond the 'supply side' of the labour market to illuminate how the capacity of educational or training institutions, as well as employers, workplaces and industry effectively shape learning/work transitions as a whole. Thus, to more clearly put our point, a critical vocationalism perspective requires attention to how transitions are affected deeply by biography, social differences, as well as institutional arrangements and forms of constrained agency or choice. And moreover, efforts to challenge and expand notions of learning/work transitions must recognize that the experience of transition is hardly universal.

Beyond the recognition of inter- and intra-institutional transitions and social differences, we feel it is equally important to also think expansively about the notions of 'learning' and 'work' themselves (e.g., Sawchuk, 2003; Livingstone, 2004; Taylor, 2005). Whereas in the past, conceptions of learning/work transitions were almost strictly rooted in conceptions of 'formal schooling' on the one hand and 'full-time paid work' on the other, it is now recognized that learning is more than 'schooling' and the complexities of employment cannot be expressed in a stagnant notion of 'full-time paid work.' Thus, we now know that formal schooling shapes and is shaped by non-formal learning (i.e., organized learning that takes place beyond the formal, state-regulated credential system) as well as by informal learning (non-organized learning that can take place through self-directed projects or can be done in groups). Furthermore, both scholars and organizations such as the OECD are increasingly registering the fact that paid work is increasingly non-standard (i.e., part-time, seasonal, precarious) and that unpaid work such as volunteering in the community or un-declared employment affects labour market participation, and that paid employment itself contains variation, includes (lateral and vertical) occupational transitions and that entire work processes frequently undergo change.

Thus to summarize the analytic points of departure of our critical vocationalism perspective we can say that it opens up the notion of learning/work transitions on several levels. First, on the specific themes of expanding previously conceptualized notions of transitions in contemporary society, across our collection we critically evaluate:

1. traditional scholarly research on inter-institutional school to work transition policy and practice
2. other inter-institutional transitions including but not limited to apprenticeship programs
3. intra-institutional learning transitions involving linkages between formal education, non-formal education as well as informal learning experiences
4. intra-institutional work-based transitions with attention to informal learning in relation to different types of work, work changes, sectors and occupations.

Second, across each of these expanded notions of 'transitions' we explore social themes oriented by our wish to critically evaluate and challenge:

1. the ***linearity*** of transitions in which either youth or adults undertake one-way progress from learning towards the world of paid work
2. the ***universality*** of transitions by highlighting how social differences including those rooted in gender, race/ethnicity, national origin, social class, disability and age.

As we indicated, we are critical of the presumption that learning/work transitions can be understood as individual, labour market 'supply-side' inadequacies. Thus, on top of these points of analysis and themes our collective argument is that problems of learning/work transitions are rooted in institutional contradictions of capitalist labour markets and labour processes themselves, as well as the economic and social implications of racial, gendered, ageist and ablest structures that are likewise central to generating disparate and inequitable experiences.

A BRIEF INTRODUCTION TO THE CHAPTERS

Each of the contributions to this volume explores aspects of the positions we have introduced above. In unique ways and via distinct empirical foci, the chapters set the stage for a better understanding of the questions inherent in the above comments; answers to which are the subject the concluding chapter of the volume. Our introductions to the two sections of the volume provides further detail, but as an initial orientation to what will come we offer a brief introduction to each chapter below.

Along with this introductory chapter, ***Chapter 2: Age, Occupational Class and Lifelong Learning: Findings of a 2004 Canadian Survey of Formal and Informal Learning through the Life Course*** completes our conceptual and empirical starting point for the volume. In it D.W. Livingstone reports analysis based on the 2004 WALL survey mentioned above. Beginning from the recognition of life course transitional elements broadly, the author suggests both proliferating sub-components and non-linearity are factors in contemporary life course. The analysis focuses on intentional (formalized and informalized) learning activities across this life course amongst cohorts from 18 to over 80 while also recognizing social class divisions. Findings reported in this chapter speak to matters of underemployment/over-education developed in earlier work by the author, and further assessed here. The dynamics between formal and informal learning alter over the life course, though this would appear to be rooted in changing formal rather than informal learning practice. In particular there is a call for greater attention to the extensive learning of both older and working-class people.

Following this, we begin the first of two major sections of the book. The goal of ***Section 1 Learning/Work Transitions – Education and Training***, is to look at critical studies of formal education and training programs designed to help participants transition into work. As with the collection as a whole, in this section there is a focus on the experiences of participants who are 'non-traditional' entrants to particular learning and work sites (e.g., women in trades, students with disabilities, black and working-class youth).

Wolfgang Lehmann and Eric Tenkorang's ***Chapter 3: Leaving University without Graduating: Evidence from Canada's Youth in Transitions Survey*** starts off this section noting that high levels of post-secondary education are seen increasingly as essential for occupational and life course success, as well as the importance of investigating the educational outcomes of groups that have been traditionally excluded from higher education. In this context, socio-economic status (SES) and access to university has tended to retain a positive relationship. However, little is known about how SES affects individuals' university experiences and chances to persist and graduate. These authors carry out an analysis of Canada's Youth in Transition Survey mentioned earlier in this chapter where we see that SES has no significant effects on university attrition when basic logistic regression models are used. The authors then offer an alternative statistical technique to find important effects on university attrition.

Alison Taylor and Evelyn Steinhaurer's ***Chapter 4: Evolving Constraints and Life 'Choices': Understanding Pathways of Students in First Nations Communities*** begins from the observation that the career pathways of First Nations youth do not conform to the linear model that is dominant in policy literature. Through interviews with high school students involved in a provincial career program and other community organizations, they examine the institutional and personal factors that influence the career pathways of First Nations youth in Alberta Canada. The authors' findings suggest that schools on Reservations were constrained by a lack of resources, high student needs, and limited opportunities for career education. Taylor and Steinhauer conclude that these institutional realities must be recognized, and the understandings of young people validated if policymakers and communities are to better support Aboriginal youth in their transitions.

In ***Chapter 5: Educating for Followership – The Hidden Curriculum in Community Colleges*** Anthony Tambureno sheds light on the role of the community college system as a reproductive force in determining employment outcomes. That is, intra-institutionally, within the college system itself, there are important determinants of transition potentials, and indeed the class structure of the broader economy. Tambureno's focus is on the hidden curriculum of the colleges that selectively prepare working-class students for working-class jobs drawing on extensive ethnographic and interview data from Ontario as well as secondary analysis of data from other provinces in Canada and the US.

Michalko and Titchkosky's ***Chapter 6: There and Not There: Presents and Absence of Disability in Transitions from Education to Work*** offers a view, rarely seen in the research literature on learning/work transitions, into the way that disability shapes and is actively produced. Indeed, as they outline, unemployment, under-employment, and labor force non-participation are enormous amongst "persons with disabilities". We see that the role of education in reproducing these dynamics is a powerful one where expectations are ratified through failed accommodation. Employing what is known as the social model of disability, the authors find that undergirding this process are the ideological assumptions of educational environments that help to constitute disability as an unexpected or as a disappearing feature of the transition from learning to work.

In our first contribution to our understanding of the apprenticeship process, in ***Chapter 7: Skilled Trade Training for Women: In Vogue One More Time*** Bonnie Watt-Malcolm analyzes the renewed discussion of women in the trades amongst multiple stake-holders including government, capital, sector councils, unions, contractors, education and training agencies, as well as employees. She offers a critical evaluation of the assumptions underlying attempts to implement training initiatives to recruit and retain women into a sector that has customarily resisted their presence. The analysis reveals that training that takes place off the jobsite may not, in fact, be the most effective means to help women learn how to work in trades work within various industrial sectors.

Karen Carter then offers a fascinating exploratory discussion in ***Chapter 8: Re-Thinking Learning-Work Transitions in the Context of Community Training and Racialized Youth***. Her argument is that traditional training and school-to-work transitions are disproportionately ineffective for racialized youth. Based on participatory observation and interview methods, her research is focuses on the role of the arts and culture industries and the value of community programs. Such programs are seeking to bridge a particularly disenfranchised social group to labour markets with a focus on community-based initiatives dealing with cultural industries such as music, film and new media in the Toronto area.

Pollock's ***Chapter 9: Transitioning to the Teacher Workforce: Internationally Educated Teachers (IETs) as Occasional Teachers*** takes a close look at the growing trend for teachers who are educated in non-western countries entering the Canadian teacher workforce. She focuses on Occassional Teachers, documents the nature of their transitions, and shows these transitions to be seriously challenging. We see that these teachers are challenged in the course of gaining access to work as well as in terms of the actual work in the classroom. The various and intersecting processes of professional marginalization are outlined.

The second section of the book is entitled ***Section 2 Learning/Work Transitions – Work, Career and Life Changes***. It is aimed at exploring social differences in the transition process 'from work to education' as well as within labour markets and the labour process itself. It highlights in several spots the role of workplace change in negotiations over learning and training opportunities.

We begin with Peter Sawchuk's ***Chapter 10: Occupational Transitions within Workplaces Undergoing Change: A Case from the Public Sector***. In keeping with the volume's orientation toward expansive understandings of learning-work transitions, his chapter focuses on what happens once people obtain a job, and how occupational and organizational transitions are interlinked. Drawing on qualitative and quantitative research on the changing nature of welfare benefit delivery work we find multiple layers of transition at play. Central to discussion are the structure of informal learning networks that are crucial for intra-occupational and intra-organizational transitions where we see the importance of changing entry requirements and age cohort divisions.

Chapter 11: Ambiguities in Continuing Education and Training in the Knowledge Economy: The Biopharmaceutical Economic Sector by Paul Bélanger and Stéphane Daniau parallels the theme introduced by Sawchuk in several ways. Their research reports on formal and informal learning trends and contradictions in the bio-pharmaceutical sector as important factors for understanding future developments over the next decade both in this and, indeed, a wide-range of other economic sectors in Canada and elsewhere. The analysis details the differential support given to informal learning among professional groups, the impact of competition between firms on knowledge transfer, as well as how these dynamics can and do shape the development of communities of practice, self-directed learning (within and outside of work).

In keeping with our focus on the transition intrinsic to particular economic sectors and differentiated experiences, in ***Chapter 12: Transitioning into Precarious Work: Immigrants' Learning and Resistance*** Kiran Mirchandiani et al. examine the dynamics of so-called flexibility associated with the new economy. The reality, as the authors point out, is that such dynamics are characterized by the use of temporary and part-time employees within contingent work arrangements which put them 'at-risk'. These workers do not receive the same protection and benefits as the full-time permanent workforce. Based on extensive interviews with female contingent workers (new immigrants) in the Toronto area across a variety of workplaces (e.g., supermarkets, call centers, garment industry) the various roles of social differences in this under-research learning/work transition topic are illuminated.

Next is Shibao Guo's ***Chapter 13: False Promises in the New Economy: Barriers Facing the Transitions of Recent Chinese Immigrants in Edmonton***. Guo expands on the theme of immigration and racialization established by Mirchandani et al. in the previous chapter. He offers a critique of the self-framing of Canada as a country of immigrants, and the land of vast opportunity. Indeed, not unlike many European countries, in the face of an aging labour force and declining fertility, Canada has little choice but to open its doors, but what awaits newcomers falls far short of the imagined 'land of opportunity' that is actively promoted abroad. The author draws on survey research on immigration from the People's Republic of China. Despite that fact that China has become the country's leading source of new Canadians over the last decade and the immigrant experiences concerning transitions remains poorly understood. Although the majority of these immigrants arrived with post-secondary education, many of them face unemployment or underemployment.

Bonnie Slade and Daniel Schugurensky's ***Chapter 14: 'Staring from Another Side, the Bottom': Volunteer Work as a Transition into the Labour Market for Immigrant Professionals*** shows how labour market participation and transitions are linked to the 'paid work bias' by focusing on volunteer work, race and immigration. The authors note that a majority of new immigrants in Canada now fall into the "Skilled Worker" category according to the country's immigration 'point system', and that although there is a good deal of information on the integration of 'highly skilled' immigrants into the Canadian labour market in general, few studies to date have explored the mediating role of volunteer work and informal learning in immigrants' work transitions from their home country to Canada. Based on interview and focus group research as well as secondary analysis of national survey data we see the significant degree to which immigrant workers orient to volunteering as a key means of fixing the broken learning-work transitions they face in Canada.

Elaine Biron and her co-authors next turn our attention to the issue of aging in their ***Chapter 15: Adult Education and the Transition to Retirement***. Extending the observations from previous chapters (e.g., Livingstone's Chapter 2 and Sawchuk's Chapter 9) their analysis shows that, even in the context of lower adult education participation amongst older adults, the contradiction between initial education in early years of one life still predict, to a large degree, not only who will remain active learners in the later portions of the life course, but also who will use adult learning to guide them amidst challenging uncertainties. The authors note important generational patterns in terms of understandings of the role and purpose of adult education.

And finally, in the last analytic chapter of our collection Tara Fenwick and Janice Wallace reconnect with the issue of disability in ***Chapter 16: Transitions in Working Dis/Ability: Able-ing Environments and Disabling Policies***. This chapter bridges many of the concerns about older workers in the previous chapter and issues raised in Chapter 6 (Machalko and Titchkosky). Here the authors point out that as workers increasingly experience age-related changes to their abilities and mobility, particularly with the removal of mandatory retirement policies in most of Canada, issues of disability in the workplace are growing in importance. However, persons with disabilities, despite employers' legal "duty to accommodate", face discrimination in the workplace including informal stigma, marginalization, insufficient provision of necessary support, and stress-producing expectations that they conform to narrow norms defining the 'good employee' and the 'acceptable body'. Fenwick and Wallace show that individuals often encounter a series of transitions between agencies and workplaces, finding themselves and their 'disability' re-inscribed at each point in the learning-work transitions process. More broadly, most workers can expect to experience transition into or out of various levels of disabling conditions that affect their well-being throughout their working lives, including invisible disabilities such as mental illness produced by workplace stress. Building on an expansive notion of formal as well as informal learning they show that issues of identity become sites of struggle for individuals finding themselves avoided and marginalized. The authors conclude that broad workplace policies can be developed to produce holistic able-ing environments.

CONCLUSIONS FOR MOVING FORWARD

Drawing from this diversity of original research allows us to effectively construct a collective, scholarly response to what, as we have argued, are frequently narrow conceptualization of transition processes. Central to constructing this volume has been our critical vocationalism approach that has the goal of illuminating the experiences of those social groups that remain effectively under-served by existing learning and work transitions processes. In our collection's division of labour, for the sake of avoiding repetition, contributors were specifically asked *not* to spend inordinate amounts of space re-hashing the range of transitions literature, but rather to focus on the detail and original contributions of their own empirical work. Situating the contributions against the backdrop of national and international literature, we felt, could be properly dealt with through effective introduction and concluding chapters further supported by concise section introductions. Where suitable, we did ask them to retain observations on method where it is necessary for critical understanding of the material and/or it serves the purpose of expanding understanding of studies in learning/work transitions directly. This way of proceeding, we feel, has yielded an illuminating look at the learning/work transition process which begins from the premise of providing voice to marginalized groups while providing clarity to marginalizing mechanisms that remain under-researched in this sub-field of scholarship.

These are the origins of our work, in brief. However, by way of moving forward into the substance of our collection we offer some final words of invitation and observation. Research on transitions can be potentially dizzying in its variation. Fantastically enough, a literature search for the term 'transition' within the many electronic indices of social science research now available reveals something that has the potential to overwhelm: over a half a million entries! The vast majority of these appear to not relate to issues of education, learning and work as such. In other words, they do not begin from what we understand as a vocationalism perspective. However, the point for us is that conceptualizations of 'transitions' has and will likely increasingly play an enormous role in how researchers come to understand the life course. For a volume of this type then, the practical as well as intellectual challenge of delimiting an understanding of transitions was a necessary and immediate one.

While encouraging readers to push forward critically to expand their own thinking beyond the resources collected here we have, nevertheless, found it necessary to draw some boundaries for the purposes of coherence. Our first tools for this are found in our discussion of vocationalism, including the new vocationalism and critical vocationalism continuum. While broad, it serves as an important orientation for us and we hope readers as well; a specific entry point into the broader field that does, however, distinguish the discussion from the sea of transitions, life course and neo-institutionalist studies that exist.

Based on this, we and our contributors have aimed to develop a perspective with careful attention to a broad array of contexts and social differences. The principles we have outlined, this type of perspective and this attention to differences, we feel, are essential for understanding learning/work transitions: transitions which remain *challenging* to an enormous proportion of the populations of virtually every country and for this reason must continue to be *challenged*.

REFERENCES

Anisef, P., Axelrod, P., Baichman-Anisef, E., James, C., & Turrittin, A. (2000). *Opportunity and uncertainty: Life course experiences of the class of '73*. Toronto: University of Toronto Press.

Becker, G. (1964). *Human capital: A theoretical and empirical analysis, with special reference to education*. Chicago: University of Chicago Press.

Bell, D. (1973). *The coming of the post-industrial society*. New York: Basic Books.

Bowlby, G. (2005). Provincial drop-out rates – trends and consequences. In *Education matters* (Vol. 2, No. 4) (Cat., 81-004-XIE). Ottawa: Statistics Canada.

Braverman, H. (1974). *Labor and monopoly capital: The degradation of work in the twentieth century*. New York: Monthly Review Press.

Breen, R. (2005). Explaining cross national variation in youth unemployment: Market and institutional factors. *European Sociological Review, 21*(2), 125–134.

Brooks, R. (2007). Transitions from education to work in the twenty-first century. *International Journal of Lifelong Education, 26*(5), 491–493.

Brzinsky-Fay, C. (2007). Lost in transition: Labour entry sequence for school leavers in Europe. *European Sociological Review, 23*(4), 409–422.

Bynner, J. (2001). British youth transitions in comparative perspective. *Journal of Youth Studies, 4*(1), 5–23.

Clark, W. (2000). 100 years of education. In *Canadian social trends* (Winter) (Cat.11-008-XIE). Ottawa: Statistics Canada.

Coffield, F. (2007). *Running ever faster down the wrong road: An alternative future for education and skills*. London: Institute of Education - University of London.

DiMaggio, P., & Powell, W. (1991). *The new institutionalism in organizational analysis*. Chicago: University of Chicago Press.

Evans, K. (2002). Taking control of their lives? Agency in young adult transitions in England and the New Germany. *Journal of Youth Studies, 5*(3), 245–269.

Evans, K., Hodkinson, P., & Unwin, L. (Eds.). (2002). *Working to learn: Transforming learning in the workplace*. London: Francis Taylor.

Frenkel, S., Korczynski, M., Shire, K., & Tam, M. (1999). *On the front live: Organization of work in the information economy*. Ithaca, NY: Cornell University Press.

Furlong, A., Cartmel, F., Biggart, A., Sweeting, H., & West, P. (2003). *Youth transitions: Patterns of vulnerability and processes of social inclusion*. Edinburgh: Scottish Executive.

Galabuzi, G.-E. (2006). *Canada's economic apartheid: The social exclusion of racialized groups in the new century*. Toronto: Canadian Scholars Press.

Gaskell, J., & Rubenson, K. (Eds.). (2004). *Educational outcomes for the Canadian workplace: New frameworks for policy and research*. Toronto: University of Toronto Press.

Gilmore, J. (2008). *The Canadian immigrant labour market in 2006: Analysis by region or country of birth* (The Immigrant Labour Force Analysis Series) (Cat. 71-606-X2008002). Ottawa: Statistics Canada.

Griffin, C. (1985). *Typical girls: Young women from school to the job market*. London: Routledge and Kegan Paul.

Griffin, C. (1999). Lifelong learning and social democracy. *International Journal of Lifelong Education, 18*(5), 329–342.

Grubb, N. (1996). *Learning to work: The case for re-integrating job training and education*. New York: Russell Sage.

Hango, D., & de Broucker, P. (2007). *Education-to-labour market pathways of Canadian youth: Findings from the youth in transition survey* (Culture, Tourism and the Centre for Education Statistics Research Paper). Ottawa: Statistics Canada.

Hannan, D. F., Raffe, D., & Smyth, E. (1997). *Cross-national research on school to work transitions: An analytical framework*. Paper presented at *1996 Workshop of the Network on Transitions in Youth*, La Ciotat.

Heinz, W. (2002). Transition discontinuities and the biographical shaping of early work careers. *Journal of Vocational Behaviour, 60*(2), 220–240.

Heinz, W. (Ed.). (1999). *From education to work: Cross-national perspectives*. New York: Cambridge University Press.

Howell, J. (2008). *The business of community*. Toronto: Imagine Canada.

Hunt, C. (1999). Candlestick and faces: Aspects of lifelong learning. *Studies in the Education of Adults, 31*(2), 197–209.

Kerr, C., Dunlop, J., Harbinson, F., & Myers, C. (1960). *Industrialism and industrial man*. New York: Oxford University Press.

Kincheloe, J. (1999). *How do we tell the workers?: The socioeconomic foundations of work and vocational education*. Boulder, CO: Westview Press.

Krahn, H., & Taylor, A. (2005). Resilient teenagers: Explaining the high educational aspirations of visible minority immigrant youth in Canada. *Journal of International Migration and Integration, 6*(3/4), 405–434.

Krahn, H. (1996). *School–work transitions: Changing patterns and research needs*. Ottawa: Applied Research Branch, Human Resources Development Canada.

Lehmann, W. (2000). Is Germany's dual system still a model for Canadian youth apprenticeship initiatives? *Canadian Public Policy-Analyse de Politiques, 26*(2), 225–240.

Lehmann, W. (2005). Choosing to labour: Structure and agency in school-to-work transitions. *Canadian Journal of Sociology, 30*(3), 325–350.

Lehmann, W., & Taylor, A. (2003). Giving employers what they want? New vocationalism in Alberta. *Journal of Education and Work, 16*(1), 45–67.

Livingstone, D. (2004). *The education-jobs gap*. Toronto: Broadview Press.

López Blasco, A., McNeish, W., & Walther, A. (2003). *Young people and contradictions of inclusion: Towards integrated transition policies in Europe*. Bristol: Policy Press.

Marsden, D. (1999). *A theory of employment systems. Micro-foundations of societal diversity*. Oxford: Oxford University Press.

McVicar, D., & Anyadike-Danes, M. (2002). Predicting successful and unsuccessful transitions from school to work by using sequence methods. *Journal of the Royal Statistical Society, 165*, 317–334.

Mortimer, J., & Shanahan, M. (Eds.). (2003). *Handbook of the life course*. New York: Kluwer.

OECD. (2004, February). *Policy brief on lifelong learning, OECD Observer*. Paris: Organization for Economic Co-operation and Development.

OECD. (1996). *Lifelong learning for all: Meeting of the education committee at ministerial level*. Paris: Organization for Economic Co-operation and Development.

OECD. (1998). Lifelong learning: A monitoring framework and trends in participation. In *Centre for educational research and innovation education policy analysis 1998* (pp. 7–24). Paris: Organization for Economic Co-operation and Development.

OECD. (2001). *Competencies for the knowledge economy*. Paris: Organization for Economic Co-operation and Development.

OECD. (2008). *OECD employment outlook 2008*. Paris: Organization for Economic Cooperation and Development.

Oliver, M. (1996). *Understanding disability: From theory to practice*. Basingstoke: Macmillan Press.

Osterman, P. (1996). *Broken ladders: Managerial careers in the new economy*. New York: Oxford University Press.

Peracchi, F. (2002). The European community household panel: A review. *Empirical Economics, 27*, 63–90.

Pohl, A., & Walther, A. (2007). Activating the disadvantages: Variations in addressing youth transitions across Europe. *International Journal of Lifelong Education, 26*(5), 533–553.

Reich, R. (1991). *The work of nations: Preparing ourselves for 21st century capitalism*. New York: Vintage.

Roberts, K. (2003). School-to-work transitions: Why the United Kingdom's educational ladders always fail to connect. *International Studies in Sociology of Education, 14*(3), 203–216.

Sackmann, R., & Wingens, M. (2003). From transitions to trajectories. Sequence types. In W. R. Heinz (Ed.), *Social dynamics of the life course. Transitions, institutions, and interrelations*. New York: Aldine de Gruyter.

Sawchuk, P. (2003). *Adult learning and technology in working-class life*. New York: Cambridge University Press.

Sawchuk, P. (2006). 'Use-Value' and the re-thinking of skills, learning and the labour process. *Journal of Industrial Relations, 48*(5), 593–617.

Sawchuk, P. (2008). Labour perspectives on the new politics of skill and competency formation: International reflections. *Asia Pacific Education Review, 9*(1), 1–15.

Schuetze, H., & Sweet, R. (Eds.). (2003). *Integrating school and workplace learning in Canada*. Montreal: McGill-Queen's Press.

Scott, W. (2001). *Institutions and organizations*. Thousands Oaks, CA: Sage.

Shaienks, D., Eisl-Culkin, J., & Bussiére, P. (2006). *Follow-up on education and labour market pathways of young Canadians aged 18 to 20: Results from YITS Cycle 3*. Ottawa: Statistics Canada.

Shaienks, D., & Gluszynski, T. (2007). *Participation in postsecondary education: Graduates, continuers and drop outs – results from the YITS Cycle 4* (Culture, Tourism and the Centre for Education Statistics Research Papers). Ottawa: Human Resources and Social Development Canada.

Sharpe, S. (1994). *Just like a girl: How girls learn to be women from the seventies to the nineties*. London: Penguin.

Shavit, Y., & Müller, W. (1998). *A comparative study of educational qualifications and occupational destinations*. New York: Oxford University Press.

Shildrick, T., & MacDonald, R. (2007). Biographies of exclusion: Poor work and poor transitions. *International Journal of Lifelong Education, 26*(5), 589–604.

Staff, J., & Mortimer, J. (2003). Diverse transitions from school to work. *Work and Occupations, 30*(3), 361–369.

Stern, D., & Wagner, D. (1999). *International perspectives on the school-to-work transition*. London: Hampton Press.

Stokes, H., & Wyn, J. (2007). Constructing identities and making carerrs: Young people's perspectives on work and learning. *International Journal of Lifelong Education, 26*(5), 495–511.

Taylor, A. (2005). 'Re-culturing' students and selling futures: School-to-work policy in Ontario. *Journal of Education and Work, 18*(3), 321–340.

Touraine, A. (1971). *The post-industrial society: Tomorrow's social history: Classes, conflicts and culture in the programmed society*. New York: Random House.

Van Berkel, R., & Hornemann Møller, I. (2002). *Active social policies in the EU: Inclusion through participation?* Bristol: Policy Press.

Walther, A., & Pohl, A. (2005). *Thematic study on policy measures for disadvantaged youth. Study for the European commission*. Tübingen: IRIS.

Willis, P. (1977). *Learning to labour: How working class kids get working class jobs*. Farnborough: Saxon House.

Zeman, K., Knighton, T., & Bussière, P. (2004). *Education and labour market pathways of young Canadians between age 20 and 22: An overview* (Education, Skills and Learning Research Papers) (Cat. 81-595-MIE2004018). Ottawa: Statistics Canada.

Peter H. Sawchuk
Professor, Department of Sociology and Equity Studies in Education
Ontario Institute for Studies in Education of the University of Toronto, Canada

Alison Taylor
Professor, Department of Educational Policy Studies
University of Alberta, Canada

D.W. LIVINGSTONE

2. AGE, OCCUPATIONAL CLASS AND LIFELONG LEARNING:

Findings of a 2004 Canadian Survey of Formal and Informal Learning through the Life Course[1]

INTRODUCTION

All societies develop rules and norms to guide their populations through the life course. Human action would be stymied if we did not rely on some such conventions. But we make our own history and in the process may chose to reproduce, modify or transform such orienting social constructions. A pertinent case in point is the notion of major transition points through the life course in the institutional context of advance capitalist societies. Through most of my life, three major transition points have been widely presumed and reproduced by most people. These are school entry, school to employment, and retirement from employment. When I enrolled in first grade a large portion of my life became increasingly regulated by a large institution outside my family. School graduation led me directly to the labour market and a steady job. Post-WWII pension and old age security programs have been designed on the assumption that most employees will retire from their jobs by their 60s, an imminent consideration for me.

The reality of life transitions is rarely as neat as norms suggest. All of these notions of major change and especially adult 'transitions' are becoming more diffuse and complex in the current period. School entry now may include stages of day care programs and junior kindergarten as well as immersion in a variety of organized pre-school activities, educational games and media. The majority of students leaving secondary schools now move back and forth between the labour market and post-secondary and further education programs, and may continue to do so through much of their careers to enhance their job prospects; married women with jobs and children to care for also increasingly move back and forth between home and jobs. Retirement from paid employment now comes in many forms from early or partial to late or never, while unpaid volunteer work by older people is being increasingly recognized as a valuable and necessary activity. The notions of retirement as a final phase of disengagement (as suggested by functionalist theories) or compulsory consignment to state-based long-term care systems (as presumed in political economy approaches) are increasingly remote accounts of the real choices for older people (see Gilleard and Higgs, 2002).

P. Sawchuk and A. Taylor (eds.), Challenging Transitions in Learning and Work: Reflections on Policy and Practice, 25–39.

Virtually all attempts to construct distinctive transition points, maturation stages or life passages are revealed on close examination as ideal types with many variants. In the present empirical analysis, we will treat respondents as active social agents who, while making work and learning choices, serve to reproduce or modify pre-established transition patterns. This agency can apply to all social actors including those in all types of marginalized groups identified in Chapter 1. The focus in this chapter will be on age and economic class differences: old and working class as well as younger and wealthy people.

The primary focus of this analysis will be on intentional learning activities throughout the life course. Such intentional acquisition of knowledge, skill or understanding occurs in sites of widely varied formality. Basic types of intentional learning include: *formal schooling*; *formal adult education*; *informal education or training*; and *non-taught individual or collective informal learning* (see Livingstone, 2006 as well as Colley et al., 2003 for further definition and critical discussion of these distinctions). Few empirical studies to date have paid comparable attention to both formal and informal learning activities, most often concentrating on more easily recorded formal education. In this chapter we will first offer a brief overview of the recent self-reported formal and informal learning activities of the Canadian adult population followed by age and class-based comparative analysis of these activities.

Age differences will be summarized using conventional five-year age cohort divisions of the population over 18 and up to the 80s, although other groupings also have been explored to detect differences in learning activities. Few prior surveys have addressed the learning practices of those adults over 65. It should be noted that the cross-sectional data used here cannot begin to distinguish individual maturation effects (aging per se) from purportedly distinctive cohort effects (e.g., 'baby boom' generation) or historical period effects (e.g., 'information age'). It may be, for example, that specific effects of the diffusion of personal information technologies over the past generation will serve to increase the incidence of learning activities significantly over the levels now found among retired people as current younger cohorts age. In any case, the incidence of learning activities found among older people in this study is unlikely to decrease as younger cohorts age in the current historical period.

For the *employed* labour force, *labour process-based occupational class distinctions* will be used because these are the most basic economic class divisions in society and therefore most likely to be associated with learning differences. The basic class division in capitalism is between the owners of means of production and those who must offer their labour to make a living. In concrete terms, few people are pure representatives of capital or labour. The boundaries are more permeable than most other nominal social distinctions such as age, sex, ethnicity, disability[2]. Many owners do some labour and many labourers own some capital. But the foundational class positions in the production process clearly perform the respective functions of capital to oversee profitable commodity production and of hired labour to produce vendible commodities. Our conceptual model of class positions is grounded in ownership, and distinguishable authority and autonomy aspects of production relations. It was initially developed during the period when Harry

Braverman's (1974) analysis of the capitalist labour process stimulated several efforts to identify contemporary class locations grounded in production relations (see Wright, 1978, Livingstone, 1983, 1999a)—before class analysis and labour process studies went their separate ways (see Carter, 1995). We can distinguish eight major class groupings: *large employers, small employers,* the *self-employed, managers, supervisors, professional employees, service workers*, and *industrial workers*. Among owners, large employers include substantial owners of capital and corporate executives who oversee investment in companies and corporations with multi-million dollar assets and many employees. Small employers, typically family firms or partnerships, tend to have exclusive ownership, small numbers of employees and continue to play active co-ordinating roles in the labour process of their firms. The self-employed remain in control of their small commodity enterprises but are reliant on their own labour. At the other end of the class hierarchy are those clearly in the working class, without substantial ownership claims and devoid of official supervisory authority or recognized autonomy to exercise specialized knowledge. This includes industrial workers who produce, distribute or repair material goods. It also includes service workers who provide a widening array of sales, business, social and other services, similarly without recognized supervisory authority or task autonomy. Between employers and those who are clearly in working class positions, other employees tend to have mixed functions. Managers are delegated by owners to control the overall labour process at the point of production to ensure profitability but may also contribute their labour to co-ordinate this process. Supervisors are under the authority of managers to control adherence to production standards by industrial or service workers but may also collaborate directly with them in aspects of this work. Professional employees have recognized task autonomy based on their specialized knowledge to design production processes for themselves and others and to execute their own work with a high level of discretion, but remain subordinated to employer prerogatives.[3] We will use these class distinctions to analyze changes in the learning practices of the employed labour force based on a recent Canadian national survey.[4] In addition, the combined effects of class and age on learning practices will be analyzed for the employed labour force, most of which is under 65 years old.

WORK AND LIFELONG LEARNING (WALL) RESEARCH NETWORK FINDINGS

The data for this analysis are drawn from the WALL research network, established at the Centre for the Study of Education and Work (CSEW) at the Ontario Institute for Studies in Education at the University of Toronto (OISE/UT) in 2002.[5] Part of the mandate of this network was to conduct comparative surveys and case studies of the changing nature of learning and work across Canada. A large-scale country-wide survey (N = 9,063) was conducted in 2004 covering an array of paid and unpaid work activities, formal and informal learning activities, and socio-demographic information (see www.wallnetwork.ca). In this paper, we will present and discuss some of the relevant findings on learning activities for the entire adult population and then by age and class.

FORMAL SCHOOLING, ADULT EDUCATION AND INFORMAL LEARNING PROFILES

Massive expansion of state-funded schooling in the post WWII era has led to near-universal attendance until near the end of secondary school and widespread participation in post-secondary institutions in most advanced capitalist economies. In Canada, with one of the highest levels of educational attainment in the world (Statistics Canada, 2003), majorities of youth cohorts now complete some form of post-secondary education. Age cohort inspection of the 2004 survey data shows that among those over 80 years of age – born before the Great Depression of the 1930s and schooled largely prior to WWII – less than 15 percent have completed any form of post-secondary schooling. About a third of those now in their early 60s—born in the WWII period and schooled mainly in the comprehensive and vocational secondary school expansion of the immediate post-war era – have completed post-secondary education, mostly university degrees. The following cohort now in their late 50s—born in the 1960s and beneficiaries of newly created community college systems in Canada—jumped to completion rates of almost half of the cohort. Younger cohorts have experienced a more gradual continuing increase in completion rates, with over 60 percent of those between 25 and 34 graduating to date.

Table 2.1. Participation in adult education by formal schooling, Canada, 18 + Population, 1998–2004

FORMAL SCHOOLING	*Taken a course 1998* [%]	*Taken a course 2004* [%]
No Diploma	18	23
High School Diploma	53	48
College Certificate	58	52
University Degree	70	63
Total	44	45
N	*1548*	*8843*

Sources: NALL Survey, 1998; WALL Survey, 2004

Participation in formal adult education courses has also expanded. Canada still has a relatively poorly organized adult education system compared to many European countries (Myers and deBroucker, 2006) but participation rates have increased rapidly from tiny numbers in the immediate post WWII era. In 1961, only around 4 percent of Canadian adults enrolled in a course; by the early 1980s, the rate had increased to around 20 percent; in 2004, over 40 percent of all Canadian adults (including students registered in degree programs) had taken a course in the past year (Livingstone and Scholtz, 2006). While both formal attainment and adult education have made very large aggregate gains since 1960, participation in adult education courses still tends to reproduce prior differences in educational attainments. As Table 2.1 shows, in both 1998 and 2004 surveys, university graduates remain three times as likely as secondary dropouts to have taken a course in the past year. However, general adult education participation differences are narrowing as greater proportions of younger cohorts complete forms of secondary and post-secondary schooling.

Popular attitudes about the need for formal education also have risen markedly in recent decades. There is now a nearly universal expectation, in Canada at least, that a post-secondary credential is needed to 'get along' in today's world – even though accessibility to both universities and adult education remain problematic for many of those from socially disadvantaged backgrounds (Livingstone and Stowe, 2003; Myers and de Broucker, 2006).

Every study ever done on informal learning has found it to be more extensive than formal education, which is hardly surprising given that learning is inherent in our species' means of coping with our changing environment. Such studies have also found little relation with formal education, which is again unremarkable since anyone can engage in informal learning at anytime without institutional or resource barriers. While there may be many variations in terms of content, intensity and competency, virtually all adults report engaging in some informal learning.

Empirical research on employment-related learning has confirmed that the vast majority of job training is done informally, much of it through mentoring by more experienced co-workers, and relatively little through formal courses (Betcherman, Leckie and McMullen, 1998; Center for Workforce Development, 1998; Livingstone and Scholtz, 2006). Recent Canadian studies have found that over 80 percent of the labour force have engaged in a specific set of job-related informal learning activities over the past year (Peters, 2004; Livingstone and Scholtz, 2006). Extensive workplace learning activities are indicated by such surveys and growing numbers of case studies (e.g., Rainbird et al., 2004; Felstead et al., 2004). Organized training programs are much less widely available. Employer and government appeals for greater lifelong learning efforts by workers to cope with an emerging knowledge-based economy (e.g., Cortada, 1998) might be more suitably directed to provision of more organized further education programs.

There is some evidence that adults' overall array of intentional informal learning efforts may have increased somewhat in recent decades. According to recent national surveys of self-reported informal learning, Canadian adults are now spending an average of around 14 hours a week in such activities (Livingstone and Scholtz, 2006), compared to around 10 hours in the many case studies and single U.S. national survey conducted in the 1970s (Tough, 1979; Penland, 1977). Whatever the reliability of such measures, there is now substantial evidence that most adults should be recognized as continuing, actively engaged informal learners, that intentional informal learning continues long past initial formal schooling, and that such learning involves many spheres beyond paid employment and is much less constrained by economic background than formal education.[6]

AGE, ADULT EDUCATION AND INFORMAL LEARNING

The connection between age and participation in further education has been one of the strongest relationships in contemporary societies (e.g., Courtney, 1992). As Table 2.2 shows, the majority of those 18 to 24 participated in at least one adult education course in the past year. But this rate now declines only very gradually, with 45 percent of those in their early 50s also taking a course. For older age groups the rate then drops more rapidly to 30 percent for the 65 to 69 cohort and under 10 percent for those over 75. While comparable historical figures are not readily available for older adults, it is safe to assume that all of these age-specific participation rates are higher than previously. Not only do people go to school longer than ever before but, with the expansion of schooling, the long established association between schooling and adult education draws evermore older adults into continuing formal adult educational activities.

Table 2.2. Age and proportion participating in adult education course in past year, Canada, 2004

AGE COHORT	*Taken a course in past year* [%]
18–24	65
25–29	56
30–34	54
35–39	50
40–44	52
45–49	50
50–54	46
55–59	38
60–64	30
65–69	21
70–74	17
75–79	9
80+	10
Total	45
N	*8757*

Source: WALL Survey, 2004

Since substantial numbers of older people have been enrolling in higher education programs, their capabilities to perform well in such programs have become a revelation to some researchers (e.g., Johnson, 1995). But direct studies of older peoples' cognitive functioning discovered decades ago that prior conceptual models focused on older peoples' less efficient recall of details had obscured the more efficient selection and distillation of usable knowledge associated with their maturity (see Labouvie-Vief, 1990). With all due respect to estimates of the doubling of the quantity of knowledge within a matter of years, the wisdom that older people typically gain through the life course surely diminishes their need to attend to a 'required curriculum' of practical knowledge with the intensity of younger people. The primary motivations for most people to take adult education courses during their middle years are job-related. Once older people leave the employed labour force, other motives assume priority but with less urgency, hence the declining adult education participation rates now beginning in the 50s age cohorts.

While involvement in intentional informal learning activities may also be increasing somewhat in recent decades, the association with age is markedly different. As Table 2.3 shows, over 90 percent of all adults and the vast majority at all ages are engaged in some form of informal learning activity. There is some evidence of declining involvement by those over 70 but two-thirds of those over 80 still report active engagement in informal learning activities. Evidence to date suggests that the youngest adults, as well as being those most involved in completing formal schooling, are the most involved in extensive informal learning—which appears self-evident since they are most likely to be experiencing multiple transitions: from families of origin to independent living situations, from initial schooling to starting careers and otherwise establishing new life styles (Livingstone, 1999b). The extensiveness of informal learning activities appears to remain fairly constant throughout later adulthood, at least as indicated by participation rates and time devoted to it.

Table 2.3. Age and participation in any informal learning activities or learning about computers in past year, Canada, 2004

AGE COHORT	*Any informal learning* [%]	*Learning about computers* [%]
18–24	95	65
25–29	95	63
30–34	96	66
35–39	96	67
40–44	94	67
45–49	95	67
50–54	94	70
55–59	90	61
60–64	86	44
65–69	86	37
70–74	78	26
75–79	72	20
80+	64	11
Total	91	58
N	*8774*	*8771*

The main contents of informal learning do shift markedly from preoccupation with job-related matters prior to retirement to 'post-occupation' focus on general interests including health issues. It is clear by virtually any direct measures that intentional informal learning is much more extensive than formal adult education for most people after they complete their initial period of intensive schooling. Tough's (1978) metaphor of the iceberg of adult learning remains quite appropriate in terms of estimated time devoted—a few hours a week of formal education versus more than 10 hours for informal learning activities on average for all adults—but the hidden part of the iceberg is even greater for older people who in a real sense have less to learn from any available formal curriculum about coping with life experience.

Table 2.3 also summarizes the proportions of each of these age cohorts that have engaged in informal learning about computers over the past year, in relation to either paid work, unpaid housework or community volunteer work or through general interest. Informal learning on any specific topic will obviously be less extensive than informal learning in general. But the majority of adults have been involved in learning about computers in this period when personal computers are making their way into most schools, most paid workplaces and the majority of households. Majorities in all age cohorts up to age 60 engage in informal learning about computers. Participation then drops rapidly in post-retirement dominated cohorts but remains detectable even in those over 80. Given the active continuing involvement in general informal learning for the majority of those over 80, this drop in learning about computers is likely an effect of older cohorts' formative years occurring in the historical period prior to the onset of the 'information age'.

A century ago, working to earn a living was a common condition in industrializing societies from adolescence to the grave. A common retirement phase of life has emerged over this period as a consequence of a more capital-intensive economy requiring less direct producers to achieve subsistence levels, widening provision of retirement benefits and extended longevity because more recent generations did not have to work themselves into the grave. Table 2.4 summarizes current employment status by age in Canada. Paid employment is now the majority status for all cohorts between 20 and 60, including both men and women. Indeed, with the rapidly growing entry of married women with children into paid employment since WWII, the labour force participation rate for these age groups is now at historically highest recorded levels. But with compulsory schooling until at least 16 and a growing norm of post-secondary completion, employment (either part-time or full-time) is now a minority status until the late teens at least and is now commonly combined with post-secondary schooling in the early 20s.

Table 2.4. Age cohort by proportion currently employed, Canada, 2004

AGE COHORT	*Males* [%]	*Females* [%]	*Total* [%]
18–19	59	41	49
20–24	71	66	68
25–29	83	72	77
30–34	90	81	86
35–39	88	75	81
40–44	91	80	85
45–49	92	80	86
50–54	84	69	77
55–59	71	57	64
60–64	45	31	37
65–69	14	7	11
70–74	15	3	9
75–79	4	1	2
80+	3	1	1
Total	71	58	64
N	*4251*	*4520*	*8775*

The retirement phase has become close to universal, with employment becoming a minority status for those between 60 and 64 and only around 10 percent continuing in employment after 65, a common legislated age for retirement benefits to begin. However, the normative age of retirement is becoming more diffuse, with early retirement provisions becoming more common as the baby boom generation has marched through the active labour force, and mandatory retirement provisions diminishing as they prepare to leave it. Paid employment remains a detectable status of at least a few of those over 80.

Before moving to consider a class perspective, one further aspect of age and learning should be emphasized. Informal education, in terms of mentoring by more experienced colleagues and friends, is commonly an age-based process. For example, according to the 2004 survey, the majority of recent young labour force entrants have actively sought advice about job skills within the past month while only a quarter of those over 55 and 10 percent of those continuing beyond 65 have done so. Much paid workplace learning tends to be collective and mutual (Sawchuk, 2003), but more experienced and typically older workers most often lead the way.

OCCUPATIONAL CLASS AND LEARNING PRACTICES

The role of formal education in reproducing social classes – at least in simple status-based dichotomous terms of middle and working classes – has been well documented. School success has long reflected the occupational and family-centred transmission of cultural codes (Bourdieu, 1984), as well as class-based access to adequate funds. Canadian research has found that children from families in higher occupational class locations, whose parents much more commonly had advanced educational attainments, have been much more likely to gain university credentials and better jobs (Curtis, Livingstone and Smaller, 1992). Table 2.5 shows that occupational classes in the current labour force continue to be clearly differentiated in terms of the proportion attaining post-secondary degrees: about 80 percent of professional employees and 70 percent large employers and managers have completed some form of post-secondary schooling, contrasted with about half of those in most other class positions and about a third of industrial workers. As previously noted, completion of some form of post-secondary certification – most notably community college diplomas – has grown rapidly in Canada since the 1960s, therefore the absolute differences in post-secondary attainment levels between large employers, managers and professional employees on the one hand and industrial and service workers on the other hand have diminished. But large gaps remain at more advanced levels. About half of professional employees have university degrees, contrasted with 10 percent of service workers and 4 percent of industrial workers.

As a consequence of post-secondary expansion, the long established association between school attainment and participation in adult education may be playing a diminishing role in the cycle of class reproduction. As Table 2.5 also shows, differences in course participation between large employers, managers and professionals on the one hand and service and industrial workers on the other hand are less than their school attainment differences; these differences also have decreased during the past decade.

Table 2.5. Post-secondary school completion, participation in adult education, and job-related and computer-related informal learning by occupational class, employed labour force, Canada, 2004

OCCUPATIONAL CLASS	*Post-secondary completion* [%]	*Course/ Workshop taken in past year* [%]	*Participate in informal job-related learning* [%]	*Participate in learning about computers* [%]
Large Employers	70	67	87	77
Small Employers	54	46	88	68
Self-Employed	54	46	87	65
Managers	71	68	92	80
Professionals	83	67	92	77
Supervisors	56	54	88	66
Service Workers	50	52	84	65
Industrial Workers	34	41	84	59
Total [%]	56	53	87	68
N	*5366*	*5436*	*5428*	*5595*

Employer contributions are widely recognized as a factor in employee course participation (Peters, 2004). While demand for adult education courses appears to be similar between occupational classes, employer contributions differ widely. In 2004, Canadian employers provided, paid for or facilitated half of all managers to receive formal training. Over a quarter of all professional employees and supervisory employees received support. Only around 15 percent of service workers and industrial workers were given any such assistance. This is presumably one factor accounting for persistent class differences in adult education participation rates. It should also be noted here that both the school attainment levels and adult course participation rates of the employed labour force are higher than those of the remaining population excluded from the active labour force; these marginalized or 'underclass' people may often find less formal education is a powerful means of their exclusion.

But it is clear that participation in both job-related as well as general informal learning is much more prevalent than participation in adult education, and does not appear to be generally linked to formal credentials or much differentiated by occupational class position. As Table 2.5 also shows, the vast majority of Canadians in all occupational classes are active informal job-related learners regardless of their formal educational attainment. This finding suggests that the continuing acquisition of skills among lower occupational classes is more prevalent than often assumed. There is also no suggestion in the survey data or related case studies (see Livingstone and Sawchuk, 2004) that those working class respondents with less formal schooling are devoting appreciably less time to job-related informal learning. Differences between class positions in informal learning about computers are somewhat more noticeable between industrial workers and others, partly because of more limited opportunities to use computers in manual jobs, but the majority of industrial workers are actively engaged in such learning even if there is little on-the-job opportunity (see

Sawchuk, 2003). There is much more detailed analysis of informal learning in other WALL survey reports (see Livingstone and Scholtz, 2006; WALL website case studies). It may be most relevant here to note that the strongest relation between work time and informal learning time for those in most class positions is found for voluntary community work, which is generally more discretionary than either paid work or housework (see Livingstone, 2001). This suggests that adults may be most likely to learn intentionally in social settings relatively free of hierarchical control.

AGE, CLASS AND LEARNING ACTIVITIES

This large-scale survey also permits further analysis of the interactive effects of age and class on learning practices. Table 2.6 summarizes the basic patterns in relation to participation in adult education courses. The first point to be noted here is that the long established decline in adult education participation with aging appears to be becoming more delayed and gradual for those actively employed in all class positions. There is virtually no consistent decline in participation rates among those aged 25 through their early 50s in either professional-managerial class positions or in working class jobs. Professional and managerial employees as well as large owners appear to have the highest sustained participation rates in all age cohorts. But participation reaches near majority levels in older cohorts of most class positions, with the notable exception the small numbers of industrial workers who remain employed into the late 50s, for whom course participation drops to around a quarter (and for whom employer sponsorship of courses appears to be almost nil).

Table 2.6. Age and occupational class position by participation in adult education courses, Canada, 2004

CLASS AGE	*Large emp.* [%]	*Small emp.* [%]	*Self-emp.* [%]	*Man-agers* [%]	*Profe ss.* [%]	*Super vis.* [%]	*Serv. Wk.* [%]	*Ind. wk.* [%]	*Age totals* [%]
18–24			54	76	71	64	62	50	62
25–29		46**	67	62	62	52	57	47	56
30–34		66	64	62	66	45	50	42	55
35–39		42	40	66	69	64	52	40	52
40–44	60*	36	48	70	68	69	42	51	53
45–49	68**	55	44	83	69	51	48	38	53
50–54		43	37	75	76	37	51	31	50
55–59		44	35	63	56	45**	48	28	45
60–64		43**	52	22**	50**		46**	23**	40
65+			24						31
Class Total [%]	64	47	45	68	67	53	51	41	53
N	*55*	*336*	*872*	*587*	*852*	*283*	*1466*	*1047*	*5498*

*Younger age cohorts combined when cell sizes less than 20 cases.

**Older age cohorts combined when cell sizes less than 20 cases.

Participation rates in informal learning activities are at similarly high levels of around 90 percent in all age cohorts in all occupational classes. Learning about computers also involves majorities of those of all ages in all class positions in the employed labour force. Paid workplace informal learning is engaged in extensively by those in all class positions throughout virtually their entire working lives.

CONCLUDING REMARKS

The current analysis does not intend to make inferences about the effectiveness of adult education courses or the quality of informal learning. It merely registers the incidence of such activities and in particular the extensive involvement of older people generally and working class employees in both types of learning activities. Those with vested interests in previously institutionalized forms of learning may well dismiss such findings as superficial. However, we can safely conclude the following:

- the most evident formal types of learning diminish in old age, but informal parts of learning persist throughout the life course. Older people in all walks of life typically remain active informal learners. In terms of recent research on neuroplasticity, their brains continue to develop. Older people warrant greater respect for their learning capacities and rights than has been generally accorded in industrial and post-industrial societies where they have been commonly regarded as cognitively deficient and socially disengaged;
- older people tend to be wiser than younger people in the 'required curriculum' of life and have less related need for formal instruction. Elders in every society are capable of providing vital mentoring instruction to younger people. In many advanced capitalist societies, they tend to be a wasted resource;
- it is evident that participation in schooling and formal adult education courses has grown rapidly in recent decades. There is mounting evidence that these increases are in excess of formal job requirements and that the 'overqualification/underemployment/underutilization/overeducation' of the entire labour force in advanced market economies, and of working class employees in particular, is also growing significantly (see Livingstone, 1999a, 2004, 2009; Green et al., 2002; Handel, 2005; Vaisey, 2006 for overviews). If the unrecognized and underutilized informal learning of many people is also considered, the waste of talent is massive;
- according to the current survey, over a quarter of all employees believe they are overqualified for their jobs. This includes over 40 percent of those ages 18 to 24. But even among those in their 50s, a quarter feel the same way. Underemployment is now a sustained problem that cannot be resolved by the maturation of workers through their employment careers;
- it is increasingly evident that further educational reforms—inherently valuable as education generally is—will be of little immediate use in addressing such education-jobs gap. More equitable distribution of paid work, design of more

decent jobs allowing more workers to utilize their current capacities, and greater valuing of now unpaid work – including creation of green jobs and mentoring by retired people – are surely part of the resolution of this growing gap.

- much further research attention to the actual learning capacities and accomplishments of older people and working class employees is needed to overcome persistent assumptions about their inferiority and irrelevance in societies in which formal education remains hegemonic.

Finally, these findings from one of the few surveys to date to have examined actual learning practices of adults across the life course and across different occupational classes provide evidence for abandoning simple assumptions of linearity, both in terms of aging and learning and also in terms of job-related learning. The findings also suggest that the heralded emergence of a knowledge-based economy with presumed demands for greater learning efforts, especially by older employees with less formal education, may be ignoring already very substantial learning efforts. Different formal educational structures and employment regulations may be related to variations in initial successful transitions between schooling and employment in respective countries (e.g., Breen, 2005). But the commonalities in adult learning practices may ultimately be more important for understanding later transitions throughout the life course.

NOTES

1 Revised version of keynote address presented at 'The times they are a-changin':researching transitions in lifelong learning' conference. Centre for Research on Lifelong Learning, University of Stirling, Scotland, 22–24 June 2007.

2 Sex, ethnicity and disability effects on learning activities will not be considered in this paper. There are significant learning differences in these terms, notably more limited recognition of the learning activities of women, visible minorities and those designated as disabled. Further multivariate analyses have found that, for the learning measures discussed here, these effects do not diminish age and class effects.

3 These class divisions based on relations of production are distinct from occupational classifications but overlap with them (see Wright, 1980). In operationalizing class divisions, ownership positions must first be separated from the rest of the active labour force. While employee positions with official supervisory authority and/or recognized specialized professional knowledge may be continually shifting, the detailed occupational censuses of most advanced industrial countries provide sufficient information to approximate most of these divisions, as well as ownership. But before proceeding to empirical data analysis, two limitations must be noted. The large employer class is not adequately distinguished in any national survey because of their very small numbers. Also, the much larger underclass of chronically unemployed and otherwise excluded from the wage labour force, but dependent on the capitalist mode of production, is also poorly represented in sample surveys and beyond the scope of this analysis.

4 For fuller comparative discussion of these occupational class distinctions, see Livingstone and Mangan (1996) and Livingstone and Scholtz (2006).

5 The 2004 WALL survey (N = 9,063) is primarily intended to provide general benchmarks for continuing studies of work and learning. Readers are encouraged to use the data in this survey in conjunction with reports on the 12 WALL network case studies and the WALL Resource Base which can be found at: http://www.wallnetwork.ca. A comparable prior national survey of adult learning was conducted in 1998 and results may be found at www.nall.ca.

6 See for example the WALL studies by Eichler (2005) and Schugurensky & Mundel (2005) on housework and volunteer community work in relation to largely informal learning activities.

REFERENCES

Gilleard, C., & Higgs, P. (2002). The third age: Class, cohort or generation? *Ageing and Society, 22*, 369–382.

Betcherman, G., Leckie, N., & McMullen, K. (1998). *Barriers to employer-sponsored training in Canada*. Ottawa: Canadian Policy Research Networks.

Bourdieu, P. (1984). *Distinction: A social critique of the judgement of taste*. Cambridge, MA: Harvard University Press.

Braverman, H. (1974). *Labor and monopoly capital*. New York: Monthly Review Press.

Breen, R. (2005). Explaining cross national variation in youth unemployment: Market and institutional factors. *European Sociological Review, 21*(2), 125–134.

Carter, B. (1995, Spring). A growing divide: Marxist class analysis and the labour process. *Capital and Class, 55*, 33–72.

Center for Workforce Development. (1998). *The teaching firm: Where productive work and learning converge*. Newton, MA: Education Development Center.

Colley, S., Hodkinson, P., & Malcom, J. (2003). *Informality and formality in learning*. London: Learning and Skills Research Centre.

Cortada, J. W. (Ed.). (1998). *Rise of the knowledge worker*. Boston: Butterworth-Heinemann.

Courtney, S. (1992). *Why adults learn: Towards a theory of participation in adult education*. London: Routledge.

Curtis, B., Livingstone, D. W., & Smaller, H. (1992). *Stacking the deck: The streaming of working class kids in Ontario schools*. Toronto, ON: Our Schools/Our Selves.

Eichler, M. (2005). The other half (or more) of the story: Unpaid household and care work and lifelong learning. In N. Bascia, A. Cumming, A. Datnow, K. Leithwood, & D. Livingstone (Eds.), *International handbook of educational policy, Part 2* (pp. 1023–1042). Bodmin, Cornwall, UK: Springer.

Felstead, A., Fuller, A., Unwin, L., Ashton, D., Butler, P., Lee, T., et al. (2004, September). *Exposing learning at work: Results from a recent survey.* Paper presented to the Work, Employment and Society Conference, University of Manchester Institute of Science and Technology (UMIST), 1–3 September 2004.

Green, F., McIntosh, S., & Vignoles, A. (2002, December). The utilization of education and skills: Evidence from Britain. *The Manchester School, 70*(6), 792–811.

Handel, M. J. (2005). *Worker skills and job requirements: Is there a mismatch?* Washington, DC: Economic Policy Institute.

Johnson, M. (1995). Lessons from the Open University: Third age learning. *Educational Gerontology, 21*(5), 415–427.

Labouvie-Vief, G. (1990). Wisdom as integrated thought. In R. J. Sternberg (Ed.), *Wisdom, its nature, origins and development*. New York: Cambridge University Press.

Livingstone, D. W. (1983). *Class, ideologies and educational futures*. London and New York: Falmer Press.

Livingstone, D. W. (1999a). *The education-jobs gap: Underemployment or economic democracy*. Toronto, ON: Garamond Press.

Livingstone, D. W. (1999b). Exploring the icebergs of adult learning: Findings of the first Canadian survey of informal learning practices. *Canadian Journal for the Study of Adult Education, 13*(2), 49–72.

Livingstone, D. W. (2001). Worker control as the missing link: Relations between paid/unpaid work and work-related learning. *Journal of Workplace Learning, 13*(7/8), 308–317.

Livingstone, D. W. (2004). Introduction: Mapping the forest of underemployment. In D. W. Livingstone (Ed.), *The education-jobs gap: Underemployment or economic democracy* (2nd edn., pp. xvii–xxxii). Aurora, ON: Garamond Press.

Livingstone, D. W. (2006). Informal learning: Conceptual distinctions and preliminary findings. In Z. Bekerman, N. C. Burbules, & D. Silberman-Keller (Eds.), *Learning in places: The informal education reader* (pp. 202–226). New York: Peter Lang.

Livingstone, D. W. (ed.). (2009). *Education and jobs: Exploring the gaps*. Toronto: University of Toronto Press.

Livingstone, D. W., &. Mangan, J. M. (1996). Men's employment classes and class consciousness: An empirical comparison of Marxist and Weberian class distinctions. In D. W. Livingstone & J. M. Mangan (Eds.), *Recast dreams: Class and gender consciousness in Steeltown* (pp. 15–51). Toronto, ON: Garamond Press.

Livingstone, D. W., & Sawchuk, P. H. (2004). *Hidden knowledge: Organized labour in the information age*. Aurora, ON: Garamond Press.

Livingstone, D. W., & Scholtz, A. (2006). *Work and lifelong learning in Canada: Basic findings of the 2004 WALL survey*. Toronto. OISE/UT, CSEW. 80 pp. Available at www.wallnetwork.ca

Livingstone, D. W., & Stowe, S. (2003). Class and learning in Canada: Intergenerational patterns of inequality. In A. Scott & J. Freeman-Moir (Eds.), *Yesterday's dreams: International and critical perspectives on education and social class* (pp. 121–35). Auckland: Canterbury University Press.

Myers, K., & de Broucker, P. (2006). *Too many left behind: Canada's adult education and training system*. Ottawa: Canadian Policy Research Networks.

Penland, P. (1977). *Self-planned learning in America*. Pittsburgh: University of Pittsburgh.

Peters, V. (2004). *Working and training: First results of the 2003 adult education and training survey*. Ottawa: Statistics Canada.

Rainbird, H., Fuller, A., & Munro, A. (Eds.). (2004). *Workplace learning in context*. London, UK: Routledge.

Schugurensky, D., & Mundel, K. (2005). Volunteer work and learning: Hidden dimensions of labour force training. In N. Bascia, A. Cumming, A. Datnow, K. Leithwood, & D. Livingstone (Eds.), *International handbook of educational policy, Part 2* (pp. 997–1022). Bodmin, Cornwall, UK: Springer.

Statistics Canada. (2003). *Education indicators in Canada: Report of the pan-Canadian education indicators program 2003*. Ottawa: Statistics Canada.

Tough, A. (1979). *The adult's learning projects: A fresh approach to theory and practice in adult learning*. Toronto, ON: OISE Press.

Vaisey, S. (2006, December). Education and its discontents: Overqualification in America, 1972–2002. *Social Forces*, *85*(2), 835–864.

Wright, E. O. (1978). *Class, crisis and the state*. London: New Left Books.

Wright, E. O. (1980). Class and occupation. *Theory and Society*, *9*, 177–214.

Dr. D. W. Livingstone
Canada Research Chair in Lifelong Learning and Work
Head, Centre for the Study of Education and Work
Director, WALL Research Network
Professor, Department of Sociology and Equity Studies in Education
Ontario Institute for Studies in Education of the University of Toronto

PETER H. SAWCHUK

SECTION 1 INTRODUCTION

Learning/Work Transitions – Education and Training

The chapters in this section explore a range of topics concerning how education and training contexts relate to transition processes. Education and training contexts are, however, treated expansively as an entry point into a series of provocative arguments that exemplify the type of critical vocationalism perspective we outlined in Chapter 1. Analyses put flesh on the conceptual bones of key themes of our approach: the recognition of social differences, non-linearity, organized as well as informal dimensions of learning and experience, intra- as well as inter-institutional transitions.

Some key points for each chapter are discussed in turn below. The goal here is to set the stage for a broad and creative reading of the chapters that further links them to the major themes outlined in our introduction. In this way, the hope is to preemptively extend the horizon of each piece of research to pose additional, productive questions to support future scholarship.

In this section of the book, both quantitative and qualitative methodologies are represented, but each chapter offers a detailed account of the way that social differences and/or particular mechanisms of marginalization, structures and conditions shape the types of transitions in which these individuals and groups are actively engaged. Some chapters offer well-bounded case studies, another offers an alternative statistical approach for understanding existing data, yet another offers a radical critique of the foundations of inequitable transitions, while still others reflect widely on key themes that intersect with Aboriginal, social class, or racial identities. As in section two of the book, we view each contribution in section one as illuminating a vital aspect of the transition process that has either been in dire need of updating, reassessment and renewal, or has been virtually absent from the literature altogether.

* * *

As we will see, despite the rhetoric of new vocationalism that we discussed in Chapter 1, as much as ever one's social and economic status still play an important role in shaping transitions within and beyond schooling. Lehmann and Tenkorang's analysis in ***Chapter 3*** establishes the current distribution of transitional chances through school attainment for students from working-class backgrounds. In relation to the literature we reviewed in Chapter 1 it achieves several additional goals as well. First, it confirms the types of relationships between paid work and school success in Canada that are the subject of similar research in other countries, notably Europe.

The findings add depth and detail to discussions in the international literature of the difficulties experienced by working-class groups within Canada's largely 'General Qualifications' oriented paradigm (as opposed to the 'Vocational Specific' paradigm, e.g., the dual system in Germany). It is important to note the contours of what might be called partial transitions, such as engaging in paid-work while attending school, and the counter-intuitive role this experience of paid work can have. Extending Lehmann and Tenkorang's analysis, it can be noted that these effects derive from not simply the experience of a particular part-time work setting, but in addition the limited or expansive forms of skills and knowledge that emerges through multiple spheres of participation. These effects also shape the distribution of time and human energy. And, finally, reflecting the macro theme of social integration and volatility referenced in Chapter 1, we see the localized and personalized equivalents and, arguably, effects that can be characterized as weak social ties.

The focus of the Lehmann and Tenkorang chapter is on working-class students and intra-institutional transitions primarily. As noted the learning associated with these transitions is both organized and informal. Moreover, we can see that the category of *working-class student* contains within it a host of social differences. As we see in other chapters of this section, working-class status is always composed of specificities; specificities of ethno-racial, immigration, disability, gendered status in addition to one's status in socioeconomic terms. Thus, in a variety of specific ways, it is these complex and overlapping fields of difference that (re)produce the types of outcomes that Lehmann and Tenkorang document. In this sense, it represents a fitting start to a critical exploration of challenging transitions.

Within the range of social differences discussed in this volume, among the most marginalized groups in Canada are those of Aboriginal heritage. Aboriginals across virtually all continents continue to experience deprivations in relation to the normative learning/work transitions in nationally specific ways. Taylor and Steinhaur's ***Chapter 4*** on Canadian Aboriginal youth, with additional attention to matters of gender and rural location, challenges the presumptions of the linearity of learning/work transitions. In this study, they call our attention to material, cultural, emotional, biographical and institutional dimensions that produce this non-linearity in specific, mutually reinforcing ways. We see how neo-colonialism deeply shapes the forms of transition that emerge for these young people. What stands out most perhaps are insights into the construction, across these multiple mechanisms of oppression, of 'discontinuity' and the complexity that multiple and severe oppressions produce; a general theme that characterizes many of the transitions of marginalized groups through unique combinations of learning/work transitional mechanisms.

In keeping with other dimensions of a critical vocationalism perspective we outlined from the start, in this chapter we see the constrained forms of agency and sense-making that Aboriginal youth engage in through which life course transitions are actively constructed. Often these instances of sense-making are understandable as informalized learning processes. These observations run against any simplistic formulation, seen in this case and several others, that Aboriginal youth 'lack a sense of purpose' per se. How well, we might ask, do even the most detailed sequential and multivariate analyses articulate the machinery of contextualized sense-making and, ultimately, choice-making that we see analyzed in this case? An invaluable tool for interpreting the details of youth actively constructing the social order beginning with the navigation of intra-institutional transitions within education and learning institutions, the dominant role of this contribution is to deepen our understanding with well-situated, qualitative analysis.

In this chapter we also obtain a glimpse at the policy challenge of effectively targeting groups that are put at-risk. There is within Taylor and Steinhaur's study evaluations of the type of programs often entertained by policy leaders in order to respond to social needs including needs related to occupationally specific educational/recruitment programs (e.g., a specific summer internship in health services), and information on the barriers to successful high school placement programs, and so on. We have yet to find a sustained, international comparative collection looking at Aboriginal learning/work transitions, and in this context the case study provided by Taylor and Steinhaur provides an invaluable response to this absence.

In the case of the North American Community College research, policy and practice, we see an institutional location where the dominance of new vocational rhetoric discussed in Chapter 1 is arguably at its most intense. Inherently challenging the new vocationalism perspective, Tambureno's ***Chapter 5*** shows multiple dimensions of the reproductive process that continues to shape the horizon of choices for a range of working-class students. Tambureno's focus is on a particular program within the heterogeneity of the community college system. He renews the literature on the class reproductive nature of these institutions in an era when many seem to believe, even if these processes existed in an earlier era, certainly they do not exist today given the short-falls in technological and vocational skills in countries like Canada. The analysis begins in the intra-institutional transitions between secondary and college systems, but Tambureno then shows how the program he investigates is implicated in serving highly differentiated labour markets outcomes. In this regard, however, these programs stand out, according to Tambureno, as the sublime expression of a 'last chance' for under-achievers still willing to persist in their search for educational attainment.

Indeed, even amongst contemporary transitions scholarship that analyzes difficulties within intra-institutional transitions and gaps in educational careers, little depth is provided as to how these gaps result exactly. Lehmann and Tenkorang fill in some gaps for us in this volume in terms of university students. However, Tambureno's study offers insights into the community college system, through qualitative analysis of interviews and observation as well as through his experience as a former teacher in this system. His work speaks to how institutions create specific forms of student culture, how this is part of the transitional process, how this culture corresponds to the needs of the economy for 'followers' as well as leaders or creative knowledge workers. The classic conception of 'cooling out' that the author references is thought to play a latent function in dissipating potentially energetic, collective responses to labour market inefficiencies such as a basic lack of good jobs. A complex institutional pedagogy is sketched: one that, at least in the GAS program, appears to depend on an intra-institutional transition process that openly ratifies and uses as a disciplinary technique earlier failures in secondary schooling. That is, the analysis offers additional details on intra-institutional transitions (i.e. within the schooling system) that in turn shape inter-institutional transitions between school and work. Finally, while in many instances the college students appear powerless to oppose class reproduction tendencies, at other times it is made clear that these students do have an acute awareness of their positioning. This prompts several questions specific to the learning/work transitions research literature as well as policy that echoes, but with a more radicalized accent, Pohl and Walther's discussion referenced in Chapter 1 of the need for 'activation'. We are compelled to ask what, beyond awareness, would 'activate' these students to engage in alterative practices, and in turn how powerful, exactly, are the forces arrayed against them? The transitions to forms of 'followership' is held in place by media campaigns, cultural production within the school itself, the symbolic coercion of the 'last chance' discourse that every student has memorized (if not wholly believed), and the coordination across secondary, post-secondary and labour market dynamics. Reading across Chapters 3 and 5, in fact the details of the intimate as well as distal, explicit but far more often implicit relations of education, the economy and social order are explored in a way that has the potential to inform new questions on learning/work transitions. It is no coincidence that (to our knowledge) none of the learning/work transitions literature we explored operationalized the pathway described in Chapter 5 as a 'cooling out' period which would cast, in our view, a stronger, critical vocationalism light on which transitional pathways are meant for whom, why and how.

Michalko and Titchkosky's ***Chapter 6*** is invaluable for its illumination of the continuing conditions of deprivation and barriers represented in relation to the intra- and inter-institutional relations of schooling and work from the standpoint of disabled people. Our review of transitions literature showed little attention beyond basic reports of educational attainment and unemployment rates amongst disabled youth or adults. At the same time, the authors argue that the chapter must offer something more fundamental than either a statistical sketch or a traditional qualitative case study. They argue this is because of the complex cultural scene in which, while there are many 'signs' of disability everywhere, disabled students or workers remain mysteriously invisible to institutional life nonetheless. In this sense, and given the nature of the literature on learning/work transitions today, what is required is to more deeply conceptualize the processes, relations and mechanism that might in turn make a detailed, informed study of disabled and disabling transitions more possible going forward. These authors show that the 'presence/absence' phenomenon of disability is constructed through artefacts like 'planning texts' (e.g., institutional policy and public legislation). Together these texts, and the practices of participation as well as learning/work transitions, pre-structure and shape the possibilities for how (all) participants in either education or work organizations interact in the context of institutionalize deficit relationships. According to Michalko and Titchkosky these types of relationships are dependent on disability as a biological, rather than a socially constructed, phenomenon.

In terms of learning/work transitions, how has the literature to date illuminated the deeper roles of planning texts, including the discourses and practice enmeshed with them, to shape how specific groups negotiate intra- and inter-institutional transitions? Not very well. The comments on the problematic role of 'job developers' discussed in Chapter 6, offer an empirical entry point into potentially invaluable transitions research through inter-institutional analysis, if this is undertaken from a conception of the limited and limiting pre-constructions of disability that the authors outline. The stream of youth culture studies that intersects with the issue of transitions beginning with, and still reflective of Willis' 'resistance theory' and certain cultural analysis scholarship within the contemporary Life Course tradition, as discussed in Chapter 1, offer the potential to analyze the living processes, sense-, meaning-making, and agency central to a critical vocationalism approach to transitions.

In North America and in Canada specifically, as we see in Watt-Malcolm's ***Chapter 7***, that despite policy attention that stretches back at least three decades, women remain 'non-traditional' participants in trades certification and employment. This is the case even in sectors that are clearly in need of an influx of new workers. In this context, supply-side policies that attempt to shape transitions between training and employment for women in the trades have not been effective in variety of countries including Canada. To make matters worse, while scholarly concern for women in the trades has waned over the last thirty years, government program support levels have been reduced over the last decade in Canada in particular.

If a key element of a critical vocationalism perspective on learning/work transitions is an expanded appreciation for learning in all its forms (e.g., organized as well as informal learning), in Watt-Malcolm's chapter we see an analysis of the potential role for work-based mentoring and informalized learning processes to support women that would appear to demonstrate positive effects. In relation to the argument of this collection as a whole we see here yet another challenge to the new vocationalism rhetoric that presumes governmental agencies or industry can and are willing to respond to skills shortages to increase the pool of willing, capable and trained workers. However, as a more critical perspective would anticipate, studies like Watt-Malcolm's show that objective 'skills needs' remain secondary to a series of marginalizing social mechanisms which consistently re-make 'durable' gender inequities. Thus, Watt-Malcolm's analysis traces the many mediating (economic/patriarchal) factors – jurisdictional, policy, program, economic as well as cultural – that consistently seem to gender and through this undermine the universality of trades training. As such this analysis adds detail to how the linearity of these specific transitions is disproportionately disrupted for women specifically. As the author (a former trades-person) notes herself, this chapter may provide the bases for asking similar questions of the disruption, lags and lapses that permeate the learning/work transitions of other groups as well (e.g., Aboriginal, disabled and racialized groups). However, in relation to the existing literature we rarely see how these latent functions of social reproduction dominate over the need to address objective skills shortages and rational economic need as we do in here.

The goals of Carter's ***Chapter 8*** are to illuminate the under-belly of transitional programming initiatives in the cultural industries for racialized, 'at-risk' youth; an under-belly that, according to the author, does not effectively appear to support the stated, long-term goals of economic success and equity. Building on the literature review in Chapter 1 we can say the goals of social integration and decreased volatility are undermined through the failure of programs of the type examined in this chapter. Additional goals of the chapter include the wish to inform the perspectives of front-line practitioners working at the community level. As with the other chapters in this section, it takes as its point of departure a specific marginalized group: young black men in urban settings. The analysis further solidifies our argument in this collection for both non-universal and non-linear perspectives on transitions. Carter takes seriously the role of community programming and informal learning which also speaks to a broadened perspective on education. She provides a clear and dynamic account of inter-institutional transitions.

However, a close reading of the chapter in relation to our overall characterization of the literature as a whole reveals something else as well. More than other contributions in this volume or elsewhere, Carter takes the specific context – what might be called the 'biography' of the city and its communities – as an important factor shaping transitional possibilities. Specifically locating the analysis in Toronto and its Regent Park community demands an account of cultural history (e.g., the city's 'Year of the Gun', and the 'Yonge Street Riots' before it) that dominated policy and programming including community-based training programming. This biography of the city is further supplemented by an assessment of urban schooling and economic changes. In providing this unique perspective, she lays important ground-work for novel dimensions of analysis of racialized youth learning/work transitions that have eluded analyses to this point. In short, in the literature far too often the specific role of 'place' is either obscured or ignored by either macro (e.g., national) or micro (e.g., organizational) frames of analysis. Carter's attempt to broaden this thinking provides a welcomed response in this regard.

In most western countries the immigration of foreign-trained professionals has the potential to provide a solution to specific labour market challenges. For immigrants, however, the challenges are often compounded. Transitions, from schooling to work, to another country, and back into schooling, unemployment, and/or the labour market, is for a disproportionate number of immigrants a particularly disruptive series of life changes. Immigrant learning/work transitions are in many ways the epitome of non-linearity. The documentation of these transitions seriously challenge the unitary character of occupational categories. In Pollock's ***Chapter 9*** the focus is on trained, immigrant high school teachers: a group that is a remarkable 10 times more likely to be unemployed than their Canadian-trained counter-parts. While many of these people do achieve successful transitions, foreign-trained teachers are nevertheless disproportionately represented in a particular labour market segment (i.e., 'occasional teaching'), where their transition all-to-often finds its terminus.

The scholarship on immigration labour market entry in Canada and elsewhere has been growing steadily over the past decade and half. Policy research in the area, however, appears to have only recently become able to generate a significant mass of critical assessments covering the role of institutionalized ethno-centrism, language-bias, racism and their many mutually-reinforcing sites of enactment (from immigration departments, to settlement service agencies, occupational regulation bodies, human resource offices and educational institutions). In her qualitative study, Pollock adds further texture to the human implications of such institutional alignments. She is correct in saying that the statistics she provides do not do justice to the dynamics she has sought to analyze. And thus, as we attend closely to the comments of these immigrant educators and the analysis provided we also begin to understand that the management of culture (e.g., in the classroom) through language, comportment, dress, and so on – so central to teacher's work *and* so open to discrimination – is also implicated in how one can construct a professional transition.

WOLFGANG LEHMANN AND ERIC Y. TENKORANG

3. LEAVING UNIVERSITY WITHOUT GRADUATING

Evidence from Canada's Youth in Transition Survey

INTRODUCTION

The employment prospects of young Canadians have long been an issue of concern for policy makers and academics. Regardless of general trends, the Canadian youth labour market is characterized by comparatively high levels of unemployment. For instance, unemployment rates for Canadians between the ages of 15 and 24 reached a high of 17 percent in 1993, compared to 10 percent for those over the age of 25 (Statistics Canada, 2006). Although by 2005 the unemployment rate for this age group had dropped to 12 percent, it was still nearly double that of the adult population (7 percent). Furthermore, those young people with educational levels below high school were at a much higher risk of unemployment (19 percent) compared to those in the labour force who had graduated from university (8 percent) (Statistics Canada, 2006).

In the policy community, this is generally considered evidence that Canada is transforming into a post-industrial knowledge economy, in which increasingly high levels of formal, educational attainment are the key to life course success for the individual, and economic success for a national economy (Sawchuk, 2006). In a post-industrial knowledge economy, it is argued, emphasis shifts from routine production processes such as manufacturing, to value-added, symbolic processes (Bell, 1973; Reich, 1991). Consequently, the cornerstone for this transformation is seen in a highly educated, skilled workforce that is prepared to innovate and gain competitive advantages in an increasingly fierce global competition. This focus on the creation of human capital is considered to result in a win-win situation: highly educated individuals will be able to obtain and secure well-paying, fulfilling, and stable employment, while the nation benefits from a competitive advantage on the global market, which in turn has trickle-down effects in terms of high levels of employment, citizenship engagement, and so forth. In Canada, this focus on the benefits of high levels of education is evident in pervasive public discourses and in policy programs at both the provincial and national levels. Stay-in-school initiatives and various cooperative programs were created to reduce the dropout rate of at-risk students. Universities and governments increased student loan, bursary and scholarship programs to attract a wider range of young people to university, although these programs have been offset by the substantial increase in tuition fees.

P. Sawchuk and A. Taylor (eds.), Challenging Transitions in Learning and Work: Reflections on Policy and Practice, 49–64.

Not surprisingly, this has struck a chord with young Canadians and their parents, who have increasingly ambitious educational aspirations (see e.g., Davies, 2005). Indeed, Canada now has one of the most highly educated workforces of all countries in the Organization for Economic Co-operation and Development (OECD, 2000). Canada's population aged 25–34 had a 26% university attainment rate in 2005, which put Canada ahead of other industrialized nations such as the UK (23%) or Germany (13%) (Usher and Cervenan, 2005, p. 39).

Although this increase in university enrolment is evident across gender, race, ethnicity, and social class categories, access to university in Canada continues to be significantly constrained for those from lower socio-economic backgrounds (Finnie et al., 2005). Access barriers to university for low-income students are often discussed as the result of the out-of-control tuition increases at Canadian universities over the past decade. Usher (2005) has shown how rising tuition fees coupled with an over-estimation of the cost and an under-estimation of the benefits of higher education keeps university out of reach for many young people from low-income families. The importance of financial constraints notwithstanding, empirical studies in Canada have shown that parental educational attainment is a key factor predicting a young person's chances of attending university. Having at least one parent with a university degree significantly increases the likelihood of a young person to be streamed into academic-track courses in high school, develop high educational and career aspirations, and ultimately enrol at university (Andres et al., 1999; Anisef et al., 2000; Lehmann, 2007a).

Despite these barriers regarding access to university for low socio-economic status (SES) youth, we have nevertheless witnessed a remarkable expansion of educational aspirations across social strata (Davies, 2005) and, correspondingly, university enrollment in the past three decades; an expansion which, every year, sees the arrival of increasing numbers of so-called first-generation students. First-generation students are students who are the first in their immediate family to enroll at university. Exploratory qualitative studies suggest that first-generation, low SES students face unique challenges as they negotiate an institutional environment that is outside their normal frame of reference (Aries and Seider, 2005; Granfield, 1991; Lehmann, 2007b), or to appropriate Bourdieu's terminology, their habitus (Bourdieu, 1977, 1990). Yet, there have been few systematic studies analyzing the role of first-generation student status in university completion or attrition. In this paper, we aim to make a contribution by analyzing Canada's Youth in Transition Survey (YITS) data for evidence of a relationship between first-generation student status, university experiences, integration, and ultimately university attrition.

FIRST-GENERATION STATUS, SOCIO-ECONOMIC STATUS AND UNIVERSITY ATTRITION

More recent research has taken into consideration various measures of socio-economic status on student retention and attrition. One of the measures of socio-economic status—parental educational attainment—has received particular attention in studies of university attendance, experiences, and retention. Across most

Western industrialized nations, parental educational attainment has been shown to be one of the most reliable predictors of a young person's own education attainment (see e.g., Shavit and Blossfeld, 1993). In Canada, there is convincing evidence that young people with at least one university-educated parent are significantly more likely to enroll at university, compared to their peers with parents who do not have a university education (Andres et al., 1999; Andres and Krahn, 1999; Anisef et al., 2000; Bouchard and Zao, 2000; Wanner, 2005).

Researchers have therefore asked if this relationship is also important in shaping university experiences and ultimately university completion or dropout. In Canada, evidence for this relationship is rather inconclusive. Although one in four Canadian high school graduates eventually becomes a post-secondary leaver (Butlin, 2000), Grayson (2003) found that the decision to drop out of university is highly individualized, based on a mix of external and institutional factors, and also highly dependent on institutional circumstances. Chen and Oderkirk (1997, p. 53), in a review of enrolment and graduation data from Canadian universities, also identified that over half of all students who dropped out of university left within their first year, although their study did not analyze the role of SES in dropout decisions. Offering a preliminary analysis of Canada's Youth in Transition Survey—the data set also under investigation in this paper—Lambert et al. (2004, pp. 13, 30) did find that—in addition to being less socially and academically integrated into university life (see also Bowlby and McMullen, 2002)—youth who had dropped out from post-secondary education were more likely to have parents with lower levels of education, as well as parents who felt it was less important to pursue further education after high school.

In a bivariate analysis of Statistics Canada's *School Leavers Follow up Survey*, Butlin (2000) showed that students with university-educated parents were significantly less likely to drop out of university. Controlling for a number of high school related variables in a logistic regression model, however, parental educational attainment lost its significance.[1] Similarly, Grayson (1997) found that first-generation students had a slight disadvantage in their grade point average and were less likely to participate in student groups and other university activities, but linked this to lower high school averages, rather than having parents without university degrees. In a 2003 follow up survey of over 1,200 young people who completed high school in Alberta in 1996, Krahn (2004) was able to confirm the relationship between parents' level of education and access to university. Once enrolled, however, the participants in his study revealed no significant differences in dropout rates by parental educational attainment.

Research in the United States shows more convincing evidence that a relationship between socio-economic or first-generation status and university experience, attrition and retention exists. This may in part be due to the fact that more education-related data are collected in the US at institutional, state and national levels. Analyzing longitudinal data from the US national study of college students, Walpole (2003) found that low socio-economic status students studied less, worked more off campus, had lower levels of academic involvement, and lower grade averages while at university. The follow-up data also showed that they achieved overall lower levels of educational attainment and had lower levels of further educational aspirations.

Using event history modeling to assess attrition behaviour of first-generation students, Ishitani (2003) documented the importance of first-generation status not only in dropping out of university, but also the timing of that decision. He found that first-generation students' relative risk of leaving university in the first year was 71 percent higher than for students with university-educated parents, but that this risk declined over time. This finding suggests that early integration is an important factor, particularly for first-generation students. This is confirmed by Berger and Milem's (1999, p. 661) analysis of institutional, longitudinal data collected from first-time freshmen at a highly selective, private, residential research university. They concluded that early integration led to higher levels of institutional commitment, which in turn made students less likely to drop out. Integration, however, was significantly influenced by family background.

In terms of university experiences, measured as 'engagement' and 'intellectual development,' Pike and Kuh (2005, p. 289) found that first-generation university students were less engaged overall at university and were less likely to become successfully integrated into university life. They also found that educational aspirations had a large indirect effect on their dependent variables, suggesting that clear and ambitious educational and occupational goals motivated students to be successful at university. Similarly, Tinto's (1975, 1987) influential conceptual framework for the study of university attrition identifies social and academic integration into university life as the most important elements of success at university. Tinto argues that the higher an individual's social and academic integration, the stronger his or her subsequent institutional and goal commitment and the higher the likelihood of university completion. Lack of integration, therefore, would lead to lower levels of institutional commitment and a higher chance of voluntary withdrawal from university.

Qualitative studies have shown that first-generation students do face unique, class-specific challenges that affect their integration at university, evident in higher levels of uncertainty (Lehmann, 2004) and fears of inadequacy because of their cultural outsider status (Aries and Seider, 2005; Granfield, 1991). Indeed, in a study comparing first-generation working-class and traditional students who left university without graduating, Lehmann (2007b) found that first-generation working-class students were more likely to leave university very early, in some cases within the first two months of enrolment. They were also more likely to leave university despite solid academic performance. Not 'fitting in,' not 'feeling university,' and not being able to 'relate to these people' were key reasons for eventually withdrawing from university. The integration problems identified in the above cited qualitative research can thus be explained as the outcome of a fundamental clash between the students' working-class social background and habitus and the middle-class culture and expectations of university, or, as Baxter and Britton (2001) have described it, habitus dislocation.

Bourdieu's theory of practice (1977, 1990) provides a useful theoretical foundation for the study of social class and university attrition. In Bourdieu's theory, the concepts of capital, habitus and field are central to determine action, or practice. Individuals' cultural capital is their accumulated knowledge of (and ease with) a society's dominant culture. An individual's habitus is based on their position in the social structure, which in turn influences their dispositions regarding, for instance, education and employment. Both combine to place individuals within a specific field (in this case, university). A deficit in cultural capital may affect individuals' successful academic integration, while a working-class habitus might create problems becoming integrated socially at university, which has been described as an essentially middle-class institution.

Based on the above literature review, a number of research questions emerge that we wish to explore using Canada's Youth in Transition Survey (YITS). Most broadly, we are interested in the relationship between social-class background and university attrition. We ask whether having university-educated parents or not (i.e., first-generation student status) is a significant direct factor in university attrition in Canada. More specifically, we explore the effect of social and academic integration, as well as clarity of career goals on individuals' decision to leave university without graduating. We hypothesize that students with high levels of social and academic integration are less likely to drop out of university, as are students with clear career goals. We further ask whether first-generation status mediates the various predictors of university dropout in a way that students with parents who do not have university degrees become less socially and academically integrated and are therefore more likely to drop out of university. Finally, we control for the impact of gender and employment during university.

METHODOLOGY

The analysis presented in this paper is based on the Youth in Transition Survey (YITS). YITS is a longitudinal survey jointly developed by Human Resources and Skills Development Canada (HRSDC) and Statistics Canada. Although YITS collected data with two youth cohorts—one age 15 and one age 18–20 at the first time of data collection—this paper will only report on findings from the older cohort. Cycle 1 of YITS, from which the data for this paper is taken, was administered between January and April of 2000. The sampling frame for YITS was 29, 164 households across Canada, drawn from a probability-based sample of the population and linked to Statistic Canada's Labour Force Survey (LFS). In total, 23,592 individuals participated in the survey, for an overall response rate of 81 percent (Bowlby and McMullen, 2002, p. 70).

The sample size for our analyses was reduced to 3819 after selecting youth who were or had been enrolled at university at the time of data collection. This represents about 16% of the overall sample size of the YITS survey. Of this subsample, 213 (or 5.6%) had left university without graduating at the time of data collection. A binary logistic regression model is used to assess the impact of the theoretically relevant independent variables on the likelihood of dropping out from university.

For the dependent variable, respondents were asked about their overall post-secondary status as of the survey date. Originally, the variable had four categories, namely; 'Graduate continuer', 'Graduate non-continuer', 'Continuer' and 'Leaver'. The first three categories were combined into a single category to be compared with our group of interest, the leavers. Independent variables used were parents' educational attainment, social and academic integration at university, social and academic integration in high school, clarity of future plans, hours worked off campus, and gender. Educational attainment of parents was used as a proxy for SES, which is common practice in educational inequality research. Parental educational attainment has been shown to be the most important factor determining university participation (e.g., Knighton and Mirza, 2002).

The YITS survey had no direct measures of social and academic university or high school integration and clarity of future plans. Instead, we created our own measures (scales) from a series of questions contained in the YITS questionnaire, using Exploratory Factor Analysis (EFA) for the actual construction of the scales. We used factor analysis to ensure that our indicators are good measures of our latent constructs, which in this research context are social and academic integration in high school, social and academic integration at university, and clarity of future plans. Clarity of future plans was measured using questions that asked respondents whether they had a better idea of their future plans; whether skills acquired in the first year of university will help them on the job market; and whether they are sure of future work. Our next latent variable, social university integration, seeks to measure how students get along with friends and cope with the social environment in general, and was measured by questions asking whether respondents made good friends in the first year of university and talked to other people at school. Academic integration seeks to measure respondents' adaptability to the academic environment and was measured by questions asking respondents the number of times they cut or skipped class per month; ask their instructors to clarify things they do not understand; relate things they were taught in their first year to their future; and whether they just felt like a number in their respective schools.

Other indices measuring the academic and social experiences of the respondents in high school were also created. The assumption here is that experiences prior to university education could impact positively by helping students stay on irrespective of challenges faced with studies at the university. Thus, a measure of the social integration of the respondents in high school was created from questions that asked whether they did little work and just wanted to get by; got along well with their teachers; and paid attention to their teachers. Academic integration was measured with questions asking whether they were interested in what was learnt in class; whether they thought many of the things learnt were useless; and whether school was generally a waste of time.

DESCRIPTIVE RESULTS

Table 3.1 shows descriptive results obtained from a cross-classification analysis of the outcome variable with the theoretically relevant predictors. Of all respondents in the YITS sample who did not have at least one university-educated parent, 5.9% had left without graduating, compared to only 4.2% of those with at least one university-educated parent. In terms of social and academic integration, the percentage differences show that respondents with lower levels of integration at high school were more likely to have dropped out of university, although the percentage differences for academic high school integration are very low. Far more pronounced were the percentage differences for the university integration variables, clarity of future plans, employment, and gender.

Table 3.1. Percentage of university students in YITS sample who left university without graduating, by various characteristics

	%
Total	5.1
Parent's Education	
Below University (both parents)	5.9
University degree (at least one parent)	4.2
Social Integration in High School	
Low	5.9
High	4.1
Academic Integration in High School	
Low	5.3
High	5.0
Academic Integration at University	
Low	6.8
High	3.5
Social Integration at University	
Low	6.2
High	3.3
Clarity of Future Plans	
Low	6.7
High	2.8
Gender	
Male	6.4
Female	4.1
Hours Worked during Term	
1–29 hours	6.4
>30 hours	15.7
Not worked at all	3.6

Note: All results have been weighted

Of the male respondents, 6.4% had discontinued their studies, compared to 4.1% of the female sample. The differences between students with low social and academic university integration compared to those with high social and academic integration were striking. While 6.2% of those who felt poorly integrated socially had dropped out, only 3.3% of socially well integrated respondents did so. The same pattern applied to academic integration: only 3.5% of the academically well integrated dropped out, compared to 6.8% of the sample who felt they were academically not well integrated. The results regarding the role of respondents' clarity about their future education and employment also showed very similar results: 6.7% of those who felt uncertain about their educational and occupational future had left without graduating, compared to only 2.8% who claimed to have a clear sense of their educational pathways and the relevance of their education to their future careers. The concerns regarding the influence of high levels of employment on dropout rates (for a discussion of this relationship at the high-school level, see Bushnik, 2003) are also confirmed in this study: 15.7% of those in the sample who were in employment situations that saw them work 30 hours or more per week during the academic year had left university, compared to 6.4% of leavers working below 30 hours per week and only 3.6% of leavers who had not worked during the term at all.

The percentage differences expressed in the bivariate analysis between the dependent variable and the independent variables to be entered into our logistic regression model thus provide some initial evidence that first-generation status has a direct negative effect on university completion. Students with university-educated parents were less likely to drop out than those without. Furthermore, low social and academic integration negatively affect university completion, students with relatively clear goals for their future career were more likely to persist, and the higher the number of hours students worked outside university, the more likely they left university without graduating. If we assume that first-generation status also affects university integration, educational aspirations, and the need to work to support one's studies, the bivariate results in Table 3.1 may also show indirect effects of first-generation status on university completion. For instance, higher hours of work may well be related to lower socio-economic status and university integration may be a substantially more difficult task for students who lack immediate role models with university experience in the family.

To investigate these assumptions, we performed cross-tabulations between parental level of education and the remaining independent variables. Somewhat unexpectedly, the results did not confirm our assumptions. Although the trends of the percentage differences go into the anticipated directions, the differences themselves are rather small. As Table 3.2 shows, students with and without university-educated parents were almost equally likely to feel academically integrated, to be clear about their future plans, and to work large numbers of hours per week. Only social integration showed a larger percentage difference: first-generation students were far more likely to have low levels of social integration, compared to students with university-educated parents.

In order to gain a better understanding of these bivariate observations, we now turn to the multivariate analysis for more detailed results.

Table 3.2. Clarity of future plans, university integration and hours worked by first-generation student status

Variables	*Parents with University Education* %	*Parents without University Education* %
Total		
Clarity of Future Plans		
Low	59.7	56.8
High	40.3	43.2
Social Integration at University		
Low	58.4	65.5
High	41.6	34.5
Academic Integration at University		
Low	48.8	50.4
High	51.2	49.6
Hours Worked during Term		
1–29 hours	39.2	42.2
>30 hours	2.4	3.5
Not worked at all	58.4	54.3

Note: All results have been weighted

MULTIVARIATE RESULTS

In our first model (Model 1), we are testing the relationship between parental level of education and dropping out of university, controlling for gender (see Table 3.3). Parental level of education is not significant in this analysis, although the direction of the coefficient is in the expected direction, as students with university-educated parents are about 30% less likely to drop out of university. The variable remains not significant throughout the other models. Similar findings are observed by Butlin (2000) and Grayson (1997) using Canadian data.

Gender is also controlled throughout the analysis, and remains significant in each model. This confirms other findings that have documented women's higher levels of educational aspirations and attainment, which is obviously also evident in their lower likelihood of leaving university without graduation.

Social and academic integration are significant (see Model 2). Students with high levels of academic integration—measured, for example, in their ability to keep up with school work and how regularly they attend classes—are about 47 percent less likely to drop out than students who are poorly integrated academically. Similarly, students with high levels of social integration are about 44 percent less likely to drop out than students who express a general sense of alienation from the institutional culture of university. The magnitude of parental education and gender diminish somewhat in Model 2.

Table 3.3. Logistic regression model of leaving university without graduating

Variables	*Model 1* exp^{β}	*Model 2* exp^{β}	*Model 3* exp^{β}	*Model 4* exp^{β}	*Model 5* exp^{β}
Parent's Education					
Below University (both parents)	1.00	1.00	1.00	1.00	1.00
University degree (at least one parent)	.695	.713	.693	.720	.714
Social Integration in High School					
Low					1.00
High					.716
Academic Integration in High School					
Low					1.00
High					.835
Academic Integration at University					
Low		1.00	1.00	1.00	1.00
High		.525***	.627**	.607**	.588**
Social Integration at University					
Low		1.00	1.00	1.00	1.00
High		.555**	.618	.686	.686
Clarity of Future Plans					
Low			1.00	1.00	1.00
High			.508**	.517**	.518**
Gender					
Male	1.00	1.00	1.00	1.00	1.00
Female	.614**	.647*	.636*	.591**	.599**
Hours Worked during Term					
1–29 hours				1.00	1.00
>30 hours				2.394**	2.388**
Not worked at all				.530**	.537**
Wald Chi-square	8.38 (2)	19.29 (4)	27.92 (5)	41.95 (7)	49.48 (9)
Log Pseudo-Likelihood	–762.78	–746.71	–738.24	–722.95	–720.59
Model Significance	0.015	0.000	0.000	0.000	0.000

Note: *** Significant at 0.01; ** Significant at 0.05; * Significant at 0.1

In Model 3, we added a variable of students' career plans, which measures respondents' clarity of future plans and how well they feel their university program relates to their goals. The logistic regression results for Model 3 show the importance of this variable for completing university, as respondents with a clear career goal and a related program of study are about half as likely to drop out of university as students without a clear sense of where university will take them. Furthermore, adding this variable reduced the impact of academic and social integration, and actually rendered social integration insignificant. This may suggest two things: 1) students with a clear future goal in mind are more likely to work toward that goal, regardless of how well they feel they fit in at university; and 2) students with a clear goal are still more likely to persist at university, even if they are not as fully integrated academically.

When we add the variable measuring work outside the university into the model (Model 4), the magnitude of social integration diminished further (and remained not significant), while that of academic integration increased slightly and remained significant. As can be expected, working a large number of hours outside of university had a tremendously negative impact on university completion. Students who worked more than 30 hours per week were almost 2.5 times as likely to drop out of university compared to the reference group of students who worked, but at a level below 30 per week. Conversely, students who did not work at all were almost 50 percent less likely to drop out than those working under 30 hours per week. Obviously, more hours of work have a negative impact on students' ability to become socially integrated. Furthermore, students who spent a substantial amount of time each week in the workplace may shift their social networks away from university and toward colleagues in the workforce. Finally, the fact that the magnitude of social integration diminished somewhat suggests that holding down a full-time job (or a job approaching full-time hours) also negatively affects university completion for those who are highly integrated.

In Model 5, we introduce two other variables measuring respondents' social and academic attitude or integration during their earlier high school years. Adding these two variables into the model follows earlier research that has shown the importance of high school marks and experiences on subsequent university completion (Butlin, 2000). In this analysis, however, neither variable is significant nor has any effects on the other variables in Model 5.

DISCUSSION AND CONCLUSIONS

Despite solid and persistent evidence that parents' level of education remains the most reliable predictor for their offspring's enrollment at university, this research supports other Canadian quantitative studies that have found no immediate statistical relationship between socio-economic background—here measured using a dichotomous variable of parental level of education—and dropping out of university. This may well suggest that the relationship between socio-economic status and educational attainment is formed in primary and secondary education and, quite likely, in the transition from high school to post-secondary education or employment. Stream placement has been shown to be significantly correlated with social class, while also exposing students to fundamentally different learning environments and socialization experiences (see e.g., Oakes, 2005). For instance, Lehmann's (2007a) study of Canadian high school students in vocational and academic streams documented how class habitus and streamed school experiences profoundly contribute to an individual's educational and occupational dispositions. The vocational students in Lehmann's study had never seriously considered university as part of their educational pathways and furthermore denied the benefits of university. They were also all working-class. The academic-stream students, in contrast, fully accepted the human capital assumptions of the knowledge economy discourse. Regardless of their social-class background, they agreed that university was mandatory for any life course success. The findings of the present study may therefore indicate that the educational attitudes, aspirations, and aptitudes of lower SES students who enter university may be closer to those of their middle-class than their working-class peers.

Nonetheless, the findings in this study may still be interpreted from a perspective of socio-economic advantages and disadvantages. The bivariate analysis did indeed show a direct relationship between parental educational attainment and university dropout, as well as between being a first-generation student and becoming socially integrated at university. Lambert et al. (2004) have found the same relationship in the YITS data. Qualitative studies in Canada and elsewhere have also discussed the role of first-generation status or socio-economic background more generally on social integration and university experiences. Lehmann (2007b) found that first-generation students left university early and often despite strong or at least solid academic performance. The decision to leave university was explained as the result of an alienation from the norms and culture of university, which they experienced as incompatible with their social backgrounds. Other qualitative research—in the UK and US—has confirmed that first-generation students, particularly those from lower-class backgrounds, can experience being at university as a form of class-cultural discontinuity (Aries and Seider, 2005; Granfield, 1991; Quinn, 2004; Reay et al., 2001). Baxter and Britton (2001, p. 99) have referred to this notion of class-cultural discontinuity as a 'dislocation between an old and newly developing habitus, which are ranked hierarchically and carry connotations of inferiority and superiority.' Although the results of this analysis do not provide evidence for this assumption, first-generation students who enter university with relatively clear and ambitious career goals that require a university education may actually be able to draw on such an instrumental attitude toward being at university.

The relatively low number of low-SES youths who enroll at university and the potential disadvantages of those who do make it, have been recognized as policy problems. Ontario's Ministry of Education has mandated that Ontario universities increase enrollment and completion of first-generation students. Relatively few formal programs have been put into place, however, to address this issue. Most importantly, universities do not have reliable information on the socio-economic (or first-generation) status of their students. Universities offer a myriad of clubs and association for women, ethnic minority students, or gay, lesbian, and transgendered students. Although social class remains a factor that significantly shapes individuals' lives and dispositions, it is not a category on which Canadians form social identities. Policies to support low SES, first-generation students therefore need to address concrete concerns these students have. As this paper has shown, effective career and educational program counseling services would create transparencies that help first-generation students develop clear career goals and develop study plans that help them accomplish these goals. Unlike students with university-educated parents in professional occupations, low SES, first-generation students lack immediate role models and insights into the careers to which they might aspire. Cooperative programs and internships would help these students to establish networks into these career fields and experience them first hand.

Finally, universities and governments have to consider more effective and redistributive loan, scholarship, and bursary programs. The data presented above have clearly demonstrated that the most powerful indicator of university dropout is long hours of work outside study. Without a doubt, for many low-SES students, this is an economic necessity that fundamentally limits their ability to become fully integrated at university and to dedicate the necessary amount of time to their academic studies. Spending long hours at work, most likely in semi- and unskilled jobs, may also contribute to the habitus dislocation students experience. Working may provide the kind of reassurance of habitus that these students miss at university, while at the same time providing an income for consumption and leisure which eludes them when they go to school.

These findings and interpretations highlight the importance of understanding the inter-institutional dimensions of school-work transitions. The formation and transformation of habitus and dispositions in an individuals' immediate social environment at home, at school, at post-secondary educational institutions and in employment all shape, enable, and restrict school-work transitions over the life course. Nonetheless, we also need to approach these findings and policy recommendations with some hesitation. The first wave of YITS data, on which this analysis is based, has only a limited number of respondents who have been to and completed university. Consequently, the relatively low number of cases under investigation may have affected our ability to find significance in the relationship between parental level of education and university dropout. Subsequent waves of YITS will offer the possibility to shed further light on this issue. The data set under investigation can also not tell us if dropout decisions are final or if students who dropped out return to university at some later point in time. The longitudinal character of YITS will offer future opportunities to further investigate the timing of dropout decisions (see e.g., Ishitani, 2003), reasons for dropping out (academic failure vs. class-cultural dislocation), and the employment and educational pathways taken up after dropping out of university. Particularly the latter is important to understand the differences between dropout and stopout decisions and the role of non-university forms of post-secondary education for the formation of successful occupational identities and life courses.

Despite the pervasiveness of the knowledge-economy discourse, it has also been argued that the labour market does in fact not create the kinds of employment opportunities we have come to associate with a knowledge-intensive post-industrial economy. In fact, lost industrial jobs are more likely replaced with low-skilled service work requiring very little human capital. Livingstone (2004) has extensively documented increasing levels of underemployment in Canada. In the UK, Brown (2003) argues that working-class students who graduate from university are at a heightened risk of falling into what he calls an opportunity trap, as post-industrial labour markets, perhaps more so than traditional industrial labour markets, use processes of social closure to exclude disadvantaged groups from access to rewarding career opportunities. In the context of this opportunity trap, the relative lack of social and economic capital of working-class university graduates restrict their ability to exchange their degree for the limited number of jobs that require this type of education.

Decisions to drop out of university have important social and individual implications if we are to take serious the debates of the knowledge economy and if we consider the originally high ambitions that led these young people to university. Equally important, the changing career trajectories of those who have dropped out and subsequently entered respected, fulfilling, and well-paying careers via community colleges and apprenticeships (Lehmann, 2007b) also suggest that we need to subject knowledge-economy discourses to a more critical debate, which ultimately may lead young people, regardless of social class, gender, race or ethnicity, to consider a larger range of educational and occupational options.

NOTES

1 What emerged as more significant predictors of university leaving were having failed a grade in elementary school, having left (but returned to) high school at some point, having experienced problems with science in high school, having received low average grades in the last term of high school, and having skipped classes (Butlin 2000, pp. 13–14).

REFERENCES

Andres, L., Anisef, P., Krahn, H., Looker, D., & Thiessen, V. (1999). The persistence of social structure: Cohort, class and gender effects on the occupational aspirations and expectations of Canadian youth. *Journal of Youth Studies*, *2*(3), 261–282.

Andres, L., & Krahn, H. (1999). Youth pathways in articulated postsecondary systems: Enrolment and completion patterns of urban young women and men. *Canadian Journal of Higher Education*, *29*(1), 47–82.

Anisef, P., Axelrod, P., Baichman-Anisef, E., James, C., & Turrittin, A. (2000). *Opportunity and uncertainty: Life course experiences of the class of '73*. Toronto: University of Toronto Press.

Aries, E., & Seider, M. (2005). The interactive relationship between class identity and the college experience: The case of lower income students. *Qualitative Sociology*, *28*(4), 419–443.

Baxter, A., & Britton, C. (2001). Risk, identity and change: Becoming a mature student. *International Studies in Sociology of Education*, *11*(1), 87–101.

Bell, D. (1973). *The coming of post-industrial society*. New York: Basic Books.

Berger, J. B., & Milem, J. F. (1999). The role of student involvement and perceptions of integration in a causal model of student persistence. *Research in Higher Education*, *40*(6), 641–664.

Bouchard, B., & Zao, J. (2000). University education: Recent trends in participation, accessibility, and returns. *Education Quarterly Review*, *6*(4), 24–32.

Bourdieu, P. (1977). *Outline of a theory of practice*. New York: Cambridge University Press.

Bourdieu, P. (1990). *The logic of practice*. Cambridge: Polity.

Bowlby, J., & McMullen, K. (2002). *At the crossroads: First results for the 18 to 20-year-old cohort of the youth in transition survey*. Hull, Quebec: Human Resources Development Canada.

Brown, P. (2003). The opportunity trap: Education and employment in a global economy. *European Educational Research Journal, 2*, 142–180.

Bushnik, T. (2003). *Learning, earning and leaving: The relationship between working while in high school and dropping out*. Ottawa: Statistics Canada. Cat No. 81-595-MIE2003004.

Butlin, G. (2000). Determinants of university and community college leaving. *Education Quarterly Review, 6*(4), 8–23 Cat#: 81-003-XIE.

Chen, E., & Oderkirk, J. (1997). Varied pathways: The undergraduate experience in Ontario. *Education Quarterly Review, 4*(3), 47–62.

Davies, S. (2005). A revolution of expectations? Three key trends in the SAEP data. In R. Sweet & P. Anisef (Eds.), *Preparing for post-secondary education: New roles for government and families* (pp. 149–165). Montreal & Kingston: McGill-Queen's University Press.

Granfield, R. (1991). Making it by faking it: Working-class students in an elite academic environment. *Journal of Contemporary Ethnography, 20*(3), 331–351.

Grayson, J. P. (1997). Academic achievement of first-generation students in a Canadian university. *Research in Higher Education, 38*(6), 659–676.

Grayson, J. P. (2003). *Research on retention and attrition*. Montreal: Canada Millennium Scholarship Foundation.

Ishitani, T. T. (2003). A longitudinal approach to assessing attrition behavior among first-generation students: Time-varying effects of pre-college characteristics. *Research in Higher Education, 44*(4), 433–449.

Knighton, T., & Mirza, S. (2002). Post-secondary participation: The effects of parents' education and household income. *Education Quarterly Review, 8*(3), 25–32.

Krahn, H. (2004). Choose your parents carefully: Social class, post-secondary education, and occupational outcomes. In E. G. a. N. G. James Curtis (Ed.), *Social inequality in Canada: Patterns, problems, and policies* (pp. 187–203). Toronto: Pearson Prentice Hall.

Lambert, M., Zeman, K., Allen, M., & Bussiere, P. (2004). *Who pursues postsecondary education, who leaves, and why: Results from the youth in transition survey*. Ottawa: Statistics Canada & Human Resources and Skills Development Canada.

Lehmann, W. (2004). 'For some reason, I get a little scared': Structure, agency, and risk in school work transitions. *Journal of Youth Studies, 7*(4), 379–396.

Lehmann, W. (2007a). *Choosing to labour? School-work transitions and social class*. Montreal & Kingston: McGill-Queen's University Press.

Lehmann, W. (2007b). 'I just didn't feel like I fit in': The role of habitus in university drop-out decisions. *Canadian Journal of Higher Education, 37*(2), 1001–1022.

Livingstone, D. W. (2004). *The education-jobs gap: Underemployment or economic democracy* (2nd ed.). Toronto: Broadview Press.

Oakes, J. (2005). *Keeping track: How schools structure inequality* (2nd ed.). New Haven, CT & London: Yale University Press.

Pike, G. R., & Kuh, G. D. (2005). First- and second-generation college students: A comparison of their engagement and intellectual development. *The Journal of Higher Education, 76*(3), 276–300.

Quinn, J. (2004). Understanding working-class 'drop-out' from higher education through a sociocultural lens: Cultural narratives and local contexts. *International Studies in Sociology of Education, 14*(1), 57–73.

Reay, D., Davies, J., David, M., & Ball, S. J. (2001). Choices of degree or degrees of choice? Class, 'race' and the higher education choice process. *Sociology, 35*(4), 855–874.

Reich, R. B. (1992). *The work of nations: Preparing ourselves for 21st century capitalism*. New York: Vintage.

Sawchuk, P. (2006). 'Use-value' and the rethinking of skills, learning and the labour process. *Journal of Industrial Relations, 48*(5), 593–617.

Shavit, Y., & Blossfeld, H.-P. (Eds.). (1993). *Persistent inequality: Changing educational attainment in thirteen countries*. Boulder, CO: Westview Press.

Tinto, V. (1975). Dropout from higher education: A theoretical synthesis of recent research. *Review of Educational Research, 45*(1), 89–125.

Tinto, V. (1987). *Leaving college: Rethinking the causes and cures of student attrition*. Chicago and London: The University of Chicago Press.

Usher, A. (2005). *A little knowledge is a dangerous thing: How perceptions of costs and benefits affect access to education*. Washington, Toronto, and Melbourne: Educational Policy Institute.

Usher, A., & Cervenan, A. (2005). *Global higher education rankings 2005*. Toronto: Educational Policy Institute.

Walpole, M. (2003). Socioeconomic status and college: How SES affects college experiences and outcomes. *The Review of Higher Education, 27*(1), 45–73.

Wanner, R. A. (2005). Twentieth-century trends in occupational attainment in Canada. *Canadian Journal of Sociology, 30*(4), 441–469.

Wolfgang Lehmann
Department of Sociology
The University of Western Ontario

Eric Tenkorang
Department of Sociology
The University of Western Ontario

ALISON TAYLOR AND EVELYN STEINHAUER

4. EVOLVING CONSTRAINTS AND LIFE 'CHOICES'

Understanding the Career Pathways of Students in First Nations Communities

INTRODUCTION

This paper examines the institutional and personal factors that influence the career pathways of First Nations[1] youth in Alberta, Canada. Our focus is on a provincial summer work experience program that was designed to interest high school students in health careers. This internship program, like many school-to-work initiatives in OECD countries, aimed to attract young people to a sector with reported skills 'shortages' and to help smooth their transition to work by making career pathways more transparent (cf. OECD, 2000). The program also made assumptions about students – for example, that they would go directly to university upon completing high school, and then secure work in their occupational area. However, our interviews between 2004 and 2006 with youth and partners involved in the internship program in an Aboriginal community challenge these assumptions.

Our intention is therefore to take a closer look at the institutional context within which such career education programs operate to understand how young people make sense of their decisions. The paper is divided into four parts: first, we discuss conceptual influences on our work; second, we describe our research methodology and introduce the case. The third section presents our analysis of the institutional and personal factors that appear to affect the 'choices' made by First Nations youth. Finally, we discuss the implications of our findings.

CONCEPTUAL INFLUENCES

The idea that young adults follow a developmental process that involves a linear and sequential movement toward their goals has been critiqued by a number of writers (Dwyer and Wyn, 2001; Looker and Dwyer, 1998; Raffe, 2003; te Riele, 2004). Raffe (2003) summarizes three main criticisms of the pathways metaphor that has dominated educational policy discourse in several OECD countries in recent years as follows: the idea of linearity ignores the complexity of transitions (e.g., many students combine work and study, many cycle between living on their own and in their parental home); in privileging the transition to paid work, pathways discourse ignores other important transitions experienced by young people; and the individualism of pathways discourse ignores social structures and mistakenly assumes that pathways are equally accessible to all young people.

P. Sawchuk and A. Taylor (eds.), Challenging Transitions in Learning and Work: Reflections on Policy and Practice, 65–84.

In contrast to the idea that youth biographies took a particular form in the past, some writers suggest that transition processes have become more uncertain, fragmented, and individualized (Beck, 1992; du Bois Reymond, 1998). However, the assertion that 'normal' biographies have been replaced by 'choice' biographies ignores the constraints on the choices available to young people (te Riele, 2004; Andres et al., 1999). As a result of theoretical debate, some researchers have focused on empirically exploring the relationship between structural factors such as class and gender, and individual reflexive decision-making in the school-to-work transition process (e.g., Lehmann, 2004; Rudd and Evans, 1998).

Other writers argue that the idea of a linear pathway was only ever applicable to a minority of young people (e.g., middle class white males in the 1950s) and therefore researchers need to explore the conditions under which different groups of young people are living and the meanings they attach to life events (Dwyer and Wyn, 2001). For example, Looker and Dwyer (1998) report findings from longitudinal studies of youth in Canada and Australia, which suggest that the transition experiences of rural youth are qualitatively different from those of urban youth and do not conform to the 'linear pathway' metaphor. This is partly because the pursuit of higher education usually has a greater impact on family relationships and can carry financial and personal burdens that impact their studies. These authors argue that the educational decisions of rural youth are not made in isolation from other decisions about work, marriage, parenting, and geographical mobility. However, they may have adverse effects; for example, in 2004/05, rural high school drop out rates were nearly twice as high as the urban drop out rate (Canadian Council on Learning, 2006).

Some of the findings related to rural youth also describe the experiences of First Nations youth. However, there is a paucity of empirical work that focuses specifically on the transition process for these youth. Gabor, Thibodeau, and Manychief (1996) suggest that a lack of housing, transportation, and employment opportunities limited the options for Aboriginal youth who wished to stay on reserves.[2] Early experimentation with alcohol and drugs were common and made it difficult for youth to pursue healthier lifestyles. At the same time, youth who left the reserve often dealt with discrimination and conflicts between their values and those prevalent in the mainstream culture. For many, the path to 'success' was perceived as becoming 'non-Indian' (Deyhle, 1992). For example, Grant and Gillespie (1993, p. 4) write:

> Native children come from homes and communities where the cultural expectations and values are different from, and discontinuous with, those held by mainstream society ... They must decide to which cultural belief system they will pledge their allegiance: the one they have learned from their community or the one promoted by the public school system. Choosing the former usually means falling further and further behind and eventually leaving school. Choosing the latter can lead to serious self-destructive behaviors of chemical addiction, violence, abuse-all typical responses of a societal group coping with cultural discontinuity.

Our study focuses on a sub-sample of First Nations youth who were on track to graduate from high school and who had expressed an interest in health services careers. We begin from the assumption that young people living on reserves are unlikely to fit the pathways metaphor, partly because the transition to a knowledge economy has meant that the transitions of all youth are more uncertain, but also because of differences in opportunity structures for these youth (cf. Deyhle, 1992). The rest of the paper explores the specific institutional and personal factors that need to be recognized by policy-makers if they are to better support Native youth in their transitions.

RESEARCH METHOD AND CONTEXT

This study began with an evaluation of a provincial work experience program that provides high school students with summer work experience opportunities in health care occupations. The program targets students who aspire to work in a healthcare occupation after completing a health-related post-secondary program (Taylor, Sabetghadam and Brigham, 2003). In 2003 and 2004, a treaty[3] area in southern Alberta piloted this program; the 2004 cohort included 12 students from three communities within the treaty area who participated in the six-week summer health internship. Eight of these students were from the largest reserve and all but two of the placements were in health facilities located on reserves. The program goals were: to increase students' awareness of careers in healthcare, to build employability and marketability skills in youth, and to grow a future health services talent pool. Like other rural sites, coordinators were concerned about attracting young people who pursue further education and training back to the community.

Our research began with an assessment of this summer work experience program based on interviews with students, workplace supervisors, educators, and coordinators in August and September 2004 (Taylor and Steinhauer, 2005). A second visit occurred in August 2005 and more follow-up interviews were conducted (with a health department representative, tribal council coordinator, and student). As 'outsiders' (although Evelyn is from another First Nation community in northern Alberta), we recognized the need to gain a better sense of the context in which this work experience program occurred. We therefore returned to the largest community in February 2006 to conduct additional interviews with individuals representing the band school, tribal college, health department, and employment and skills training department, as well as with students who had been involved in the internship in 2004. Five of the six students interviewed were female, which is representative of overall program enrolments.[4] In total, we conducted 30 interviews and focus groups between 2004 and 2006.

The reserve that is the primary focus of our research is one of the largest in Canada with a population of approximately 10,000 people. Interview participants from this reserve suggest that the education level in the community has been increasing over time with more young people continuing their education beyond high school. A comparison of this treaty area with others across Canada found that education was marginally higher than the overall average while the employment ratio and income were marginally lower (Armstrong, 2001).[5] However, this information needs to be placed in context since 'First Nations communities in the best of socio-economic circumstances compare only with the poorest regions of non-aboriginal Canada' (Armstrong, 2001, p. 22). Table 5.1 below summarizes data that support this conclusion.

Table 5.1. Comparison of first nations communities with other Canadian communities

Indicators	On-reserve population	Canadian population overall
Population >15 years old with less than grade 9 education	29%	12%
Population >15 years old with high school diploma or some post-secondary education	36%	65%
Employment to population ratio	37%	59%
Average annual income	$12,245	$25,196
Lone parent families	26%	13%
Crowded dwellings	31%	5%

(Based on figures provided in Armstrong, 2001)

EVOLVING CONSTRAINTS

> In this supposedly post-colonial world, what does it matter if the reserve is run by Indians, so long as they behave like bureaucrats and carry out the same old policies? Redefined and reworded, the 'new' relationship still abuses indigenous people, albeit more subtly. In this 'new' relationship, Indigenous people are still bound to another power's order. The rusty cage may be broken, but a new chain has been strung around the Indigenous neck; it offers more room to move, but it still ties our people to white men pulling on the strong end. (Alfred, 1999, p. xiii)

We begin our discussion with this quotation because it resonates with our analysis of the institutional factors that affect youth pathways in a First Nations community. For example, although the term 'band control'[6] was used by respondents to describe areas of education and healthcare on the reserve, it appeared that the institutionalization of federal practices as well as the continuing control by the federal government through funding relations made it very difficult for communities to move forward in a self-directed way. One respondent from the health department described the process of moving from very tight federal regulation of programs to more open agreements as the 'evolution of constraints.' Therefore, the legacy of colonial relations persists. This section describes the institutional context that shapes the realities of First Nations youth. Our discussion focuses on compulsory schooling, access to post-secondary education (PSE), and access to employment.

SECONDARY SCHOOLING ON AND OFF RESERVE

> What the data suggest is that less than half of the [First Nations] students in Grade 12 reach Grade 12 in 'normal' progression and less than 10% of students actually graduate from Grade 12 in 12 years. Additional examination of the data suggests that some students will stay four years beyond 12 to complete graduation requirements. (Breaker and Kawaguchi, 2002, p. 16)

The provinces in Canada have jurisdictional control over education except with respect to First Nations education, which is the responsibility of the federal government. At the same time, provincial governments may enact education laws that affect First Nations students in the provincial school system, and most schools on reserves follow provincial curriculum (Morgan, 2002). Further, the federal government may delegate responsibility for education to bands. For example, the reserve that is the focus of our research has had 'band control' over education since 1988. The school board is able to hire teachers and operate schools on the reserve within the constraints of funding provided by the federal government. However, the band does not educate all students living on the reserve. In fact, a representative from the school board reported that an increasing proportion of children from families living on the reserve attend provincial schools (off reserve)—reportedly, 40 percent of all students and 60 percent of high school age students. The band has 'tuition agreements' with provincial school districts and the department of Indian Affairs, which govern the transfer of monies associated with the education of First Nations students attending provincial schools.

Participants suggest that students attend schools off reserve for a variety of reasons. For example, because of the size of the reserve, some families live closer to schools located off the reserve. Access to housing is reportedly a significant problem for new generations of families who work on the reserve and want to live and have their children educated there. For high school age students, schools in urban centres with amenities close by are appealing. Further, students who plan to pursue post-secondary education may attend school off reserve in an effort to ease their transition. For example, two student participants living on reserve attended high school in a nearby city—a commitment that involved catching a bus daily at 6:30 am and arriving home at 5 pm. One commented on this 'choice' as follows:

> Like with these reserve schools, you know, you're just around Natives, and then, when you go to … an off-reserve school you're in a minority. It really feels different, and going to that school and getting used to that helped me get used to university being like that.

Although students agreed that there was a higher level of comfort associated with attending school on reserve, this participant felt that the reserve schools provided less rigorous preparation for post-secondary education because they 'are a little more lenient' with students. A few participants noted that 'the standard of education' is perceived to be higher in the provincial schools. To some extent, this perception becomes self-fulfilling since the 'choices' of families to attend school on or off reserve has an effect on student mix, which, in turn, affects programming. For example, a school district representative comments:

> We spend a whole lot of time meeting the needs of our children. Some of them have a lot of high needs. ... And there's a tendency for the reserve system to be dumped on with high needs, or you know, special education kids. And the public systems don't want to take them—it's more work and stuff. And it's not where they just go and say, 'hey, you go to the reserve system.' The way I see it is they seem to get a rough time, parents and students, when they take them to the other systems ... And it's basically open arms [here]—we'll work with them, we'll do what we have to do and they end up staying. So we're getting an audience, a fairly large audience of that kind. So we teach to that end.

These comments, along with those of students, suggest that disproportionate numbers of high achieving students living on reserve may attend provincial schools while disproportionate numbers of students with special needs attend schools on the reserve. The student mix necessarily impacts programming. For example, a participant from the high school on reserve suggested that just over a third of students were taking advanced level courses (required for university entrance), around a quarter were in 'intermediate courses' (qualifying them for some college programs), and the remaining 40 percent were taking Integrated Occupations Program (IOP) courses leading to a certificate of achievement (requiring fewer credits than a high school diploma). The 40 percent figure is substantially higher than the range of 4 to 8 percent of students in provincial schools across Alberta reported to be enrolled in IOP courses in 1998 (Taylor, 2003). School choice therefore appears to affect the mix of students in schools, and ultimately, school programming (cf. Taylor, 2006).

Further, participants suggest that the resources provided to on-reserve schools compare unfavourably with those of provincial schools. For example, a representative from the school board commented that although the district has chosen to provide Aboriginal language immersion programming at the elementary level in an effort to maintain culture, the federal government does not provide additional funding support. Further, this participant quotes a 'senior official from INAC [Indian and Northern Affairs Canada]' as saying 'we'll never be able to keep up with [Premier] Klein's education budget,' particularly in the area of funding for students with special needs.[7] Similar to other rural districts that lack the economies of scale of urban centres, there are also challenges associated with trying to offer the required range of courses to small numbers of students. One indication of resource deficiency is the fact that teacher salaries on reserve are reportedly 'six to seven thousand [dollars] less on average' than those in provincial schools. Further, because of funding uncertainties, teachers are hired on limited-term contracts. In these ways, conditions of work are less favourable in reserve schools.

Reserve schools also face challenges in trying to provide work experience and other career exploration opportunities for students because of the size of the reserve, a lack of public transportation, limited placement opportunities, and scheduling challenges. For example, a provincial coordinator who was working to promote high school apprenticeship programs in Aboriginal communities noted that it was difficult to find qualified journeypersons and placements for students interested in skilled trades work on reserves because of the lack of employer base. Placements off reserve were also difficult to secure because reserve schools were competing for employers with provincial schools and students. Arranging transportation for students and providing time for work experience coordinators was also highly problematic. Further, comments from school personnel suggest that work experience opportunities were seen as most important for students who were unlikely to pursue post-secondary education. These observations are consistent with the finding that rural communities across Canada find it difficult to implement effective school-to-careers strategies (Canadian Council on Learning, 2006), although the student mix and poor employment conditions within First Nations communities arguably add to their challenges.

The summer internship in healthcare was a unique program in three aspects: its focus on students who plan to pursue post-secondary education, its emphasis on career planning, and central coordination by the tribal council. For example, the band with the largest number of interns required students to attend a one-week science camp at a university located several hours drive from the reserve as a way of introducing them to health careers and university life. The program operated successfully for two years. However, changes in tribal governance resulted in the discontinuation of this program in 2005. In the absence of central coordination, support, and funding, participants from schools, the health department, and other agencies agreed that it was more difficult to provide students with opportunities for career exploration.

Educators saw the loss of the program as detrimental because they felt that many students lack a sense of purpose in their education. Youth living in First Nations communities were perceived to have less well-defined horizons for action[8] than other students, as a school district representative suggests in the following exchange:

> I[9]: Are students living on reserve different from non-Native students? Or do you think all teenagers are having more difficulty nowadays thinking about the future?
>
> P: I believe it's coming from the home. I don't think we on the reserve discipline our children to the point where, you know, you've got to have something in mind, we've got to have a goal. You have to kind of instil that into our children to plan something that they want to do… you know, to help them explore things. I see it more as parents just letting—they've got this idea as long as the kids are going to school every day, everything is fine. They, in a sense, expect [educators] to handle all that aspect and we do, you know, the career education, career fairs … But there isn't that drive to really want to say 'this is what I'll do right now and maybe I might change my mind twenty times by the time I'm finished high school.' It's not like that. And I see that in [name of neighbouring town] and some other places with non-Native families. And it's happening with some of our families as well, but not to the extent it should be.

I[9]: And is it related to the education level of parents?
P: Yeah, a lot of them don't have a lot of that training. But a lot of them, the challenge on the reserve is related to alcohol and drugs.

Students involved in the internship saw themselves as choosing a different path from many of their peers who had become involved with alcohol and drugs. Participants tended to come from families that encouraged further education. Of the six students interviewed in February 2006, four came from families where a parent was a teacher, and a couple had older siblings who were attending college or university. However, even among this select group, most were not following a direct pathway from high school to university.

One student had started university in a 'transition program' but dropped out (partly because of the death of a community member). At the time of our interview, he was living with his parents while attending a condensed six-month program at the college on the reserve. A second student started a two-year certificate program at a college in a nearby city but dropped out (partly for financial reasons) and was working full time in a retail position and living with her mother. This participant hoped to return to college within a year, but noted also that she would soon be living on her own and caring for her 14-year old brother. A third was enrolled in a three-year diploma program at a college in a nearby city and was living there with her boyfriend. A fourth had been unable to graduate from high school on the reserve as expected because of illness and had taken an additional year to upgrade and complete her diploma. She planned to apply to university for general arts. A fifth (who was 16 years old) was attending high school off reserve, was taking advanced level courses, and planned to pursue post-secondary education. However, in the course of a year, she had changed her career goal from paediatrician to massage therapist. The last student was attending her first semester of university in a general arts program and had changed her career goal from psychiatrist to psychologist. This student was the only one following the path assumed by internship program coordinators.

It is noteworthy that no student was enrolled in a science program at university. Three of the students would need to take pre-requisite courses or upgrade to enter such a program. One of these young people commented, 'I kind of don't push myself as much as I should, yeah. I wouldn't mind being in school to be a doctor but it kind of seems long.' The decisions made by student participants are consistent with the words of a representative from the health department in an earlier interview:

> I asked the students one time, I said, 'why isn't there an interest in the health [area]?' and they're all saying, 'Well we really want to take care of our Elders and we enjoy this but it's so hard because of the sciences. We never do well enough in science...' You know, then they have to repeat, and they don't want to repeat, and they get accepted into another program. So they just want to start something.

The preceding discussion highlights some of the institutional challenges that affect the experiences, attitudes, and horizons for action of First Nations youth.

The student mix on reserve affects programming, and students who aspire to post-secondary education find themselves leaving most of their peers behind. Further, students who attended schools on reserve reported facing questions from people inside and outside the community about whether their aspirations were attainable, partly because of negative perceptions about the quality of schooling on reserve. Finally, there are challenges to schools providing career education because of a lack of resources, and the distance to and availability of placements. These factors and others discussed in the next few sections provide insight into why it is more difficult for students attending school on reserves to develop clearly-defined horizons for action with respect to future education and work.

ACCESS TO AND CHALLENGES ASSOCIATED WITH POST-SECONDARY EDUCATION (PSE)

> Status Indians are theoretically eligible for funding of their post-secondary education, but many do not receive it. The limited resources of the Student Support Program mean not all interested Aboriginal people can access band funds. The Assembly of First Nations estimates that approximately 8,475 Aboriginal applicants didn't get funding for post secondary education in 2000–2001. ... The number of students supported by the post-secondary program has increased from about 3,600 in 1988–1978 to approximately 27,500 in 1999–2000. Funding has not increased since 1994, when $20 million was added. (Malatest and Associates, 2004, pp. 19–20)

When asked about the destinations of high school graduates who had attended school on reserve (34 students in 2006), a school administrator responded that, in the past, about half have gone directly to a post-secondary institution, some took a year off with the intention of pursuing further education, while others looked for work. An administrator at the band-operated college added that over half of funded students attend college or university in the closest urban centre (less than 100 km from the centre of the reserve). Of these students, just over half attend the college and the remainder attend university. Although educators encourage students to go directly to university, several participants suggested that a more common route for students is to take two-year college programs that transfer to university programs. According to a school administrator, it is easier to get accepted to some college programs and is a more comfortable transition for many students as opposed to going directly to university. This is consistent with the finding that American Indians and some other minority groups in the US disproportionately rely on community colleges as their point of initial access to higher education (Richardson, 1990, cited in Archibald et al., 2002).

Despite the fact that First Nations education levels are increasing, students' pursuit of PSE is affected by the availability of student funding, the availability of further education opportunities on or near the reserve, and the support provided by institutions for Aboriginal students. In the community that is the focus of our study, a representative of the band-controlled college that administers post-secondary funding confirmed that money is scarce:

> P: We'll have 380 post-secondary students around the country and in the US… masters, doctorate, and undergrad programs. … We have between 700 and 800 applicants [for funding] and we reject 60 percent.
> I1: [From my experience] it is usually a large number and those are the ones that just applied and there's still some that just don't bother applying.
> P: Yeah, there's some that applied maybe two years ago and they're told 'you are Priority 3.'
> I2: How do you make the decision, what criteria?
> P: We have priorities 1, 2, and 3. Priority 1 is continuing and high school students. … [Priority 2's tend to stay there] because you can't get enough [funding] to get to them. … There's about 200 waiting and then there's another 200 at priority 3 so it's kind of got stuck there—we've got no more monies.
> I1: And you're finding now the trend is a lot of younger kids are going directly to university, because before we never used to have that in our communities.
> P: Exactly.

Ironically, the increasing educational attainment of First Nations students means that more students are competing for fewer resources. Citing an increase in costs and the number of eligible students, the federal government introduced the Post-secondary Student Assistance Program in 1989, which apparently tightened eligibility and funding restrictions for Indian and Inuit post-secondary students (Wotherspoon and Satzewich, 2000). Further, the assumption within funding guidelines of a linear, direct pathway penalizes students who drop out, transfer institutions or programs, or fail their year. For example, a representative from the employment and skills training department suggests that a lot of students drop out if their studies are not going well and then are 'placed on low priority,' which makes it difficult for them to re-enter the system.

Two of the students interviewed were in this situation. A participant who dropped out of college reports that she 'lost her funding' and would be ineligible for the next three years. This student dropped out because she decided that the program 'wasn't for me.' She had also found it difficult to cover her expenses (including accommodations and car payments) with the funding provided. The other student fell behind in his university courses after a death in his community but did not follow the correct withdrawal procedures. He also noted that while he had found the internship stimulating, the chemistry course at university was less interesting than expected. Both students were unsure about their future education and career interests.

It is interesting that most of the students who had been involved in the health internship in 2004 did not carry through on their plans to pursue further education in health-related programs. Although a key goal of the health internship was to attract students to health careers, efforts to ensure that students are well prepared for post-secondary education and are supported in pursuing health-related programs appeared to be limited. For example, although a representative from the health department commented that administrators would like to see post-secondary funding priority given to students entering health-related post-secondary programs, this did not appear to be in place. One student participant stated that the health department tried to facilitate further education and training for him but it did not work out because of transportation problems and the inability to provide sufficient work. The example of the health internship suggests that the development of viable and transparent pathways for young people includes providing adequate academic preparation for post-secondary study, opportunities for career exploration, support for the pursuit of post-secondary education, and ultimately, a commitment to providing work for successful graduates.

An important aspect of the development of career pathways more generally for First Nations students concerns access to post-secondary education for students living on reserves. Although the Royal Commission on Aboriginal Peoples (1996) recommended that post-secondary policies be reviewed, this has not yet occurred. On the reserve in our study, a band-operated (tribal) college opened in the latter part of the 1980s in an old residential school building. Although it initially offered only upgrading, it has been brokering courses through local colleges and universities for several years.

A representative from the college listed the programs offered and enrolments at the time of our interview in February 2006 as follows: high school upgrading (not including advanced science courses because of a lack of lab facilities)[10] (average of 200 students); two-year Arts and Science program that can transfer to university) (60–75 students); oil and gas petroleum administration course in partnership with a nearby college (14 students), a two-year post-diploma cultural program that can transfer to certain university programs, and social work degree programs. The college also ran an off-campus program in a nearby city (75 students). The employment and skills training department offers short-term training programs leading to employment. For example, in recent years, it partnered with the health department and a local college to provide a 16-week Personal Care Attendant course on reserve. For youth who are not in school (including those who drop out of a post-secondary program), this agency also provides a work experience program.

One significant concern for some students taking programs at the tribal college is whether their certification will be recognized off the reserve. Aboriginal institutions may obtain accreditation of programs through an affiliation agreement with an accredited university or college (usually for a single course or program) or they may apply to provincially-established accreditation agencies or bodies, which is a more complicated process (Morgan and Louie, 2006). As the president of a tribal college commented, 'The only way to get recognition is to work as a mainstream institution' (Barnsley, 2005). Alternatively, colleges can seek accreditation through the First Nations Accreditation Board (FNAB), which involves carrying out a self-study report followed by an on-site audit by the board. However, the current status of the FNAB is unclear (Morgan and Louie, 2006) and provincial governments do not necessarily recognize this accreditation. Therefore, tribal colleges appear to face a 'catch 22' situation in that they are often established in opposition to mainstream institutions yet must harmonize with these institutions if their students' credentials are to be recognized off the reserve.

Beyond programs on the reserve, there were at least three colleges and two universities within 300 km of the centre of the reserve. When asked about the support provided for Aboriginal students by off-reserve institutions, an administrator from the college on reserve noted that most institutions have a centre for Native students. However, the issue of whether off-reserve colleges and universities should designate a certain number of seats in programs specifically for Aboriginal students was contentious. For example, while a representative from the tribal council was pleased that this was occurring at one university in certain health related programs, a representative from the band college was concerned about the 'stigma' that is usually attached to 'affirmative action' programs and to the students who participate in these.

Participants agreed that off-reserve institutions offered some support for Aboriginal students and most acknowledged that this support was very important. For example, a school administer recounted his own experience of the transition to university:

> P: I remember transferring to [university several hours away] in my third year and went to the [name of building] and there's too many people there. I just left, I went back to my apartment and I phoned in and somebody helped me get through it, the registration process. It's hard. You know and at that time I was like 27 years old, and it's tough. Just imagine somebody 18 or 19 coming off the reserve and going through that. …
> I1[9]: So could there be more done to support them do you think?
> P: Yeah, I think so. I think there's a lot being done, like at the [name of university], they had the [name of Aboriginal student centre] and [name of other university] has a very good support system there.

Students also recognized the importance of support as they adjusted to the demands of post-secondary programs. For example, one participant compared high school to university:

> I had to be responsible about classes, be on time, and get these assignments done and everything. Like in high school the teachers they were always like you know are 'right, this is due next week,' and like every day they're telling you 'okay, this is due in four days, two days, you know, this is due tomorrow, do it' … But at the [university] you know you have to go through internet and make phone calls and everything. Phone one of your buddies, have study groups and everything and… you know, check the books out at the library, you know, parking passes all these permits and everything.'

In addition, students who move away from the community must deal with the challenges associated with leaving home.

The comments of First Nations students confirm Looker and Dwyer's (1998) suggestion that youth in rural communities who want to pursue PSE usually face higher financial costs and are likely to feel cut off from social support networks. In defining rurality, authors identify characteristics such as an identification of the community as separate and distinct, more homogeneity, and more internal social networks with fewer external connections. These characteristics fit the community that is the focus in this study very well.

Like other rural students, the transition to post-secondary education involved a giant step into adulthood for many students. Younger students were concerned about leaving the support of family. For example, when asked what might hold her back from achieving her career goals, a 16 year-old participant replied:

> Um, maybe schooling. If I wanted to go that way [nursing], I think to get a good one [program], I'd probably, like go to the U of A [approximately 500 kilometres away]. But I'm the baby of the family, so it'll be kind of hard for me like to let go of that whole support system of my family.'

A few of the older students felt a sense of responsibility to their families, which probably reflects the fact that five of six students were female. For example, a student who was attending college and living in the city spoke about the need to come home often to help her mother, who lived alone and had health problems. Her father was recovering from a stroke in a continuing care facility. As mentioned, another student planned to become the guardian of her teenage brother. A third student, who was the eldest of seven children, had deferred starting university for a term because she was caring for her three-year old sister. Interviews with young people (and young women in particular) suggest, therefore, that the emotional as well as financial 'costs' of further education are significant.

First Nations students (especially those who attended school on the reserve) also tended to be uncertain about their ability to successfully complete post-secondary programs. For example, one student refers to the response of others to her post-secondary plans:

> I was kind of debating whether I should go onto university, because I have this group of people saying, 'you can do it'...But I also have these other groups saying, 'oh no, you can't do it, you know, you're Native and you won't be able to do that.'

While this student adds that the negative comments push her to try harder, her initial statement suggests that the responses of others also create doubt. Another student commented that she had been told that the 'work was hard' in the college program to which she applied and 'it kind of scared me.' In addition to these challenges, First Nation students represent a minority within off-reserve institutions and many feel alienated (Smith, 1999). The preceding discussion helps us to understand the reasons for the extended and non-linear pathways of many Aboriginal students (cf. Breaker and Kawaguchi, 2002). Given the challenges associated with further education, pathways that involve incremental steps make sense. The fact that further education does not guarantee work in the community is also important to our analysis of pathways.

WORK OPPORTUNITIES ON RESERVE

> One of the biggest problems I find on the reserve is just lack of work. ... What I find is if you take, for instance, a city you'll see that 80 to 90 percent

> of its work comes from the private sector, and our private sector is very small. (Representative from employment and skills training department)

The main employers are the tribal administration, departments and entities (e.g., health, education), and an agriculture project. However, the unemployment rate on the reserve is high—estimated by this participant at 40 to 50 percent. This statistic is consistent with that reported in the 2001 Aboriginal Peoples Survey (Statistics Canada, 2001). Youth unemployment is also a concern. For example, although the Employment and Skills Training department runs a summer employment program for students, out of approximately 300 clients, only about 100 work placements are available. Since the band is apparently 'keeping up' with the province in terms of education rates, this information raises the question of where the education will lead.

It is difficult to attract professional people back to the community when much of the available work on the reserve is said to be unskilled, and opportunities, even for professional work, are limited in certain ways. For example, two of the largest employers are health and education departments, which each employ approximately 200 people on the reserve. Both departments seek to hire Aboriginal people and have seen their numbers increase over time. A participant from the school district notes that when they gained band control in the late 1980s, about ten percent of teachers employed were Aboriginal, whereas by 2006 this had grown to 90 percent of certificated teachers. In other words, the board of education is 'running out of positions' on reserve for newly trained teachers.

In the health area, although most of the nursing staff is Native, there were projections that almost one third of this group would be retiring in the near future. Similar shortages were projected in a number of other areas. The summer health internship was partly a response to the concern that young people were not going into PSE health programs and that those who did may not return to the reserve to work. For example, the college respondent said that a new nursing graduate who had just completed her program at a university that is several hours drive from the reserve has had job offers 'up that way.' A key constraint, also noted by other participants, is the lack of available housing on the reserve.

Another challenge was that although the reserve once operated a hospital, the federal government closed it in 1999. Therefore, the health department is unable to deliver the range of services and to offer professionals the range of work experience that is available off reserve. Like education, health department staff point out that while they compare favourably to other reserves, the level of resources (and hence service) is not comparable to the provincial system. For example, when asked if there are opportunities for current staff to ladder into more skilled positions by going back for training, participants suggested that the department does not have the resources to support that.

Like provincial health authorities, the areas of greatest staff turnover in the department tend to have less favourable working conditions (e.g., shiftwork). But unlike RHAs, the health department has a much higher ratio of full time to part time and casual staff. Therefore, even where there is the rhetoric of shortage, actual opportunities for new graduates may be limited. This was confirmed in part by the experience of a high school participant who was encouraged to pursue post-secondary training in a specialized area after completing a summer internship but found his hours and pay cut when the unit was able to hire a university graduate.

LIFE TRANSITIONS AND CULTURE

> A focus on young people's identities and on their subjective assessments of their situation provides a mechanism for acknowledging the complex ways in which young people themselves shape and change their world. (Dwyer and Wyn, 2001, p. 127)

The preceding discussion tends to accept the assumption within contemporary educational policy discourse that, as a society, we need to be more concerned about the career pathways of youth. Within this frame, our goal has been to identify some of the institutional constraints faced by First Nations youth in the areas of compulsory education, post-secondary education, and work. But while this analysis is useful in highlighting reasons for their 'non-linear' pathways, it is important to acknowledge that youth participants do not give the same priority to career transitions as do policy-makers (cf., Dwyer and Wynn, 2001).

For example, when students were asked how they saw their past and future pathways, one replied, 'I won't' follow a straight path in the future, but added, 'I don't mind it; I like trying different things.' Another student expanded the idea of pathways when she said, 'I'd say that my educational path has been pretty straight but my spiritual journey and my personal path has been kind of wavy—you know, not really figuring out if I should do this or if I should do that.' Further, participants valued family and community as well as a satisfying career. For example, when asked about career goals, one participant stated, 'I think my career goals are to follow and help our community.' The other student participants echoed this strong sense of responsibility to community. Similarly, as mentioned, a number of female participants were already taking responsibility for family members (parents, siblings, grandparents) and were clear about the priority given to these relationships. Therefore, the value of further education and career success were not necessarily primary.

Although young people did not perceive a tension between their collectivist values and individual career goals, a participant from the school district spoke about the price of success, as defined by mainstream society:

> The reserve is getting more work oriented and professional as adults. The problem with that, and I think that goes more to the society in general, and I saw it with my children, like we get so caught up in our work that we neglect the time spent with our children. That time spent orienting them to what they want to do in life, protecting them against the challenges we have in society.

He added that another price is the loss of culture because as schools and families become better at grooming their children for success, youth often have no choice but to leave the reserve. Therefore, cultural programs (e.g., immersion programs) appear as exercises that are 'not really going anywhere.'

The comments of student participants, on the other hand, demonstrate that culture and spirituality have been and continue to be critical in their pathways to adulthood. For example, most of the young people attended and took part in traditional ceremonies and/or had accepted or aspired to take on respected roles within cultural societies. Most spoke about their cultural and spiritual traditions as foundational for their development to date and future lives. For example, one participant reflects:

> Actually my family is pretty traditional so I've always been going to [name of spiritual ceremony], stuff like that. ... I'm planning to be a [role within a cultural society]. And you know, my culture is really important for me and I realize that there are not really a lot of Elders or adults around right now that really teach it to their kids. My dad and my mom have always, you know, like I grew up with my dad talking [name of indigenous language]. So I understand the language pretty good and I notice that, like our language and our culture are really disappearing and it really scares me because once we lose that, we don't really have anything after that.

The words of First Nations youth suggest that the priorities and values of students are not those of policy-makers. Career transitions are part of broader life transitions and students clearly feel the need to balance work goals with other goals related to family, spirituality, culture, and community.

IMPLICATIONS

The comment of a student participant that 'I just go step by step' is typical of the incremental approach to pathways exhibited by the First Nations youth in our study. Although these young people were no doubt different from many of their peers in that they had expressed post-secondary aspirations early and had either completed or were on track to successfully complete high school, most of their pathways were not linear. Our analysis identifies some of the institutional and personal factors that affect inter-institutional transitions between compulsory schooling, post-secondary education, and work. The preceding discussion therefore highlights the social conditions under which youth 'choices' are made (see Introduction, this volume).

For example, schools on reserve were constrained in terms of resources for programming, higher than average numbers of students with special needs, and limited opportunities for career education. Students attending these schools had to deal with the perception that the quality of education was lower than that provided in provincial schools. Access to post-secondary education was limited by the increasing scarcity of federal funding for First Nations students and the limited availability of programs on reserve. Further, the additional financial and emotional costs of moving away from home, and leaving behind peers, family and culture posed challenges for youth. Finally, although five of six student participants wanted to return to work on the reserve, it was not clear that further education guaranteed work. Given these factors, youth did not make educational decisions in isolation from other decisions related to work, family, and community (cf. Looker and Dwyer, 1998).

The example of the health internship suggests that facilitating career pathways for First Nations youth requires greater attention to ensuring that students are made aware of and are able to meet the requirements for entry to post-secondary programs, and that post-secondary institutions support Aboriginal students. Ideally, a broader range of PSE program options would be available on reserves. But given the incremental process followed by young people and the large number of adults that are involved in upgrading on the reserve, it is equally important for employers (with government support) to provide opportunities for workers to gain further education and training in order to 'ladder' into more highly skilled positions. Access to PSE is related to government funding for First Nations students, which has been declining in relation to the demand. Finally, it must be clear to graduates that they will find rewarding work.

The need for partnership across institutional spheres, coupled with the priority given to community by the First Nations students that were interviewed, challenges the characterization of youth transitions as individual. Rather, *community pathways* that involve a holistic approach to facilitating life transitions while meeting community needs may be a more appropriate metaphor for First Nations youth transitions (cf. Evans and Furlong, 1997). Community often comes first for First Nations students, perhaps because 'our survival [as First Nations peoples] rests on the fact that each Indian is at heart a king or queen that serves the people' (Hampton, 1995, p. 31). A student in Hampton's study elaborates on what this means,

> The quality of the group is dependent on the qualities of the individuals. And the strength of that group and the clarity of that group depends on the strength and clarity of the individuals. And somehow, I don't know how, but being Indian, being Native American, there is an essence to that. You know, that no matter how much we can change of the inessentials, there is a core of being who we are that makes us who we are. (p. 31)

The critical expansive approach to transitions introduced in the introductory chapter of this volume discussed problems with the universalistic, linear, economistic pathways model which is often assumed in youth transitions policy. Our analysis supports this perspective and adds that expanded definitions of transitions outcomes that look beyond 'success' as measured by an individual's educational attainment, occupational status, and earnings is also needed. In this regard, the idea of community pathways warrants further exploration.

NOTES

1 The term 'First Nations' refers to the various governments of the first peoples of Canada. This term is preferred by many Aboriginal peoples over the terms 'Indians,' 'Tribes,' and 'Bands,' which are frequently used by the federal, provincial, and territorial governments in Canada.

2 In Canada, a reserve is specified by the Indian Act (1876) as a 'tract of land, the legal title to which is vested in Her Majesty that has been set apart by Her Majesty for the use and benefit of a band.' A band is defined as a body of Indians for whose collective use and benefit lands have been set apart or money held by the Crown. There are currently over 600 First Nations governments or bands in Canada and roughly half of these are located in the provinces of Ontario and British Columbia.

[3] Treaties are legal documents between government and a First Nations that confer rights and obligations on both parties. No two Treaties are identical but the western Treaties provide certain rights including, but not restricted to, entitlement to reserve lands and hunting, fishing, and trapping.

[4] While the gender imbalance no doubt reflects the association of females with health services work, it also matches the finding that Aboriginal post-secondary students are disproportionately women (Malatest, 2002).

[5] In this report (Armstrong, 2001), education is defined as the percentage of the population aged 20–64 with less than grade 9 education as their highest level of schooling. The employment ratio was defined as the percentage of the population aged 20–64 that was employed in the week prior to the 1996 census. Income is defined as the average annual income from all sources in 1995.

[6] Aboriginal peoples in Canada have struggled to be self-governing for many years, and more recently the federal government has endorsed the idea of Aboriginal self-government in principle. Self-government is based on the idea that Aboriginal peoples of Canada have the 'right to govern themselves in relation to matters internal to their communities, integral to their unique cultures, identities, traditions, languages and institutions, and with respect to their special relationship to their land and their resources' (Indian Affairs and Northern Development, 1995).

[7] The comments of the INAC official are ironic given that several public education advocacy groups have developed over the past decade to protest the lack of resources allocated to education by the province.

[8] Horizons for action refer to the areas within which youth see themselves taking action and making decisions (Hodkinson, 1998; Ball, Maguire and Macrae, 2000).

[9] 'P' stands for participant while 'I1' and 'I2' stand for interviewer 1 and interviewer 2.

[10] At the time of our interview, the representative from the college on reserve noted that they are currently fundraising to raise the money required to build a new facility that will increase the possible range of programs that can be offered.

REFERENCES

Alfred, T. (1999). *Peace, power, righteousness. An indigenous manifesto.* Don Mills, Ontario, CA: Oxford University Press.

Andres, L., Anisef, P., Krahn, H., Looker, D., & Thiessen, D. (1999). The persistence of social structure: Cohort, class, and gender effects on the occupational aspirations and expectations of Canadian youth. *Journal of Youth Studies, 2*(3), 261–282.

Archibald, J., Pidgeon, M., Janvier, S., Commodore, H., & McCormick, R. (2002). *Teacher recruitment, retention and training: Implications for First Nations education. A literature review.* Prepared for the Minister's National Working Group on Education and Northern Affairs Canada.

Armstrong, R. (2001, March). *The geographical patterns of socio-economic well-being of First Nations communities in Canada.* Prepared for Statistic Canada, Agriculture Division. Cat. No. 21-601-MIE01046. Minister of Industry, Ottawa.

Ball, S., Maguire, M., & Macrae, S. (2000). *Choice, pathways, and transitions post-16: New youth, new economies in the global city.* London: Routledge/Falmer.

Barnsley, P. (2005). College dispute upsets students. *Windspeaker News, 22*(11).

Beck, U. (1992). *Risk society: Towards a new modernity.* London: Sage.

Breaker, R., & Kawaguchi, B. (2002). *Infrastructure and funding in First Nations education: Education renewal initiative. A literature review, summary and recommendations.* Prepared for The Minister's Working Group on Education, on behalf of The Minister of Indian Affairs and Northern Development Canada Education Renewal Initiative.

Canadian Council on Learning. (2006, February). *The rural-urban gap in education.* Paper accessed Retrieved March 3, 2006, from www.ccl-cca.ca

Deyhle, D. (1992). Constructing failure and maintaining cultural identity: Navajo and Ute school leavers. *Journal of American Indian Education.* Retrieved October 28 from http://jaie.asu.edu/v31/V31S2con.htm

Du Bois-Reymond, M. (1998). 'I don't want to commit myself yet': Young people's life concepts. *Journal of Youth Studies, 1*(1), 63–78.

Dwyer, P., & Wynn, J. (2001). *Youth, education and risk.* London: Routledge/Falmer.

Evans, K., & Furlong, A. (1997). Metaphors of youth transitions: Niches, pathways, trajectories or navigations. In J. Bynner, L. Chisholm, & A. Furlong (Eds.), *Youth citizenship and social change*. Aldershot: Ashgate.

Gabor, P., Thibodeau, S., & Manychief, S. (1996). Taking flight? The transition experiences of native youth. In B. Galaway & J. Hudson (Eds.), *Youth in transition: Perspectives on research and policy*. Toronto: Thompson.

Grant, A., & Gillespie, L., (1993). Joining the circle: A practitioner's guide to responsive education for native students. Retrieved August 29, 2007, from http://clas.uiuc.edu/fulltext/c100192/c1000192.html

Hampton, E. (1995). Towards a redefinition of Indian education. In M. Battiste & J. Barman (Eds.), *The circle unfolds*. Vancouver: UBC Press.

Hodkinson, P. (1998). How young people make career decisions. *Education and Training, 40*(6/7), 301–306.

Indian Affairs and Northern Development. (1995). *The government of Canada's approach to implementation of the inherent right and the negotiation of Aboriginal self-government*. Document Retrieved June 7, 2006 from www.ainc-inac.gc.ca

Lehmann, W. (2004). 'For some reason, I get a little scared': Structure, agency, and risk in school-work transitions. *Journal of Youth Studies, 7*(4), 379–396.

Looker, E., & Dwyer, P. (1998). Educational and negotiated reality: Complexities facing rural youth in the 1990s. *Journal of Youth Studies, 1*(1), 5–22.

Malatest & Associates Ltd. (2002). *Best practices in increasing aboriginal postsecondary enrolment rates*. Prepared for the Council of Ministers of Education, Canada (CMEC).

Malatest & Associates Ltd. (2004). *Aboriginal peoples and post-secondary education: What educators have learned*. Canadian Millennium Scholarship Foundation.

Morgan, N. (2002). *If not now, Then when? First Nations jurisdiction over education: A literature review*. A report to the Minister's National Working Group on First Nations Education.

Morgan, N., & Louie, M. (2006). *Post-secondary quality assurance practices*. Prepared for the Indigenous Adult and Higher Learning Association. Vancouver, BC.

OECD. (2000). *From initial education to working life: Making transitions work*. Organisation for Economic Cooperation and Development. Paris: Author.

Raffe, D. (2003). Pathways linking education & work: A review of concepts, research, and policy debates. *Journal of Youth Studies, 6*(1), 3–19.

Royal Commission on Aboriginal Peoples. (1996). *Report of the royal commission on aboriginal peoples*. Ottawa: The Commission.

Rudd, P., & Evans, K. (1998). Structure and agency in youth transitions: Student experiences of vocational further education. *Journal of Youth Studies, 1*(3), 39–62.

Smith, L. (1999). *Decolonizing methodologies: Research and indigenous peoples*. London: Zed Books.

Statistics Canada. (2001). *2001 Aboriginal peoples survey: Community profiles*. Retrieved August 17, 2007, from http://www12.statcan.ca/english/profil01aps/highlights.cfm

Taylor, A. (2003). 'Adding value' to the high school diploma. In W. Antony & L. Samuelson (Eds.), *Power and resistance* (3rd ed., pp. 293–314). Halifax: Fernwood.

Taylor, A. (2006). 'Bright lights and twinkies': Career pathways in an education market. *Journal of Education Policy, 21*(1), 35–57.

Taylor, A., Sabetghadam, A., & Brigham, S. (2003). *Career pathways in health services: Report of 2003 survey data for student interns*. Prepared for CAREERS the Next Generation. Edmonton, Alberta.

Taylor, A., & Steinhauer, E. (2005). *Aboriginal health services internship program: Report based on interview data*. Report prepared for CAREERS the Next Generation, Edmonton, Alberta.

te Riele, K. (2004). Youth transitions in Australia: Challenging assumptions of linearity and choice. *Journal of Youth Studies, 7*(3), 243–257.

Wotherspoon, T., & Satzewich, V. (2000). *First Nations: Race, class, and gender relations*. Saskatoon, Saskatchewan: Houghton Boston Press.

Alison Taylor
Department of Educational Policy Studies
University of Alberta

Evelyn Steinhauer
Aboriginal Teacher Education Program
University of Alberta

ANTHONY TAMBURENO

5. EDUCATING FOR FOLLOWERSHIP:

The Social Relations and Labour Process in a College Program

INTRODUCTION

Community colleges have been lauded for their alleged role in democratising post-secondary education (PSE). With open admissions, affordable costs, and local proximity, they provide non-traditional student's access to PSE and the hope of upward mobility. In this sense they are believed to alleviate social inequality and inter-institutional transition barriers from secondary to PSE, and have been described favourably in Ontario as 'separate but *equal*' to universities.

This chapter builds on the 'class conflict tradition of community college scholarship', which is critical of this characterisation, and suggests that the expansion of colleges has lead to increased PSE stratification and labour market segmentation as students eventually transition to paid work, rather than a reduction of social and labour market inequities.

While the development of colleges has allowed unprecedented PSE access to non-traditional students, their growth may have permitted universities to become more socially selective (Anisef et al., 1992, pg. 71; Clift, 1999, pg. 2; OCCSPA, 2001, pg. 4, Smith, 1989, pg. 2), leading to a increasingly hierarchal, and unequal PSE system.

Universities expose already relatively advantaged youth to a better funded (ACAATO, 2003, pg. 1; Easton, 2002, pg. 9; Moore, 2004, pg. 50), more rigorous, broader, and theoretically oriented education, grooming them for transitions into leadership positions, where three-quarters will be employed in professional-managerial occupations (Allen, 1998, p. 16; Donner and Lazar, 2000, p. 27).

Working-class and socially marginal populations are frequently streamed into colleges and other non-university institutions (Clift, Hawkey and Vaughan, 1998, p. 3) where limited work place preparation replaces liberal education, and a 'hidden curriculum', reflecting in a number of key respects, the social relations of lower to intermediate levels of the workplace often prevails.

The focus of this chapter is a general arts (GA) program in the province of Ontario. Somewhat distinctive, these are one of the only academically oriented programs in the Ontario college sector, and have historically been one of the few programs with university transfer as one of the mandates. These programs thus

P. Sawchuk and A. Taylor (eds.), Challenging Transitions in Learning and Work: Reflections on Policy and Practice, 85–108.

occupy a rather exceptional and contradictory position in an institution engulfed in a discourse of narrow instrumentalism, 'hands on skills', and tailing after the immediate labour market needs of local employers.

The chapter expands the critical analytical literature on colleges in the new millennium in the context of the *new vocationalist* discourse discussed throughout this book. It is particularly relevant as a critical social, cultural and economic analysis in the context of the intensified 'new economy' rhetoric dominating the literature on colleges. It attempts to unravel the particularities of how the social relations, 'hidden curriculum', and distinct sub-culture of a college program are actively produced and played out through the daily interactions between students and faculty, the curriculum and institution.

The 'last chance' pedagogical climate, instructor and student sub-cultures, and 'client' markets consisting of student's with marginal academic histories, are actively created in the context of a unspoken, subtle awareness that participants may have regarding the socially reproductive nature of the program, and its unique role in eventually transitioning students from PSE to the labour market.

The analyses is concerned with the role played by PSE institutions in transitioning youth into the labour market by focusing on the way one program may integrate students into the social relations of production. Post-secondary schooling often functions as a social-sorting mechanism, where students of different social backgrounds are separated and streamed into different educational institutions and prepared for divergent labour markets and roles in the labour process. As Donner and Lazar state; "There are significant differences between universities and colleges in terms of their roles, their objectives and the socio-economic demographics of their students" (2000, p. 21).

Through enrolling students of modest social origins, linking their programs to occupational strata's below university credentialed ones, and most critically, emphasising behaviours and relations required in lower to intermediate levels of the production process, colleges contribute to social stratification, the maintenance of class boundaries, the unequal distribution of resources, and the division of labour which characterizes the contemporary capitalist production process.

In this way, this chapter exposes the myth of universality of PSE learning-work transitions, and the tendency of new vocationalism to obscure differences in PSE paths and transistions amongst different social groups. It highlights, as Sawchuk and Taylor describe in the opening chapter: "how transitions are affected deeply by biography, social differences, as well as institutional arrangements and finally forms of constrained agency or choice".

Of particular concern is the *form* of education, its correspondence to the labour process, and the role in transitioning students into workplace norms and hierarchies characterized by alienated conditions and restricted autonomy. Qualitative and quantitative literature is reviewed in conjunction with highlights of original interviews conducted with a number of students and teachers from a GA program. In readying students for occupational sectors where the carrying out of applied tasks is paramount, this chapter sheds light on the way, at least one program, may contribute to the mental-manual division of labour by preparing students for 'educated followership'.

SOME BRIEF METHODOLOGICAL NOTES

While the central focus of this chapter is a GA program, the quantitative data cited for contextual purposes is often college wide, and frequently national. Thus, the intra-institutional heterogeneity within colleges is at times conflated. College, (and university) programs are relatively internally stratified; there is somewhat of a range of student socio-economic status (SES), post graduation incomes, occupational status etc. between programs. It should be noted that the inclusion of Quebec in the national data skews the average SES (and other related variables) of Canadian college students much higher, as university bound students in that province first study in colleges (Raman et al., 2005, p. 15).

Many one-year programs enrol students of lower SES compared to longer programs for example, and the emerging 'applied degree' programs tend to attract students of more moderate SES and pay fairly greater economic dividends. The same of course can be said about university programs; medical programs enrol students of higher SES compared to teacher training, for example, and some programs lead to occupations with greater authority, remuneration and the like.

This research does not conduct a detailed university-college comparison, but at times refers to universities to make broad, relative contrasts between the two institutions in key areas such as student SES, occupational outcomes, and the tendency of curriculum to broadly reflect the division of labour of the advanced capitalist labour process.

The analyses is contextualized in the *class reproduction* tradition, and thus it will be noted that the range of works cited cover an extensive thirty-year period, incorporating US based ethnographies and the classic texts of the tradition, which provide a necessary historical backdrop to the arguments which characterize the debates on the nature of colleges. The older works further offer a theoretical and analytical framework which provides critical insights not found in the quantitative data, or much of the qualitative work which dominates the contemporary literature, which tends to pre-suppose 'new economy', 'human capital', and technological functionalist assumptions discussed throughout this book.

THE SOCIAL ORIGINS OF COLLEGE STUDENTS

> Everyone's parents (at my college) are usually just, what did you say? Average workers? No one is no head of nothing or whatever. Like my mom … she's not the – what do you call it? … the president or anything. You won't see *their* son at our school you know! (GA student, personal interview, 2004).

A marked increase in Canadian PSE participation has occurred in recent decades. This has not however, diminished social and economic inequality, which has, it can be argued, been intensified and exacerbated. Enrollment growth has led to further PSE stratification and inequality of outcomes. While 'new vocationalist' discourse pre-supposes homogeneous and comparable school to work transitions across social groups, the PSE paths taken, the differing returns on various credentials, the opportunities for educational and occupational advancement, and the social and economic dividends reaped are divergent, and not spread evenly amongst PSE graduates.

Ontario students of lower SES have been disproportionaly concentrated in colleges and non-university institutions (Anisef et al., 1992, p. 75; Armstrong and Armstrong, 1989, p. 4; Clift et al., 1998, p. 3, Rahman et al., 2005, pp. 15, Smith, 1989, p. 2). College students have lower parental educational levels in comparison to university students; close to a quarter of college students fathers did not complete high school for example (PRA Inc., 2004). College students are often the first generation in their family to enter PSE (Malatest and Associates, 2007, p. 31), and first generation students are frequently from lower SES families and at a decided educational disadvantage (Looker and Thiessen, 2004).

Frequently having been placed in the non-academic tracks in high school, they have achieved lower grades, have less academic confidence, receive less educational support, have high levels of absenteeism and report lower levels of interest in school compared to university students. (ACCC, 2007, Anisef et al., 1992, p. 75, Looker and Thiessen, 2004, Lambert et al., 2004). Many have limited PSE preparedness; upwards of 40% require remediation and enter college at 'high risk' for failure (Schulze, 1999, Donner and Lazar, 2000, p. 21).

Literacy deficiencies are common; a quarter of Ontario college students in the late 1980's had reading and writing levels at or below a 9th grade level (Gerson, 1989, A 36); 60% read below the 11th, and 80% below the 12th grade level (Easton, 2002, p. 26). A recent study found more than 1/3 failing or marginally passing their first year math course (Brown, 2008, p. A 10). Underdeveloped study skills and limited math, computer, and science proficiencies have hampered the prior scholastic success and confidence of many.

In comparison to university students, research finds college students spending less time studying in high school (and in college); having less educational resources and having more trouble in school and at home; being less academically motivated and being less engaged in extra curricular activities in high school; and of critical importance, spending less time researching PSE and career options, as well as making the decision to attend PSE late (ACCC, 2007, p. 29, Looker and Thiessen, 2004, Lambert et al., 2004). Such behaviours have all been linked to lower SES, poor PSE performance, and high risk of incompletion.

College students frequently originate from socially marginal backgrounds; A high number have learning disabilities for example (Schulze, 1999), 2% have elementary school as their highest pre-college level of education, while 2% reside in shelters and group homes, and 6% self identify as being physically or mentally disabled (SIAST, 2004, p. 14). Aboriginal students are twice as likely to attend a college than a university (HRSDC, 2001, p. 2). The college student body has been described by one college committee as including:

> Illiterate Ontarioan's, basic and general level graduates, women in non-traditional areas, under-prepared secondary school graduates requiring remediation or upgrading, people with learning disabilities, developmentally handicapped persons seeking job-oriented programs, recently released

> psychiatric patients, native students, special need students, and student populations with increasingly diverse multicultural backgrounds (Corelli, 1989, p. 4).

Students from marginal backgrounds tend to have less well defined educational plans and strategies (See Taylor and Steinhauer's discussion in this book regarding the poor preparation, limited academic confidence, and low expectations of educators in regards to Native students) and are described by the teachers in my interviews as lacking educational and occupational focus.

THE LABOUR MARKET OUTCOMES OF COLLEGE STUDENTS

> They would end up in like service sector type jobs, not very high-end . . . it's not much of a credential if you think about it. It's not much more than high–school . . . it's not like . . . a BA or something; college GA is pretty basic stuff (college teacher, personal interview, 2004).

> I think it was generally understood that you go to college and then you get a job and you're never really destined to . . . be a manager or any sort of professional (college-university transfer student, personal interview, 2004).

> "University and community college graduates head for very different kinds of occupations in the labour market" (Anisef et al., 1992, p. 77).

Marketing campaigns have persuaded many that the 'practical' orientation of colleges and vocational centres leads to comparable post-graduation success when contrasted to universities (Allen, 1998, p. 7; Walters, 2004, p. 5). The empirical evidence however, suggests otherwise. College attrition rates are universally high; A Ontario college student has just over a 50% chance of graduating from their program (Donner and Lazar, 2000, p. 5; Drea, 2004, p. 2). More than 40% of those who do graduate will be unemployed, working part-time or out of the labour market, while a third of employed graduates work in an occupation unrelated to the field of study (MTCU, 2002). Thus, a student entering a Ontario college has roughly a 20% chance of graduating and becoming employed full time in a field related to their course of study.

College graduates earn less and have higher unemployment rates compared to their university counterparts (Allen, 1998). On average, university graduate incomes are more than a 1/3 higher (Ferrer and Ridell, 2002, p. 9), and *"even income in the least remunerative university program exceeds the income earned by the average college graduate*" (italics provided) (Allen, 1998, p. 32). Allen, Harris, and Butlin (2001) confirm that: "Unemployment rates for young community college graduates follow a pattern similar to rates for young adults in general through economic upswings and downturns, while the rate for university graduates is less likely to be affected by the business cycle" (pp.'s 6–7).

Those who combine multiple college credentials *still* earn less than bachelor degree holders, and there is evidence that college attendance is counter productive for university graduates as the earnings of BA holders who proceed to obtain a college diploma is *less than those with just a degree* (Walters, 2003, p. 9). College graduates also lack the salary growth potential, flexibility, and mobility that university graduates enjoy in the labour market (Allen, 1998; NGS, 2001, p. 2; Silver et al., 1999, p. 21) and they are frequently employed in precarious, unskilled, low-status and poorly paid occupations. The most common occupations Ontario college graduates are employed in include cashiers, retail sales, restaurant and amusement employees, customer service, general office clerks, receptionists and aides and orderlies in nursing homes (MTCU, 2002).

Many of the most remunerative occupations include traditional 'blue collar', skilled and semi-skilled jobs, such as mechanics, repairmen, hairdressers, construction workers and autoworkers (ibid.). College students are more likely to be employed in goods and service industries, and are less likely to be in knowledge and managerial categories compared to university graduates (HRSDC, 2001, p. 3). Walters (2004), surveying the Canadian National Graduate Survey writes:

> There does not appear to be any clear evidence that college and trades graduates have narrowed the earnings gap when compared with graduates of university programs. Trades, and then college, graduates are clearly at the bottom of the earnings hierarchy… In fact, the gap between them and university undergraduates appears to have widened slightly…When comparing the earnings of graduates of different fields of study, there does not appear to be solid evidence that the new economy has increasingly favoured graduates with technical and applied skills (pp. 11–13).

POST-SECONDARY STRATIFICATION AND THE DIVISION OF LABOUR

> The universities were perhaps the better place to teach people "to think", the colleges should cover core courses . . . basic electronics, basic use of machines . . . (summation of Ontario employers statements) (Gill, 1989, p. 15).

> University students are meant to go on to dominate other people who have lower levels of education . . . it is understood that university students are more highly educated than other people, than college students for example . . . and that they should be in charge of them and making decisions (college-university transfer student, personal interview, 2004).

Universities and the Preparation of Mental Labour

Close to 3/4 of Ontario university graduates are employed in professional-managerial occupations (Allen, 1998, p. 16; Donner and Lazar, 2000, p. 27). Often reflecting the conceptual side of the labour process, greater emphasis is placed on preparing students to perform theoretical-analytical labour, including long range planning and organising, in positions generally characterised by wider degrees of autonomy. University students are encouraged to comprehend and contrast the larger contexts events and ideas occur in, and to evaluate various interpretations of these, and at senior levels, they are taught to *create* conceptual knowledge.

Colleges and the Preparation of Applied Labour

Colleges however, were explicitly constructed and mandated to transition students into occupations and positions in local industries where they are commonly responsible for the execution of applied tasks, and are frequently subordinate to university educated professionals[1]. They are often socialised to work under conditions characterised by restricted autonomy and discretion, where procedure following and deference to authority are frequently stressed. In this respect, colleges have been noted to contribute to the separation of theoretical knowledge from the direct producers, and its monopolisation by management (Robinson, 1982, p. 145).

The *highest* layers of the labour market accessible to college graduates have frequently been those occupations designated as assistant, technician, and technologist; positions of various skill levels limited to the carrying out of applied tasks, and characterised by "little control over the direction and organisation of work" (ibid. p. 151).

College advisory boards have viewed universities as being oriented towards the perceived 20% of the population believed to be abstract thinkers, who enjoy the intrinsic value of education. Colleges however, have been characterised as being directed towards 'concrete thinkers and doers'. Similar to Anyon's (1980) findings regarding elementary and secondary teachers, college personnel have often perceived these dispositions as fixed and unalterable by education (Murphy, 1983, pp. 220–221).

Compared to their university counterparts, college students are given less discretion and greater direction from teachers, more program guidance, and less choice in course selection (Easton, 2002, p. 22). Haggerty (1998) explains that typically "college programs are highly structured. Students proceed in 'lock step fashion' as a class, through a number of prescribed courses" (p. 171). More time is spent in classroom activities and less time engaged in independent work. Many are in class 30–40 hours a week, for example (SIAST, 2004, p. 2, Murphy, 1983, pp. 267–269, 296). Ethnographic literature describes form taking precedence over content, while procedure, routinization and the close following of instruction is emphasised, prompting Shor to comment that 'imagination is held in low esteem in the community college, where training replaces education' (1980).

Some vocational programs have replicated their classrooms on workplace environments. The classrooms of one secretarial arts program for example, were arranged to mirror office environments, with students evaluated on their ability to answer phones, take messages, interact with superiors appropriately, and demonstrate understanding of workplace norms (Coffin, in Konrad, 1974, p. 54). Some programs have required students to maintain a 90% attendance record, with advisor-instructors responsible for closely supervising students and being able to account for their whereabouts throughout the day (Ibid. p. 56), extending the social relations established in the earlier grades of working class schools into PSE.

The Intermediate Social Relations of College General Arts

The architects of the Ontario college system described their vision of colleges as occupying a position *in-between* high school and university (Dennison and Gallagher, 1986, p. 245, Oppenheimer, 1989, p. 2, 4) and this intermediate position appears aptly reflected in the curriculum and social relations. Asked how much input they are given in course selection, for example, the accounts of these students suggests that it is limited: "first semester they just give you your schedule and say 'show up at this time'" (personal interview, 2004). The following students, who had successsfully transferred to university, contrast the amount of direction and structure of their college and university curricula:

> (College) is probably closer to high school. For example, you're given a essay to write, it was suggested to you the number of pages and words you had to write, and the topic you had to write on. And even that confused a lot of people, who became very worried that they didn't have enough direction . . . very structured, but less structure than you had in high school. So a lot of people felt lost without that little bit of extra structure . . . you got to vaguely choose a topic, out of a list you were given, and that's about all the discretion you were given . . . I think a lot of people that did go to college were looking for structure, and whenever they were presented with something to do at their own discretion, they suffered badly for it. I think they got very nervous about it . . . when you say 'write a five page essay on something to do with TV', they would always ask you 'how should I do it? How many words? How do I begin it?' I think they were threatened and nervous because they didn't want to leave any structure actually (personal interview, 2004).

This transfer student contrasts his college and university experience, noting a greater regimentation of college curriculum and an emphasis on form over content

> University courses are much more independent. In GA we're going to school *every day* of the week. It was more regimented . . . it had more of a high-school feel to it, where as university is much more independent. . . you don't necessarily have to attend every class. There were more hours of instruction in GA, and the amount of work and tests was more frequent . . . they would go over process so much! Constantly! Spending a lot of time going over the process of *how* to present something, where in university it's just like – present it! They expect you to know a lot more (at university) I think. It was (college) very slow paced too (personal interview, 2004).

In this respect, the organisational environment and structuring of social relations is a extension of patterns first established in the primary grades of working class schools, where more time is spent in class, and 'practical', procedural routines are stressed over innovative, challenging and creative work. In these environments, student choice and autonomy is restricted, and activities often take the form of copying, taking diction and the like (Duke, 2000, pp.s' 447–462).

Illustrating the socialisation that working class students have often been subjected to and the normalization of disengagement in their previous school experiences, this student explains that a well-liked teacher was one who "actually taught us *exactly* what to do, *exactly* how it was done, *exactly* what everything means", while vocational courses were often preferred over academic ones as "some people don't care about, like philosophy, where it comes from and all that, where everything comes from. They're like; 'yeah, whatever, that's just to confusing for me', where they like, say, computers, where they're told what to do" (personal interview, 2004).

Where the previous observations were made by exceptionally articulate and perceptive transfer students, this non-transfer student describes pedagogical styles disliked by students, illustrating the very points made by the previous students:

> Nothing was explained! I don't like when teachers do that. They just say what they want done, and they expect you to do it. Then if you do it the way you think they expect you to do it, then they're like 'no that's not they way I wanted it done at all', and you are like, 'okay, you didn't explain you know, when people asked you, you just said "just like this, this is essays and stuff"' (personal interview, 2004).

Such variation in student perception speaks to a number of pertinent issues that are worth commenting on here. The intermediate nature of the curriculum is reflected in that students appear to be afforded *less direction* then previously accustomed in their pre-college experiences, a fact that clearly leads to anxiety for some. However, they appear to be given less autonomy and discretion than their university counterparts.

It further speaks to the uneven academic preparation of students attracted to such a program; university aspiring students, with stronger academic backgrounds, may experience the social relations as over structured and less challenging, while those from less rigorous high school streams may struggle when given some discretion in their work, causing stress and demoralization for many. It further suggests a fairly wide variation in pedagogy and curricular intensity from course to course, with some teachers viewing their role as one of university preparation, and others as remedial.

'*Fundamental Skills*'

> The biggest suggestion is that you learn how to type, you learn how to take information and present it, but not create your own information. You use information from other people that is handed down to you, and you are the one who figures out how to present it, but that's about it. More clerical type work. Not something where you will be digging holes all day, but its not going to be a professional position (college-university transfer student, personal interview, 2004).

College discourse centres around 'skills' and frequently, occupation-specific training. The term 'skill' however, is not necessarily used in the artisan-craft sense, but is often employed to refer to generic and basic literacy, communication, numeracy, computer usage, and non-cognitive attitudes in the workplace (Armstrong and Armstrong, 1989). The learning of *specific* occupational skills are believed by many on college advisory boards to be best learned 'on the job', while colleges are encouraged to emphasize non-specific, 'fundamental' skills and *attitudes*, to better facilitate continuous re-adaptation to changing job requirements and a precarious labour market (Donner and Lazar, 2000, p. 13).

In ch. 1, Sawchuk and Taylor suggest that the labour process tends to diminish workers use of control, judgment and discretion, while the 'flexibility and use of skills is not as important as the direct and immediate control exerted by industry over the use of these skills'. Gill (1989) and Wolfe (1989) documented that employers have frequently appealed to colleges to encourage desired attitudes, outlooks and behaviours in students more so than job-specific skills.

Employers in the construction industry for example, complain that young workers 'have no work ethic', and lack appreciation and respect for workplace hierarchies and norms. Other employers suggest that workers must improve their ability to read complex manuals, write basic proposals, and learn new production techniques. As one states: "The role of colleges is to make high school graduates functional in the work world" (Gill, 1989, p. 15). Employers who lament about skill shortages are often referring to workers lacking acquiescent attitudes (Avis, 1981, p. 154).

Colleges have been noted by some to play a role in socializing students to adapt to precarious employment and perpetual re-training (Margolis, 2001, Santiago, 2000). Learning to position themselves to the dictates of the labour market and employers appears itself to be a important 'skill' that colleges attempt to instill. Muller (1990) suggests that learning to position themselves to the dictates of the labour market and employers appears itself to be a important 'skill' that colleges attempt to instill. In this sense, colleges integrate students into the *social* as much as the *technical* relations of production. The adherence to deadlines, perseverance through uninteresting work (referred to in upcoming pages) and the presentation of *received* information produced by others, as succinctly described by the university transfer student previously, are an extension of the labour process established in earlier grades discussed by Anyon (1980).

Curricular Intensity

> It is called a college, but elementary grade subjects – arithmetic, reading and writing rank high in terms of courses offered and student's enrolled (Lombardi, cited in Brint and Karabel, 1989, p. 129).

College promotional materials speak of 'uncompromising dedication to academic excellence' and a 'invigorating environment which opens your mind to new possibilities'. Such characterisation has been disputed by the critical literature, which has described frequently basic courses, often taught by under-prepared teachers with little pedagogical training or support.

Close to half of Ontario college students who read below the 10th grade level pass their courses (Ophenheimer, 1989, pp. 42, 49). Campbell (Konrad, 1974, p. 18) described the gap between college promotional rhetoric and the reality of the curriculum as 'acute', while Brint and Karabel (1989), Luker (Muller, 1990), Pincus (1980), and Shor (1980) cautioned students to be wary of the 'linguistic hocus-pocus' of college marketing.

I asked a number of students and teachers to describe the complexity and breadth of their curriculum. The characterizations ranged from rudimentary to more challenging than high school courses. This teacher suggested that "the emphasis is more on 'hands on', definitaly. It's more relaxed here, and I don't think a great deal of studious work is expected of them. They are not given a great amount of studies and research – it's *very basic*! (personal interview, 2004)[2].

Students also described a frequently less than rigorous curriculum. One noted for example that "some Prof's conducted their lessons like a kindergarten teacher, very slow paced" (personal interview, 2004). Others described courses which failed to challenge them:

> The mathematics course . . . seemed like it was all adding and subtracting, it was pretty much from the beginning all over again. . . It seemed like it was grade three work, and it was like 'well, anybody can do this kind of stuff'! . . . there were a lot of students who were just like 'why am I here? I mean, I feel like I am in kindergarten again' (personal interview, 2004).

While introductory classes in sociology, philosophy and other liberal arts courses are frequent, and may expose students to more theoretical subject matter, numerous course titles are reminiscent of high school subjects; 'Math', 'Science', and 'English' are frequent offerings (Murphy, 1983, p. 9, Tambureno, 2004).

Students Transferring to University are Under-Prepared

Students who transfer to university have high attrition rates and see a substantial drop in grades. A Ontario study of nursing transfer students for example, found most experiencing academic shock and transition stress. These students quickly learned that their college experience did not prepare them for university level studies, including the increased workload, reading, writing, academic quality and expectations of independent work and critical thinking. Many found that they lacked the elaborate speech codes and theoretical sophistication for the transition (Cameron, 2005, pp.'s 28–32). A separate Ontario study found that many GA students who transfer to university also fare poorly (Decock and Greene, 1998, p. 14).

Disengagement and Alienation

> They didn't want to waste time studying or growing intellectually. They would just want to know what's going to be on the test and regurgitate it back and memorize it, (and) that would be enough to pass (college teacher, personal interview, 2004).

The classic ethnographies of Anyon (1980) and Weis (1985) describe alienated and disengaged students in working class schools passing courses with minimal effort, as long as regular attendance was maintained, assignments submitted, and proper deference was given to authority. Poor quality work was assigned a passing grade 'as long as they handed something in', and teachers often 'looked the other way' as students copied each other's work.

In such environments, students learned alienated and instrumental attitudes and work habits early on and were rarely given the 'tools' and opportunity to develop academic and leadership qualities. The hidden curriculum instilled in these youth a vision of work as an unpleasant activity to be suffered through, where one does as little as possible in exchange for a reward. Teachers were less concerned that students developed their creative capacities or leadership abilities than they followed procedures and rules.

The following observations of a teacher and former student, suggest that such cultivated attitudes and practices may be carried over into college. Asked how this was interpreted, this student comments:

> It would have been thought as reflective of the second-class status of college itself. It's very much like high school . . . you could not pay attention, not read the book and get by, with the bare minimum . . . For most college courses, the expectation was not very high, so it was not difficult to get an A, when a lot of the work you had to compare it to was not very well done to begin with. Most students *understood* that there was not much expected of them (personal interview, 2004).

Similar sentiments were echoed by this teacher, who recognized that many students rejected the very legitimacy of the college itself due to this, amongst other reasons:

> Students expected to be graded in the higher echelons based solely on attendance; that showing up and trying should be graded with at least a B. There is a small core of students who find it a mark of status to pass a course with out ever having done a required reading. They think that's a funny thing, they laugh about it . . . that's about getting by with out having to do the work, it's a sign of victory. It's a sign of putting one over on the dumb professors, it's a sign to them that this stuff is all bullshit, that you really don't need to be in school to know this stuff because I can pass a course without reading the text book (personal interview, 2004).

Asked what qualities most students favoured in teachers, the response of this transfer student points to a 'punching in and out' attitude towards school, reflective of the most alienating occupations and being rooted in the previous school experiences of many who enroll in the program:

> To be straightforward and more available with answers, and not so much to challenge the class. They wanted teachers just to present what was in the textbook, something that's not too challenging intellectually or work wise. Most of them would have preferred to not do *any* work, as far as I saw . . . so I think an intellectual challenge was perceived as a bit threatening to them . . . because . . . that's not what they came for! . . .They don't want to be challenged in that way, they want to be *taught* rather than *educated.* They want to be taught something that they could easily regurgitate, rather than having a tool that they could use . . . they went to college to get a job and anything that wasn't really going to help out getting a job or that they couldn't put on a resume, I don't think they were interested in . . . they wanted teachers who would give easy answers, not posing challenging questions to the class, they wanted true and false tests, or something of that nature (personal interview, 2004).

Easton (2002) found many students expressing shock when asked to engage in challenging work, as college is believed by many to be an easy way to obtain a credential (p. 29)[3].

Emphasising Non-Cognitive Behaviours

Apple and Kings 1990 ethnography of a kindergarten in a working class community found teachers emphasising alienated behaviours and attitudes more than cognitive and intellectual development; children learned that work is compulsory, requires following instructions, must be followed in prescribed procedure, and is neither interesting, fulfilling, or related to students needs and interests. Youngsters learned that they had to "share, to listen, to put things away, and to follow the classroom routine" (Chafel, 1997, p. 6).

The demonstration of these attitudes is not a uncommon theme in GA course outlines, which recurrently stress respect for teachers, decorum, deadlines, school property and norms patterned after the work place. Outlines warn students that 'outbursts in class will not be tolerated' and 'deadlines must be respected'. Employer and workplace expectations are frequently cited as rationale for assignments, skills and classroom behaviours; 'employers require employees who can follow instructions'; 'lateness will not be tolerated in the workplace'. Punctuality, attendance, 'listening' and the *ability to persevere through uninteresting tasks* are frequently cited, at times literally, as required traits that students must demonstrate to pass their courses and succeed in the workplace.

Bowles and Gintis (1976) suggested that students being groomed for the professional/managerial class are socialized to internalise the norms, mores and non-cognitive behavioural traits of this group, and strongly identify with them.

College curricula however, tends to limit significant theoretical knowledge, and in a manner familiar to the working class students in the ethnographies of Anyon (1980), college students are socialized to work under conditions of minimal autonomy and discretion; learning to follow procedure, deferring to authority and carrying out sets of tasks, *responding to external motivations*, and in short, developing the non-cognitive behavioural and attitudinal traits associated with the alienated forms of labour in the service, blue collar, assistant, and office administration sectors that many will be employed in.

'And Another Thing; They have no Manners!'

> The structure of social relations in education not only inures the student to the discipline of the work-place, but develops the types of personal demeanour, modes of self-presentation, self-image, and social-class identifications which are crucial ingredients of job adequacy (Bowles and Gintis, 1976, p. 131).

Also frequent in outlines and my interviews is the implication that students lack proper etiquette, decorum, modes of communication, social capital and self-presentation. Outlines inform students that they must refrain from making 'knee jerk' comments, eating in class, speaking out of turn, interrupting and verbally abusing each other. This student re-counts:

> One class . . . called 'personal hygiene' or something, presented a film ... it was a stuffed (mascot) walking around the campus showing people how to pick up garbage and throw it in the garbage can, and how to treat other people well. Even in the washrooms . . . there are signs saying 'wash your hands'! (personal interview, 2004).

Asked what was required of students to pass courses, the response of these teachers indicates an emphasis on self-control rather than mastery of a body of knowledge:

> Attitude matters. A student does him or her self in with the wrong attitude. So we stress in the outline that the attitude should be 'blah blah'. So committed to the work. Respecting others views in class. Being able to listen and to participate, and openness to new ideas. Because some time students come and they are very rude to other people who may have an idea they don't agree with! (personal interview, 2004).

The comments of this teacher suggests that students are disarticulated from academic norms, and that the cultural capital, and behavioural expectations of teachers are rejected by students:

> And another thing is they have no manners! They talk incessantly in class, they arrive late, they eat food in class – and not just like a bag of chips, I mean they are eating chicken and pizza, and they are not taking notes! (personal interview, 2004).

An under-lying student-teacher conflict may be noted in these comments, a tension recognized in all the critical ethnographies, and to be elaborated on here shortly.

'Grade 14' and the Lack of Status Transition

In his classic college ethnography, London (1978) described the status transition undergone by elite university students as a necessary component of the social and cultural integration into the professional-managerial middle class. Schlossburg, Waters and Goodman define transition: "broadly, is any event, or non-event, that results in changed relationships, routines, assumptions and roles", while Cameron suggests "students initiate the transition process by leaving the past behind, separating, dissociating, and distancing themselves from their membership in past communities…" (Cameron, 2005, p. 24).

Elite students traditionally move away from the family home and come in contact with new ideas, colleagues, and experiences, often undergoing a rapid period of self-growth and development of new identities. London (1978) and Zwerling (1976) found community college attendance requiring little, if any, status transition, and described the experience as 'gr. 14' or 'high-school with ashtrays'.

Shor (1980) suggested that the social patterns and relations students encounter in community colleges did not require a significant rupture from the ones they had been accustomed to, as they frequently continue residing in the same communities and maintain the same part-time jobs and social circles. Over half of Canadian college students live with their parents, while many more are older students with families of their own. Half commute less than 25 km to get to school (SIAST, 2004, p. 13). Commenting on this alleged continuation of pre-college social patterns and asked if students underwent status passage, this transfer student explains:

> Definitely not! Because most of the people were from the area, most people drove or walked there. So it wasn't really a coming out experience, it wasn't a radical departure from what you were doing. It was basically like going to grade 14. It is done locally, you don't really go somewhere else and you don't really try to learn new ideas . . . It has become a given now that you have to go to high school, and now a lot of people see it as you *have to* go to PSE, but they really don't know why . . . so why not do it conveniently right in your backyard, where you can walk there (personal interview, 2004).

College Aesthetics and the Hidden Curriculum; 'It looks like a prison'

Ethnographic descriptions of community colleges have depicted uninspiring buildings often interpreted by students as indicative of the low status of colleges, and frequently reminiscent of high-school buildings (Easton, 2002, p. 49).

The physicality of college campuses was believed to be an integral component of the hidden curriculum in the work of Shor (1980), London (1978), Weis (1985), Zwerling (1976), and Costello (Margolis, 2001[4]). Frequently described in these works as dreary and industrial looking, buildings were viewed as being 'cheaply constructed in the genre of welfare institutions' (Shor, 1980).

Often housed in shopping malls (Ryval, 2005, p. E4), high schools, store fronts, trailers and former factories, the aesthetics contribute to what Zwerling (1976) described as the 'perpetual down feeling that permeates the college environment'. Early research found that the administrative, curricular, pedagogical *and physical* environment of colleges directly affect student attitudes and perceptions (Russell, in Konrad, pp. 79–90, 1974).

I asked these former students to describe the appearance of their college and its affect on the educational and intellectual environment. The following responses are illustrative:

> There were open pipes and cables, it was very industrial looking. It was an environment that you had to grow use to. I find that now, because I work in a lot of factories, *that's* what you find in the ceilings in factories. So I think that's what it is leaning you towards, having very low expectations, even of your surroundings. Like you shouldn't *expect* that you're going to get luxurious surroundings or anything like that . . . (it) was not a comfortable place to be. It's getting you ready to work in an environment like that all day. So you get exposed to being in there 3–4 hours a day instead of 8–12, so you can get used to it (personal interview, 2004).

Transfer students contrasted their university buildings being named after individuals of stature and importance with the less ambitious, generic and anonymous names given to college buildings such as the 'B Building':

> It seemed really low budget . . . it was a big, long port-a-pack pretty much. Very cold in the winter. It looked kind of like high school; plastic chairs, one big long table, you don't get your own individual desk...it's not the most conducive to learning as compared to university (personal interview, 2004).
>
> The whole school was basically classrooms and a parking lot . . . where ever there was a field, or a place to sit, it was covered in garbage. A lot of the buildings themselves were actually falling apart . . . There were holes clear through the wall to the outside . . . the cafeteria was usually covered in garbage as well, it was not really a place where you would want to go eat. The building itself . . . looks like a prison, it has a very prison like appearance to it (personal interview, 2004).

TEACHER-STUDENT CONFLICT

Ethnographic literature describes a minority of profoundly alienated and disengaged students in ongoing conflict with teachers, who repeatadly express frustration with students' apparent resistance to their attempts to educate them. Attendance begins diminishing rapidly in the initial weeks of the semester and many unofficially 'drop-out' (Schulze, 1999, p. 2). Only a minority are described as taking notes, participating in class, or attempting required readings. While students are often described as non-engaged, some are antagonistic, disruptive and openly articulate disdain towards academic courses and teachers[5].

Classroom interactions are described by the following interviewees in a manner consistent with the literature, highlighting the ongoing attempts of many teachers to engage students who frequently lack the academic preperation or focus to respond accordingly:

> Maybe only 3–4 people participating - *if* that many! And teachers? Huh! *Desperately* trying to get something going with other people, maybe picking students at random . . . and getting in response maybe a one or two word answer...there probably were 3–4 really enthusiastic people that did participate, while the rest were not interested, and just basically put there heads down on the table and ignored what was going on around them (student, personal interview, 2004).

A minority of students are described as quite uncooperative:

> A lot of people were just *completely* disinterested in class and just let loose! Like a lot of people made and received cell phone calls in class, this is openly, without any regard to anyone else. One class . . . people in the back were breaking chairs and scattering the pieces while the teacher was teaching and not doing anything about it! Not making a suggestion to leave or anything (ibid.).

Teachers described high attrition, low attendance, disruptive and non-participating students:

> I was used to the university environment . . . and I was surprised at how little these students knew, and how badly they wrote . . . it was more like babysittsing than really academic. I was disappointed . . . they would be laughing in class, joking around and talking...Maybe 10% were . . . good, bright. The others . . . definitley were not university material (personal interview, 2004).

'The last qoute suggests that the social origins of students was a persistent theme for teachers, and just as in the case with primary and secondary teachers in other research (Oakes and Guiton, 1995), was a central explanation for the behaviour of students, often described in definciency discourse. The same teacher for example, comments that'

> The local kids . . . are from that background; working class and lower middle class, and/or not that bright . . . I think it's just the way their minds work, they don't have those kind of *intellectual* minds, they have more *hands on* kind of minds you can say. They are going to end up in those kinds of jobs anyway, for them to think abstractly is *hard*. They are not cut out for that. If they were they would probably go to university (ibid.).

Teachers often express deep frustration, and stress when confronted with collopsed classes.

The following remarks were made by a first-time teacher in only her second month at the college. The antagonistic relationship with students is evident as she describes her experiences:

> I am just totally overwhelmed with what I am seeing . . . This is really unbelievable . . . There's just (referring to students abilities and potential) (pause) nothing! (pause) It's really distressing! We have a lot of – not even poorly educated, but just (pause) it's like they're empty! There is no interest in anything . . . They do not read. They do not read the newspaper, they know very little about what's going on, with the exception of a few, and they shouldn't even be here, they should be in university . . . I am burned out . . . I am going home and sleeping, for the last 2 months, and another teacher here says she needs to go just sit on the couch after class, and two hours later she is still there! She is trying to teach Chaucer and Keats and sort of give students appreciation of English. But it's just blank stares . . . They are not motivated. They are not disciplined . . .Ughhh! (personal interview, 2004).

These comments are striking in that they are near identical to teacher depictions of immigrant students in US 'ghetto' schools and working class elementary students in the early 20th century (Anyon, 1980). A common theme running through teacher descriptions in both the ethnographies, and my interviews, is one of student deficiency.

'STRUCTURED FAILURE'

> "I think it just sort of robbed people of their interest in PSE" (student, personal interview, 2004).

> The process of "cooling-out" is sophisticated thought control. It transfers the locus of failure from the institution to the individual. At issue is the students setting of goals and the student's perceptions of who is responsible for the place he or she reaches in society. As it functions in the schools for worker-students, "cooling out" is depressant tracking. It is the ironic counter-point in a schizoid system which stands you up only to knock you down, which needs you to believe in a Dream that won't come true...Sights have to be lowered because unmet needs and frustrated aspirations generate alienation and rebellion (Shor, 1980, p. 17).

While teachers frequently cite student deficiency as explanations for their lack of success, some students noted the curriculum quality, instructional climate, teacher attitudes, and low-status of colleges as contributing to high attrition, disengagement and lack of commitment, success and interest of many. The proceeding comments of students suggest that apathy and indifference may be a *rational* response and penetration into the underlying character of mass education:

> A lot of the classes in the program left a lot to be desired . . . just *very* uninteresting. A lot of people saw that, and they thought they couldn't put up with another few years of doing that over and over . . . In a lot of the classes taught by part timers, they didn't know their topic very well . . . I think people just lost interest, and in the more challenging classes, they really lost interest because they saw it as pointless; it wasn't going to give them anything, so why go (personal interview, 2004).

Another transfer student comments:

> There were one or two prof's . . . that could hold student's attention, where in university almost every class was like that, where the class was *into it.* I think because (university) was going at a faster pace and you were forced to tune in or else. It was just more rapid and kept people's attention. The slow pace (of college) made student's lacksidsical (personal interview, 2004).

London (1978) theorised that students in his study frequently mocked teachers, cheated on exams, withheld effort and participation and refused to 'play the game' as they perceived the status of the institution and the frequently non-challenging curriculum as second-rate. Two students explained to him for example, that: "this isn't a *college* college. It just seems more like high-school…For a lot of kids this school is the joke of the year . . . they admitted everyone that applied didn't they?" (p. 22). A parallel will be noted between those comments and the ones expressed by this student:

> I sort of understood community college as being sort of second class to the university and I think other people did too. I think that maybe 60% perceived it that way, and they began treating it sort of as a joke. Like, if it's just going to be second place then why try! There's no point in trying if you are just going to finish second place behind university anyhow. I really think people did the bare minimum to get by because there is no point in coming in first (personal interview, 2004).

Such sentiment speaks directly to the 'cooling-out function' addressed in the literature. The institutional, pedagogic, curricular, and administrative culture of colleges are believed to 'cool-out' students who aspire to upward mobility and university transfer, and quickly 'turn them off' PSE all together.

'They realize that this is their Last Chance'

> It is a ... second *chance* program . . . That's the way it is in fact designed; That it is a second chance program for students to have another go at school, and do it in a liberal arts atmosphere . . . very few students show up not having that attitude and perception. They realize that this is their last chance (teacher, personal interview, 2004).

Many students perceive college as their 'last chance', especially those in GA programs. Some seek self-improvement and the opportunity to heal some of the 'hidden injuries' inflicted upon them in their previous school experiences. As one student explains:

> I was out to prove to a lot of people, not just myself, but to the people that originally were of the opinion that I couldn't do it. I wanted to prove to them that I could do it . . . the colleges and the universities that didn't accept me, I wanted to prove that I was at their level. I have been going back to my high school and talking to my old teachers, trying to prove to them that I can do it, 'you guys just didn't give me a chance' (personal interview, 2004).

London (1978), Shor (1980) and Zwerling (1976) suggested that much of the disengagement and rejection of teachers interpretation of success might be viewed as 'defensive-pessimism', attempts by working class students to protect injured pride, dignity and honour in an institutional environment that has often mistreated them and made them question their self-worth. An English teacher explained this underling tension the following way:

> They have this bravado, this outer veneer . . . it's hard to know if it's real or not . . . They put on this outward toughness . . . 'it doesn't matter to me, I am *cool'*. It's easy to see through this, because sometimes one senses a tension during the exam, that it *really* matters deep down. When I speak to them in private sometimes, it comes across (personal interview, 2004).

CONCLUDING REMARKS

Colleges have been noted to play a legitimating role in the 'post-industrial economy' by obscuring social divisions and class inequality in their institutional and marketing discourse, promising students the rewards traditionally enjoyed by the middle strata's (Muller, 1990).

The 'new economy' rhetoric of 'hands-on training', 'skills', and 'high-tech', so favoured by colleges can not alter the reality that most jobs continue to be characterized by a lack of power, and large numbers of 'followers' are required by capital to process received information in the growing service, office administrative, hospitality, data-entry and other sectors colleges are linked to. An examination of the social origins and outcomes of students suggests that these institutions may be better understood as facilating intra-class, or *horizontal* mobility, and the integration of working class youth into working class jobs.

Of particular importance in reference to GA programs is the issue of university transfer. While never having been a major priority of college administrators, it is increasingly the desired goal of many students. More than a third of all students and *three quarters* of GA students at one Ontario college for example, hoped to transfer to a university (Decock, 2004). Yet while the majority of GA students desire transfer, only 11% will obtain it. The *possibility* however, gives colleges an air of legitimacy (ibid. p. 1) and GA programs often serve as a 'feeder' program, drawing students in to the college where they are then frequently counselled into vocational programs.

The empirical evidence demonstrates that a university degree is a prerequisite for entrance into the professional-managerial class, yet enrolling in a college frequently prevents students from obtaining this.

GA programs are contradictory in this respect. While they continue social streaming and re-produce the social relations of alienated labour, they also expose working class youth, in a limited way, to liberal arts and academic courses, and the possibility of critical thinking. Given the life experiences and chances of this student base however, such pursuits often appear foreign, irrelevant, or potentially harmful to their perceived needs, as they often feel that they must aggressivley assert what employers demand. As some of the interviewees quoted here have suggested, students at times feel threatened by the abstract nature of liberal arts courses and their apparent disconnect from students lives, past educational experiences and the labour market.

How one program may contribute to the reproduction of class relationships by inadvertally continuing certain aspects of the hidden curriculum first established in elementary grades, was considered here. The process however, is not a linear or uncontested one, and is wrought with contradictions and conflict between teachers and students, who recognise the increasing necessity of PSE credentials in the labour market, and enrol in their local college as few alternatives are open to them.

Many refuse to 'play the game'; passive sabotage, non-engagement, withholding effort, and resistance to the expectations of teachers are widespread, often taking forms similar to the ones found in earlier grades, and the workplace itself. That some teachers may perceive these behaviours as confirmation of their belief that students lack intelligence, sophistication, and work ethic, parallels other research of middle class perceptions of workers (Gorman, 1998).

Despite numerous institutional barriers, GA programs do provide a potential avenue to university transfer and mobility into the professional-managerial class for working class students. This possibility is often eluded to by teachers, who uphold university and university students as a measuring stick used to remind students of past failures, that 'this is their last chance', and the subtle implication conveyed that college is legitimate only as a stepping stone to university. In the rejection of their teachers interpretations of success, useful knowledge, and appropriate attitudes, students, through their resistance, actively participate in their own streaming and cooling-out, validating teachers belief that they were not 'cut out' for a university education and deserving of their eventual fate in 'those kind of jobs', thus confirming a self-fufilling prophecy.

Shor (1980) has conceptualised working-class student outlooks and behaviours as being rooted in their prior educational and class based experiences; pre-shaped by 12 years of mass schooling, which has done little to foster leadership qualities, self-confidence, and the social capital expected by their college instructors – as evidenced by the quotes of teachers here. The institutional and organisational culture of colleges provides limited opportunity for students to develop the advanced literacy, cultural capital and academic skills required for transfer to university and the upper layers of the labour market.

The expansion of colleges, have reduced barriers to the equality of *opportunity* to enter PSE by increasing access to non-traditional students, and may be perceived as a democratic gain for the working class in this respect. However, inequality of *conditions* and *outcomes* remain intact, as a university education is still oft the privilege of the advantaged, while colleges enrol 'the rest', ensuring that class of origin is a major determinate to the type of education received.

The social relations of education outlined here augment the existing social relations of production, and do not simply ready students for the work place; they prepare them for particular layers in the class hierarchy of power and division of labour in the advanced capitalist labour process. While university students often learn that they were 'born to lead', the students examined here may have learned that they were 'born to be lead' before they even entered PS.

This leader-led dichotomy is captured in recent marketing campaigns of a Ontario university and college respectively. The university add, depicting a relaxed student in a pleasant outdoor environment, reads 'The world *belongs* to those who *understand* it' (emphasis added). The more humble college add reads 'college gets you the job', with depictions of administration assistants and kitchen workers. The university slogan stresses ownership, leadership, curiosity, intellectual vigour and broad based understanding and the *connection* between these. The college add however, is quite explicit in it the limitations of its offerings and the social location and function its graduates are destined for.

NOTES

1 Course descriptions often inform students of the limitations of their training and credentials, stating that graduates will be working under the supervision of university educated professionals.

2 See Taylor and Steinhauer's discussion in ch. 5 of this book on the secondary education of Canadian Native peoples, and Anyon's work cited in this chapter, both of who suggest that marginalized communities are not given a challenging education that would prepare them for the rigours of university.

3 Taylor and Steinhauer (ibid.)found that many Native students and their teachers also viewed college as a less challenging alternative to university

4 See Costello's chapter in Margolis (2001) for a in depth discussion comparing the hidden curriculum of the buildings of a elite law school and social work program on the same campus of a US university.

5 According to the research of Grubb et el, (1999) large numbers of US community colleges classes are described as being completely disengaged or 'collapsed'.

REFERENCES

Allen, M., Harris, S., & Butlin, G. (2001). *Finding their way: A profile of young Canadian graduates*. Ottawa: Culture, Tourism and the Centre for Education Statistics Division. Retrieved May, 2005, from http://www.statcan.ca/english/research/81-595-MIE/81-595-MIE2003003.pdf

Allen, R. C. (1998). *The employability of university graduates in the humanities, social sciences, and education: Recent statistical evidence*. Discussion paper no. 98-15, Department of Economics, University of British Columbia. Retrieved May 2005 from http://www.econ.ubc.ca/dp9815.pdf

Anisef, P., Ashbury, F. D., & Turrittin, A. H. (1992). Differential effects of university and community college education on occupational status attainment in Ontario. *Canadian Journal of Sociology, 17*(1), 69–83.

Anyon, J. (1980). Social class and the hidden curriculum of work. *Journal of Education, 162*(1), 67–92.

Armstrong, P., & Armstrong, H. (1989). *Choosing equity and prosperity: access to college and the Ontario economy*. A report prepared for the Ontario Council of Regents Vision 2000 Review of the Role and Mandate of the CAATs. Toronto: Ontario Council of Regents for the Colleges of Applied Arts and Technologies.

Association of Canadian Community Colleges. (2007). *Pan-Canadian study of first year college students: Student characteristics and the college experience*. Human resources and Social Development Canada. Retrieved September 2008, from http://www.accc.ca/ftp/pubs/studies/200708StudentStudy.pdf

Association of Colleges of Applied Arts and Technology of Ontario. (2003, October). *Colleges commit to working with new minister to address workforce needs*. Retrieved May 2005, from www.acaato.on.ca/new/pr/2003/collegescommit-oct23.htm

Avis, J. (1981). Social and technical relations: The case of further education. *British Journal of Sociology of Education, 2*(2), 145–161.

Bowles, S., & Gintis, H. (1976). *Schooling in capitalist America*. New York: Basic Books.

Brint, S., & Karabel, J. (1989). *The diverted dream: Community colleges and the promise of educational opportunity in America; 1900–1985*. New York: Oxford University Press.

Brown, L. (2008, February 13). High school grads adrift in math. *Toronto Star*, p. A 10.

Cameron, C. (2005). Experiences of transfer students in a collaborative baccalaureate nursing program. *Community College Review, 33*, 22–44.

Chafel, J. (1997). Schooling, the hidden curriculum, and children's conceptions of poverty. *Social Policy Report, 11*(1), 1–18.

Clift, R., Hawkey, C., & Vaughan, A. M. (1998). *A background analysis of the relationship between tuition fees, financial aid, and student choice*. Retrieved July 2007, from http://www.cufa.bc.ca/Clift/A_Background_Analysis.html

Clift, R. F. (1999). *Who goes? Who pays? A primer on tuition and student aid policy research*. Presentation to the Canadian Association of Student Financial Aid Administrators Conference. Retrieved July, 2007, from http://cufabc.harbour.sfu.ca/Clift/CASFAA99.html

Coreli, F. (1989). *Summary of submissions received in response to "an invitation to participate"*. A report prepared for the Ontario Council of Regents Vision 2000 Review of the Role and Mandate of the CAATs. Toronto: Ontario Council of Regents for the Colleges of Applied Arts and Technologies.

Decock, H. (2004). Calculating the college-to university transfer rate in Ontario. *College Qaurtley, 7*(1).

Decock, H., & Greene, I. (1998). *The York University – Seneca College partnership in context*. Paper presentation to the Canadian Institutional Research and Planning Association, St. John's Newfoundland. Retrieved June 2007, from http://www.cirpaacpri.ca/images/stjohns98/98_proceedings/decock.htm

Dennison, J., & Gallagher, P. (1986). *Canada's community colleges*. Vancouver: University of British Columbia Press.

Donner, A., & Lazar, F. (2000). *Measuring graduation and attrition at Ontario colleges. A discussion of measurement issues and their usefulness as indicators of student success*. Retrieved July, 2007, from http://www.collegesontario.org/Client/CollegesOntario/Colleges_Ontario_LP4W_LND_WebStation.nsf/resources/Measuring+Graduation/$file/CO_MEASURING_GRADUATION.pdf

Drea, C. (2004). Student attrition and retention in Ontario's colleges. *College Quarterly, 7*(2).

Duke, N. K. (2000). For the rich it's richer: Print experiences and environments offered to children in very low- and very high-socioeconomic status first grade classrooms. *American Educational Research Journal, 37*(2), 441–478.

Easton, L. P. (2002). *Disciplining a working subject: An examination of English curriculum at two Canadian community colleges* (Doctoral Dissertation), University of Toronto, Toronto, Ont.

Ferrer, A., & Riddell, C. (2002). *The role of credentials in the Canadian labour market*. Department of Economics, UBC. Retrieved August 2007, from http://www2.arts.ubc.ca/cresp/riddell1.pdf

Gerson, M. (1989, March 8). Faced with rising deficits and falling enrolment, Ontario's community colleges begin rapprochement. *The Chronicle of Higher Education, 35*, 26 (p. A33).

Gill, A. (1989). *Role of the colleges in the changing economy report on consultations*. A report prepared for the Ontario Council of Regents Vision 2000 Review of the Role and Mandate of the CAATs. Toronto: Ontario Council of Regents for the Colleges of Applied Arts and Technologies.

Gorman, T. (1998). Social class and parental attitudes toward education; resistance and conformity to schooling in the family. *Journal of Contemporary Ethnography, 27*(1), 10–44.

Human Resources and Social Development Canada. (2001). *Special edition to the National Graduates Surveys*. Retrieved June 28, 2005, from http://www.hrsdc.gc.ca/en/cs/sp/hrsd/prc/publications/bulletin/2001000024/page16.shtml

Grubb, N., & Associates. (1999). *Honored but invisible: An inside look at teaching in community colleges*. New York: Routledge.

Haggerty, F. D. (1998). *Current developments and future directions of general education in Ontario's colleges of applied arts and technology*. Doctoral Dissertation, University of Toronto, Toronto, Ontario.

Konrad, A. G. (1974). *Clientele and community: The student in the Canadian community college*. Willowdale, Ontario: Association of Canadian Community Colleges.

Lambert, M., Zeman, K., Allen, M., & Bussiere, P. (2004). *Who pursues postsecondary education, who leaves and why: Results from the youth in transition survey*. Ottawa: Culture, Tourism, and the Centre for Education Statistics Division.

London, H. (1978). *The culture of a community college*. New York: Praeger.

Looker, D., & Thiessen, V. (2004). *Aspirations of Canadian youth for higher education*. Human Resources and Skills Development Canada, Gatineu, Quebec. Retrieved September 2008, from http://www.pisa.gc.ca/SP-600-05-04E.pdf

Malatest, R. A., & Associates Ltd. (2007). *The class of 2003 high school follow-up survey*. The Canada Millennium Scholarship Foundation. Retrieved September 2008, from http://www.millenniumscholarships.ca/images/Publications/070614_class_of_03_en.pdf

Margolis, E., Soldatenko, M., Acker, S., & Gair, M. (Eds.). (2001). *"Peekaboo: Hiding and outing the curriculum." The hidden curriculum in higher education*. New York: Routledge.

Ministry of Training, Colleges and Universities. (2002). *Provincial overview of survey results: Employment profile: 2001–2002 graduates*. Retrieved July 2, 2007, from http://www.edu.gov.on.ca/eng/document/serials/eprofile01-02/007e.pdf

Moore, J. E. (2004). *General education within Ontario's community colleges: Second class citizens?* Doctoral Dissertation, University of Toronto, Toronto, Ontario.

Muller, J. (Ed.). (1990). *Education for work education as work: Canada's changing community college's*. Toronto: Garamond Press.

Murphy, M. N. (1983). *An analysis of the general education component in curricula of the Ontario Colleges of Applied Arts and Technology*. Doctoral Dissertation, University of Toronto, Toronto, Ontario.

Ontario Community College Student Parliamentary Association. (2001, February). *Submission to the standing committee on finance and economic affairs*. Retrieved November 2003, from the Ontario Community College Student Parliamentary Association: http://www.occspa.org/publications/Submission_FinanceCommittee.pdf

Oakes, J., & Guiton, G. (1995). Matchmaking: The dynamics of high school tracking decisions. *American Educational Research Journal, 32*(1), 3–33.

Oppenheimer, J. (1989). *The relationship between schools and colleges report on consultations*. A report prepared for the Ontario Council of Regents Vision 2000 Review of the Role and Mandate of the CAATs. Toronto: Ontario Council of Regents for the Colleges of Applied Arts and Technologies.

Pincus, F. (1980). The false promises of community colleges: Class conflict and vocational education. *Harvard Educational Review, 50*(3), 332–361.

PRA Inc. (2004). *Canadian College Student Survey*. The Canada Millennium Scholarship Foundation and the Canadian College Student Survey Consortium. Retrieved August 2008, from http://www.kwantlen.ca/__shared/assets/College_Student_Survey_20046326.pdf

Rahman, A., Situ, J., & Jimmo, V. (2005). *Participation in postsecondary education: Evidence from the survey of labour and income dynamics*. Statistics Canada Human Resources and Skills Development Canada. Retrieved September 2008, from http://www.statcan.gc.ca/pub/81-595-m/81-595-m2005036-eng.pdf

Robinson, D. (1982). Community colleges and the division between mental and manual labour. *Alternative Routes*, *5*, 133–166.

Ryal, M. (2005, September 26). Getting Canada ready for work. *Globe and Mail*, p. E4.

Santiago, S. J. (2000, August 2). *The changing role of community colleges in America and a comparative look at the system of higher education in China*. Paper presentation to the Chinese Academy of Social Sciences, Beijing. Retrieved April 2006, from http://www.necc.mass.edu/noncredit/wfdce/pdf/Changing%20Role%20of%20Community%20.pdf

Saskatchewan Institute of Applied Science and Technology. (2004). *Canadian college student survey*. Retrieved June, 2006, from http://www.siast.sk.ca/about/reports_statistics/documents/0404_2003cdncollegsurvey.pdf

Shor, I. (1980). *Critical teaching and everyday life*. Montreal: Black Rose.

Shulze, J. (1999). *Riding the winds of change: Responding to the remedial needs of at risk community college students*. Retrieved November 2003, from http://www.collegesontario.org/Client/CollegesOntario/Colleges_Ontario_LP4W_LND_WebStation.nsf/resources/Peer/$file/SCHULZE_WINDS_OF_CHANGE.pdf

Silver, I., Lavallee, L., & Pereboom, B. (1999). *Labour market transitions of graduates*. Human Resources Development Canada. Retrieved September, 2005 from http://www.hrsdc.gc.ca/en/cs/sp/hrsd/prc/publications/research/1999-000062/r-00-1-9e.pdf

Smith, S. (1989). *Skilled and educated: A solution to Ontario's urgent need for more polytechnic programs*. A report prepared for the Ontario Council of Regents Vision 2000 Review of the Role and Mandate of the CAATs. Toronto: Ontario Council of Regents for the Colleges of Applied Arts and Technologies.

Walters, D. (2003, July). *"Recycling": The economic implications of obtaining additional post secondary credentials at lower or equivalent levels*. RDC working paper for Statistics Canada. Hamilton. Retrieved November 2003, from http://socserv.socsci.mcmaster.ca/rdc/RDCwp2.pdf

Walters, D. (2004). A comparison of the labour market outcomes of postsecondary graduates of various levels and fields over a four-cohort period. *The Canadian Journal of Sociology*, *29*(1), 1–27, 15.

Weis, L. (1985). *Between two worlds: Black students in an urban community college*. Boston: Routledge and Kegan Paul.

Wolfe, D. (1989). *New Technology and education: A challenge for the colleges*. A report prepared for the Ontario Council of Regents Vision 2000 Review of the Role and Mandate of the CAATs. Toronto: Ontario Council of Regents for the Colleges of Applied Arts and Technologies.

Zwerling, S. (1976). *Second best; the crisis of the community college*. New York: McGraw Hill.

ROD MICHALKO AND TANYA TITCHKOSKY

6. THERE AND NOT THERE:

Presence and Absence of Disability in the Transition from Education to Work[1]

INTRODUCTION

The central question of this chapter is, how is disability configured in the transition from education to work? The high unemployment and underemployment rates of disabled Canadians compared to our non-disabled counterparts, points to at least one answer to this question – disabled people are significantly absent from the workforce.[2] Thus, the transition or movement of disability from the realm of education to that of work is significantly minimal. Disability does not routinely move between these two realms as a matter of course. When disability is conceived as a strictly biological phenomenon, any collective interest in pondering this lack of transition can become as absent as are disabled people themselves. This chapter examines the variety of ways that disability remains absent from the workforce. Like the other chapters in this volume, ours too will demonstrate the essential need to consider critically the rhetoric of the knowledge economy. We will also examine the accompanying assumptions that individual prosperity flows directly from individual skills and knowledge acquisition in a "linear, roughly homogenous and comparable" way (Sawchuk and Taylor, p. 1). In the face of the persistent belief that skill, knowledge, and other forms of individualized training will straightforwardly equip disabled people to move from education to work, our chapter will show how these mechanisms of educational inclusion serve to reproduce the disabled worker as excluded.

Paradoxical as it may seem given its significant absence, disability *is* present in the workforce. Disability's presence, however, does not ordinarily take the form of "actual" disabled workers. Instead, the presence of disability in the workforce is expressed in the form of "signs" that point to its presence despite its absence. Some organizations, for example, have wheelchair ramps, the universal accessible sign on bathroom doors, Braille markings on elevator pads, and even "talking" elevators. And yet, wheelchair users or blind people are rarely present in such organizations, especially as employees. Job advertisements often encourage "persons with disabilities" to apply, but such applications are rarely successful. Signs of disability do mark its presence in the workforce but do so within the simultaneous social situation of its absence. This chapter also examines the various ways disability is made present, or is represented, in the workforce.

In this chapter, then, we explore the social significance of how disability figures as physically absent, but simultaneously present in signs, programs, policy, posters, and other texts. While the absence of disabled people[3] from the

P. Sawchuk and A. Taylor (eds.), Challenging Transitions in Learning and Work: Reflections on Policy and Practice, 109–124.

workplace is egregious, the devalued status of disability that makes it into an expected, or even unnoticed, absence remains in need of theoretical consideration. We address the presence of ordinary textual renderings of disability in education and in the workplace as a way to interrogate what is being moved from education to work by commonplace representations of disability. Such an exploration leads to the methodological need to make the "common and the ordinary [...] our primary concern, the daily food of our thought" (Arendt as cited in Hill, 1979, p. 175). This allows us to show how the absent/present character of disability is made manifest in the inter-institutional transition from education to work.

Our examination ends by incorporating a little twist to the expected. We conclude by demonstrating that disability representation is itself a space of education insofar as we can learn about some of the ways contemporary society connects education and work, especially the connection that is found in the assumption that one automatically and universally leads to the other. Taking a disability studies perspective, our underlying commitment is to show the political value of understanding disability as a fully social phenomenon. We thus expose the more objectifying or medicalized conceptions of disability as they are expressed in the transitions between education and work. Such conceptions operate with an unquestioned assumption that disability is essentially an individual deficit. From this unquestioned assumption, educational programs and workplace policies locate all employment problems (as well as all the solutions) in and on the individual lives of disabled people. By regarding disability as a lack of proper function, or as an inability to fully measure up to a version of the expected worker, some people are systematically reproduced as costly deficiencies. The ways in which disability is made both present and absent in the work place have their own educational force, since people must learn to regard disability as a cost and little else. Our chapter will show how education programs are engaged in transmitting this limited and limiting conception of disability to the workplace. It is this deficit version of disability which continuously makes the transition from education to work and back again (since both education and work are understood as solutions to the problem of deficit that disability is assumed to be). Our analysis of the representations of disability in both education and in work challenge notions of the 'universality' of learning/work transitions and challenges, as well as the rhetoric of the knowledge economy and its reliance on human capital theory. The market-place, after all, remains beholden to its rather singular version of the productive citizen, a version which is continuously disrupted by the actual interpretive and diverse bodied beings that we are.

We begin by turning to a consideration of a commonplace representation of disability in the workplace.

THE INDIVIDUATION OF DISABILITY IN THE WORKPLACE

The "absent/present" character of disability in the workplace makes an appearance in many ways. In the face of low employment rates of disabled people, provincial, territorial, and federal governments require organizations to address this issue by making accessibility plans and by requiring that these plans be made public by publicly funded institutions, such as hospitals, schools, and universities. This means that disability makes an appearance in the workplace through these "planning texts"[4] aimed at the inclusion of disabled people at sometime…in the future.

In many Ontario workplaces for example, the Accessibility for Ontarians with Disabilities Act (AODA) has made it necessary for organizations to develop an "accessibility plan" with regard to disability. Consider the following planning text, a table-of-contents excerpt taken from a University's accessibility plan. This type of plan is a common feature of many workplaces:

"Accessibility Plan for 2005–2006"

- 5.1 Physical Facilities
- 5.2 Awareness and Outreach
- 5.3 Information Resources and Adaptive Technology
- 5.4 Academic and Non-academic Student Support Services
- 5.5 Human Resources Initiative for Faculty and Staff (www.uoguelph.ca/web/accessibility 2005.shtml [accessed 6/29/07]).

This way of addressing access issues, clearly makes accessibility for disabled people into an issue of adaptation. It has initiatives regarding adapting the physical space of the organization, providing disabled people with adaptive technology and resources, as well as adapting its human resources activities to disability. The plan also intends to develop an initiative oriented to providing "awareness" and information, as well as "outreach" regarding disability.

This accessibility plan is not unique to this University since the AODA makes it necessary for all public organizations receiving provincial funding to develop such a plan (Opini, 2006). The case is similar in other provinces and territories, and the federal government also makes it necessary for organizations they support to develop such plans. While there are many such plans being made, and being made public, these plans are not qualitatively different from each other. The difference they make to disabled people entering the workforce is insignificant; disabled people remain as absent from the workforce today, as they did in the past. (Canada: *Advancing the Inclusion of Persons with Disabilities 2004*; Canadian Council of on Learning, 2007).

These accessibility plans maintain a singular conception of disability, namely, disability is a problem in need of a solution (Mitchell, 2002, p. 15). Moreover, the problem of disability is understood in terms of lack – as bodily, sensory, intellectual, or emotional lack – located in individuals. Such lack is understood as a problem requiring the solution of adaptation. Workplaces develop plans to adapt their physical environments, their human resources practices and policies, and their attitudes toward disability. Organizations also develop public awareness and information initiatives regarding disability. Presumably, this "public" refers to their non-disabled workforce and presumably, this "public" is unaware of disability. Instead, it is understood as requiring awareness programs and information regarding disability. The solution to the problem of disability, then, is two-fold – (1) adapt the workplace environment to disability and (2) make the workforce aware, inform it about disability. Clearly, the workplace lacks structures that will accommodate disability and thus must adapt in order to include disability. But the inherent sturctural lack of the workplace is deposited onto disabled people as their lack which, nonetheless, serves as a way to address the workplace lack. Disability awareness programs are a mechanism to inform people of the problem of disability, understood as lack, as well as how to rationalize this workplace by focusing on lack as an individual problem. Thus, the workplace lacks only because disability does.

The workforce is being made aware and informed about a particular and singular conception of disability; disability is being regarded as a highly individualized notion of biological lack or malfunctioning. This individualizing conception is in stark contrast to, and critiqued from the perspective of, what Mike Oliver (1990) and other disability studies scholars call the Social Model of Disability. The Social Model of Disability emphasizes that a society's failure to respond appropriately to impairment is a process of disablement; defining disability as individual lack is thus part of a disabling process. Oliver says:

> There are two fundamental points that need to be made about the individual model of disability. Firstly, it locates the 'problem' of disability within the individual and secondly it sees the causes of this problem as stemming from the functional limitations or psychological losses which are assumed to arise from disability [...] Of course, nothing could be further from the truth [...] It is not individual limitations, of whatever kind, which are the cause of the problem but society's failure to provide appropriate services and adequately ensure the needs of disabled people are fully taken into account in its social organization [...] Further [...] disabled people as a group [...] experience this failure as discrimination institutionalised throughout society. (Oliver, 1996, pp. 32–33).

Workplace plans to adapt to disability, whether they are eventually implemented or not, are nonetheless vehicles for moving a singular conception of disability as an individual problem into and around workplace organizations.

While disabled workers may be hard to find in workplaces, the conception of disability as an individual problem is quite easy to find; it is not rare but powerfully and consistently present. Consider the following excerpt from an interview we conducted with a "job developer."[5] His job was to develop employment opportunities for disabled people, in part, by speaking with potential employers about hiring disabled people. Jeremy (a pseudonym), the job developer, received training in job development from people already working in this area. One of these trainers, described by Jeremy as a "young white woman," gave him the following advice:

> Look, you are not really a job developer. You are really in sales and so what you need to learn is how to find ways of how to sell broken people.

Given that "specially trained" job developers are trained to convince employers to hire disabled people attests to the fact that disabled people are an *unexpected type* in the workplace (Michalko and Titchkosky, 2001, p. 216ff). They are not expected to show up. Employers must be "sold" on hiring disabled people and this is a "hard sell." After all, who among us would buy anything that is "broken?" Jeremy's trainer did not suggest that job developers could sell "broken people" to employers by convincing them that they could "fix" these people. Instead, the notion of "broken people" makes reference to a conception of disability as a static bodily condition, steeped in the (un)natural individual condition of a "body-gone-wrong." For the trainer, disabled people are "broken" or, as Robert Murphy puts it, disabled people are conceived of as "damaged goods" (1987, p. 85ff). It is this conception of disability that makes convincing an employer to hire a disabled person such a "hard sell," for who would buy "broken or damaged" goods unless they are convinced to do so. Human capital theory and its basic assumption that investing in the development of the skills, knowledge, education, and experience of the potential worker leads to increased opportunities, rewards, and success for the worker so invested, is ironically operating in exactly the opposite fashion. The concept of investing in people, that is, believing in humans as things or processes which can gain value, is a concept whose development and exchange relies on the production of the opposite also being true. Some humans are conceived of as inherently empty of value. A conception of humans as valueless can be regarded as a background necessity for human capital theory to "work" or reproduce itself.

It is ironic that in adapting the workplace to the possibility of increasing the presence of disabled people, the plans and procedures for this change require that people learn to regard disability in a singular and debilitating fashion. Disability enters the workplace through accessibility plans and it enters as an individual, biological, functional lack. Moreover, this concept of disability exists as a taken-for-granted feature of our society. Assuming that nature, not culture, has provided us with this conception of disability means learning to not pay attention to learning; it means that we must treat the natural character of disability as self evident and not as a conception that we have learned. This taken-for-granted relation to disability as body-gone-wrong helps to produce the sense that disability is 'naturally' excluded while non-disability is 'naturally' included. This is why it is good to remember Lennard Davis' admonition that easy ways of knowing disability (taking what it is for granted) are "really another aspect of discrimination against people with disabilities" (1995, p. 2).

Having explored how disability appears in the workplace as an individual problem, we turn now to an analysis of a common and ordinary way that workplaces aim to solve the problem of disability constructed as such.

DISABILTIY AND THE NEED FOR PREVENTION

Some versions of disability emerge out of attempts to solve the problem disability is assumed to be in and for the workplace. Disability, insofar as it is conceived of as individual lack, malfunction, brokenness, and something not readily fixed, makes the prevention of disability a common solution to the always-already imagined problem it is assumed to be.

Recent years, for example, have been witness to the emergence of several private companies oriented to selling training programs and guides for the development of a "safe workplace." Here is but one example:

Work Smarter, Not Harder. Ergonomics in the Workplace

> A Business Case for Ergonomic Change [...] Musculoskeletal Injuries (MSIs) are quickly becoming the leading cause of discomfort, injury and disability in Canadian workplaces [...] This guide is dedicated to the demonstration of a sound business case for ergonomics [...] Topics covered in the guide include [...] – A demonstration of the benefits derived from ergonomics including employee retention, reduced absenteeism, reduced disability and injury claims costs, improved production, and improved quality consistency. (National Seafood Sector Council, http:/www.nssc.ca/erg/ products.html [accessed 6/29/07]).

This advertisement relies on a version of the worker as potentially harmed by non-ergonomically oriented workplaces. Such harm leads to costs and such costs should be prevented. The prevention of such costs means, among other things, the prevention of disability. Along with the workforce's conception of disability as individual lack, we now see the understanding of disability as some *thing* that must be prevented. Disability is conceived of as a lack that is costly, and ergonomics is understood as a way to prevent such costs. In this sense, disability and cost are conflated and become one – disability *is* cost; prevent the former and the latter is prevented as well. This conception of disability treats it as a condition that costs; it costs individuals a worthwhile life and it costs workplaces insofar as the cost of disabled workers is not worthwhile.

Such a conception of disability is ubiquitous in our society and is made use of by such organizations as Worker's Compensation Boards. Their advertisements appear not only in workplaces, but also on television, in newspapers and magazines, and in all sorts of public venues, such as washrooms and public transportation. These advertisements depict, often in graphic form, various disabilities – missing hands, missing limbs, missing eyes – all due to the carelessness that is believed to result in workplace injuries. As one such compensation board advertisement campaign explicitly says: "There really are no accidents." (WSIB Ontario http://www.wsib.on.ca/wsib/wsibsite.nsf/public/2006 CoreCampaign).

Ruling accident out in favor of carelessness as the cause of workplace injury, suggests very strongly that the individual worker is wholly responsible for any disability which results from a workplace injury. Disability thus becomes a sign of individual carelessness, leading to a life not worth living where the individual worker cost a workplace must bear regarding disability. From the scores of ways that disability is made manifest as worthy only of prevention, let us consider one in detail. The Nova Scotia "Work Safe. For Life" (Workers Compensation Board of Nova Scotia, 2007, http://www.worksafeforlife.ca/) campaign, for example, features a white woman at a meat cutting station holding her bloody arm. She has apparently severed her hand while working. Fore-grounded by paramedics, standing holding her arm against her chest, she looks into the camera while calmly but sadly saying: "All I can think about is how much I am going to miss helping my baby look pretty for school." It is unclear whether she will not be able to help her child because she has died or because she is now a person with one hand. The woman with the bloody arm is fore-grounded by a team of paramedics, but the paramedics are not attending to the injured woman. The woman is in the background of the video, and is almost ghostly in appearance. She may have died from her injury and the video may be portraying what her death has taken from her. What has been taken from her is that she will not be able to help make her baby look pretty for school. The prosaic character of what this woman is missing is what gives the video its power; the woman, because of a workplace injury, is now "missing" the very thing that is most valuable to her – raising a child. Dead or disabled begins to amount to the same thing – no life.

The campaign which is oriented to prevent disability in workplaces is framed by a boldly ambiguous message: "Work safe. For life." This ambiguity situates disability between death and a life emptied of life, a kind of living death. These sorts of advertisement campaigns, along with other "health and safety" programs for the workplace, stress that disability must be prevented at all costs and that the life derived from disability is not worth living. Even when the death/disability connection is not depicted quite so starkly as it is with the woman with the severed hand, workplace safety and worker's compensation advertisements across Canada depict disability as needing prevention. And, ordinarily and commonly, disability needs to be prevented because disability entails a death of some sort, of pleasure (e.g., cannot hear your music, cannot attend your daughters wedding) or participation (cannot bike with friends, play video games, or get out of the hospital) (Association of Workers Compensation Boards of Canada, 2007, http:// www.awcbc.org/english/whats_new_WCBs.asp). Disability is located firmly in the notion of a body-gone-wrong whose only worth, and thus only solution, lies in its prevention.

We want to emphasize that we are not arguing against workplace health and safety legislation and policy as such. Such legislation and policy are the result of hard fought battles on the part of unions and labour movements and are a necessary part of workplaces. We are, however, against safety campaigns that blame the individual worker for workplace injuries. Workplaces and those who legally own and control them must be responsible for providing safe environments. Yet, we are perplexed with the ubiquitous use that safety campaigns make of disability. As Lennard Davis suggests, disability is used as a *momento mori*, as a reminder of the death that disability *is* (1995, p. 1). So, what are we against when disability is made use of in this way?

When disability is used in this way, there is a "narrative prosthetic" at work (Mitchell and Snyder, 2000, p. 1ff). Disability is being used as a prosthetic, as a "crutch" to narrate the story of the "good life," of the life worth living. The story being told here is, of course, the story of non-disability and "normalcy." Disability is used as a prosthetic to narrate the story of non-disability as the only life worth living. The setting for this non-disabled life is the workplace, inclusive of its pathways into and through paid work, and this is significant. The significance of such a narrative lies in the implicit adherence to capitalist notions of production. Adults must work and must be productive, and whatever prevents such production must itself be prevented. When workers are productive they have family, friends, and ordinary pleasures, not to mention that workers are assumed to have similar forms of embodiment. When workers become disabled, they lose their productivity and thus they lose the good life. As David Mitchell and Sharron Snyder suggest, disability "has been attributed to all 'deviant' biologies as a discrediting feature, while also serving as the material marker of inferiority itself" (2000, p. 3). Disability marks, for example, the body of the white woman meat cutter who says that "all she can think about" is a normative return to helping her daughter look pretty. The viewer is left not knowing if the meat cutter is dead or alive, thus positioning the missing hand as a deep mark of inferiority itself. Within such a narrative, there is no room for disability except as the character that must be prevented. This narrative does not even provide for the conception of disability as the need for adaptation – the woman with the bloody arm cannot, as the advertisement suggests, take care of her child with one hand.

Thus, while disability is absent from the workforce as is indicated by high unemployment rates among disabled people, it is also present. Its presence, though, is more symbolic than actual. Disability is symbolized in the workforce through such understandings of it as requiring prevention, as lack, and as a problem in need of a solution. As this chapter demonstrates, the transition from education to work tacitly relies upon disability understood as a pre-established deficit awaiting the arrival of the body of the disabled worker. For the most part, this solution takes the form of adaptation. Disabled people must adapt to their disabilities, workplaces must adapt by becoming accessible, and such adaptation is understood as the only way for disabled people to make the transition from education to work. But these versions of disability – as an individual problem, as something to be prevented – are already in the workforce, albeit symbolically. This means that disability has made the transition from education to work. Disability has moved to the workplace. But what has moved, what has made the transition?

What has moved from education to work is a conception of disability. Disability's presence in the workplace is framed by both its significant absence and its symbolic presence. The absence of disability in the workforce is constructed as "natural" insofar as it is reasonable for it not to be there, and disability itself is often evoked as the reason for its own absence. For example, we often hear "he's on disability," "she's on disability." "On disability" is reason enough for disability not to be in the workplace. Still, it is necessary to understand the configuration of disability in the transition from education to work. As a way to develop this understanding, we now turn to a discussion of a common and ordinary way that disability appears in education.

DISABILITY IN EDUCATION

In this section, we want to examine the ways in which university education departments depict disability in their curricula. We turn to one realm of education, namely, the teaching of "pre-service teachers,"or teachers-to-be; that is, future actors in and enactors of the education system. Such an examination will give us some understanding of the versions of disability that education students are given in these programs, and thus what versions of disability they take with them into the school system. In other words, we want to explore how education plays a role in supporting the absent/present character of disability as is found in workplaces. We begin our exploration of the conception of disability moving from education to work, by making use of course descriptions from education departments in Canadian universities.

> "Introduction to Special Education and Adaptive Instruction"
> In Ontario, the regular education classroom is currently the placement of choice for students with disabilities. This movement toward inclusive education has occurred for a variety of reasons; legal, educational, moral and philosophical. In this course, we will consider special education from the perspective of the regular classroom teacher. From this perspective, special education is not 'special' but is effective teaching that benefits all the students in the class. It is the provision of instruction that is adapted to the diverse needs of the students in the class. Therefore, we will not consider how to identify disabilities, or how to interpret psycho-diagnostic tests to confirm learner difference. Instead, we concentrate on how instructional assessment can be used to calibrate instruction to meet the needs of individual students, how to accommodate learner differences and how to collaborate with other professionals to meet the provincial requirements for inclusion of students and teaching, programming and assessment. (Ontario Institute for Studies in Education of the University of Toronto, *Calendar 2007*)

Unlike the workforce, there are a significant number of disabled students in Ontario schools. This is because, as the course description above suggests, the regular classroom, for legal, educational, moral, and philosophical reasons, is currently the placement of choice for students with disabilities. Whether it is disabled students or professionals "working with" disabled students who are making this "placement of choice," the contemporary orientation that animates education for disabled students is "inclusion." Disabled students *must*, like their non-disabled counterparts, attend school and they *must* be included in the regular classrooms. The mandate for including disabled people in the workforce, however, is not nearly as strong.

Now that disabled students are included in regular classrooms, the question becomes: how are they included? First, terms and activities such as "special education" and "adaptive instruction" have been invented as a way to address the presence of disability in the classroom. Interestingly enough, the above course description treats "special education" from the perspective of the teacher. The claim is that the teacher's perspective allows special education not to be seen as "special," but as effective teaching, benefiting all students. Special education provides instruction, according to the course description, that is adapted to the diverse needs of students. Special education, in this sense, while recognizing "learner difference" does not see these "different learners" as "special." Thus, *what* is taught remains the same for all students; it is *how* what is taught that differs because of "learner difference." This version of special education concentrates "on how instructional assessment can be used to calibrate instruction to meet the needs of individual students, how to accommodate learner differences." All of this is done in order to meet the "provincial requirements" for inclusion.

Adaptation is the orienting principle for inclusionary education. Instruction must be adapted to meet the needs of learner difference where "learner difference" acts as a euphemism for disabled students. Claims, such as special education is not "special" since it benefits all students, act to legitimate the invocation of "calibrated" instructional programs for disabled students as "really" beneficial to all students. It is interesting that such calibration did not take place for anyone's benefit until "irregularity" made an appearance in the "regular classroom." From this course description, we can begin to understand that the conception of disability that makes the transition from education to work is the understanding that disability-adaptations benefit all.

The following two course descriptions emphasize the individual nature of disability and the need to teach teachers how to teach disabled students.

> "Psychology and Education of Children and Adolescents with Learning Disabilities"
> Psychological and educational characteristics of children and adolescents with learning disabilities and ADHD with an emphasis on the constitutional and environmental factors that contribute to these disabilities and enable optimal functioning. Emphasis is placed on the concept of learning disability and on the educational implications of the research literature in the field. (University of New Brunswick, *Calandar 2007*)

> "Introduction to Special Education and Adaptive Instruction"
> A critical analysis of current issues related to identification and programming for children with special needs. The emphasis is on using well-founded research to inform instructional practices and decision-making. This course is designed to promote reflective thinking about key topics in Special Education that educators must conceptualize from both theoretical and practical perspectives. It is intended to provide students with knowledge, skills, and attitudes that will enable evidence-based understanding of what is involved in working with exceptional learners across a variety of settings, but primarily in an inclusive classroom situation. Focus is placed on curriculum being flexible in responding to diversity, so that teachers are guided to make appropriate accommodation and modify expectations for the various categories of exceptionality. (Ontario Institute for Studies in Education of the University of Toronto, *Calendar 2007*)

Both of these course descriptions provide a conception of disability as a "thing" that resides in an individual. The courses are also based on "well-founded research" on disabled children. This suggests that disability is an object of study, something about which knowledge can be gained and expertise developed. Thus, those becoming teachers can acquire "knowledge, skills and attitudes" together with "evidence-based understanding" necessary for "working with exceptional learners." These courses constitute disability as a "mysterious thing" that happens to some children and that generates "special needs," needs that can be met only through developing an expertise. Disability thus becomes a field of inquiry and disabled people become those about which only a few experts know, and know how to unravel the mystery of their "special needs." In the workplace we noted the common necessity to learn a singular conception of disability, but to forget that this conception was, indeed, learned, and not natural. Non-disability thus becomes the knower, whereas disability becomes the mysterious thing in need of experts. This version of disability makes the transition from education to work and does so prior to the arrival of actual living people who are, through such mechanisms, constructed as deficient. It is no surprise, then, that workplace "accessibility plans" always include public awareness and information initiatives; whereas classrooms include special educators.

The following course outline reflects the need for control and discipline:

> "Behavioural/Emotional Disorders: Introduction"
> An overview of various emotional and behavioural disorders of children and young people and the ways in which coping and monitoring strategies can be applied to develop self-discipline and control. (University of New Brunswick, *Calandar 2007*)

What is interesting about this course description is the portrayal of the need to discipline and control the body. Emotional disorders yield behavioural disorders and these need to be controlled in order to regularize classroom practices. The same notion of the "excessive body" frames popular understandings of disability (Erevelles, 2000). It is as though the Cartesian privileging of the mind has been reversed in disability; the uncontrollable body now indicates an uncontrolled mind. The excess of disability is often framed within the concept of "too much or too little." Someone's eyes see too little; others' legs are seen as not moving enough; and still others' bodies are repulsive or too out of control. This generates and ratifies a version of disability as an individual problem that must be coped with, disciplined, and controlled, a version that also makes the transition between education and work. Recall the work-safe campaigns which suggest that "there really are no accidents." Again, disability serves as a narrative prosthesis holding up the idea that good workers remain in control, remain safe. The management of disability in the classroom, refracted in the prevention of disability in the workplace, is then one way the notion of the good of self-control makes the transition from education to work.

The following is one more example:

> "Technology for the Visually Impaired"
> Preparation of teachers to work with a variety of technological devices designed for students who are blind or visually impaired, e.g., computers, electronic reading devices, and closed circuit television. (University of British Columbia, *Calendar 2007*)

We end our discussion on course descriptions from Departments of Education with the above which stresses the conception of disability as a technical problem. With the above course description as a specific example, the understanding of disability as a technical problem moves in the following way: blind people cannot read with their eyes; eyes are a technical apparatus for reading that blind people do not have; this technical apparatus must be replaced; technology is invented to allow blind people to read. Disability, then, is based on the understanding of the human body as a "set-of-functions" where disability is understood as the lack of one or more of these functions. This conception of the body generates a version of disability as the "body-gone-wrong" where the "wrong" can be remedied with technology. This conception of disability also makes the transition from education to work. Though we suggest that such conceptions gain force through their prominent role in the education of teachers, these conceptions of disability are ubiquitous and are not restricted to university education programs.

We want to end this section with an illustration of how disability is presented to elementary school students. Like all social institutions, education is committed to some notion of the "normal" and expresses this commitment in its desire to "normalize" students (Ferri and Connor, 2006, p. 128ff). Within the idea of the normal and average person, resides the notion that we are all limited, that we are all disabled. This sentiment is captured nicely in the following:

> I am fat, I am thin, I am short, I am tall
> I am deaf, I am blind, hey, aren't we all? (Rogers et al., 2002)

These are lines from a song which accompany a book on difference and diversity titled *Don't Laugh at Me*, written for elementary school-aged children as part of an inclusive education program , (Rogers, 2000 [a creation of Peter Yarrow of Peter, Paul and Mary fame]). As is readily noticeable in these lines, the book emphasizes sameness. While we are different from one another and while our differences are cogent and negatively so, this cogency is superceded and thus erased by our sameness. This suggests that the ideal body is the interchangeable one (Davis 2002, p. 105). The only response to difference this book imagines is negative, in particular, laughing at those who are different.

"I am deaf, I am blind, hey, aren't we all?" suggests, albeit tacitly, that there is something wrong with all of us, and so we should not laugh at bodily differences which, at first blush, do not appear as average difference. Any bodily difference that falls at either extreme of the bell-curve is a difference which is erased by invoking the contemporary method of saming, namely, we are like everyone else. Yet, that we are all like everyone else, while serving to erase difference, does not necessarily produce interchangeability. We end this chapter with a discussion of the interchangeable body and how the disabled body can serve as a site for the interrogation of the notion of interchangeability.

THE QUESTION OF THE TRANSITION: DISABILITY AS TEACHER

Lennard Davis says:

> The operative notion of equality, especially as it applies to the working classes, is really one of interchangeability. As the average man can be constructed, so can the average worker. All working bodies are equal to all other working bodies, because they are interchangeable. This interchangeability, particularly

> in nineteenth-century factories, means that workers' bodies have been conceptualized as identical. And able-bodied workers came to be interchangeable with able-bodied citizens [...] If all workers are equal and all workers are citizens, then all citizens must have standard bodies to be able to fit into the industrial-political notion of democracy, equality, and normality. Clearly people with disabilities pose problems to work situations in which labor is standardized and bodies conceptualized as interchangeable. (2002, p. 105)

The "normal" possibility of embodied difference is provided for by the invocation of the concept of the norm. Hence, the normative notion – we are all different, but we are all the same. This paradox is easily resolved by invoking the concept of the norm and its subsequent materiality of homogenous embodiment. In order to escape the formulation of abnormal or pathological, our individual differences must be understood and represented as "average difference," thus meeting the standard of homogenous embodiment. But when the labour of education and work, including the transition from one to the other, is understood as the doing of normalcy, all labour becomes standardized labour.

The concept of the norm permits us to "see" the citizenry as made up of average citizens. The idea of the "average citizen" is the consequential material manifestation of the abstraction known as the norm. This abstraction reflexively flows from the need and desire to know, to control, and to postulate the average citizen. The requirement for the "average citizen" is socially located and produced insofar as its genesis is to be found in the socio-political organization of the societal institutions of education and work. We can calibrate the average classroom so that it can fit special education that no longer appears special, since it helps to regularize, control, and adapt learner differences to the mainstream educational system. Again, "if all workers are equal and all workers are citizens, then all citizens must have standard bodies to be able to fit...". Industrial and post-industrial notions of equality and democracy, require both the norm and the average citizen in order to equalize and democratize people so that everyone can be counted as "everyone else." This notion of an average citizenry brings with it the sense that disability is a problem, an individual problem, that does not fit with versions of productivity, unless such bodies receive a special education to make them want to fit and desire interchangeability.

The idea of the "interchangeable body," then, finds its grounds in the social organization of industrial and late capitalist society inclusive of its mutually constitutive relationships with the development of mass schooling. This is why such an understanding of the body is found not only in work situations but in all social situations, including education. Recall the lines from the children's song "*Don't Laugh at Me*" – we are all blind, we are all deaf. These lines suggest that differences, and severe ones at that, can be erased. We are all "blind" or "deaf," but only metaphorically. This metaphor constitutes the societal need for interchangeable bodies by invoking a conception of every self as limited. However, bodily limitation, particularly in the work place, is conceived of as a limitation that should go unnoticed. This is one method for producing the interchangeable body, the average citizen, and the idea that all workers are equal.

Yet, that we are all like everyone-else, while serving to erase difference, does not necessarily produce interchangeability. You may be blind, but you are not blind like me and my blindness is not like yours. Our eyes (bodies) are definitely not interchangeable. The idea that we are all blind or all deaf, even those who are neither, fails to imagine a life of blindness or deafness as anything other than negative.

The inability to imagine the life of disability as nothing other than negative, stems from the ubiquitous cultural representation of disability as a problem in need of a solution. "Nearly every culture," David Mitchell writes, "views disability as a problem in need of a solution" (2002, p. 15). It is virtually impossible to think of disability without simultaneously thinking of problem and of solution (Michalko, 1998, 2002, *forthcoming*; Oliver, 1990; Titchkosky, 2003, 2007). The utilitarian and pragmatic sensibility of contemporary society serves to linguistically pair the ideas of problem and solution since this contemporary sensibility cannot imagine the good of a problem, or even the good problem. This lack of imagination cannot create the cultural adage – a solution in need of a problem. The book *Don't Laugh at Me*, for example, treats all non-average difference as a problem in need of a solution. It isolates the problem of non-average difference as that of laughing, and recommends the solution that we are all different and thus all the same, making laughter an inappropriate response. This solution may or may not solve the problem of laughing at difference. Despite the rhetorical character of this solution, however, it does not solve the problem of difference insofar as it never raises it in the first place. *Don't Laugh at Me* never problematizes difference or disability. It merely submits to the cultural representation of difference and disability as problems, problems of laughter, problems of whatever. The solution recommended by the children's book *Don't Laugh at Me* is itself in need of a problem. Problematizing this solution would begin the work of uncovering the sense of difference and disability that is being socially generated by the solution.

What is interesting is that "absolute sameness" is not a ubiquitous feature of contemporary Western culture and it is certainly not pervasive. What is pervasive is our familiarity with the human body; everyone, including us, has one and bodies come in a variety of shapes, sizes, colours, and the like. And yet, despite this familiarity, we "see" some bodies as representing "absolute difference." We have ideologically constructed (normed) the human body so that it complies to a culturally dominant view of "normal human variation." This norming process, together with the resulting sense of a "normatively-ordered body," is what produces the familiar as strange, the human as inhuman, and the pervasive as exceptional. So strong is the cultural desire for a normatively-ordered body, that social institutions such as education and work search for any technical solution to disability in order to make it a "normal" part of their policies and practices. And this, ironically, continues to be done in the face of the significant absence of disabled workers from the work force.

The challenge for both education and work is not only the development of techniques and technologies for the adaptation of disability. This may be necessary, but what is essential is that education and work develop a conception of disability as teacher. Disability does disrupt all social institutions. Rather than conceiving of this disruption only as a problem in need of a solution, it can be understood as a space through which the normative order can be "viewed," understood, and ultimately changed. As teacher, disability is a "good problem;" it is an occasion to problematize and thus uncover the tacit conceptions of the human body that already moves us from education to work.

NOTES

1 We thank SSHRC for support of our work, "Organizing Disablement: Disability and University Experience." We also thank the editors Peter Sawchuk and Alison Taylor for their insightful comments which have improved our analysis.

2 With little variation since at least the 1980's, the combined unemployment, under-employment, and non-labour force participation rates for "persons with disabilities" in Canada, the USA and UK is upwards of 70% (Barnes and Mercer, 2003, p. 47). As Mike Oliver (2001, p. 153) demonstrates, the unemployment rate among disabled people "remains similar to that during the period of fordism." In the more prosaic terms of the Canadian government, "... 44% of working-age adults with disabilities (aged 15 to 64) are employed, compared to 78% of those without disabilities... Adults with disabilities are over three times more likely to be out of the labor force than adults without disabilities." (Advancing, 2004: 39 [PALS 2001]) The flesh and blood figure of the disabled worker in the everyday work world is not a prevalent one. (Consider also, http://www.mcss.gov.on.ca/mcss/english/topics/pop_ado_stats.htm and for world disability rates and fates, consider Priestley, 2001, and Disability World, http://www.disabilityworld.org/links/Employment)

3 We use the term "disabled people" rather than the more popular term "people with disabilities." The latter termininology, refered to as "people-first language," aims to separate people from their embodied differences (as the government of Canada and WHO constantly and consistently recommend [e.g., http://www.mcss.gov.on.ca/mcss/english/how/howto_choose.htm]). This act of separation puts some distance between the meaning of disability and the meaning of people but leaves the oppressive everyday meaning of disability unchanged. For an analysis of the social significance of disability labels as they constitute different relations to the politics of the body, consider McColl and Jongbloed, 2006; Michalko, 2002; Overboe, 1999; Pothier and Devlin, 2005; Titchkosky, 2001.

4 In Ontario, these planning texts are increasing in number and becoming more particular with the advent of accessibility regulations.

5 This interview is part of our SSHRC funded research project considering the experiences of disabled university students.

RERFERENCES

Association of Workers Compensation Boards of Canada. (2007). *What's new*. Retrieved October 6, 2007, from http://www.awcbc.org/english/whats_new_WCBs.asp

Barnes, C., Mike, O., & Len, B. (Eds.). (2002). *Disability studies today*. Cambridge, UK: Polity.

Canada. (2004). *Advancing the inclusion of persons with disabilities 2004*. Ottawa: Human Resources Development Canada.

Canadian Council on Learning. (2007). *Canada slow to overcome limits for disabled learners* Retrieved July 16, 2007, from http://www.cclcca.ca/CCL/Reports/LessonsInLearning/ LinL20070222_Slow_overcome_limits_disabled_learners.htm

Davis, L. (1995). *Enforcing normalcy: Disability, deafness and the body*. London: Verso Press.

Davis, L. (2002). Bodies of difference: Politics, disability, and representation. In S. Snyder, B. J. Brueggemann, & R. Garland-Thomson (Eds.), *Disability studies: Enabling the humanities* (pp. 100–108). New York: The Modern Language Association of America.

Disability Archive, Leeds University. Retrieved July 2, 2007, from http://www.leeds.ac.uk/disability-studies/archiveuk/

Erevelles, N. (2000). Education unruly bodies: Critical pedagogy, disability studies, and the politics of schooling. *Educational Theory*, *50*(1), 25–47.

Ferri, B., & Connor, D. (2006). *Reading resistance: Discourses of exclusion in desegregation and inclusion debates*. New York: Peter Lang.

Garland-Thomson, R. (1997). *Extraordinary bodies: Figuring physical disability in American culture and literature*. New York: Columbia University Press.
Hill, M. A. (1979). *Hannah Arendt: The recovery of the public world*. New York: St. Martins Press.
Hughes, B., & Paterson, K. (1997). The social model of disability and the disappearing body: Towards a sociology of impairment. *Disability & Society, 12*(3), 325–340.
McColl, M. A., & Lyn, J. (Eds.). (2005). *Disability and social policy in Canada* (2nd ed.). Toronto: Captus Press.
Michalko, R. (1998). *The mystery of the eye and the shadow of blindness*. Toronto: University of Toronto Press.
Michalko, R. (2002). *The difference that disability makes*. Philadelphia: Temple University Press.
Michalko, R., & Titchkosky, T. (2001). Putting disability in its place: It's not a joking matter. In J. C. Wilson & C. Lewiecki-Wilson (Eds.), *Embodied rhetorics: Disability in language and culture* (pp. 200–228). Carbonsdale, IL: Southern Illinois University Press.
Mitchell, D. T. (2002). Narrative prosthesis and the materiality of metaphor. In S. Snyder, B. J. Brueggeman, & R. Garland Thomson (Eds.), *Disability studies: Enabling the humanities* (pp. 15–30). New York: The Modern Language Association of America.
Mitchell, D. T., & Snyder, S. (2000). *Narrative prosthesis: Disability and the dependencies of discourse*. Ann Arbor, MI: University of Michigan Press.
Murphy, R. (1987). *The body silent*. New York: W. W. Norton.
National Seafood Sector Council. (2007). *Work smarter, not harder: Ergonomics in the workplace*. Retrieved July 29, 2007, from http:/www.nssc.ca/erg/products.html
Oliver, M. (1990). *The politics of disablement*. Hampshire, London: The MacMillan Press Ltd. Retrieved from http://www.leeds.ac.uk/disability-studies/archiveuk/Oliver/in%20soc%20dis.pdf
Oliver, M. (1996). *Understanding disability: From theory to practice*. New York: St. Martin's Press.
Oliver, M. (2001). Disability issues in the postmodern world. In L. Barton (Ed.), *Disability, politics and the struggle for change* (pp. 149–159). London: David Fulton Publishers.
Opini. B. M. (2006). Strengths and limitations of Ontario post-secondary education accessibility plans: A review of one university accessibility plan. In *International journal of inclusive education* (pp. 1–23).
Overboe, J. (1999). 'Difference in itself': Validating disabled people's lived experience. *Body & society, 5*(4), 17–29.
Pothier, D., & Richard, D. (2005). *Critical disability theory: Essays in philosophy, politics, policy, and law*. Vancouver: UBC press.
Priestley, M. (Eds.). (2001). *Disability and the life course: Global perspective*. Cambridge: Cambridge University Press.
Rogers, F., Steve, S., & Allen, S. (2002). *Don't laugh at me*. Berkley, CA: Tricycle Press.
Titchkosky, T. (2003). *Disability, self and society*. Toronto: University of Toronto Press.
Titchkosky, T. (2007). *Reading and writing disability differently: The textured life of embodiment*. Toronto: University of Toronto Press.
University of Guelph. (2005). *Accessbility plan 2005–2006*. Retrieved July 29, 2007, from www.uoguelph.ca/web/accessibility 2005.shtml
Workers Compensation Board of Nova Scotia. (2007). *Work safe. For life*. Nova Scotia. Retrieved July 16, 2007, from http://www.worksafeforlife.ca/
Workplace Safety and Insurance Board. (2007). *There really are no accidents*. WSIB Ontario. Retrieved July 16, 2007, from http://www.wsib.on.ca/wsib/wsibsite.nsf/public/2006CoreCampaign

Rod Michalko
Equity Studies, New College
University of Toronto

Tanya Titchkosky
Sociology and Equity Studies in Education
Ontario Institute for Studies in Education of the University of Toronto

BONNIE WATT-MALCOLM

7. SKILLED TRADE TRAINING PROGRAMS FOR WOMEN:

In Vogue One More Time

INTRODUCTION

Recent demands for skilled trade workers in Canada has, once again, brought to the forefront the idea that non-traditional workers such as women are an available labour pool. An ageing working population combined with a shortage of skilled labour concerns construction sector stakeholders (e.g., governments, owners, sector councils, unions, contractors, education institutions, and training agencies). To alleviate this situation, supply-side mechanisms such as training programs are key methods used to introduce pertinent skills and knowledge to potential workers. Although training programs seem to be a viable recruitment strategy, it is questionable whether these training initiatives are an effective retention strategy. Unfortunately, reliable statistics documenting the career paths of graduates are difficult to find.

Framed within the present economic, political, and social conditions in Canada, this chapter examines the use of pre-apprenticeship training programs as a technique to introduce non-traditional workers to construction skills and knowledge. The first section outlines pertinent regulations, definitions, and related concepts of Canada's apprenticeship system. Then an overview of Canada's current construction industry is presented, followed by an introduction of women-only skill trade training programs within the Canadian context and a succinct description of my research method. The next section details observations made by 14 research participants (26 interviews) representing employers, educators, training providers, government representatives, and skilled trade workers. Here, I draw on scholarly literature to critically examine stakeholders' attempts to implement training initiatives to recruit and retain women in a sector that has customarily resisted their presence. The purpose of this discussion is to investigate the assumption that training programs help women learn about skilled trades and, with this knowledge, transition to apprenticeable skilled trade work in the construction field. I then outline approaches that, according to the research participants, could help training programs promote women's successful transitions to the skilled trade workforce. The last section offers implications for women's transitions to construction work.

P. Sawchuk and A. Taylor (eds.), Challenging Transitions in Learning and Work: Reflections on Policy and Practice, 125–143.

CANADA'S APPRENTICESHIP SYSTEM: REGULATIONS, DEFINITIONS, AND RELATED CONCEPTS

An integral aspect of recognizing skill levels in the construction industry is its governance through apprenticeship processes and subsequent attainment of journey level status. The current apprenticeship process in Canada is comprised of 13 systems, one for each province and territory, because apprenticeship training is classified under the education delivery umbrella. The British North America Act (BNA) of 1867 outlined particular policy boundaries between federal, provincial, and territorial governments and education is deemed to be the responsibility of provinces and territories. Hence, the onus is on each Canadian province and territory to legislate, regulate, and monitor its apprenticeship system.

Throughout the various jurisdictions, an apprenticeship program is typically a formalized system where the employee enters into a contractual agreement with a provincial or territorial government and an employer. Upon entering this contractual agreement, the apprentice then completes a series of on-the-job and in-class training over a period of three to four years to obtain a government-issued journey qualification. Further, a Red Seal Interprovincial designation, available in 45 of the 150 apprenticeable trades in Canada, provide workers mobility across provincial and territorial borders if the Red Seal qualification is recognized in the receiving province or territory (Human Resources Partnerships Directorate, 2004).

Apprenticeship refers to two distinct but related concepts. First, apprenticeship in this context is a formal process to achieve a qualification in a skilled trade and, second, apprenticeship is a recognized approach to learning. Learning is a social practice that involves relations between the person, community, and surroundings (Lave and Wenger, 1991; Illeris, 2003). Apprenticeship training embodies this holistic learning definition because it is a learning method that encourages a learner to learn by practice (Bunn, 1999). Pre-apprenticeship training is premised on these same notions. Some would suggest that one way to gain access to the construction sector is pre-apprenticeship training, which is a form of pre-employment or bridging training. For the purpose of this discussion, I use these terms interchangeably.

A skilled trade bridging program is a structured pre-apprenticeship training process designed to help people learn basic skills and knowledge of one or more skilled trades to work on construction worksites and subsequently apprentice as, for example, carpenters, welders, steamfitters-pipefitters, plumbers, electricians, boilermakers, and sheet metal fabricators. Upon completion of pre-apprenticeship training, the goal is for learners to be employed and obtain skilled trade apprenticeships. However, skilled trade careers are still considered non-traditional occupations for women. A non-traditional occupation is where women account for less than 30 percent of the workers (McKinnon and Ahola-Sidaway, 1995). The percentage of Canadian women working as skilled trade apprentices meets this criterion. In support, according to data available from Statistics Canada (2003), in 2001, approximately two percent of registered apprentices in the building construction trades (2.8 percent), the industrial and mechanical trades (1.6 percent), and the metal fabrication trades (1.8 percent) were women. The following section presents an overview of Canada's construction industry.

CANADA'S CONSTRUCTION INDUSTRY

Canada's construction industry is growing at a phenomenal rate and there is a tentative consensus among stakeholders that this rate of growth will continue for another decade. This is especially true in western Canada where the projected development of non-renewable resources is estimated in the billions of dollars, which, in turn, has a profound effect on Canada's economy. Current employees are able to maintain their employment status or perhaps seek opportunities that align with their career aspirations. Jobs are purportedly available for non-traditional workers such as women, youth, Aboriginals, ethnic minorities, and persons with disabilities. Skilled labour shortages create a situation where employers who need qualified trade people and unskilled labour are at a disadvantage in that they may not have the labour to meet their contractual obligations. Further complicating the current issue of skill shortages is the prediction that by 2020 there will be a shortage of one million workers because there are fewer people choosing trades as a career and the current working population is getting older (Skilled Trades, 2005). In May 2001, 41 years was the average age of a construction worker (Construction Sector Council, 2004). Labour shortfalls are particularly acute in the metal trades where it is predicted that 50,000 workers will be needed in the next five years as well as 400,000 manufacturing workers in 15 years (Skills Trades, 2005). Labour shortages, in some trades, continue despite political actions by means of government and corporate policies to encourage non-traditional workers (e.g., women, Aboriginals, and youth) to consider trades as a career, socio-cultural awareness campaigns, past and present market demands for more skilled trade workers, and women-only pre-apprenticeship training programs designed to prepare women for careers in the skilled trades.

Despite promising employment forecasts, there is a caution that coincides with these present and anticipated labour shortages that needs to be articulated. The construction industry is cyclical with periods of high labour demands followed by declines in labour requirements. Even though there may be a demand for labour not all trades will need additional personnel; in fact, there may be a surplus of skilled labour in a particular trade. Notwithstanding the uncertainties inherent in the construction labour market, governments and employers have a stake in ensuring there are adequate numbers of employable people to meet employers' labour needs. Not only do governments and employers have a vested interest in the labour market, construction associations, labour organizations, trade unions, employees, and potential workers are also concerned about labour requirements. Through the combined efforts of these stakeholders, training programs, especially for non-traditional labour groups (e.g., women, Aboriginals, and youth), are seen as one approach to help upgrade Canadian's skills. The next section reviews recent actions concerning women-only pre-apprenticeship training in Canada.

PRE-APPRENTICESHIP TRAINING IN CANADA

There is limited scholarly research studying bridging programs or pre-apprenticeship training programs with the intent to introduce women to the skilled trades in Canada (Betcherman, McMullen, and Davidman, 1998; Sweet and Schuetze, 2003) and, in a similar manner, there is a lack of scholarship examining the success of these programs. Yet government, for-profit, and not-for-profit training programs continue to be put in place to introduce women to skilled trade careers (cf. Cohen and Braid, 2003; Sweet, 2003a; Little, 2005; Watt-Malcolm, 2005). Policy development depends on labour market demand and the 'just in time' nature of policy implementation does not produce quality programs. Development of a quality program takes time and once the program is designed and the length of program is determined (typically three to 10 months long), it is quite possible that one year (or longer) has lapsed before the first training program students graduate.

Nor is it obvious that these initiatives have significantly increased the percentage of women employed as skilled trade workers in the construction sector during the past century (cf. Statistics Canada, 2003). The construction sector is the bastion of men workers (often single white men) and embedded masculine practices continue. Within this context, women-only pre-apprenticeship training programs appear to offer a much-needed service for women who want to work in the construction field and for employers who need willing, knowledgeable, entry-level workers.

The recent promotion of skills training is somewhat contradictory because government-sponsored training for women was significantly reduced in the 1990s (cf. Stephen, 2000; Lior and Wismer, 2002; ACTEW, 2003; Critoph, 2003). Three examples provide evidence of this assertion. First, the Designated Group Policy (DGP) was eliminated. This policy was put in place to support the training of women, Aboriginals, ethnic minorities, and persons with disabilities. Second, the federal government's Employment Insurance Act (EI) was revised regarding the distribution of monies to unemployed Canadians. Perhaps the most significant change in the EI legislation that reduced women's access to training opportunities was the narrowing of eligibility conditions. To be eligible for EI, fulltime workers are now required to record more weeks of work and, similarly, part-time workers must give proof of more hours worked. Many women find it difficult to meet these eligibility standards. Additionally, prior to the revised EI, the federal government's Consolidated Revenue Fund (CRF) provided monies for non-EI eligible persons. Since 1995, CRF monies available for labour market training programs have drastically decreased (ACTEW, 2003).

Third, Labour Market Development Agreements (LMDAs) were implemented. With the introduction of LMDAs, skill training has increasingly fallen under provincial and territorial jurisdictions. Under the guidelines of the LMDAs, federal monies are transferred to the provinces and territories and subsequently managed within the parameters of these agreements (ACTEW, 2003; Critoph, 2003). Due to the strong links between LMDAs and EI, provinces and territories have little leeway in how they distribute training dollars. Unfortunately, women who work part-time or are trying to re-enter the workforce may not meet EI requirements thus are ineligible for training monies. Despite this situation, there are provinces and territories (Yukon, Saskatchewan, Newfoundland-Labrador, Ontario, Nova Scotia) that support training programs for women (Ursule Critoph Consulting, 2002).

It is within these political and economic conditions that employment training programs are designed. They are organized interventions calculated to develop the skill and knowledge base of potential employees according to their interests and current and projected labour requirements. Training quality determines, in part, the degree of personal growth, skill attainment, employment possibilities, and career advancement. In Canada, numerous training programs are designed and implemented to increase workforce skill levels, which, given the present need for skilled labour in the construction sector (cf. Construction Sector Council, 2006), could be beneficial for people who enrol in training programs to boost their employment prospects.

Although there are an increasing number of training opportunities for Canadians, people who have weak relationships with their employers or little formal education tend not to pursue formal training and/or do not have access to job-related training (Betcherman, McMullen, and Davidman, 1998). By way of illustration, only 18 percent of Canadians with less than or equal to high school qualifications enrolled in formal training programs in 2002. In contrast, 38 percent of Canadians with college or trade credentials and 52 percent with university qualifications participated in formal training programs in 2002. As well, in 2002, employers across all provinces decreased their sponsorship of workers in job-specific skill training thus adults are using their own resources to acquire additional skills (Peters, 2004). Despite people's educational attainment and their access to formal learning opportunities, most paid workers engage in informal learning at work to learn related knowledge and skills (Livingstone, 2003). As a means to increase employment potential, especially for women who have experienced little success in the elementary and secondary school system (mandatory schooling required of Canadian youth), pre-apprenticeship, pre-employment, and bridging programs ideally present trainees a way to learn employable skills and transition into the labour market. Yet this group may not be eligible for government funding nor have the financial means to enter into training programs.

Despite the apparent labour shortfalls in specific occupations including skilled trades, there are few programs in operation with the mandate to teach women the skills considered necessary to work in the construction field; albeit, the number of programs is increasing. Programs and initiatives to encourage women to consider skilled trades as an occupation are offered by governments, technical institutes, private training delivery agents, and not-for-profit organizations. For example, the Yukon College delivers the Women in Trades and Technology program and, in Alberta, the Journeywomen Start program is developed and presented by Women Building Futures. Manitoba Women's Directorate sponsors the Trade Up program. Other sponsors of this program include Manitoba Education and Training, Employment and Training Services Branch, and the Gateway Group. In Ontario, the Women in Skilled Trades program is delivered by the college system and is managed by the Ontario Women's Directorate and the Newfoundland and Labrador's Women in Resource Development Committee offers the Orientation to Trades and Technology program (Canadian Council on Learning, 2006). Other programs that are available for women interested in learning and working in the skilled trades are the British Columbia Institute of Technology's (BCIT) Trades Discovery for Women program (BCIT, n.d.), and the Northwest Territories' Status of Women Canada's Northern Women in Mining, Oil and Gas program (Status of Women Canada, Northwest Territories, n.d.). The quality of these programs is difficult to determine in that program duration (approximately three to 10 months) and content varies and women's continuation in the construction field has proven to be difficult to track. Nonetheless, typically, the goals of these programs are to help women upgrade high-school credentials and learn job skills.

RESEARCH METHOD

Data include 26 face-to-face and telephone interviews with 14 participants that were audio-taped and transcribed. The participants were educators/trainers, employers, government representatives, employees (journeypersons and apprentices) from western Canada as well as representation from northern and eastern Canada. All participants were associated with the Canadian construction sector, which includes, but not limited to, the petroleum, petrochemical, pulp and paper, and chemical industries. More than 60 percent of the participants had one or more trade tickets and women represent greater than 50 percent of the total interviews. Over 50 percent started working in the industrial field in the late 1960s and 1970s while the remainder entered into this sector in the 1980s through to the 2000s. Work experiences consist of working with union and non-union large and medium-sized contractors on industrial and commercial jobsites.

The following section presents observations made by employers, educators, training providers, skilled trade workers, and government representatives as to the viability of training programs and related policies. It also highlights, according to these research participants, what needs to be considered if training programs are used as a recruitment and retention strategy for a sector that tends to hire women only in times of acute labour shortages. If training is the method of choice to help women access construction work, then it is necessary to reiterate employers' roles in this process – to hire these trainees and further help them complete their apprenticeships.

WOMEN LEARNING TO WORK AS SKILLED TRADE WORKERS

Gendered inequities still exist in Canada's workplaces and skilled trade careers are more often than not viewed as unsuitable occupations for women. Tilly (1998) labels these deeply-rooted views as 'durable inequities' (p. 6). Abilities and capabilities are based on categories such as women's work and men's work and assumptions that suggest women are not capable of undertaking construction-type work. Inherent in these classifications are associated expectations and restrictions imposed by governments and their funding targets, employers and their organizational mandates, and workers who characteristically adhere to employer and government guidelines (Tilly). Within this context, throughout the 20th century and into the 21st century, governments, industry, and society anticipated and responded to economic decline and growth. At times, industry has needed skilled labour to meet the demands of a growing economy; therefore, government-funded training policies were implemented. Conversely, according to an employer of a medium-sized company (less than 500 employees), the current lack of skilled trade workers is a result of the downturn in the economy in the 1980s and early 1990s (I-3)[1].

People were unable to find jobs in the construction sector and, with a surplus of skilled labour, training non-traditional labour groups was not a high priority on provincial or federal governments' policy agendas.

From another perspective, an educator believes there is not a shortage of labour; rather, there is a shortage of *skilled* labour. Women are, once again, considered to be an untapped labour source but they lack the required skills (I-5, Educator). It is difficult for women, who often do not have pre-requisite skills, established networks, or the confidence, to apply for trade-related positions; therefore, training programs are one way to help women learn appropriate skills. The following sections highlight underlying issues in training initiatives related to funding and access, and social constraints.

TRAINING PROGRAMS: FUNDING AND ACCESS

More women-only training programs have been established to introduce women to non-traditional skilled trades in the past few years, often on a cost-recovery basis. The reason, in part, for this influx of training initiatives sponsored by federal, provincial, and territorial government agencies as well as private and not-for-profit organizations is to alleviate the shortage of skilled trade workers occurring in many parts of Canada. Women among other non-traditional workers, for example, Aboriginals, youth, persons with disabilities, and ethnic minorities, as mentioned previously, are viewed as untapped labour resources.

An employer working for a mid-sized contractor mentions that recent federal government initiatives, specifically LMDAs and the now defunct DGP, have hindered funding schedules that might have made monies available for training non-traditional workers (I-4). In support, a training provider is concerned that their program is dependent upon government funding, 'which means that it is under review each year as to whether they will do it for the following year. In other words, the program is not in place as a continuing program' (I-20). Another employer states that government-training initiatives do not increase the number of skilled trade workers and strongly believes that policies implemented in Canada to promote skilled trades to women and other non-traditional workers have not made a difference (I-3). For different reasons, the viewpoint that government-initiated training policies are ineffective is prevalent among the employers who participated in this research. For example, one employer comments that mid-sized companies 'haven't really spent much time on recruiting workforce [or] development training. Its bring people in, hire them, get the job done and move on, to the next job I mean. They're preoccupied with keeping the business going' (I-12). I argue that employers are also apprehensive about return on investment. Monies spent for employee training are withheld because employers cannot guarantee a return on investment. This is particularly true in the construction sector because of its highly mobile workforce. Thompson (2003), in a similar manner, maintains that there are studies that indicate employers are contributing less to training as well as skill development due to redundancy or people leaving their employ.

From another perspective, a training provider expresses misgivings in response to 'all kinds of programs springing up' (I-7). Specifically:

> [T]here have been lots of programs before. In the 70s there was a ton of programs for women getting in the trades and typically in the long haul, in the bigger picture, they were not successful and we know that because of the [low] number of women in trades ... So the retention rate is poor. (I-7)

Although numerous programs were established in the 1970s to introduce women to skilled trade work, the success of these training programs is uncertain. I suggest that the programs were unsustainable because the need for skilled labour decreased due to a downturn in construction activity. Another reason for the demise of programs is women's lack of interest in the skilled trades as a career path and employers' resistance to hiring non-traditional labour when other labour sources were available.

Eliminating inequitable hiring, retention, and promotion activities have proven to be difficult. Existing structures resist the fundamental tenets of inclusiveness in the workplace thus inequalities still exist (Armstrong, 1997). As noted in the above quote, there is an underlying question as to the effectiveness of training programs intended to introduce women to the skilled trades. Many training organizations only take on trainees that are, for the most part, fundable by government agencies. Hence, training programs tend to attract low-skilled and unemployed people and because of the current funding schedule, working people, even the poorly-paid, are not eligible. These people cannot access training and may well be the people who would benefit greatly from this training. This is not to suggest that those people who are eligible for training funding do not benefit from the opportunity to acquire additional skills and knowledge. Nonetheless, a training provider maintains that funders are jumping 'on that band wagon for funding more trades programs for women' (I-7). However, if the program is government driven:

> [T]hen more than likely it won't work because it won't have the money or the components that will work because government tends to be very band-aid in their approach. So they'll want to say, '... we'll give them some industrial first aid and maybe a day or two on workplace culture.' Or something like that, but just get them out there working. They don't realize how deep the barriers still are and how systemic those barriers still are ... Someone who is not feeling really confident. Someone who maybe does not have a significant amount of drive because she's been beaten down there in her life. Those kinds of obstacles that you encounter might kill her intention [to succeed]. (I-7, Training Provider)

Training programs are used as a means to recruit and retain women in the skilled trade sector but as noted by this training provider, systemic barriers still exist in an occupational field that has proven to be resilient to change. Systemic barriers include negative attitudes towards skilled trades, hostile workplaces and training settings (Canadian Apprenticeship Forum, 2004), women's perceptions that trades are not a career option, and employers' resistance to hiring women as skilled trade workers. Without sustained funding from governments or other sources and committed long-term employer support, awareness of entrenched systemic barriers, and programs designed with defined links to the construction sector, pre-apprenticeship training programs are essentially short-term band-aid measures to meet short-term labour requirements – just-in-time training for just-in-time labour needs.

However, an employer working for a medium-sized company contends that these policies and programs are proactive but more needs to be done. Even though training unskilled Canadians, particularly women, for construction trade work has typically been left to federal, provincial, and territorial governments this same employer advises that the responsibility for training belongs to industry. Instead of concerning themselves with government policies, this employer is of the opinion that it is more important for companies to promote apprenticeships. Although this employer advocates apprenticeship training, his company does not specifically target women for skilled trade training (I-3). For the most part, this phenomenon is the norm for Canadian employers in that they do not take on the responsibility to fund formal pre-apprenticeship skilled trade training. Typically, pre-apprenticeship training programs are funded by governments as dictated by the LMDAs. Other training programs may be offered on a cost-recovery basis by open shop associations, technical institutions, and private delivery agents. Unions do not often participate in women-only pre-apprenticeship training programs. In their defence, there are unions as well as employers who take the time to offer their apprentices well-rounded on-the-job training experiences.

To counteract the short-term funding measures of government initiatives, a few training organizations have established strategic partnerships with employers, colleges, past-graduates, government personnel, and community agencies. There is an express need to build partnerships to ideally promote effective use of organizational resources. Partnerships and relationships also influence the degree of integration into occupational and organizational cultures (Taylor, 2006). Nonetheless, where partnerships exist, there are tensions because of conflicting motivations and contradictions. In spite of the tensions inherent in partnerships, a program organizer illustrates the continuing efforts undertaken to ensure quality relationships. They liaise 'with government on policy issues, advocating and lobbying with them. Doing the same with industry … if the numbers of women are to be increased. Working with post-secondary institutions for the … same goals' (I-10, Training Provider).

The role that employers have in the apprenticeship process, as mentioned previously, is crucial. For an employee to become an apprentice, the individual enters into a contractual agreement with his/her employer and the provincial government. Yet, training providers, regardless of their location in Canada, comment that persuading employers to hire women graduates has been difficult even when it is obvious that entry-level skilled workers could help employers alleviate some of their labour concerns. Moreover, this is one stakeholder group that seems to avoid active involvement in apprenticeship training, which is not exclusive to supporting women in their construction apprenticeships. Thompson (2003) highlights that employer investment for training, in general, is lessening. Toner (2003) and Taylor, McGray, and Watt-Malcolm (2007) more specifically examine employers' hesitance to actively support apprenticeship training especially for adult and high school apprenticeships, respectively. Without employer buy-in, even a quality program will not be successful. Employers are essential part of the training process.

The research participants draw on both supply-side and demand-side arguments for the lack of employer participation to help women gain construction employment and apprenticeships. Supply-side comments include those related to employers' beliefs that training is inadequate and that the program graduates are not qualified to be paid entry level construction wages. There is also the idea that investment in training is governed according to cost-benefit analyses (Toner, 2003). For example, research participants note that employers repeatedly hire journeypersons who have required skills, which can be more cost effective than hiring apprentices who need supervision and training. To thwart this trend, one training organization invites employers to critique their curriculum and offer suggestions (I-7, Training Provider). This approach helps educate employers and support ongoing efforts to strengthen partnerships, which will ideally advance women's learning and their access to jobs and apprenticeships. Also from a supply-side perceptive, participants suggest that women tend to choose occupations that allow them to assume familial responsibilities (Kirton and Greene, 2000). Construction work typically is organized around multi-day shifts, long hours, and jobsites that are often out of town. This organization of work denies many women access to these lucrative positions.

The demand-side arguments similarly create inherent barriers for women attempting to enter the construction field. Kirton and Greene (2000) contend that employers have preferences for certain kinds of workers and women are not the preferred worker group. Women, according to some employers and skilled trade workers, are costly employees because of absenteeism, lateness, maternity leave – all founded on the historical roles attached to women around family obligations. Additionally, employers believe that women frequently leave their employment thus creating a situation where they are required to find and then train new employees. Many employers do not view women as construction workers and, if women are hired, they bring with them more issues than their male co-workers. Other demand-side institutional and structural factors are economics, historical work relationships, full and part-time workers, and organizational structures (Toner, 2003).

The following section further elaborate ideas that continue to restrict women's construction sector participation.

TRAINING PROGRAMS: SOCIAL CONSTRAINTS

Current pre-apprenticeship training programs introduce women to skilled trades such as, but not limited to, electrical, carpentry, sheet metal fabrication, welding, boilermaking, steamfitting-pipefitting, plumbing, crane and hoisting, and heavy equipment operation. They work with various hand and power tools central to these trades and learn the basics (I-8, Training Provider). Learners may also receive their certification for Standard First Aid, CSTS (Construction Safety Training System), WHMIS (Workplace Hazardous Materials Information System), scaffolding, and fall protection. Main strategies to advance women's learning are women-only classes, role-modeling, hands-on skill training, introduction to workplace culture, exposure to worksites, job-shadowing, career investigations, labour market research, financial management, safety training, construction fitness training, personal development, and conflict resolution. Another critical element is highlighted by an employer where women must be given opportunities to build self confidence and know they are capable of doing this work (I-4). Further support is offered by a ticketed trade person in that her biggest challenge was to learn how to 'jump right in and try it' (I-6). Implementing learning techniques such as hands-on training is often easier than strategies to build self-confidence and to learn how to eagerly tackle unforeseen challenges. Many women enrolled in pre-apprenticeship programs have struggled with low self-esteem due to hardships they have encountered in their lives (I-7, Training Provider).

Women's career choices are influenced by social pressures and familial responsibilities and construction-related trades are not typically seen by many as occupations women are involved in. Fuller, Beck, and Unwin (2005) document in their study of youth and employers, and their perceptions of non-traditional occupations, that although stereotypical viewpoints exist, young people believe they could go into non-traditional careers but prefer not to. These authors suggest that this approach 'tends to mask the reality of the obstacles (e.g., teasing, feeling isolated and workplace conditions) to making such choices, and is likely to affect individuals' response to policies designed to dismantle them' (p. 307). Sweet (2003a) points out many women, if they have the means, choose college training as opposed to skilled trade training because of their interests. Women will enrol in service or business-related training programs. Occupations linked to these formal education routes include recreation, early childhood, computer applications, teaching, and nursing. Equally, women steer clear of construction skilled trade work because of perceived and/or real difficulties in learning and working in unfamiliar work environments. Another aspect of employment training is that men are often invited by their employers to upgrade their skills; whereas, women tend to be overlooked by employers (Hart and Shrimpton, 2003). Women's lack of training, especially in the trade area, also hinders job promotions and increases the possibility of job layoffs, which perpetuates the myth that women are not skilled trade workers.

Biases are noticeable in employment training. Butterwick (2003) argues that training for non-traditional groups assumes 'one size fits all' in that 'all participants in government-funded job training programs have the same needs and social biographies' (p. 162). To become a skilled tradesperson, a person must learn the skills and knowledge of the trade (Riemer, 1979), which typically occurs through daily interaction with more experienced trade people and frequent use of trade tools. The transition from student to employee, from training to employment, is an essential part of establishing and maintaining an occupation. Recently this transition is becoming more an individual responsibility (Sweet, 2003a). Cohen and Braid (2003) confirm that for a training program to be effective, links between training and employment must be clear. Programs that seem to have numerous genuine learning activities provide the impetus to motivate a woman to gain status as a legitimate peripheral participant – motivation is sustained through quality participation and an aspiration to be acknowledged as an expert (Lave and Wenger, 1991). But to be considered an expert, first, the learners must complete their pre-apprenticeship training and, second, obtain employment that leads to apprenticeships and journeyed status. In this transition from the training environment to the workplace, women need to have support of their training organizations and employers and ask for assistance if required (I-10, Training Provider). Exposure to employers allows these potential employees to demonstrate their knowledge and employers are likely to hire people with relevant workplace knowledge (Sweet, 2003a).

However, frequently, program developers ignore the lived realities of women and give them first-aid training and a few days of workplace culture (I-7, Training Provider) and expect them to be ready for construction work. Correspondingly, often overlooked in developing an effective training program, as Little (2005) describes and similar to Butterwick's (2003) comment above about employment training biases, are the difficulties women encounter in the workplace, which also are present in training situations. Hardships include, especially for low-income and/or marginalized women, a group often targeted for skill training, lack of childcare, little family support, poverty, and low self-confidence. These issues are present even when women have opportunities to experience the workplace and its idiosyncrasies and given the means to use their skills, safety training, and to situate their newly-acquired skills and knowledge in the workplace. Further, the organization of construction work repeatedly inhibits women's workforce participation. Work locations, hours of work, and extended periods away from home, are systemic barriers that continue to be hidden or disregarded as inconsequential. When women encounter the realities of workplace structures, the accepted norms, they meet resistance from employers to accommodate home responsibilities – because that is the way construction work is organized. Thus it is expected that women who enrol in these programs and complete them will be able to access jobsites and put in place strategies to work around these organizational structures to meet their familial responsibilities.

Few women take on construction work, an observation supported by statistics that indicate that women make up less than three percent of the construction workforce (see above). An individual's approach towards her pre-apprenticeship training strongly affects how she will transition from training to employment. Individual agency is necessary to successfully complete a training program and gain subsequent employment in a related career. One apprentice articulates how her pre-apprenticeship training program gave her the confidence and the agency to see herself as a construction worker:

> I think its [training program] great just for women because it is getting the women out there. I mean I know women who would have loved to have gone into a trade but went into a more traditional setting because that was what society expected of them. So at least with a program like this it is exposing women to the trades. And though I really think that it is you know something that everybody can benefit from in terms of trade work. … I haven't actually been out in the workforce with it yet but that's where I'm headed. I think the

> fact that the [training] program was there and then I got the hands-on and then I was in the shops and I was out there with the guys with my coveralls on getting dirty you know with steel toed boots and my hard hat.

The previous excerpt exposes how this woman took on the responsibility for learning the necessary skills, knowledge, and attitudes to promote her career in the skilled trades. However, in order for her to succeed in this field, there must be opportunities to access jobsites.

The following section outlines strategies that, according to the research participants based on their experiences, will promote successful training program design, implementation, and evaluation to help women access trade work.

TRAINING PROGRAM DESIGN, IMPLEMENTATION, AND EVALUATION

Despite the shortcomings of many women-only bridging programs, Sweet (2003a) maintains that training programs may be successful if they recognize and coincide with students' interest, motivations, and abilities. To prepare students for careers in the skilled trades and to ensure student success, program organizers put in place training that deals with not only safety, basic theory, skills, and construction terminology, but programs that include courses on workplace culture, financial management, and physical fitness. Wismer and Lior (1994) purport that implementing a learner-centered curriculum is central to advancing women's success in training programs. Building into the curriculum appropriate teaching/learning strategies and course content that value diversities and differences, both in the classroom and the workplace, is critical (Women in Trades and Technology, 1993).

Well-designed bridging programs implement helpful strategies such as formalized 'back-up' plans for childcare, eldercare, and transportation. Additionally, there are organizers of women-only bridging programs who are aware of the deeply-entrenched masculinized workplace culture of the construction field. Disregarding the overwhelming masculinized work environment by not incorporating related workplace culture courses is often the downfall of less successful women-only skilled trade training programs (Braid, 2003). Grzetic (1998) adds that incorporation of gender-neutral policies into the training program and techniques to improve communication skills for learners, instructors, and support staff will aid in promoting a positive learning environment. Underlying all of these strategies is the need to provide trainees with the skills to survive in the workforce (Madsen, 1999) – an approach that is not always evident in short-term generic training programs. In addition to educating trainees, a government representative suggests it is also necessary to find ways to educate employers and their on-site supervisory personnel about effective ways to make workplaces more equitable for everyone (I-9).

Women trade instructors familiar with trade jargon and trade-specific skills are often used as role models. Nonetheless, this strategy does not always work. An employer states: 'if you think that you're going to rely on some successful role models, women, to manage other women in that regard, I am not so sure that it's going to be a natural phenomena ... you're going to have to work hard at it' (I-12). In spite of this employer's experience with women role models, training organizers believe that all-women classes make a difference where students start with the basics, the hands-on work, in a non-threatening environment (I-8, Training Provider). Some women-only pre-apprenticeship training programs have proven to be successful because:

> [W]hen we grow up we are conditioned to think that men grow up knowing how to use power tools. Women miss a lot of the experiences that men have in that respect and what we are giving them are the first baby steps and once they get over the initial trepidation, hesitancy, shyness ... they are so willing to try and they look forward to trying in a very non-competitive space. (I-8, Training Provider)

From another perspective, since women are entering workplaces that employ mostly men, trainers also bring in men trade instructors (I-8, Training Provider). This training provider's argument assumes that students who have the benefit of working with skilled women and men in the training environment have greater exposure to workplace dynamics. Students also learn about how women are received and treated on jobsites and have more opportunities to learn techniques to overcome obstacles that may arise.

In the skill training portion, an introduction of a skill or knowledge component should provide the foundation for the following activity. From a localized perspective, this activity organization is similar to one interpretation of Vygotsky's zone of proximal development, the difference in demonstrating acquisition of knowledge or skill between learners solving problems alone or in the presence of more experienced practitioners (Guile and Young, 1999). Further, these organizational practices emphasize connections of the changing historical relations between apprentices and journeyed people in the process of practice (Lave and Wenger, 1991; Engeström, 2001). Progressive learning activities are structured to move learners towards legitimate participation in the construction field. Women are more than capable of shifting from newcomer status to active participants, if given the opportunity.

To reiterate, the strategies previously listed are intended to engage the learners by addressing a variety of learning styles (I-2, Educator). For example, pedagogical strategies should include tours to jobsites because most students have never seen a jobsite (I-8, Training Provider). Reinforcing skills and knowledge acquired in the shop environment are the job-shadowing and work experience placements. Worksite visits, prior to graduating from a training program, offers women an opportunity to explore their future worksites. Eisenberg (1998), in her research of women who work in the construction trades, states: 'Since construction sites are off limits to the public, most new tradeswomen's first day on the job was also their first glimpse of its sights, smells, and sounds. Just navigating the worksite could be a series of new experiences or challenges' (p. 41). Providing opportunities for women to visit jobsites and then, upon completion of the core program, secure work experience or job shadowing placements demonstrates sound pedagogical practices – a combination of practice and theory, which promotes transitions from school to work. The training programs in this study expose their students to workplaces, incorporate effective teaching and learning strategies, and there is evidence of qualified and supportive program staff. It is also essential for women to engage with the program content and gain confidence in their ability to meet or exceed occupational skill and knowledge requirements. Women, upon entering training programs introducing non-traditional skilled trades, according to Sweet (2003b), need to believe there will be a return, emotionally, physically, and/or financially for the time they have invested.

An ideal bridging program contains, most if not all, the following components: a) choice of training program based on an individual's interests and career aspirations, b) flexibility and consideration of family and personal commitments, c) learner-centered and holistic program, d) longer program duration, e) safe learning environment, f) instructors who are role-models, and g) training that promotes success (Little, 2005). Pre-apprenticeship training should also: a) offer women the means to learn entry-level trade skills, which will help them obtain work as apprentices, b) present women opportunities to move out of poverty, and c) give women techniques to promote positive and healthy personal development. Graduates need to have the necessary entry-level skills and knowledge to obtain long-term employment as trade apprentices and achieve, in a timely fashion, their journey qualifications. Pre-employment preparation programs with a cursory overview of trade occupations and brief introduction to skills and tools tend to be less successful than programs with a more in-depth examination of skilled trade careers, tool use, skill application, safety training, financial management, physical fitness, workplace culture, and specific reference to employer expectations. Just as important, 'We are aware that it would be irresponsible of us if we weren't vying to get policy changes that were going to make it easier for [our students] … to also be employed. So we work on all the levels, everything from the training for women right through to policy' (I-10, Training Provider). Success of pre-apprenticeship training programs is in the accomplishments of the graduates. However, it is unknown, for the most part, how many women who have completed their pre-apprenticeship training are working as skilled trade workers in Canada's construction field. The lack of concrete evidence as to the effectiveness of these programs is a concern and deserves further investigation.

CONCLUDING COMMENTS

The purpose of this discussion is to explore the assumption that training programs are effective recruitment and retention strategies for employers requiring skilled labour and useful mechanisms for women wanting to work in Canada's construction sector. Overall, training programs seem to be the method of choice for many stakeholders to meet current labour requirements, but the success of Canadian training programs designed to introduce the skilled trades to women and to promote their participation in related apprenticeships is unknown for the most part. Moreover, training programs are founded on the notion that inter-institutional transitions are different depending on the worker group. Women are viewed as non-traditional workers for construction-related occupations thus bridging programs are needed in order to gain entry to the construction workforce. Although many formalized bridging programs that train women in non-traditional occupations are limited and further restricted by accepted norms and traditions of the workplaces (Hart and Shrimpton, 2003).

Even with the training undertaken by the women trainees, and whatever strategies are pursued, employer involvement continues to be a concern. There are employers who do not hire women as skilled trade workers unless they are in dire need of *bodies* for their jobsites because of the perceived unsuitability of women for construction trade work. Training women for skilled trade work does not guarantee employment. Compounding this resistance are the realities of the organization of construction work with its long work hours and out of town or inaccessible jobsites. There is also the masculinized work culture. All of these factors cause women to avoid construction-related careers. Additionally, biographical agency differs across gender and class lines. Learners may have had little success in the formal secondary education system often because connections between school and work were not made clear and, as a result these women have not been able to access and maintain sustainable well-paying jobs. Pre-apprenticeship training developers need to seriously consider these ideas before selecting learning strategies.

Despite the lack of evidence for program success, there are indications that some programs may be more effective than others. These exceptions offer insights into how programs with effective strategies (i.e., choice, flexibility, learner-centered, long-term) and awareness that women do not typically have the necessary skills and knowledge or confidence to apply for positions in the construction field can further student success. These programs have developed strategies to aid women in their transition to the workplace from their formal training. A key awareness of workplace conditions must dictate the choice of learning strategies, for example, employers' resistance to hiring women apprentices, work locations, organization of work, and physical nature of the work.

Critical program content includes skill application, trade knowledge, safety training, financial management, physical fitness, and workplace culture courses detailing jobsite social, political, and economic constructs and the entrenched masculinized culture. Opportunities to learn entry-level skills, tool use, trade terminology, and exposure to jobsites within a safe learning environment are important considerations. This approach to training is reflective of a philosophy that merges training and job expectations through partnerships with industry and community, and for students, work experiences and job shadowing, jobsite tours, and interactions with guest speakers. Nonetheless, training that takes place off the jobsite may not be the most effective means to help women learn how to work in the construction field especially programs that are put in place to meet 'just in time' labour requirements.

In contrast, long-term, well-designed, structured training and mentoring programs on jobsites in conjunction with formal in-class training may better serve the needs of the stakeholders as well as promote women's transitions to construction workplaces. Here, it is necessary to establish links with unions and employers willing to sponsor training through financial support, hiring of potential apprentices, and/or on-site work experiences for women. These commitments also lessen the heavy reliance on governments to fund training. Research is required to examine how unions and employers could play a more significant role in pre-apprenticeship training for women. Another research possibility is to formally explore women's experiences and subsequent career paths upon graduating from their training programs. A detailed study of program outcomes is also needed. Lastly, an investigation is necessary to consider underlying assumptions that, first, women need to participate in skills training in order to be considered viable workers and, second, that training programs are an effective way to recruit and retain women in a sector that has traditionally resisted their presence.

NOTES

1 Reference indicates research participant interview (I), interview number (e.g., 3), and participant status (e.g., Educator).

REFERENCES

Andres, L., Anisef, P., Krahn, H., Looker, D., & Thiessen, D. (1999). The persistence of social structure: Cohort, class, and gender effects on the occupational aspirations and expectations of Canadian youth. *Journal of Youth Studies, 2*(3), 261–282.

ACTEW. (2003). *Putting women in the picture – Labour market policy and the women's training sector*. Retrieved May 2005, from http://www.actew.org

Armstrong, P. (1997). Restructuring public and private: Women's paid and unpaid work. In S. Boyd (Ed.), *Challenging the public/private divide: Feminism, law, and public policy* (pp. 37–61). Toronto: University of Toronto Press.

Betcherman, G., McMullen, K., & Davidman, K. (1998). *Training for the new economy: A synthesis report*. Ottawa: Renouf Publishing Co. Ltd.

Braid, K. (2003). The culture of construction: Or, etiquette for the nontraditional. In M. Griffin Cohen (Ed.), *Training the excluded for work: Access and equity for women, immigrants, First Nations, youth, and people with low income*. Toronto: UBC Press.

British Columbia Institute of Technology. (n.d.). *Trades discovery for women*. Retrieved June 2007, from http://www.bcit.ca

Bunn, S. (1999). The nomad's apprentice: Different kinds of 'apprenticeship' among Kyrgyz nomads in Central Asia. In P. Ainley & H. Rainbird (Eds.), *Apprenticeship: Towards a new paradigm of learning*. London: Kogan Page Limited.

Butterwick, S. (2003). Life skills training: 'Open for discussion'. In M. Griffin Cohen (Ed.), *Training the excluded for work: Access and equity for women, immigrants, First Nations, youth, and people with low income*. Toronto: UBC Press.

Canadian Council on Learning. (2006). *Apprenticeship training in Canada*. Retrieved June 2007, from http://www.ccl-cca.ca

Canadian Apprenticeship Forum. (2004). *Accessing and completing apprenticeship training in Canada: Perception of barriers*. Ottawa: Author.

Cohen, M., & Braid, K. (2003). The road to equity: Training women and First Nations on the Vancouver Island highway. In M. Griffin Cohen (Ed.), *Training the excluded for work: Access and equity for women, immigrants, First Nations, youth, and people with low income*. Toronto: UBC Press.

Construction Sector Council. (2004). *Building tomorrow's workforce*. Retrieved March 2005, from http://www.csc-cs.org

Construction Sector Council. (2006). *Building tomorrow's workforce*. Retrieved June 2006, from http://www.csc-cs.org

Critoph, U. (2003). Who wins, who loses: The real story of the transfer of training to the provinces and its impact on women. In M. Griffin Cohen (Ed.), *Training the excluded for work: Access and equity for women, immigrants, First Nations, youth, and people with low income*. Toronto: UBC Press.

Eisenberg, S. (1998). *We'll call you if we need you: Experiences of women working construction*. Ithaca, NY: Cornell University Press.

Engeström, Y. (2001). Expansive learning at work: Toward an activity theoretical reconceptualization. *Journal of Education and Work, 14*(1), 133–156.

Fuller, A., Beck, V., & Unwin, L. (2005). The gendered nature of apprenticeship: Employers' and young people's perspectives. *Education and Training, 47*(4/5), 298–311.

Grzetic, B. (1998). *Women in technical work in Atlantic Canada.* Retrieved March 2003, from http://www.curricstudies.educ.ubc.ca

Guile, M., & Young, M. (1999). Beyond the institution of apprenticeship: Towards a social theory of learning as the production of knowledge. In P. Ainley & H. Rainbird (Eds.), *Apprenticeship: Towards a new paradigm of learning.* London: Kogan Page Limited.

Hart, S., & Shrimpton, M. (2003). Women's training and equity on the Hibernia construction project. In M. Griffin Cohen (Ed.), *Training the excluded for work: Access and equity for women, immigrants, First Nations, youth, and people with low income.* Toronto: UBC Press.

Human Resources Partnerships Directorate. (2004). *The interprovincial standards 'Red Seal' program.* Retrieved June, 2006, from http://www.red-seal.ca

Illeris, K. (2003). Workplace learning and learning theory. *Journal of Workplace Learning, 15*(4), 167–178.

Kirton, G., & Greene, A. (2000). *The dynamics of managing diversity: A critical approach.* Oxford, UK: Butterworth-Heinemann.

Lave, J., & Wenger, E. (1991). *Situated learning: Legitimate peripheral participation.* New York: Cambridge University Press.

Little, M. (2005). *If I had a hammer: Retraining that really works.* Vancouver: UBC Press.

Lior, K., & Wismer, S. (2002). *By design or by default? Women's labour market training needs and the role of community-based training.* Toronto: Labour Education and Research Network.

Livingstone, D. (2003). *Hidden dimensions of work and learning: The significance of unpaid work and informal learning in global capitalism.* Toronto: Centre for the Study of Education and Work.

Madsen, K. (1999). *Yukon women in apprenticeship and trades.* Retrieved March 2003, from http://www.gov.yk

McKinnon, M., & Ahola-Sidaway, J. (1995). 'Workin' with the boys': A North American perspective on non-traditional work initiatives for adolescent females in secondary schools. *Gender & Education, 7*(3), 327–339.

Peters, V. (2004). *Working and training: First results of the 2003 adult education and training survey.* Ottawa: Statistics Canada, Human Resources and Skills Development Canada.

Reimer, J. (1979). *Hard hats: The work world of construction workers.* London: Sage Publications, Inc.

Skilled Trades. (2005). *Fact sheet.* Retrieved August 2007, from http://www.careersintrades.ca

Skilled Trades. (2005). *A career you can build on.* Retrieved September 2005, from http://www.careersintrades.ca

Statistics Canada. (2003). *The Daily, November 20, 2003: Registered apprenticeship training programs.* Retrieved March 2006, from http://www.statscan.ca

Status of Women Canada, Northwest Territories. (n.d.). *Q & A.* Retrieved June 2007, from http://statusofwomen.nt.ca

Stephen, J. (2000). *Accessed diminished. A report on women's training and employment services in Ontario.* Toronto: ACTEW.

Sweet, R. (2003a). Pathways to employment for women: Apprenticeship or college training. In M. Griffin Cohen (Ed.), *Training the excluded for work: Access and equity for women, immigrants, First Nations, youth, and people with low income.* Toronto: UBC Press.

Sweet, R. (2003b). Women and apprenticeships: The role of personal agency in transition success. In H. Schuetze & R. Sweet (Eds.), *Integrating school and workplace learning in Canada: Principles and practices of alternation education and training.* Montreal: McGill-Queen's University Press.

Sweet, R., & Schuetze, H. (2003). New policy and research directions. In H. Schuetze & R. Sweet (Eds.), *Integrating school and workplace learning in Canada: Principles and practices of alternation education and training.* Montreal: McGill-Queen's University Press.

Taylor, A. (2006). The challenges of partnership in school-to-work transition. *Journal of Vocational Education and Training, 58*(3), 319–336.

Taylor, A., McGray, R., & Watt-Malcolm, B. (2007). Struggles over labour power: The case of Fort McMurray. *Journal of Education and Work, 20*(5), 379–396.

Thompson, P. (2003). Disconnected capitalism: Or why employers can't keep their side of the bargain. *Work, Employment, and Society, 17*(2), 359–378.

Tilly, C. (1998). *Durable inequality*. Berkley, CA: University of California Press.
Toner, P. (2003). Supply-side and demand-side explanations of declining apprentice training rates: A critical overview. *The Journal of Industrial Relations, 45*(4), 457–484.
Watt-Malcolm, B. (2005). Women learning to work in Canada's industrial sector: An analysis of bridging programs introducing the skilled trades to Canadian women. In P. Hager & G. Hawke (Eds.), *Conference papers: 4th international conference on researching work and learning*. Retrieved June 2006, from http://www.oval.uts.edu.au/rwl4
Wismer, S., & Lior, K. (1994). *Meeting women's training needs: Case studies in women's training*. St. John's, NFLD: Government of Newfoundland and Labrador, Women's Policy Office.
Women in Trades & Technology. (1993). *Proceedings of the western regional women in trades & technology conference*. Victoria: South Island Women in Trades & Technology.
Ursule Critoph Consulting. (2002). *Women's access to training and employment programs in the post-labour market development agreement era*. Edmonton: Author.

Bonnie Watt-Malcolm
Department of Secondary Education
University of Alberta

KAREN CARTER

8. RE-THINKING LEARNING-WORK TRANSITIONS IN THE CONTEXT OF COMMUNITY TRAINING FOR RACIALIZED YOUTH

INTRODUCTION

The belief that community programs are an effective preventative response to the crisis of disenfranchised racialized youth has led to calls for better funding of such programs. These calls have been fuelled by an increase in youth gun crime in Toronto. In Canada's largest city, the year 2005 was dubbed the '*Year of the Gun*' due to the striking increase in violent, gun related crime among youth in the Greater Toronto Area (GTA), a disproportionate number of the youth involved were black and male. Toronto had 78 homicides in 2005; 57 were male and 48 percent of the fatalities were black men (Toronto Star, 2005). Compared to the USA, in Canada gun crime is considerably less frequent. Nevertheless, the disturbing rise in gun violence in 2005 resulted in a public outcry for more police presence in neighbourhoods where such incidents have occurred in order to arrest and convict perpetrators. This outcry has been accompanied by a call for an increase in preventative programming for "at-risk youth" in the hope of keeping them away from criminal activity. As 2006 ended there were considerably fewer youth gun-related deaths, a substantial increase in funds to community programs and increased policing. But while community programs may be a factor in the decrease in gun deaths among youth, the question of the long term effectiveness of these measures as a response to youth violence begs analysis.

The goal of this chapter is to illuminate a specific, under-studied example of what was termed in the introduction of this volume as an 'inter-institutional learning-work transition'. In connection to this a further goal is to assist community leaders and workers who are on the frontlines of the development and delivery of arts and cultural programs that engage and educate disenfranchised youth in many of the low income communities in the greater Toronto area. My objective is to give voice to some of the challenges facing those on the frontlines, in part, so that government funders and policy makers will pay attention to these needs when setting funding criteria and writing policy. Thus I examine the effectiveness and long term viability of community programming as a response to the problems faced by disenfranchised youth, specifically Black youth. Given the lack of employment skills that are a consequence of high dropout rates among this group in Canada, (Dei, Mazzuca, McIsaac and Zine 1997; Lewis, 1992;

P. Sawchuk and A. Taylor (eds.), Challenging Transitions in Learning and Work: Reflections on Policy and Practice, 145–163.

Royal Commission on Learning, 1994), I look at how community programs contribute to employment opportunities for youth by providing them with employable skills, and in so doing establish viable and, in Canada under-studied, transitions from learning to work. The core of my analysis is rooted in a specific racialized, low-income community: Regent Park. Specifically, I examine challenges facing Regent Park Focus (RPF), one example of the myriad of community organizations in the Toronto area that are engaging youth with a focus on introducing youth to work in cultural industries. The RPF program provides education and training opportunities for youth in film, new media or music industries, all of which have a strong presence in the GTA.

As I'll show, RPF provides a relevant case study of the challenges facing organizations that are trying to provide opportunities for youth. These challenges include operational issues such as managing organization growth and operational funding. For example, while it may be relatively easy to find project funding, these organizations need a operational funding structure that is flexible and allows them to create programs that respond to and plan for their constituency's needs which may be emergent or shifting. Project funding is short term and limits an **organizations' (organization's)** ability to engage in long term planning. Beyond organizational and funding issues, however, this chapter will pay particular attention to the challenges facing the youth who are learning marketable skills at RPF. The hope is to share some information and ideas to encourage policy makers and community leaders to think about the steps that may be taken to develop an overall plan for effective youth engagement in the creative industries. For the current myriad of community programming to be worthwhile and not a fad to keep young people busy, it must include a viable plan for the learning-work transition: transitions from community programs to forms of apprenticeships or further education and eventually paid work within the cultural industries.

One of the desired outcomes is to see policy changes that encourage recognition of training within grassroots programming on a broad scale as an option for youth who have not been successful in traditional education settings. What we see is the value in recognizing the unique dimensions of learning-work transitions that racialized, **disenfranchise (disenfranchised)** and 'at-risk' youth face; that these individuals are frequently pushed off of conventional, prescribed pathways toward becoming a productive member of society; and, that for those who veer toward unproductive, unsafe or criminal behaviour, the societal response should not automatically be one of judicial punishment. These considerations are especially relevant when there is documentation to show that cultural programming can be effective in deterring youth from crime.

The Jobs Ontario Community Action program initiated by the Bob **Ray (Rae)** Government (the **Ray (Rae)** government was in provincial office from October 1990 to June 1995) in response to the Yonge Street Riots in 1992[1] is a good example of how cultural programs can equip youth with skills that enable them to pursue a career in a particular cultural field. One particular program, Fresh Arts, gave youth the opportunity to work and develop their skills in a discipline of their choice. Many of the young people who are now celebrities in Canada's urban music industry were given the opportunity to write and produce their own music and later went on to successful careers in the industry based on experiences in this and similar programs. Thus, governments are not being asked to test an initiative that has not been already proven in our own country.

The existence of disenfranchised youth in any society speaks to familial, governmental and institutional failures to provide for the most vulnerable; and in the case of the isolation, alienation and resulting disenfranchisement facing young, black men this may be especially so. The expectation that "young people will be propelled through the education system in pursuit of credentials and as a consequence, emerge out the other end able to both enjoy the individual benefits of their education as well as contribute usefully to the economy" (Smyth 2003, p. 128), simply fails to acknowledge that this will not be the experience or transitions of many youth, disenfranchised or not (Taylor, 2005; Staff and Mortimer; Wentling and Waight, 2002). As Looker and Dwyer (1998) argue, this model, perpetuated by organizations such as the Organization for Economic Cooperation and Development (OECD), is problematic; and that furthermore, such expectations have set many youth up to fail as they do not provide for differing responses or levels of engagement within society. In fact, the 1990 initiatives launched by the OECD focusing on the skills required for success in the technological age of the 21st century have resulted in education policies in many Western countries that have an overwhelming focus on service based economies. Thus, the argument presented in this chapter that the predominant focus **is (add "is")** on the service economy is further evidence of the cookie cutter response to the economic tide which can negatively influence education and training initiatives. If the economy is going in a particular direction then the expectation is that certain types of skill sets and qualifications will be molded within the education system in response to the "market." This leaves little room for innovation and creativity, either within our education and training institutions or within the broader economy. This in turn is yet another factor which supports the continued lack of attention to the increasing numbers of youth who will not fit into this mold **,(add ",")** including the young people who are ~~**being**~~ engaging with community arts programs **(add: and of whom)** we **(will, add "will")** focus on in this chapter. As such, we see the perpetuation of transitions policy and practice that ignores the differentiated experiences across youth groups and in so doing both normalizes and ratifies exclusions that are as predictable as they are inequitable.

This chapter will show how urban, community programs focusing on the cultural industries such as RPF operate, how they fill a vital role in expanding learning-work transitions to meet the needs of those so often pushed off fulfilling and productive pathways, and the unique challenges, such as the ones introduced above, that they face in carrying out their work. However, before proceeding it is important to recognize the specific political and social context – inclusive of the role of provincial and municipal government and emergent social 'crises' such as Toronto's so-called *Year of the Gun* – in which these types of programs operate. Indeed, unusual in scholarship on learning-work transitions is the recognition that is registered here that sees the history and cultural identity of specific locations – such as a town, a city, state or province – as playing an active, even constitutive role in how these transitions operate.

POLITICAL CONTEXT AND THE ROLE OF SOCIAL CRISIS IN UNDERSTANDING LEARNING-WORK TRANSITIONS

As context for the argument of this chapter it is important to note the role played by the Ontario Conservative government's policy changes in the mid-to-late 1990s, (Mike Harris was Premier of Ontario from June, 1995 to April 2002), which reflected a shift in focus towards learning-work transitions and service-based economies. In a special issue of the magazine *Orbit*, titled "School to Work Transitions", these matters are summarized nicely. Contributors looked at the educational reform agenda of the Conservative government of the time, and raised questions about curriculum implementation and delivery during the early stages of policy changes to education. The co-editors of the issue ask: "How can links between schools and work-places be established and sustained, and what contributions should firms be making as education faces the challenges of technological and structural change?" (Russell and Wideman, 2000, p. 5). This question suggests that governments have the capacity to work with business and education, if motivated. Government has a role to play in creating the environment that will encourage educational institutions and the private sector to work with community organizations who are training youth to work in the creative sectors, including the cultural industries, to assist in bringing those skills to the marketplace. But, how this relationship works, the resources and broader social changes it requires, and the other significant societal challenges that need to be addressed to move this discussion forward, remain. This dilemma is more recently becoming recognized by policy makers and decision makers in local governments, and the projects are resulting in projects that are initiated by local governments. However most of their initiatives **replicates (replicate)** the programs that community organizations are presenting.[2] While others attempt to bring together the organizations that are providing community cultural programs for youth to try and advance policies and practices**, (delete ",")** through research prospects for policy makers.[3]

At the same time, however, government policy directions do not give a full picture of the context, indeed the crisis, which has led to the need to take a closer look at the role of targeted community programs. Of course, at a general level, government policy-making with regards to learning, labour markets and work is the target of pressure from business circles regarding shortages of labour in certain fields (Livingstone, 2006). However, government also responds to its reading of public opinion. The importance of this emerges for this chapter in the case of Toronto specifically in relation to the public outcry over gun violence that arose largely based on the death of a young middle class white woman on Boxing Day 2005. The way this reaction affected policy, in fact, betrays additional complexities regarding whose 'public opinion' mattered in this context, and in turn the type of community program responses that would eventually be brought forward. In this sense, the specific biography of the city is deeply intertwined with the learning/work transitions process. In order to flesh this out further it is relevant to note some particular details.

The public outcry and political response linked to this death fixated on several factors: it took place on a busy city street; it took place on a busy shopping day; and it occurred as a random result of the crossfire as one black male tried to shoot another. These factors, it would seem, were a potent combination. In fact, prior to her shooting, a young man was shot at a church during the funeral of his friend the previous week. These earlier shootings received less but also distinct forms of media attention: the first was characterized as a gang related incident, highly racialized as yet another in the string of shootings that had plagued Toronto in 2005; while the second was characterized differently as a young man who was the supposed witness in the shooting of the friend whose funeral he was attending when he was shot. The fact that this crime took place at a house of worship was highlighted in the media and used to further vilify the shooter as particularly inhumane for taking a life while friends ~~a~~ **(and)** family mourned the loss of another. As 2005 ended the overriding sentiment with the rash of murders that had taken place was that these were young (black) "thugs" who were killing each other and the problem was not one that concerned the law abiding citizens in Toronto. The church killing barely disturbed this logic; that is, until an innocent white woman from a middle class family was randomly killed while shopping. The sense that society gives greater value to the life of a young middle white woman over that of a young black man is underscored when such events take place so close together and the level of response and outcry is so obviously different (Toronto Star, 2005: Section A 22).

The newspaper coverage at the end of 2005 also took an interesting look at the broad picture by mapping the homicides over the year in the city and briefly profiling some of the black male victims. The impact of the conservative Government's tenure was linked to the marked increase in gun crime. The view that the cuts to social assistance programs, general cuts in education and specifically the zero tolerance policies in the school system during Mike Harris' Conservative Government, is responsible for the society these youth, that come of age during the Harris years, (1995–2002), grew up in, lends further credibility to critical education theory which we review briefly below. Many of these policies adversely affected black students in particular. The Toronto Star's profile of one of the black men killed in 2005 points to the impact that adverse education cuts and policy changes had in low income neighbourhoods such as Jane and Finch[4], which has a large Black population. Where previously the school was seen as a part of the community and was accessible for after school programs, the cuts resulted in a lack of space for community to gather and for accessible programming for children and youth in ~~may~~ **(many)** low income GTA neighbourhoods. The article also highlights the continued systemic racism raised in the Stephen Lewis report published in the 1992:

> It is Black youth that is unemployed in excessive numbers, it is Black students who are being inappropriately streamed in schools, it is Black kids who are disproportionately dropping out, it is housing communities with large concentrations of Black residents where the sense of vulnerability and disadvantage is most acute, it is Black employees, professional and non-professional, on whom the doors of upward equity slam shut. Just as the soothing balm of "multiculturalism" cannot mask racism, so racism cannot mask its primary target. (Lewis in Toronto Star, 2005: Section A 22)

Lewis' report underscores the fact that when social exclusion and marginalization are impacting youth at large, the impact on black youth is greater than on other marginalized groups. **These issues – in terms of their public policy connections and linkage to public outcry – set the stage for a deeper understanding of the community programs and learning-work transitions that they support. (not sure what you want to say, but it's a sentence fragment)** However, before proceeding to this research, it is important to take a moment to outline the basic theory and research that can inform this deeper understanding.

THEORETICAL FRAMEWORK: A STARTING POINT

Critical educational theory is concerned with how institutions, societal culture and political processes reflect and reproduce broader social systems such as racism and capitalism (Hayes and Way, 1998). It is this observation that provides the initial framework for my analysis. Such systems tend to support the status quo and reinforce the inter-locking nature of racist and capitalist power structures that are difficult to break through to affect social change. In a 2005 **D (make it "d")**octorial dissertation Plastaras analyses the difficulty in challenging the capitalist power structure **is (change to "in")** the United States in response to the education crisis of African-American students. Plastaras' analysis is particularly relevant to the discussion here as it specifically points to how capitalism is benefiting from the diversity in the United States, since American students are being prepared to be leaders in the global market. However, what we see is that educational success does not translate to provision of opportunities for all students to be successful. Instead the power structure **take(add "s")** lessons from the diverse cultures and people that make up the United States and uses that knowledge to reinforce their power on **<u>and</u>(change to "an")** international scale (Plastaras, 2005). This position is an important point to note when discussing critical education theory since it recognizes that even when those in the echelons of power are appearing to recognize the benefit of inclusion and one may think more access and openness is possible, too often that inclusion benefits those in power and does not truly **<u>providing</u> (Change to "provide")** access for all people. In fact, Toronto is regularly applauded as one of the most diverse cities in the world where people from various cultures live and work together in relative harmony. However if the surface is scratched, ever so slightly, one finds that tensions are present that speak to the need for a re-defining of the power structure to impact decisions and outcomes not only for the positions of this paper but for a whole host of other critical social issues.

Critical education theory and particularly those who have taken a close look at how schools function to reproduce the social order has a significant history. Theories of reproduction as well as resistance as outlined decades ago by Willis (1980), Giroux (e.g., 1981, 1983), and Livingstone (1987; also Curtis, Livingstone and Smaller, 1992) noted **(add "that")** the latent function of schooling was a type of differential inclusion where outcomes were systematically distributed unequally across a class and gender hierarchy. Curriculum, **(delete ",")** policy as well as cultural practice and broader economic and family systems were all implicated.

Several scholars took inspiration from the work of Paulo Friere (e.g., 1970), Illich (1971) and others. At the same time it became clear that issues of race were not well represented (Wotherspoon 2004). Canadian anti-racist educational scholarship has emerged over the last two decades and by the 1990s it reached critical mass with the work of Dei (e.g., 1996) and James (1993; see also James and Haig-Brown, 2004); James (1993) taking issues of black youth transitions to employment as a core focus. Important to note here is that critical educational scholarship has, however, focused on the role of traditional schooling primarily, leaving much to be examined in terms of the interlocking nature of race/class analysis in relation to extended pathways and transitions toward employment, including those paths that run through community-based programs. One of the goals is that this chapter is to encourage further scholarship in the area of study to shine light on the influence community programs are having in response to the barriers within the credential system. Such scholarship would give policy makers the evidence needed to encourage the support of local governments and their agencies in formalizing ~~of~~ community programs to fill~~ing~~ some of the gaps in the current credential system.

Returning to the findings of Lewis' report discussed in the previous section and linking the critical educational tradition with it, we see several points which are echoed in the research. Speaking about systemic racism in the Ontario education system, Dei (2004) points out that: "[i]n spite of the addition of multicultural education, Canadian educational system serves to produce and reproduce racial biases, discriminations, exclusions and ultimately, inequalities" (p. 195). Such findings are highlighted time and again in Dei's research. In fact, what may be central to these debates is the promise of grassroots organizing for change which links parents, students and the community with the education system, and recognizes that forms of alternative education outside of the regular education system has value as an alternative for students to succeed. Dei (2004) points to Black parents' use of Afrocentric home schooling as an example of alternatives to mainstream schooling. It must be noted however that Dei speaks of schooling in the limited sense of gaining educational credentials. Lewis's commentary and Dei's research shows how critical education theory relates to perpetuating systemic racism. And in this chapter I extend their observations suggesting that this same systemic racism may be what is hindering policy-makers from developing and implementing policies and practices that can support and expand the work of community organizations that are working with disenfranchised youth.

What emerges from my discussion of context and the initial introduction of critical educational theory is the need to better understand community sites as an important link in the chain of alternative learning-work transitions that might speak to the needs of racialized youth directly. So, before our look at a specific initiative it is important to extend my discussion of a theoretical framework to these alternative sites, and to introduce broader notions of learning beyond schooling.

Community organizations as I use the term, refers to the existence of a group of people knitted together by their geographic location, socio-economic condition and some common social goals. The community organizations referred to in general and specifically here all have these common threads in that they are located in a particular neighbourhood and give access and a sense of ownership to a facility and/or services offered by and for the people of the neighbourhood. This does not mean ~~to~~ that programs offered in Jane and Finch for example may not be utilized by people from another Toronto neighbourhood, however in the case of the programs that will be discussed here, the impetus for their start-up is the recognition of a need within the geographic boundaries of the community that they wish to serve. The raison d'être for the ongoing existence of the programming offered, is to serve the immediate community.

Learning as it takes place within community organizations, gives youth access to knowledge through informal, non-formal and tacit learning; a significant gap exists within critical education theory's understandings of learning and its connection to labour markets. This type of education may be at odds with dominant perspectives that hold fast to the idea that formal education, for example represented by a high school diploma, is essential for the development of young people. In this chapter I challenge the strictness of these dominant educational values by showing that education outside of the traditional institutional setting can impart valuable skills and knowledge to youth and develop good citizenship which is of particular importance to disenfranchised youth. Since one might argue that their disenfranchised state is at the core of their destructive behaviour (Lewis, 1992). Thus, my argument is much more aligned with**,(delete ",")** Bourdieu's notion of how schooling contributes to the reproduction of cultural inequality in society**,(delete ",")** (Plastaras, 2005).

The work of Carl James and Celia Haig-Brown (2004) also serve to reinforce the need to approach formal education with a more open mind. The authors contend that "[w]hile it is obviously desirable to complete grade 12, youth need to know that school is waiting when they are ready" (James and Haig-Brown 2004, p. 221), In fact, many community-based educational efforts shatter the lock-step educational myth expressed in dominant educational values when they provide youth with both developmental opportunities in their own right as well as a second chance to revisit credentials that otherwise simply represent missed opportunity. In other words, the approach to learning explored here shows that the formal educational institutions are not the only place that can help youth, particularly disenfranchised youth, in attaining positive personal outcomes as well as employable skills.

Expanding our appreciation for community as a site of learning, in turn, demands a consideration of different ways of knowing. It has been well documented that education systems in Canada (and elsewhere) are structured toward success for a certain type of learner, leaving a large portion of students and the future labour force marginalized (Livingstone, 2004; Galabuzi, 2006). Giving legitimacy to informal, non-formal and tacit learning for developing skills that may be taken into a paid work environment is an essential change that needs to take place in policy generally speaking, and may be particularly important for a full understanding of the dynamics of learning-work transitions. Since many community organizations are approaching training in an informal or non-formal way, "lived experience" becomes an essential part of the maturity and life lessons required for a young person to contribute to civil society in a meaningful way through their work.

Some community programs have managed to make this connection, acting as the intermediary between youth and employers or educational institutions to provide access to employment or credentials that create opportunities and options for employment. While other programs give youth the hope to see they are able to play a productive role in society.

The transition from school to work is, of course, more difficult for those young people who have not been successful in high school largely because they learn in ways that the educational system does not accommodate (Bourdieu, 1989; Curtis, Livingstone and Smaller, 1992). Much of the research into school-to-work transition and the dialogue around a "new vocationalism" has attempted to remove the stigma of the route of the so-called 'low-achieving' high school student's avenue to employment from vocational education (Lehmann and Taylor, 2003; see also the introductory chapter of this volume). However, despite the inclusion in this new vocationalism school of thought of the concern for re-directing high school students who are not university-bound, what remains neglected is the sub-group of students who do not go into traditional vocations such as the skilled trades. I argue here that this narrow fixation on giving greater credibility to students who are largely being streamed into the skilled trades emerges largely because it is safer than dealing with the much more difficult – and more socially radical – task of addressing the more extreme needs of young people who increasingly in a country like Canada cannot find success anywhere in the current academic structures and who, in turn, are barred from apprenticeship and related occupational opportunities. In these cases, it would appear that only a social crisis – for example, as in the case of Toronto's *Year of the Gun* – holds the potential to open opportunities for public discourse on providing a broader ranger of opportunities for the disenfranchised. At the same time, it seems equally clear that crisis, while perhaps necessary, is not sufficient for solving the problems at hand. What is also needed is a policy response that will truly engage business, government and community stakeholders so that the approach to the issue of disenfranchised, and perhaps particularly racialized, youth is proactive and expansive rather than reactive, misdirected and ultimately ineffective. With that stated we will now move to highlight our case study of RPF.

REGENT PARK FOCUS: LINKING COMMUNITY PROGRAMS TO CREDENTIAL INSTITUTIONS AND THE LABOUR MARKET

Earlier it was suggested the biography of a place matters, when an analysis of the least fortunate is taking place it is particularly poignant to see how the past is related to the present circumstances. Time has been taken to explain a particular moment in the biography of the city of Toronto by highlighting its social crisis. However, the effects of this biography are enacted not simply in the city, but more specifically neighbourhoods as well in relation to the make-up, the history and the existing programming that will be detailed further here. Regent Park Focus (RPF) was established in 1989 as a part of a provincial ~~governments'~~ governments **(add "'s")**-initiated strategy to promote health in vulnerable communities across Ontario. This program is funded through the Ministry of Health and Long-Term Care to address the rise in violence and drug addiction in the neighbourhood. The organization is located in

Regent Park, Canada's largest and oldest public housing community having been built in the late 1940s. It is a lower income neighbourhood located in downtown Toronto. It is bound~~ed~~ by Gerrard Street East to the north, River Street to the east, Shuter Street to the south, and Parliament Street to the west. It is an extremely culturally diverse neighbourhood, with more than half of its population being immigrants. It is home to approximately 7,500 people. Over 50% of the population living in Regent Park are children 18 years and younger (compared to a Toronto-wide average of 30%). The average income for Regent Park residents is approximately half the average for other Torontonians. A majority of families in Regent Park are classified as low-income, with 68% of the population living below Statistics Canada's Low-Income Cut-Off Rate in one of its census tracts, and 76% in the other (compared to a Toronto-wide average of just over 20%). Poverty is a reality for seven in ten Regent Park families. Regent Park's residential dwellings are entirely social housing, and cover all of the 69 acres (280,000 m^2) which comprise the community. The city government developed a plan to demolish and rebuild Regent Park over the next ten years, with the first phase having started fall 2005. The addition of market units on site will double the number of units in Regent Park. Former street patterns will be restored and housing will be designed to reflect that of adjacent and **afuent (affluent)** neighbourhoods (including Cabbagetown and Corktown), in order to end Regent Park's physical isolation from the rest of the city. RPF is one of the many community programs offered in Regent Park for underprivileged children. Being the oldest social housing complex in Toronto this community has many lessons to teach others about community activism and organizing. RPF is a good example of the level of community excellence possible with very little resources. RPF provides a community-based facility for training in new media, video production, music and photography. Youth are also able to engage in production of a radio show which airs on a local station as well as publish a community newspaper. In a number of cases, with the support and guidance of the staff at RPF, youth have been able to use the skills acquired in the program to enter post-secondary institutions and eventually the labour market.

The following are brief testimonials documented through ongoing discussions with Adonis Huggins, the Director of RPF. My discussions with Huggins, in turn gave rise to observations of his program and further informal contact ~~wit~~ **(change to "with")** program participants. Huggins spoke at length about some of the success stories of youth that have gone on to work in a sector of the creative economy after initial training at RPF:

> Carl[5] started with Regent Park Focus in 1997. He was interested in video production and trained with RPF for three years before going on to Centennial College's Film and Television program in 1999. Currently he is working as a segment producer with Much Music.
>
> Robert also started with RPF in 1997 and was with the program for three years. He went on to work full-time with the youth video production organization "Global Hood" in Dufferin Mall. Now, he is studying at the Academy of Design and Technology.

These profiles are interesting as they point to the Tchibozo's notion of hedonistic variant ~~where by~~ **(change to one word "whereby")** youth choose a training model and later deduce the occupational target that is revealed through their training (Tchibozo, 2002, p. 338). Tchibozo's analysis of the ~~of the~~ principles governing the process of learning-work transition espouses four key concepts, the determinist approach which is dictated largely by familial and social roots; the random approach, leaving the matter to chance; the chaotic approach, ~~where by~~ **(change to one word "whereby")** a prior predictable outcome is cancelled by a major live altering experience and finally the strategic approach where intentional choices of the agent result in a desired outcome. The ~~St~~rategic **(change to lower case "strategic")** version of school-to-work transitions is relevant here as it places emphasis on the agent as one adapts and is complex in relating to social history and environment. However the strategic variant is further dissected by the author into two more variants: the hedonistic and the utilitarian. The utilitarian variant assumes that people chose an occupational target and then decide on the appropriate training model. While with the hedonistic variant a method of training is chosen allowing individuals to find their occupational target through the training process. This approach to training for youth at risk is fairly safe as it usually allows low risk of failure, which is key for youth who have not had good experiences with traditional methods of learning (2002). This model is repeated in communities all across the GTA. Drop-in programs allow young people to freely commit as much or as little of their time to learning a new skill or exploring an interest without any pressure as to the outcome. Youth are not coming into RPF expecting to get a job if they learn how to make a CD or a video. They come to explore without the pressure of an expected outcome. This is not to say that there is no structure or boundaries to provide youth with a learning outcome and a clear sense of achievement. Instead of being linked to making life changing decisions from the outset, the structure gives clear boundaries for youth so they know what is acceptable within the environment in which they are working. This hedonistic variant is an essential component of what draws these youth in and creates a safe space to experiment and explore without the demands of acquiring credentials or beginning to plan for the future.

According to John Smyth (2003), the ability to explore and discover outside of the linear school environment is markedly different from the deterministic structural process seen within mainstream schooling. Smyth's argument points out that more young people are drawn to a complex process that allows them more agency than currently exists in mainstream schooling. Smyth's position is one of the ~~may~~ **(change to "many")** that **put accurately to the shortfalls of the currently school system.<PREVIOUS SENTENCE IS CONFUSING>** Yet, the policies and structures that guide mainstream schooling persist, despite the high dropout rates that suggest that they are not effective for all youth. As such, it is time to rethink the definition of success as it is currently defined. The navigation of the credential system in a linear way as the model for effective preparation for work is leaving many young people behind. Many youth are either detouring from that path or disengaging from education altogether, increasing their marginalization in society which has dire consequences for any form of successful learning-work transition as well as other more damaging societal implications.

In the case of Toronto, it can be argued that the education system along with zero tolerance policies[6] have further intensified these dynamics, and contributed to a rise in the expulsion of black students and to dropout rates among this group specifically. While studies have not been conducted to look at the link between dropout rates among Black students and gun crime, there is a common belief that these black youth who dropout from school make up a disproportionate number of the youth involved in gun violence, and the disproportionate rate of homicide among this group in Toronto. According to Gartner and Thompson (2004), "the homicide rate per 100,000 blacks in Toronto average 10.1 between 1992 and 2003. This was almost five times greater than the average overall homicide rate of 2.4 per 100,000 [people]" (Gartner and Thomas, 2004, p. 33). Zero tolerance was introduced in 1999, providing some suggestion that links the increase in expulsions to the rise in violent crime. This data further supports the position that links Harris Government policies to the increase in gun crime among some Toronto youth.

In continuing with the analysis of the findings from the RPF discussions, it became clear that not all of the youth who come to RPF are past recognizing the value of educational credentials. Some find the community training a safe environment to explore job interests and later are able to re-enter the education system and acquire the needed credentials for securing a job of their choice, while others have no interest in the formal credential process. Robert is a clear example of this as he is now at the Academy of Design and Technology after three years at RPF. Robert detoured from the credential path **(add ",")** was on the fringes of society but had the skills and knowledge to be engaged again after finding a meaningful path. RPF gave him an~~d~~**(change to "an")** opportunity to explore in a pressure free environment,(delete ",") ~~the~~**(change to "The")** program not only gave him an opportunity to learn new things, he was also able to take a leadership role in teaching younger peers the skills he had acquired, which further re-enforced his knowledge and built his confidence about the knowledge he had gained. RPF keeps records of the students that have been through their programs and Adonis has also written letters of reference ~~to~~ for many young people. Many youth who have gone on to further their education have come back to share with Executive Director, Adonis Huggins that the knowledge they gained at RPF gave them an edge with college or university programs since they had more practical training than most of their fellow classmates.

Another group of youth are those who have left the credential path all together and have no desire to re-engage with formal education. Their capabilities are often not identified within the school system. What we learn from the research on RPF is that these are the young people that the education system has failed because it is not geared towards their learning style or structured to meet their needs. The community organizations offering training in the cultural industries often provide an environment of multi-tasking and experiential learning opportunities that appear to suit many of these youth. These young people are often less confident in their abilities because they have been unsuccessful in the school system (Curtis, Livingstone, Smaller, 1992). Therefore, success in this new informal learning environment provides a much needed boost to their self-esteem. Program Director, Huggins of RPF shared an example of one such young person:

> Kevin is a high school drop out and former drug dealer who came to RPF in 2004 and was with the program for one year. He is a rapper who wrote and produced his CD at the music studio at RPF. RPF was able to get this young person enrolled into George Brown College based on an assessment of the learning he had acquired at RPF. However, Kevin was not successful at the college and dropped out shortly after enrolling.

The RPF Director pointed out that he was not surprised that Kevin was not successful at one of the local community colleges he had initially enrolled in because he was always adamant that school was not for him and, he just wanted to work. Huggins admitted that if he was able to help Kevin get some work experience, he would have pursued this option over the academy. Adonis sees RPF's role as creating as much access and opportunities as possible for these young people to give them choices to find what they want to do with their lives. He added that the choice they make as agents of their own destiny is preferable to blind obedience.

Creating these choices is the reason RPF is in the process of developing ~~of~~ a new pilot project with the aim of creating more options within learning-work transitions than are currently available for disenfranchised youth. RPF has links to the education system but the organization does not have links to employers for those young people who do not wish to go back to school. RPF is in the preliminary stage of developing a three year pilot project with the Toronto Community Housing Corporation to take 12 youth per year who are identified as "having potential." They will receive career development opportunities in new media and digital production through a training program that will see the youth from start to finish with a work-based apprenticeship with a local media business. In the first year of the pilot, the curriculum will be structured for four to six months to prepare the youth for a two-month apprenticeship with a production company where they can take an idea through the development process from concept to completion. This project will see 36 youth over three years go through this program and track their placement in jobs after the six to eight month training program in informal settings. The hope is that this project will provide a model that will allow young people such as Kevin the access to training for work that is happening outside of the confines of the academy. Such innovative projects recognize that not every young person will want to learn in a school setting and is seeking options and opportunities for them.

As noted earlier, Canadian policy makers have typically failed to come up with alternatives for acquiring schooling credentials outside of the mainstream education system. In their comparison of work transition policies in Germany and Canada, both Heinz and Taylor (2005) and Lehmann (2000) found that compared to European countries of the OECD, North America is ineffective at developing training initiatives that partner educational institutions with employers and labour. Heinz and Taylor (2005) maintain that North American "employers are noted as underinvested in long-term employee training programs and [are] less active in education programs compared to those in most other OECD countries" (Heinz and Taylor, 2005, p. 5). They highlight the fact that high youth unemployment and a desire to increase the number of high school graduates have created a climate of urgency driving policy makers to address these challenges through vocational programs within secondary schools. Currently, in Canada, there is no significant body of research on grassroots community education and training programs that are working with young people who were previously unsuccessful in the school system but are now finding successful learning outcomes through informal, non-formal ~~and~~ or tacit learning. Nor does research focus on the disenfranchised youth who may be involved in petty crime, but who are increasingly being engaged by community arts education programs that may deter them from further criminal activity.

ESTABLISHING STANDARDS FOR COMMUNITY EDUCATION AND TRAINING PROGRAMS

Partnerships are needed between community program deliverers and employers for providing opportunities to young people that engage them in non-formal and informal learning environments. These partnerships may be an effective way of determining some standards for the myriad of cultural training programs popping up across Toronto and other major cities across Canada, or elsewhere. Such standards would be invaluable in providing indicators to strengthen the linkages between the program being delivered and employment opportunities, by ensuring that the programming is truly preparing youth for the work environment or imparting skills that lend themselves to good citizenship **what ever ("whichever")** road their career path may take. In much the same way as there is a comprehensive approach to preparing youth for work in the skilled trades, a similar approach for the cultural industries would serve to give ~~clear an~~**(replace with "a clear")** indicator as to the value of working in the creative economy. As well as outline paths that ~~lead~~**(replace with "led")** to enhanced skills development or recognition of the skills that are transferable to another sector of the economy.

On this point, it is useful to share some of the findings from the *Imagine a Toronto* report which was published after a team of cultural leaders and policy makers in Toronto and London (England), came together to study the potential opportunities that existed in the creative economy of their respective cities. The report provides some key data about the value of working in the creative sector. The report was launched in July 2006 and provided a summary of the research findings from the *Strategies for Creative Cities Project* that informed the strategic opportunities articulated in the document. The project team studied a range of creative activities and interventions used in cities around the world. The report grouped these areas of study into five broad categories: People, Enterprise, Space, Connectivity and Vision (Imagine a Toronto, 2006).

The section on Enterprise is particularly relevant as it acknowledges that "creativity often produces economic opportunity and that cultural entrepreneurs start and grow creative business. Commercializing creative talent enhances wealth and employment generation…" (Imagine a Toronto, 2006, p. 8). The report also provided statistics that compared the economic growth within the creative sectors in Toronto with other more traditional sectors such as finance and information technology, showing that between 1991 and 2004 the creative industries grew faster than financial services and was catching up to information technology. Within the creative sector the fastest growing industries in Toronto are Performing Arts Companies (at 7.1%), Motion Picture and Video industries and the Sound recording industry (at 5.4%) and finally the Broadcasting (at 4.6%) (Imagine a Toronto, 2006, p. 17–18). Indeed, such figures show the growth potential that is often used by policy makers to encourage workers into certain fields, and make a compelling argument for support of grass roots community programs that are introducing some of our most vulnerable young people to work in cultural industries.

While one might hope that it would not have taken a crisis of gun violence as seen in 2005 in Toronto for policy makers to recognize the need to make the changes which would support non-traditional transitions into working in the creative sectors; in many ways these events – their timing, sequencing and character specific to the Toronto context – have served a contradictory function in this regard. It is contradictory in this specific case in the sense that while public funding and public attention has come to be focused on the issue of marginalized youth, they have emerged in ways that may be problematic should more expansive, long-term support and a recognition of multiple ways of knowing and school-based marginalization continues to be under-appreciated. The fact remains that long before the crisis there was a desperate need among black youth in Toronto especially young black men who are looking for something meaningful in life, in some ways this has become obscured. Some of these youth are looking for a new start after encountering some dangerous and potentially deadly detours in life. Others have not yet reached such extremes but are on the cusp of making decisions that could irrevocable impact **(add "on")** their lives. This urgency is evident by the tragic loss of so many young lives in Toronto in 2005. The need for concrete change to provide a range of meaningful opportunities for young people to become productive citizens is essential now. If there is not a systematic response to the issue of disenfranchised youth who have not been successful along the paths that society has set out we will simply increase the pool of marginalized people facing broken transitions from learning to work; a societal context of turbulence, destabilization and injustice in which the loss of innocent life (of all colours) will become less of an exception. "An increasing number of young people are diverging from the white middle-class pattern. Educational institutions and workplaces must adapt to changes in the youth population. Education and workplace training that are typically effective with advantaged youth will not necessarily enable disadvantaged youth to reach their full potential (Wentling and Waight, 2001, p. 72)

CONCLUSION

The evidence is there to support the position that the creative industries are growing and thus provide viable career path options for the 21st century. Community organizations are responding with interesting and innovative programming for many marginalized youth. There are aspects of this situation that are comparable across different locations and times which was, in part, demonstrated by the *Imagine a Toronto* (2006) report. But the specificities of location also matter. In the Toronto case, we have been here before, after the young street riots in 1992 the NDP government funded programs such as Fresh Arts[7] which was a part of the Jobs Ontario Community Action program. With the renewed initiative at the grassroots toward arts and cultural programming in the wake of the increase in gun crime in Toronto it is an important time for pointed action.

Programs like RPF with the potential to do what Tchibozo describes as a 'hedonistic variant,' by providing youth a place to acquire some skills and **~~there in~~ (replace with "therein")** determine a potential career path, are in need of support to ensure their long term viability as a part of the learning-work transition in Toronto. Support for such programs could provide a model towards a remedy for the crime and violence that is on the increase in other Canadian cities. The necessary next step is for business and government to recognize the opportunity to support the development of these programs into valuable alternatives that reintegrate marginalized youth into society.

There are some obvious gaps in the literature concerning learning and work transitions and the cultural sector. In recent years some OECD nations have began to recognize the value of the cultural sector to their economies (2006 Imagine A Toronto). The focus on manufacturing and skilled labour reflected in the literature is in direct response to the labour environment that have dominated OECD economic markets for much of the 20th century. As we begin the 21st century and the creative economy continues to mature studies will reflect the new challenges that are particular to the creative economy. The biography of place may emerge as an area of interest for learning and work scholars as they consider the ways governments and policy makers choose to engage youth in non-traditional ways with the economy **~~along side~~(replace with "alongside")** the social issues that may impact policy.

The youth who have benefited from Regent Park Focus are a testament to possibilities that are untapped if governments are willing to provide solutions that see community organizations take a more active role in policy and practice. In an age where information is so readily available to all youth, our marginalized young people are very aware of the options and opportunities' that are not being made available to them. The tragedy would be to have our business leaders and policy makers continue to believe that creating programs on a project by project basis is sufficient to engage and assist the next generation of youth who are on the margins of our society. This research has **lead (replace with "led")** to various opportunities to see first hand what can happen when a young person in on the border between productive citizenship and criminal offender. Finally there is an anecdote that illustrates the tragic outcome that is too often occurring in Toronto neighbourhoods **(add ".") ~~it~~ (replace with "It")** involves a young black man who was a leader in initiating a theatre project in the Alexander Park community, a low income housing project in the heart of Toronto at Spadina and Dundas. He had written much of the script for the theatre program that was to tell the story of how the youth in that community felt about the recent increase in gun violence in Toronto. He was arrested while we were developing the project. The ~~**centres**~~**(replace with Centre's)** ~~director~~ (replace with "Director") was aware that he was still engaging in petty drug crime and hoped the theatre project would motivate him to leave that lifestyle altogether. One has to wonder if that young man could have seen an opportunity to pursue a career as a writer, or actor or director, or some other professional. Would he have stopped dabbling in petty crime if he ~~**say**~~ **(replace with "saw")** another way to make money that did not involve the risk of incarceration?

NOTES

1 The Yonge street riots in down town Toronto took place after the verdict for the Rodney King ~~**trail**~~ **"trial")** in the United States came back.

2 The Mobile City was a digital photography project/competition aimed at enhancing youth participation in community building in the twin cities of Milan and Toronto. Ten winners from Toronto travelled to Milan in July to participate in a group exhibit. A week later, the winning photographers from Milan ~~**came**~~ **(replace with "to come")** to Toronto to take part in the July 16 exhibition, to visit with famed Toronto photographer Michael Awad and to travel throughout the GTA. Selections from the winning photographs were published in a book in the fall of 2008. The winning photographs are posted at www.mobilecityphoto.org. The Mobile City was a joint initiative of the Italian Chamber of Commerce of Toronto, the Chamber of Commerce of Milan, the City of Toronto: Toronto Culture and Toronto Economic Development, the City of Milan, and the Province of Milan (with the support of the Region of Lombardy).

3 The Ignite C.Y.A.N. (Canadian Youth Arts Network Youth Arts Forum) took place June 12 & 13, 2007 in Toronto. The purpose of the forum was to advance policies and practices that support youth arts practitioners in Toronto. The forum also sought to:

- Provide networking opportunities for youth arts practitioners to get/stay connected, share resources, review best practices, talk to policy makers and funding bodies.
- Provide the policy community with the research and evidence to support investment in youth-relevant cultural activities and programs and identify other policy areas where targeted support could leverage further benefits in this area.
- Shorten the gaps between "on the ground" experience of youth-relevant and youth-led cultural activities and researchers, policy makers and funding bodies.

4 Jane and Finch is a neighbourhood located in the North West area of Toronto centered around the intersection of two arterial roads, Jane Street and Finch Avenue. The community is commonly referred to as the most ethnically diverse of all of Toronto's communities, with 120 nationalities and ethnic populations and over 100 languages spoken. The community is also home to Canada's largest concentration of gangs. The community has been stigmatized as one of those Toronto neighbourhoods that has long had a reputation for violence, drugs and racial tensions.

5 Pseudonyms are used for all of the youth referenced in the paper.

6 In 2001 under the Ontario Progressive Conservative Government of Mike Harris a zero tolerance safe schools act was introduced. This act outlined strict rules and consequences for students breaking the rules. The act was brought before the human rights commission due to the disproportionate number of students of colour and students with disabilities who were suspended and expelled under the act. In 2007 the Liberal Government introduced changes to the safe schools act to eliminate the zero tolerance approach and instead introduced a progressive discipline policy.

7 Under the ~~**fresh-arts**~~ **(replace with "Fresh Arts")** program youth were paid to work on various arts projects in the summer, the programs ranged from the fine arts such as visual art and theatre to creative industries such as film and music. Fresh Arts was administered by the Toronto Arts Council (TAC), the program gave rise to musicians and poets who went on to create an urban music scene that did not exist previously in Canada. Toronto hip hop recording artist Kardinal Official is one example of an internationally successful artist who was introduced to the possibility of becoming a professional at his craft after acquiring the training and support in the Fresh Arts summer program. The Fresh Arts program was a public private partnership, the TAC worked with local business to give youth time in a recording studio with producers to develop their work.

REFERENCES

Apple, M. W. (2007). Social movements and political practice in education. *Theory and Research in Education, 5*(2), 161–171.

Begin, M., Caplan, G., Bharti, M., Glaze, A., & Murphy, D. (1994). *Royal commission on learning.* Government of Ontario.

Bourdieu, P. (1989). How schools help reproduce the social order. *Current Contents/Social and Behavioural Science, 21*(8).

Curtis, B., Livingstone, D. W., & Smaller, H. (1992). *Stacking the deck: The steaming of working-class kids in Ontario schools.* Toronto: Our Schools/Our Selves Education Foundation.

Dei, G. S. (2004). The challenge of promoting inclusive education in Ontario schools. In B. Kidd & J. Phillips (Eds.), *From enforcement and prevention to civic engagement: Research on community safety* (pp. 184–202). Toronto: University of Toronto Press.

Dei, G. S. (1996). *Anti-racism education: Theory and practice.* Halifax: Fernwood.

Dei, G., Mazzuca, J., McIsaac, E., & Zine, J. (1997). *Reconstructing 'Drop-Out'-A critical ethnography of the dynamics of black students' disengagement from school.* Toronto: University of Toronto Press.

Dwyer, P., & Looker, D. E. (1998). Rethinking on the educational transition of youth in the 1990s. *Research in Post Compulsory Education, 3*(1), 5–23.

Freire, P. (1970). *Pedagogy of the oppressed.* New York: Continuum.

Galabuzi, G. E. (2006). *Canada's economic apartheid.* Toronto: Canadian Scholars' Press.

Gartner, R., & Thompson, S. (2004). Trends in Homicide. In B. Toronto Kidd & J. Phillips (Eds.), *From enforcement and prevention to civic engagement: Research on community safety* (pp. 28–39). Toronto: University of Toronto.

Giourx, H. (1981). Hegemony, resistance, and the paradox of educational reform. *Interchange, 12*(2–3), 3–26.

Giroux, H. (1983). *Theory and resistance in education.* Massachusetts, MA: Bergin and Garvey.

Haig-Brown, C., & James, C. (2004). Supporting respectful relationships: Community-school interface and youth "At Risk." In B. Kidd & J. Phillips (Eds.), *From enforcement and prevention to civic engagement: Research on community safety* (pp. 216–234). Toronto: University of Toronto.

Hayes, E., & Way, W. (1998). *Negotiating the discourse of work: Women and welfare-to-work educational programs.* University of Wisconsin-Madison. Retrieved from http:www.adulterc.org/Proceedings/1998/98hayes.htm

Heinz, W. R., & Taylor, A. (2005). *Learning and work transitions policies in a comparative perspective: Canada and Germany.* University of Bermen, Germany; University of Alberta, Canada.

Illich, I. (1971). *Deschooling society.* New York: Harper and Row.

Imagine a Toronto. (2006). *Imagine A Toronto: Strategies for a creative city.* Toronto: University of Toronto Press.

James, C. (1993). Getting there and staying there: Blacks' employment experience. In P. Anisef & P. Axelrod (Eds.), *Transitions: Schooling and employment in Canada* (pp. 3–20). Toronto: Thompson Educational Press.

Krahn, H., & Taylor, A. (2005). "*Resilient teenagers: Explaining the high educational aspirations on visible minority immigrant youth in Canada.* PCERII Working Paper Series: Prairie Centre of Excellence for Research on Immigration and Integration. Working Paper No. WP02-05.

Layder, D., Ashton, D., & Sung, J. (1991). The empirical correlates of action and structure: The transition from school to work. *Sociology, 25*(3), 447–464.

Lehmann, W. (2000). Is Germany's dual system still a model for Canadian youth apprenticeship initiatives? *Canadian Public Policy-Analyse de Politiques, 26*(2), 225–240.

Lewis, S. (1992). *Stephen Lewis report.* Toronto: Government of Ontario.

Livingstone, D. W., & Contributors. (1987). *Critical pedagogy & cultural power.* Massachusetts, MA: Bergin & Garvey Publishers Inc.

Livingstone, D. W. (2004). *Education-Jobs gap* (2nd ed.). Toronto: Garamond Press.

Livingstone, D. W., & Scholtz, A. (2006). *Work and lifelong learning in Canada: Basic findings of the 2004 wall survery.* Centre for the Study of Education and Work: University of Toronto.

Moliner, M. (2007). *Presentation to I Reunion Extraordinaira del Sector Cultura de la CECC Foro Taller "Arte y Cultura como estrategia para prevenir la violencia social.*" Department of Canadian Heritage, Ontario Region.

Plastaras, H. M. (2005). *Cross-race friendships and segregated peer groups among teens: An educational anthropology study of race relations in two "integrated" U.S. High Schools.* Doctoral Dissertation, Emory University, USA.

Russel, H., & Wideman, R. (2000). School to work transitions. *ORBIT: OISE/UT's Magazine for Schools, 31*(2), 6–12.

Rankin, J. (2005). A loving mother's son. *Toronto Star Newspaper*, p. A22.

Smyth, J. (2003). The making of young lives with/against the school credential. *Journal of Education and Work, 16*(2), 127–146.

Staff, J., & Mortimer, J. (2003). Diverse transitions from school to work. *Work and Occupations, 30*(3), 361–369.

Tchibozo, G. (2002). Meta-functional criteria and school-to-work transition. *Journal of Education and Work, 15*(3), 337–350.

Willis, P. (1980). *Learning to labour: How working class kids get working class jobs.* Hampshire, England: Gower Publishing Company Limited.

Wotherspoon, T. (2004). *The sociology of education in Canada: Critical perspectives.* Don Mills: Oxford University Press.

Karen Carter
Ontario Institute for Studies in Education
University of Toronto, Canada

KATINA E. POLLOCK

9. TRANSITIONING TO THE TEACHER WORKFORCE:

Internationally Educated Teachers (IETs) as Occasional Teachers

INTRODUCTION

The Ontario teacher workforce is becoming more diverse. Teachers who are educated in non-western countries are entering the Ontario teacher workforce in greater numbers than ever before. However, their transition to the Ontario English-speaking, public education system can be challenging; it is neither straightforward nor easy. This case demonstrates how work transitions are differentiated and non-linear, rather than linear, homogenous or comparable across social groups. Many internationally educated teachers (IETs) have emigrated from non-western countries, speak English as a second or third language, and do not represent or reflect the existing teacher population in Ontario. Many of those IETs who manage to successfully obtain Ontario College of Teachers (OCT) certification, however, are relegated to the occasional teacher workforce (McIntyre, 2006). These 'occasional' teachers are certified, non-permanent teachers working in the Ontario, English-speaking public education system, who replace full-time teaching staff when absent from the classroom (Section 1(1.1) Education Act, R.S.O. 1990, c. E.2).

Working as an occasional teacher is challenging at the best of times. Occasional teachers are challenged in two significant ways: getting access to daily work and in the actual work in the classroom. The challenge of gaining access to teaching work plays out in two ways. The more immediate concern is securing occasional work on a daily basis and the latter, more long-term goal, involves acquiring a full-time permanent position. The second challenge of occasional teaching is in the actual classroom work that includes managing the classroom and delivering lessons. While these challenges exist to some degree for all occasional teachers, they are heightened for IETs because of issues around language and culture (Koroma, 2004). This chapter explores certified IETs transitional barriers as they engage in occasional teaching. First, it presents a snapshot of Canada's evolving immigration policy, followed by a brief description of the research that provides the basis for the chapter. Next, I illustrate how structures and policies create systemic barriers for IETs, and how barriers to access and work are influenced by differences in language and culture.

P. Sawchuk and A. Taylor (eds.), Challenging Transitions in Learning and Work: Reflections on Policy and Practice, 165–182.

IMMIGRATION AND TEACHING

Long standing institutionalized beliefs, values, and practices shape certified IETs experiences. These values are reflected in Canada's immigration policies. Immigration has been a part of Canada since its colonization. Initially colonized by Europeans, Canada became home mostly to British, French and northern Europeans looking mainly for economic opportunities (Derwing and Munro, 2007). Initially, there were no restrictions on who could immigrate to Canada until 1885 when a head tax was placed on Chinese immigrants. At that same time

> White Americans and Europeans were preferred, and northern Europeans were preferred over those from eastern and southern Europe. Canada later implemented further discriminatory immigration policies favouring Whites from Europe and the United States. In 1910 an Immigration Act was introduced that gave the cabinet the right to refuse "immigrants belonging to any race deemed unsuited to the climate and requirements of Canada" (Canada 1910, s. 38, para. C.) (Derwing and Munro, 2007).

Canada continued to employ these discriminatory practices for many years. In 1923, countries of origin were officially divided into preferred and non-preferred. Immigrants from Britain, the United States, the Irish Free State, Newfoundland, Australia, New Zealand, and South Africa experienced no restrictions, while immigrants from the non-preferred countries had to meet certain conditions (Green and Green, 1996). While Canada favored those immigrants who were thought to best serve its economic interests at the time, these immigrants had to be a particular 'type', that is, they had to reflect the existing white European Canadian population.

Coinciding with the social movement of the 1960's, immigration policy began to change. The *New Immigration Act* of 1978 was meant to meet "the country's demographic, social, economic, and cultural goals in a nondiscriminatory fashion and to meet humanitarian goals by facilitating family reunification and refugee resettlement in Canada" (Derwing and Munro, 2007, p. 94). Further changes took place with the passing of Canada's *Immigration and Refugee Protection Act* of 2002. This Act focused on selecting immigrants for their 'human capital' characteristics. These relatively new policies have changed the source countries for Canadian immigrants; most now come from non-Western countries. Citizenship and Immigration Canada (2002) reported in 2001 the top five source countries included: China (16.10%), India (11.11%), Pakistan (6.13%), Philippines (5.15%) and the Republic of Korea (3.84%). Many Canadian immigrants choose to settle in large urban centers such as Toronto, Montreal, and Vancouver (Harvey and Houle, 2006).

Immigration affects education on a number of fronts. Historically, Canada's population growth, and the evolving belief in educating all children in the 1850s-60s (Davey, 1991; and Prentice, 1991), required more teachers. Teachers for Canadian children were drawn either from Canadian citizens or recent immigrants, both of which were from specific pools of white European men, and then women (Abott, 1991), many of whom wanted to "spread the British culture to the inhabitants of the Canadian backwoods (Prentice, 1991). Therefore, internationally educated teachers in Canadian schools before the 1960s were white and reflected the European population. Recent changes in immigration patterns, however, have affected education in two ways. First, urban centers are experiencing growing diversity in their student population (Statistics Canada, 2005, 2007). In some school districts, the visible minority population exceeds 50% of the total student population (Cheng and Yau, 1999). Second, there has been a growing diversity in immigration teacher population as well. Teaching represents the fourth largest occupation of immigrants arriving in Ontario (Citizenship and Immigration Canada, 2003). Of the 162,240 teachers in Ontario in 2001, 12,055 were identified as visible minority[1] (Statistics Canada, 2005, 2007).

These statistics, however, do not reflect the difficulties certified IETs experience transitioning into the teacher workforce. A recent five-year study conducted by the Ontario College of Teachers (sponsored by the Ontario Ministry of Education), reported that IETs are 6 times more likely than other Ontario graduates to be unemployed in their first year of teaching, 10 times more likely to be unemployed because they could not find a teaching job, 3 times more likely to be underemployed, 3 times more likely to be in daily occasional teaching and, and 3 times less likely to have found a regular teaching job. Only 1 out of 5 (20%) have found teaching jobs, and of those, more than half (57%) are teaching only on an occasional daily basis. Certified IETs currently represent 48% of the occasional teacher workforce compared to new Ontario graduates (18%), teachers educated in other provinces (23%) and teachers educated at border-colleges (24%) (McIntyre, 2006).

These issues are significant for two reasons. First well educated, certified, and experienced IETs have difficulty finding work. According to current immigration policies immigrant selection is through "a point system, which favours highly educated, younger, skilled workers who are fluent in at least one of Canada's official languages" (Owen, 2005). Many IETs are not only trained and certified, but 96% reported one or more years of teaching in another jurisdiction prior to certification in Ontario (McIntyre, 2006). Yet, even new Canadians who held high-demand qualifications in secondary math, physics or chemistry or French do not fair well in finding work. Their overall unemployment rate is 43%, compared with 3% of Ontario graduates who specialize in French language. The occasional teacher workforce has an overrepresentation of certified, often well trained teachers, who also have some teaching experience, and can speak one of the two official languages of Canada, yet they have difficulty transitioning into the full-time permanent teaching. According to those who have coined the term 'new' and/or 'knowledge' economy, IETs would have the required skills and knowledge needed to successfully participate in the teacher workforce. In reality, though, they do not have what it takes to participate. Obviously there is something else at play here. Can it be that the knowledge economy that emphasizes knowledge and skill appears to ignore other influences such as differing beliefs, assumptions, and cultural practices and that these other influences contribute to transitions a) that can occur at any time within an individual's work life and b) not all individuals or groups experience transitions in the same manner or with similar degrees of success? In this case, all of the IETs in this study were essentially experiencing transitioning at mid-career and the challenges they faced were not necessarily due to lack of technical knowledge or skills.

IET difficulties do not end when and if they find work. They continue to experience challenges with their transition in the schools and classrooms (Pollock, 2006). Such challenges are different from what most full-time, majority culture teachers face.

These problems are a concern for another reason. In 2004, the Ontario Ministry of Training, Colleges and Universities, predicted that immigration will account for 100% of net labour force growth by 2011 and 100% of the net population growth by 2031. The Ministry also predicted a teacher shortage by 2010 as approximately 56,000 teachers are expected to retire. If this is the case then it stands to reason that that hiring pool for teachers will predominantly come from both the existing reserve of teachers and from the occasional teacher workforce that includes a large number of IETs.

This article explores the difficulties that certified, occasional IETs experience in their attempts both to find daily work and when they do find work, in their school encounters.

THE RESEARCH

The data used in this chapter was generated from a qualitative study focusing on occasional teachers. Participants in this study were part of the Ontario English-speaking public school system. All occasional teachers in this study participated in the teacher workforce through daily teaching; none of them held a permanent teaching position at the time of the interviews. In fact, participants were selected only if they had taught occasionally within the previous 12 months (in the Ontario English-speaking public education system). In addition, participants could not be working at the time in a Long-Term Occasional (LTO) position.

Eighteen educators were interviewed, 15 of which were occasional teachers from the southern Ontario region. Of the 15 teachers interviewed, four were internationally educated teachers (IETs) seeking full-time teaching employment, five individuals who had retired from permanent teaching posts and were presently doing occasional work, and six who were career occasional teachers, many of whom also held executive positions on various local Occasion Teachers' Bargaining Units (OTBU). In addition, a union representative from the Ontario Secondary School Teachers' Federation (OSSTF) who used to bargain on behalf of occasional teachers was interviewed. In an attempt to understand the practices within this particular work sector, an employee from the Toronto District School Board and, a past director for ***TeachinOntario*** (bridging program for internationally trained teachers seeking work in Ontario), were also interviewed. These interviews sought to capture the lived experiences of occasional teachers and gain insight into their work.

During the interview process occasional teachers were asked why they were teaching occasionally, what steps they took to get on the "eligible to hire" list, to describe a typical day teaching, detail some of the strategies used to get on the occasional teacher list and to get occasional teaching work, and to describe some of the barriers that they faced. The remaining interviews with the OSSTF representative, the board employee and ***TeachinOntario*** director were somewhat different. They were asked how they were associated with occasional teachers, what they saw as the benefits for individuals participating in occasional teaching, the issues that have arisen, and the supports that were available to occasional teachers. As it turned out, issues involving IETs proved to be one of the significant themes. Both IETs and non-IETs discussed the issues that the former faced.

POLICY BARRIERS

Many transitional barriers IETs face are due to racist beliefs, attitudes and practices. "Contemporary racism assumes many forms and shows up in many different situations, practices, and discourses" (Ryan, 1999). Shoshat and Stam (1994, p. 23) argue racism plays out in a complex interwoven manner where,

> Racism…is both individual and systemic, interwoven into the fabric both of the psyche and of the social systems, at once grindingly quotidian and maddeningly abstract. It is not merely an attitudinal issue, but a historically contingent institutional and discursive apparatus linked to the dramatically unequal distribution of resources and opportunities, the unfair apportioning of justice, wealth, pleasures and pain. It is less an error in logic than an abuse of power, less about 'attitudes' than about the deferring of hopes and the destruction of lives.

Canadian immigration policies of the late 1800s and early 1990s reflected this individual and structural racist practice. They proceeded under the assumption that this idealized (European) Canadian population constituted "a group or groups of people who shared certain valued characteristics with one another, while at the same time setting themselves apart from others who did not share these same positive traits" (Ryan, 1999, p. 76). In these policies, only immigrants from particular countries who were considered to have desired characteristics were given access to the country. Immigrants from other source countries were given access only if they met a set of particular criteria. Doing so, symbolized a separation of those who belong from those who do not (Morely and Robins, 1995). Historically, Canadian immigration policies promoted a particular kind of whiteness. In this context, 'whiteness' means more than skin colour (Dei, 1996). It is also "'space of positions', a strategic, flexible and privileged location from which to view and to keep 'others' at a distance. From this privileged space both viewer and the viewed are constituted from the norms of whiteness" (Ryan, 1999, p. 86). Like most public institutions, the Canadian education system, including the teacher workforce, promoted a particular type of citizenship associated with whiteness.

Things began to change in the 1960s when Canada was forced to deal with its own demographic, social and economic challenges. One of the responses was to change immigration policy. However, these changes did not bring about a change in cultural beliefs, attitudes or practices, that is, in the institutional biases that dominated the social landscape. The prevailing white Eurocentric culture with its explicit and implicit discriminatory attitudes and practices continued to shape the organizational culture of the Ontario, English-speaking public education system. The result was that it perpetuated negative attitudes toward teachers who do not mirror the present teacher workforce. This chapter reports on the consequences for IETs. Despite newer and more enlightened policies, the older discriminating practices continue to make transitioning into a new teacher workforce difficult for these occasional IETs.

Since the changes in immigration policy, there have been a number of initiatives and programs set up to assist Internationally Educated Professionals (IEPs), including IETs. For instance, in 1994, York University and the University of Ottawa received funding from the Provincial government for pilot projects that enabled IETs to upgrade their credentials. Seven out of 35 IETs graduated from Ottawa's program and were certified within a few months, but it is not known whether these IETs were successful in gaining access to teaching. York's program graduated twenty IETs in its second program, but again it is not clear whether these graduates secured any teaching work. Overall, it appeared that too few IETs were targeted, given the cost of the programs. The program ended in 2005. In 1995, the Access to Processions and Trades (APT) unit of the Ontario Ministry of Education was created to help promote recognition of qualifications of internationally trained professional and trades people and speed their access to the Ontario Labour market. The following year, the College of Teachers Act was passed and the college assumed responsibility for assessing teachers' credentials, English Language proficiency and awarding teacher certification. Eventually, a number of reports indicated that merely allowing professionals access to the country does not guarantee employment in the area of expertise. Indeed, many internationally trained professionals, including teachers, were in fact NOT successful in finding work in their designated profession (National Organization of Immigrant and Visible Minority Women of Canada (NOIVMWC, 2001, 1999). Response to growing concerns over access to professions led both the provincial government and federal government to invest millions into bridging programs (Ministry of Citizenship and immigration, 2006, Ministry of Training, Colleges, and Universities, 2005a, 2005b), programs meant to help assist IEPs, including IETs, gain access to their profession. Yet the success of IETs attempting to gain full-time permanent teaching work is still dismal. The problem, however, does not rest entirely with the 'individual' IETs', as a number of programs designed to help them assume, but rather with the built-in systemic barriers within the education system.

ACCESS, WORK, LANGUAGE, AND CULTURE

Internationally Educated Teachers face systemic barriers in their transition from their previous work to work in their new communities. Institutional expectations and values around culture and language create barriers around access and with the actual work in the classroom (Deters, 2006; Walsh and Brigham, 2007). Access conceptualized more broadly means securing full-time permanent teaching and this is what the majority of IETs seek (McIntyre, 2005, 2006, Unpublished Ministry of Education Report, 2007). As a steppingstone to this full-time, permanent teaching, many IETs utilize occasional teaching to learn about the Ontario, English-speaking public education system, gain experience teaching in this new system, network with other teachers, and make connections with administrators who might potentially hire them (Pollock, 2008; Ramlal, 2003; Turnbull andBrown, 2006). More narrowly conceived, access includes securing daily occasional work. Daily work, the frequency of it, and the location of this work will have an impact on IETs' overall goal. If an IET works only a few days, and only in a limited number of schools, then the ability to learn about the system and network is substantially reduced. To avoid this, occasional IETs engage in practices that will secure as much daily work as possible.

Occasional teaching is invisible and largely misunderstood (Betts, 2006; Duggleby, 2003; Damianos, 1998; St. Michel, 1995). Not only do IETs have to figure out how this new education system works, but they soon also realize, like many other people who do occasional teaching, that this is different from full-time permanent teaching. IETs encounter two significant differences in their transition – one between their home and their new community and between permanent, full-time teaching and occasional teaching. These differences have consequences for their practice. For instance, occasional teachers need to utilize particular classroom management strategies (Arnold, 2006; Clark, Antonelli, Lacaera, Livingstone, Pollock, Smaller, et al., 2007; Clifton and Rambaran, 1987; Collins, 1982, 1989; Herbst, 2001; Pronin, 1983; Ramsey, 1997; Sigel, 1997), while useful in full-time teaching situations, are *essential* for daily occasional work. As well, many teaching and learning strategies and classroom management techniques included in teacher training programs are not appropriate for daily occasional teaching because they all assume an element of consistent, ongoing contact with students, something that does not exist in occasional teaching work (Pollock, 2008). Within this environment IETs encounter barriers associated with culture and language that will prevent them from getting and performing their jobs.Occasional IETs also struggle with issues of culture. Culture is a complex concept. It has numerous contested meanings (Williams 1958; Kroeber and Klockholm, 1952). For the purposes of this chapter, culture is conceptualized as "a signifying system, through which necessarily a social order is communicated, reproduced, experienced, and explored (William, 1981, p. 13). It is "embedded in a whole range of activities, relations and institutions" (Williams, 1981, p. 209) and is not so much a set of things as a process, a set of social practices (Hall, 1997). However, there is never just one culture. In any organization there are a number of competing cultures. In this case, not only does the Ontario, English-speaking public education system have a dominant culture that includes all aspects of what it means to be 'white', but within this system there are other non-dominant cultures such as student cultures, and the culture of daily occasional teachers. These cultures exist in the same space and time. Darder (1991), for example, maintains that

> The structures, material practices, and lived relations of a given society are not in themselves a unified culture, but rather a complex combination of dominant and subordinate cultures (p. 29).

In this case, the dominant full-time teacher workforce culture marginalizes other sub-cultures associated with teaching assistants, daily occasional teachers, or IETs. This relationship between dominant and subordinate cultures perpetuates an internal teacher workforce hierarchy (Pollock, 2008). This dominant culture revolves around the beliefs, attitudes, behaviors and practices of whiteness. Other teacher sub-cultures, on the other hand, are marginalized as they compete with the dominant culture of the full-time teacher workforce and other sub-cultures as members of the various groups attempt to make sense of their work arrangement and control their work environment.

The structure of the teacher workforce has created an environment that fosters the perpetuation of competing, but unequal cultures. Schein (1986) argues that, "the environment thus initially influences the formation of the culture, but once culture is present in the sense of shared assumptions, those assumptions, in turn, influence what will be perceived and defined as the environment" (p. 51). This dominant culture creates and perpetuates particular attitudes toward IETs, and various relationships among and within the various teacher groups. While IETs are not a homogenous group, from the perspective of the existing teacher workforce, they are perceived as such and this affects all IETs. The following section considers how cultural differences influence IETs transition into the teacher workforce. Language, while a part of culture, is highlighted first because discourses around language use and proficiency play a key role in access for many IETs. In the subsequent section, culture refers to the common sense notions around practices and knowledge, excluding language.

LANGUAGE AND ACCESS

Language was reported as one of the most obvious challenges for IETs. All participants reported issues around language. Zahra, for example, said "First of all, the language proficiency problem is a barrier for us". Many IETs remain uncertified because they have not reached the required language proficiency needed for certification. In other cases, IETs have passed the proficiency test for provincial certification only to fail language proficiency tests at the board level. Thus, while they have provincial certification, they may be denied access to the occasional teacher list at the board level.

The language proficiency test is not the only barrier for IETs. In fact, certified IETs would have already passed this test in order to meet accreditation requirements. IETs cannot work if they do not meet this requirement. However, even for these teachers, language continues to be an issue. Ping, for example, claims, "because I speak English as a second language, so this is why it will be very difficult for me to find a job." IETs are not the only ones who recognize language as a barrier. Daniel, a board employee, maintains that:

> Language barrier is still our major one; in fact that's the number one obstacle for folks who were trained outside of Canada. It's not their pedagogy, it's not their knowledge background…

Kelly, a union representative, also recognizes the barriers around language. She contends that:

> So if you're an immigrant who does not speak good English you're probably not going to start right into the regular teacher workforce. You're going to start as an occasional teacher, and you are going to become the career

> occasional because it's so hard to break past that language barrier. ...And so our occasional teacher workforce is disproportionately [exaggerated voice] loaded with people with poorer English skills.

In both cases, the school board member and union representative indicate that not only is language one of the biggest barriers for IETs, it is also probably the biggest reason why many of them do not secure full-time teaching. The consequence of this is that if they do stay in the teaching profession, they do so as occasional teachers.

While proficiency may be the most obvious challenge around language, other language barriers exist. In order to apply for teacher certification, IETs must pass the TOFEL test for language proficiency. Therefore, for those IETs certified in Ontario, language should not be an issue. This, however, is often not the case. While many IETs may be proficient enough in English to navigate the community, teaching and learning have their own occupation-specific language. Miscommunication occurs when IETs fail to comprehend the subtle nuances of word meanings or when they are unaware of the present 'politically correct' discourses. When this happens, English-speakers perceive IETs in a negative light, believing them to be not well-educated or as having prejudicial and discriminatory attitudes. When others see IETs in these ways they may not call them back for occasional teaching work or hire them for any type of permanent teaching position. Mawhinney and Xu (1997) argue that IETs "should be aware that job-related oral proficiency in English is essential".

LANGUAGE AND WORK

Language issues can also create challenges for occasional IETs in the classroom. Language is not uniform. "...it varies according to social characteristics of groups of people, such as their cultural background, geographical location, social class, gender, or age" (Adger, Wolfram and Christian, 2007, p. 1). For many IETs, it is more than just proficiency that is at issue; there are issues around dialect and accent[2] as well. Everyone speaks with a dialect. "A person cannot speak a language without speaking a dialect of that language. Everyone is part of some group that can be distinguished from other groups in part by how group members talk. If a person speaks the English language, that person necessarily speaks some dialect of the English language" (Adger, Wolfram and Christian, 2007, p. 2). The interesting piece to the language puzzle is that while Adger, Wolfram, and Christian (2007) argue that dialects have complete linguistic systems and structural integrity (p. 2), not all dialects are considered equal. Social evaluation confers some dialects with a higher status than others and this occurs on social rather than linguistic grounds (p. 2). Accents are also not neutral. They are also evaluated socially; some are more preferred than others. Not surprising, but reflective of the dominant white culture, is that "many North Americans hold a British accent in high regard" (Adger, Wolfram and Christian, 2007, p. 4). Most IETs speak English with an accent and it tends not to be British. They also have many dialects different from that found within the full-time teacher workforce. Mawhinney and Xu (1997) report that IETs in their study constantly faced questioning about their accent. Those accents most reflective of the general teaching population are considered more appropriate than accents from non-western countries. Most of the IETS are from countries like China, India, Pakistan and the Philippines and carry with them non-Western accents. Brian, a board employee, reflected on the attitudes associated with accents.

> Language is a barrier, and not in terms of proficiency. I think it's clear that it's important to have a proficiency level when in a classroom, but there are cultural barriers that people face around accent; many may not necessarily get a job because they have an accent.

While people who hire teachers may hold particular accents against IETs in job interviews, these negative attitudes also surface elsewhere. As Katherine contends, students also hold particular attitudes surrounding accents as well.

> Unfortunately, if you do not speak good English, or let's say, comprehensible English, something which is good enough, and if you go into the classroom, the students make fun of you. I've seen it, I've heard about it many times…

This ridiculing of dialect or accent can be an example of discriminatory attitudes. According to IETs, many students held the belief that language reflects teaching competency; those IETs who spoke a particular way were considered to be less competent (Koroma, 2004). These discriminatory attitudes and behaviours reduce IETs engagement in two ways. First, they are unable to gain access to actual daily occasional work in ways proficient English-speakers can. Second, when they do find employment, they often experience difficulties in the work environment because of students' and teachers' negative perceptions of their accents. From a workforce perspective, this leaves IETs on the margins.

CULTURE AND ACCESS

Barriers for IETs extend beyond language, however. They are also entangled in culture. The present teacher workforce culture is dominated by values associated with whiteness. Those of the dominant culture are not only English speaking; they are also predominantly Eurocentric and Caucasian. This in turn means that the predominant culture of the teacher workforce is grounded in this particular group's way of being and tends to exclude different others. IETs, however, bring with them different cultural proclivities and knowledge. Unfortunately, this can lead to discrimination against IETs on a number of fronts. For instance, some parents and students may not want to be taught by teachers of particular ethnic or racial backgrounds. Sonia retells a story of how an IET covering for a full-time teacher going on maternity experienced racism. When a group of parents found out the occasional teacher was an IET from a minoritized group, they opposed the hiring of this individual, and they put tremendous pressure on the school and board to hire someone else. This movement began even before the teacher stepped inside the classroom. Therefore, their actions were not based on her ability to teach.

However, the local union supported the occasional teacher and she kept her position. This issue, however, did not rest then. During the long-term occasional term, one male student approached the teacher and stated that his father told him that if they were back in the 1800s she, the teacher, would be a slave to his family. In this case, these racist attitudes did not influence the IETs access to work, but they did little to promote positive interactions within the classroom environment.

Discriminatory attitudes from both school staff and students impact IETs' ability to find work and their job performance in the sense that many students misbehave more when occasional teachers of particular ethnicities or races are in the classroom. An excerpt of an interview with Helen, an Ontario educated, English-speaking, career-occasional teacher provides a glimpse of the attitudes that exist in the system. She says:

> ...someone did make a comment to me at one point when I walked in to [name of school] when I introduced myself to the secretary, and she goes 'oh, it's somebody that speaks English'

CULTURE AND WORK

Besides language, there are other cultural issues that influence IETs' work experiences. One of these differences centres around the issue of respect. Different cultures have different conceptions of respect. Many IETs entering Ontario's English-speaking, public education system comment on the differences in how they are received and perceived both in the school and within the classroom. For instance, Zahra was working in a long-term occasional position at a local elementary school. She mentioned having communication problems with her principal. She believed that her principal did not like her. She felt that this administrator was cold and that a certain amount of tension existed between them. Zahra explained that when she would meet the principal in the hall, she would always put her head down, look away and address her as Ms. So and So as a sign of respect. Not understanding her formality, the principal told her to "Call me by my first name,' but Zahra could never bring herself to do this.

Zahra eventually spoke to her principal and explained some of her behaviors. She told the principal that she was brought up to treat principals formally and that she was very uncomfortable interacting with her in an informal way. She explained she could not make eye contact with her or go over to her house for a social event because that would indicate disrespect. Since Zahra's conversation with her principal, things have improved because much of the miscommunication had been resolved. She confided "because there was an understanding now that the principal understood where she was coming from and then she understood now where the principal was coming from". The misinterpretation was now clarified and they were able to work well together. The stress of the relationship was greatly reduced.

Issues around respect also play out in the classroom as well. As an administrator commented in Schotte's (1973) study "they [IETs] have little control and discipline and just fail to command any respect from the children" (p. 65). Ping commented that students would sometimes say things like "You're not a teacher...why are you pressuring me to learn....leave me alone, I don't want to learn [from you]". Unfortunately, many IETs also do not receive support from administration or teaching staff. Schotte (1973) pointed out "principals do not feel that all [occasional] teachers deserve the support they can give them" (p. 65). One such principal commented,

> I usually have problems with [occasional] teachers from India and the West Indies. They are not trained in our system and are not used to it. I hate to say it, but there is not much I can do for them. (p. 65)

POLICIES FOR IETS

In response to an increase in diversity, and as a way to meet the needs of the diverse student population, there has been a call for a more diverse teacher workforce from the provincial government and local school boards. For example the Ontario provincial government stated that amendments to *The Education Act* of 1992 occurred in response to an awareness that "systemic inequities exist[ed] in the school system that limit the opportunities for aboriginal and other students and staff members of racial and ethnocultural minorities to fulfill their potential" (PPM 119, July 1993). The policy was designed to ensure that the "workforce in the school board should reflect and be capable of understanding and responding to the experience of Ontario's culturally and racially diverse population" (PPM 119, July 1993). Local school districts also have policies that promote a diverse workforce. For instance, the Toronto District School Board's Employment Equity policy P. 029 EMP states that the board is committed to policies, practices and procedures that "result in and sustain a workforce that, at all levels, reflects, understands and responds to a diverse population". Ryan, Antonelli and Pollock (2007) argued four reasons (symbolic, relationship, pedagogic, and political) for why diversification of the teacher workforce is critical. Yet, it appears that these calls for diversification have not been put into practice because the teacher workforce in Ontario is still predominantly white (Bascia, 2001; Bedard, 2000; Ryan, Antonelli and Pollock, 2007). However, Ontario does have a pool of teachers to draw upon. They are IETs. Yet, the recent report from the College of Teachers describes the experiences of those certified IETs as "dismal" and the outcomes of their job searches as "disastrous." The report claims "despite the fact that they (IETs) are highly experienced in teaching, many of them appear shut out of their profession" (p. 23). One of the study participants summed the immigrant experience up well by stating "There is an undeniable preference for non-immigrant teachers over immigrated ones. This fact despite the experience and qualifications I hold" (McIntyre, 2006, p. 28).

If school boards are sincere about promoting equitable hiring practices, then IETs should be more evenly represented through the teacher workforce. Unfortunately, we know from the Transition to Teaching Study (McIntyre, 2005, 2006) that this is not the case. The largest concentration of IETs is still found within the occasional teacher workforce at the bottom of the teacher hierarchy and in positions with the least power, influence, and prestige. The difficulties that IETs face, however, come as a surprise to them. Many come to Canada expecting to be hired as full-time teachers. It seems that they have been misled at some point. Zahra and Ogus reported misinformation about both the teacher shortage and access to the teaching profession in the immigration process. Zahra pointed to an assumption perpetuated through immigration that because a potential immigrant is certified as a teacher and has had a teaching career in their homeland that this will be an advantage to them in finding a teaching position. Katherine, an advocate for IETs, stated "...many of them will say that they have been told by immigration that they'll be teachers in Ontario. And that's a big problem for us right now... because becoming a teacher in Ontario is not as easy as they had been lead to believe." While none of the IETs outwardly stated that they felt discriminated against, their stories indicate that there is room for such an interpretation. Emily, an occasional teacher who is not an IET, indicated that racism might be at play in the process.

> ...I'm very privileged compared to most people who are supply teaching, ... Well, a lot of people are quite racist in their assumptions about supply teaching, so if they see somebody who is "whiteish" and who speaks English with the same accent that they speak English, and who is doing this because they are doing a graduate degree, rather than because they couldn't get a job teaching, and all of the assumptions that they might have around supply teaching are sort of ... there, I play into them just by existing and having my body so, I don't ever see a sort of big shock on people's face as I'm walking through the door and supply teach...

IETs have had to adapt to this racism. They also reported having to learn the 'cultural capital' associated with teaching in Ontario. There is a fine line between gaining an understanding of how an organization functions and assimilating into a particular culture and set of dominant values. IETs encounter contradictory pressures to "acclimatize" to a particular way of doing things in Ontario, as one interviewee indicated. Rather than assuming that IETs bring shortcomings, it may be in the interests of schools to approach IETs as an educational asset.

IETs level of education and experience may not help them find work. Many occasional IETs new to the Ontario teaching system tend to be well-educated. They have a number of years of teaching experience outside of Ontario and/or teaching experience in Ontario in the private school system. IETs who participated in this study also had many teaching credentials. Ping, for example, received her teaching certificate in Hong King, where she taught for 17 years. After immigrating to Canada, she chose to upgrade her teaching certificate and completed a Bachelor of Arts in Linguistics. While studying for her Bachelors degree at an Ontario University, she also worked as a teacher in a Heritage school in an attempt to gain more teaching experience. She then participated in five summer institute courses, so she could qualify for a Long-Term Occasional (LTO) position. Zahra had a Masters of Education, a Bachelor of Science in Mathematics and Physics and Bachelor of Education in Physics and Mathematics. She taught 15 years in her home country before immigrating to Ontario. Since being here, she has completed an

Additional Qualification (AQ) course from a local university and even participated in a grade 12 mathematics class at a local night school in an attempt to make herself more marketable. Despite all this, she continues to struggle to find daily occasional work.

Zahra and Ping are not the only IETs with experience. Another IET, Ogus, from the Middle East, commented

> I was 24 when I started teaching at university. I was the youngest teacher. And in a year I became ... I got my permanent employment, so at the age 25 I was a university teacher, with permanent employment, full-time permanent... I was about to become the Director.

This teacher has since completed Additional qualification (AQ) courses at the Ontario Institute for the Studies of Education of University of Toronto (OISE/UT) and volunteered in a number of public schools in an attempt to gain experience in the Ontario context. Within the sample of IETs interviewed, with the exception of teachers of French (McIntyre, 2005), the majority of IETs are reported to be over qualified and underemployed. Even so, access to permanent teaching positions appears to be restricted.

IETs have considerably less success than Canadian-born teachers finding jobs in teaching. Teachers who were successful in gaining work in Ontario tend to be Canadian-born, Caucasian, and have English as a first language. This is reflected in the Ontario College of Teachers', Transition to Teaching study where "only eight per cent of new-Canadian teachers certified in 2004 report that they have been unable to find any type of teaching job. However, of those who have obtained jobs, a mere 20 per cent have regular teaching positions less than half the success rate Ontarians or teachers from other provinces" (McIntyre, 2005). IETs find themselves at a disadvantage from the mere fact that they do not mirror the existing teaching population and therefore often find themselves at the bottom of the internal teacher hierarchy.

The general positioning of IETs within the teacher workforce hierarchy reflects a 'lesser than' value. Because of the large numbers of IETs found at the bottom of the workforce hierarchy, it would appear that most school boards and administrators view IETs as less than desirable candidates for teaching positions. Many assume that in order for IETs to contribute positively to the school system, specific supports must be in place that requires more management time and financial spending, both of which are rare resources. Often overlooked are their valued assets. IETs bring with them a wealth of professional and cultural knowledge, skill sets, and experience that can be utilized, especially in diverse school environments. This knowledge, however, has largely gone untapped.

Policy initiatives designed to assist IETs may initially focus on IETs themselves, but there are other complicated issues in play as well. There is an expectation for IETs to learn Western cultural capital. Access to the teaching profession is denied to those who do not 'assimilate' into the prevailing culture of the existing educational system. It may be beneficial in pragmatic terms to provide support in the form of additional training for IETs, but there must also be some way of approaching the issue of access not from a deficit model but by targeting the system.

Professional development for the regular teaching workforce and educational institutions that focuses on understanding the needs of IETs can have more of a positive impact on IETs than delivering PD directly to IETs themselves. The 'system' needs to reflect on its discriminatory attitudes and beliefs as well. Assimilation only recreates specific types of teachers that already exist in the system and defeats the very purpose for wanting IETs in the system in the first place – their own cultural capital. Certified IETs tend to be quite sound in their pedagogical knowledge, content area and skill-sets learned on the job, but they also bring cultural, religious and social ways of knowing that can assist schools that are attempting to be democratic, equitable and inclusive.

Local school districts can generate policies that promote a diverse workforce. However, these policies may have their own unintended outcomes. For example, the Toronto District School Board Employment Equity policy focuses on assisting with hiring teachers' who best represent the student body. Ogus, one of the IETs in the study, volunteered in a school that taught students with a similar ethnic background. He stated

> …the school is good and many Iranians go to that school, so it's policy of the Board also to have persons of the same nationality there. So teachers know me, and there are people who support me. So, I hope I get an interview.

Apparently, the board is actively seeking individual teachers who reflect certain student populations. Despite this stated intention, such teachers are not hired. However, even if they were, this particular policy can lead to other equity issues. Can equitable hiring practices create a trend where only schools with particular populations seek teachers from those populations? Will other traditionally Euro-centric homogenous schools (and boards/districts) not see the need for a diverse teaching staff? This hiring practice can in turn lead to a form of segregated schooling, which can lead to other equity issues.

CONCLUSION

This chapter demonstrates how prevalent discourses strongly supported by post-industrialist, human capital, rational choice theory and neo-classical economics fail to capture the complexity of learning/work transitions that particular groups experience. For instance, this case introduces the idea that learning/work transitions occur throughout an individual's work career and not just as people move from formal schooling into full-time employment. It also demonstrates that not all social groups have similar experiences. A particular sub-group of certified teachers – those who are internationally educated – tend to experience unique challenges transitioning from one teacher workforce to full-time teaching within the Ontario English-speaking public teacher workforce that other groups of teachers do not. Internationally Educated Teachers tend to have few, if any, networks to build upon and often face discriminatory attitudes and practices. While many certified IETs do teach, they do so at the margins – as occasional teachers. Occasional teaching, however, need not be seen as necessarily negative. It provides the opportunity for new teachers to learn about the current school system, decide what type of school environment to which they are suited, and provides a way to network with other teachers. Working as an occasional teacher becomes problematic when teachers want to transition into full-time, permanent work, but are somehow not able to acquire it. This is the case for many certified IETs; they tend to work for long periods of time as occasional teachers before securing full-time, permanent work (if ever). The findings in this research indicate that certified IETs from non-Western countries encounter many obstacles when transitioning from their previous education system to the Ontario, English-speaking public education system. However, viewing IETs simply as assets will have little to no impact in helping IETs gain access to the profession if it is not accompanied by professional development and policies that target the system. Even though the struggles of IETs have been recognized for a number of years, and strategies such as bridging programs have been implemented, success has been limited. More work is required in changing attitudes of regular teachers and administrators from within the system. In other words, meaningful change requires systemic alterations.

NOTES

1 The Canadian Employment Equity Act defines visible minorities as "persons, other than Aboriginal peoples, who are non-Caucasian in race or non-white in colour."

2 The words accent and dialect are often used interchangeably in causal conversation, however, accent is used to refer to how people pronounce word. For example someone who has learn English as a second language may speak English with a French accent, etc., Dialect refers to the variation within a single language. Accent is limited to pronunciation only while dialect includes variation in pronunciation but also includes differences in vocabulary use and grammatical structure (Adger, Wolfram, & Christian, 2007, p. 4).

REFERENCES

Abott, J. R. (1991). Accomplishing "a man's task": Rural women teachers, male culture and the school inspectorate in turn of the century Ontario. In R. Heap & A. Prentice (Eds.), *Gender and education in Ontario: An historical reader* (pp. 49–70). Toronto: Canadian Scholar's Press.

Adger, C. T., Wolfram, W., & Christian, D. (2007). *Dialects in schools and communities* (2nd ed.). Mahwah, NJ: Lawrence Erlbaum.

Arnold, R. (2006). *Treasury of tips*. Mustang, OK: Tate Publishing.

Bascia, N., & Jacka, N. (2001). Falling in and filling in: ESL teaching careers in changing times. *Journal of Educational Change, 2*, 325–346.

Bedard, G. (2000). Deconstructing whiteness. In G. J. S. Dei & A. Calliste (Eds.), *Power, knowledge and anti-racism education: A critical reader* (pp. 41–57). Halifax, Canada: Fernwood.

Betts, R. (2006). *Lived experiences of long-term supply beginning teachers in New Brunswick: A hermeneutic phenomenological approach*. Fredericton, NB: The University of New Brunswick.

Cheng, M., & Yau, M. (1999). *The 1997 every secondary student survey: Detailed findings*. Toronto: Toronto Board of Education.

Clark, R., Antonelli, F., Lacaera, D., Livingstone, D. W., Pollock, K., Smaller, H., et al. (2007). *Beyond PD Days: Teachers' work and learning in Canada*. Toronto: Ontario Teachers Federation.

Clifton, R. A., & Rambaran, R. (1987). Substitute teaching: Survival in a marginal situation. *Urban Education, 22*(3), 310–327.

Collins, S. H. (1982). *Classroom management for substitute teachers*. Eugene, OR: The Garlic Press.

Collins, S. H., & Wilde-Oswalt, L. (1989). *Substitute ingredients: A journey through the soup, salad, main course, and dessert of substitute and classroom teaching*. Eugene, OR: Garlic Press.

Damianos, M. (1998). *Substitute teachers in elementary schools and their professional discourse*. Unpublished MA, OISE/UT, Toronto, ON.

Darder, A. (1991). *Culture and power in the classroom: A critical foundation for bicultural education.* Toronto: OISE Press.

Davey, I. (1991). Trends in female school attendance in mid-nineteenth-Century Ontario. In R. Heap & A. Prentice (Eds.), *Gender and education in Ontario: An historical reader* (pp. 1–24). Toronto: Canadian Scholar's Press.

Dei, G. (1996). *Anti-racism education: Theory and practice*. Halifax, NS: Fernwood.

Derwing, T. M., & Munro, M. J. (2007). Canadian policies on immigrant language education. In R. Joshee & L. Johnson (Eds.), *Multicultural education policies in Canada and the United States.* Vancouver: UBCPress.

Deters, P. (2006). *Immigrant teachers in Canada: Learning the language and culture of a new professional community.* Paper presented at the V Congreso Internacional de AELFE (Asociación Europea de Lenguas para Fines Específicos). Academic and Professional Communication in the 21st century: Genres, rhetoric and the construction of disciplinary knowledge, Zaragoza.

Duggleby, P. A. (2003). *Expectations and experiences of substitute teachers: A Saskatchewan urban context.* Regina, SA: University of Regina.

Green, A., & Green, D. (1996). *The economic goals of Canada's immigration policy, past and present. Research on immigration and integration in the Metropolis Working Paper 96-04.* Vancouver: RIIM.

Hall, S. (1997). The work of representation. In S. Hall (Ed.), *Representation: Cultural representations and signifying practices* (pp. 13–74). London: Sage.

Harvey, E., & Houle, R. (2006). *Demographic changes in Canada and their impact on public education.* Toronto: The Learning Partnership.

Herbst, J. (2001). *Substitute teacher's organize: A comprehensive resource to make every teaching assignment a success.* Huntington Beach, CA: Creative Teaching Press.

Koroma, K. (2004). The West African supply teacher as 'other' in London secondary schools. *FORUM, 46*(3), 86–91.

Kroeber, A., & Klockholm, C. (1952). Culture: A critical review of concepts and definitions. In *Peabody Museum Papers XLVII.* Harvard University Press.

Mawhinney, H., & Fengying, X. (1997). Reconstructing the professional identity of foreign-trained teachers in Ontario schools. *TESOL Quarterly, 31*(3), 632–639.

McIntyre, F. (2005, December). *Transition to teaching 2005: Underemployment in a mixed Ontario job market.* Professionally Speaking.

McIntyre, F. (2006). *Transition to teaching 2006 Report.* Toronto: Ontario College of Teachers.

Ministry of Citizenship and Immigration. (2006). *New bridge training investment means better opportunities for newcomers.*

Ministry of Training, C., & Universities. (2005a). *McGuinty government helps secure future career success for newcomers.*

Ministry of Training, C., & Universities. (2005b). *New bridging projects help people in more professions, communities.*

Morely, D., & Robins, K. (1995). *Spaces of identity: Global media, Electronic landscapes and cultural boundaries.* London: Routledge.

National Organization of Immigrant and Visible Minority Women of Canada (NOIVMWC). (1999). *Recognition and accreditation of foreign qualifications: Case studies of the nursing, teaching and social work professions, "Case studies".* Retrieved October 11, 2007, from http://pch.gc.ca/progs/multi/pubs/sra-ras/accred_e.cfm

National Organization of Immigrant and Visible Minority Women of Canada (NOIVMWC). (2001). *Recognition and accreditation of foreign qualifications – finding a solution, "Activity report".* Retrieved October 11, 2007, from http://pch.gc.ca/progs/multi/pubs/sra-ras/accred_e.cfm

Owen, T. (2005). *The labour market experience of immigrants.* Paper presented at The Future of Lifelong Learning, Toronto.

Pollock, K. (2008). *Occasional teachers' work engagement.* Unpublished Thesis. OISE/UT.

Pollock, K. (2006). *Access to the teaching profession: Internationally educated teachers (IETs) experiences.* Paper presented at the ICSEI 2006 Embracing Diversity: New Challenges for School Effectiveness and Improvement in a Global Learning Society, Fort Lauderdale, FL.

Prentice, A. (1991). From household to school house: The emergence of the teacher as servant of the state. In R. Heap & A. Prentice (Eds.), *Gender and education in Ontario: An historical reader* (pp. 25–48). Toronto: Canadian Scholar's Press.

Pronin, B. (1983). *Substitute teaching: A handbook for hassle-free subbing*. New York: St. Martin's Press.
Ramlal, S. (2003). *Report of think tank meeting on internationally educated teachers*. Toronto, ON.
Ramsey, R. D. (1997). *501 tips for teachers*. Chicago: Contemporary Publishing Company.
Ryan, J. (1999). *Race and ethnicity in multiethnic schools*. San Francisco: Jossey-Bass.
Ryan, J., Antonelli, F., & Pollock, K. (2007). *Teacher and administrator diversity in Canada: Leaky pipelines, bottlenecks, and glass ceilings*. Paper presented at the CSSE, Saskatoon, Saskatchewan.
Schein, E. (1986). *Organizational culture and leadership*. London: Jossey-Bass.
Schotte, F. (1973). *An investigation into some aspects of the occupation of substitute teaching*. OISE/UT, Toronto.
Shohat, E., & Stam, R. (1994). *Unthinking Eurocentrism: Munticulturalism and the media*. New York: Routledge.
Sigel, M., & Routh, P. (1997). *Dear substitute teacher*. Fort Bragg, CA: Lost Coast Press.
St. Michel, T. (Ed.). (1995). *Effective substitute teachers: Myth, mayhem, or magic?* Thousand Oaks, CA: Corwin Press.
Statistics Canada. (2005). *Population projections of visible minority groups, Canada, provinces and regions, 2001–2017, Cat. No 91-541XIE*. Ottawa: Statistics Canada.
Statistics Canada. (2007). *Community profiles*. Retrieved from http://www12.statcan.ca/english/profil01/CP01/Index.cfm?Lang=E
Turnbull, H., & Brown, S. (2006). *Connections to action: Report on the 2006 Internationally Educated Professionals (IEP) Breaking Barriers Building Bridges Conference Think Tank*. Toronto, Ontario.
Walsh, S., & Brigham, S. (2007). *Ways that female internationally educated and trained teachers are constructed in the Atlantic Canadian context: One woman's story*. Paper presented at the British Educational Research Association (BERA), Institute of Education, University of London.
William, R. (1981). *Culture*. Glasgow: Fontana.
Williams, R. (1958). *Culture and society*. London: Chatto & Windus.

Katina E. Pollock
Faculty of Education
University of Western Ontario

ALISON TAYLOR

SECTION 2 INTRODUCTION

Learning/Work Transitions – Work, Career, and Life Changes

The chapters in this section explore topics related to learning and work transitions of different groups of workers in different economic sectors. The goal of this section introduction, as in the previous one, is to support a broad and creative reading of the chapters that links them to the major themes outlined in our opening literature review and extends the horizon of their contributions by posing additional questions to guide future scholarship.

The type of transitions explored in this section include intra-institutional transitions as workers adapt to changes within their workplace or try to access professional development opportunities, and inter-institutional transitions as different groups of workers try to match their knowledge and skills with paid and unpaid work opportunities. Authors explore the factors that contribute to particular outcomes within organizations and for groups that have been traditionally excluded from access to valued knowledge and highly skilled work. In the broadest sense, the argument supported in this and the previous section is that while patterns of transition are discernable, key forms of social differences – and in particular, a concern for the disproportionate numbers of people for whom transitions are challenging or prohibitive if not virtually impossible and painful – must serve as a much stronger guide-post for empirical investigation as well as policy-making. Transitions are, in other words, a core mechanism of social differentiation based on gender, race/ethnicity, dis/ability and class, mediated further by matters of age and generation, labour process, sector, immigration status, health and so on. Research on transitions that orients to a normative, discrete and finite set of transition types is thus called into question. Categorical boundaries of 'discernable' transitions must be softened to allow for a broader appreciation of multiple-mediations that, in turn, pave the way to the recognition of agency, deviation from categorical norms, and, ultimately, the movement from description to explanation. All these, and other points highlighted below, add further substance to the critical vocationalism perspective we are attempting to develop in this volume.

* * *

Peter Sawchuk's analysis in ***Chapter 10*** looks at intra-institutional transitions associated with technological change in welfare benefit delivery work in Ontario. In this research we see an instance of a large group undergoing transition of an occupation as a whole. His case study, involving interviews and a survey of workers, focuses on how the introduction of a new work system changed a labour process.

This labour process, once more deeply rooted in autonomy, skill, and judgement associated with professional social work, was transformed into a labour process where work was more fragmented, systematized, and in many ways 'deskilled' making clients more difficult to address. Thus, Sawchuk's work challenges the 'knowledge economy' assumption that technological change necessarily involves 'upskilling.'

At the same time, Sawchuk does not believe workers are passive or 'dupes.' Rather, he uses data from his case to suggest that, in contrast to the centralization of knowledge associated with increased supervision as well as additional control by private sector consultants, workers developed local knowledge and 'workarounds' to cope with problems with the technology and its potentially adverse effects on clients. In this sense, technology has both upskilling and deskilling effects: it promotes both engagement and alienation, and gives rise to both cooperation and conflict. Sawchuk's analysis confirms that changes in labour processes are experienced in distinct ways for newer and more seasoned workers, depending on the particular relations of power and knowledge at work. It is consistent with critical vocational ideas which focus on the need to democratize practices in the workplace as well as education and informal learning. At the same time, he recognizes important forms of social difference (i.e., the younger, novice worker versus the older more expert worker).

On a broader level, his analysis also suggests that some clients do not 'fit' the new standardizing and regularizing government system—he comments that the new system could not accommodate the 'irregularities of clients' lives.' Therefore, government systems (including social services, education and training) do not appear to work well for some groups of people, as we see also in other chapters of this book. Sawchuk's observation about worker resistance through the collectivisation of knowledge is interesting to consider in terms of how this knowledge might be used to form alliances across groups.

In ***Chapter 11***, Belanger and Daniau also examine intra-institutional learning dynamics. The authors focus on the education and training of production operators and researchers in the biopharmaceutical sector in four different companies in Quebec. Their findings suggest differences between production employees and scientific staff related to the type of knowledge deemed important for them to do their work successfully and the forms of learning available to them. The authors note that the education and training provided for production staff tends to promote a 'logic of conformity,' while that supported for scientific staff promotes a 'logic of reflexivity.'

The authors contribute to a critical vocational approach by asking three key questions: Who has access to what kinds of learning in the workplace? Whose learning (formal and informal) is encouraged, supported, and rewarded in the workplace? And, what are the implications of this? They raise concerns about the social distribution of knowledge across employee groups, across organizations, and across different work sectors. By asking how differences in the patterns and logics of educational and training can be explained, with a focus on occupational and organizational differences, this chapter provides a perspective which complements other chapters focusing on groups (identified by gender, race/ethnicity, class and dis/ability) that occupy particular occupational and organizational locations. Clearly, attention to institutional logics and social divisions are key to a more complete understanding of learning and work transitions.

The question of which groups come to occupy which occupational locations is taken up by Mirchandani et al., Slade and Schugurensky, and Guo. In ***Chapter 12***, Mirchandani et al., explore the transitions of immigrant women (half of whom had university degrees in their home countries) into contingent workers as garment sewers, cashiers, and call centre operators. The authors suggest that immigrant women in Canada encounter pressures to accept work where they are underemployed because of pressures to earn income, language issues, gendered family dynamics, difficulties finding work commensurate with their education and experience, and the easy availability of contingent work. However, this trend raises important questions about immigration policy which, as authors say, seeks to attract the 'best and the brightest.' The 'downward' mobility of highly educated immigrants also disputes the knowledge economy presumption that the skills of highly-educated people will be valued and rewarded in the workplace.

Slade and Schugurensky explore another response of skilled immigrants to barriers in the Canadian labour market in ***Chapter 14***. The focus of these authors is on transitions from 'labour market undesirables' to 'volunteer workers' that skilled immigrants make in order to address the 'deficits' they are perceived to have in terms of language skills, social capital, and Canadian experience. However, the authors' interviews with immigrants who have pursued this strategy show that many, though certainly not all, of these workers found that it was not successful in terms of providing a stepping stone to appropriate work. Further, as in the case of contingent workers, immigrant workers in the Slade and Schugurensky chapter were open to heightened exploitation by employers. These findings prompt us to question our conceptions of work (as paid), of volunteer work (e.g., as freely chosen), of transitions (as linear and direct), and of education and training (as developing human capital that will be rewarded in the labour market).

Guo's ***Chapter 13*** reinforces the message that gender, race, and nationality have an impact on individuals' perceived skill levels with reference to his study of Chinese immigrants' transitions to work. Like Slade and Schugurensky, he finds that for a disproportionate number these transitions are lengthy, costly, and painful. All three chapters (12, 13 and 14) raise questions about how skills and knowledge are valued and rewarded in the Canadian labour market and who is being 'left out.' They highlight the ways in which credentials can be a mechanism for exclusion or social closure that acts to legitimize existing power relations. Linking to our discussion of critical vocationalism, these chapters highlight problems with human capital assumptions about education and employment outcomes and the problems of education-jobs mismatch. They also point to the need to explore how different groups, immigrants in this case, come to occupy certain locations within the labour market, and thus the importance of gender and race/ethnicity for learning and work opportunities and outcomes. The multi-faceted understanding of transitions associated with critical vocational approaches of authors in this section will hopefully encourage more multi-faceted policies that provide opportunities for learners to participate and to transform inequitable social practices.

Biron et al., help us move from 'transitions to paid work' to 'transitions from paid work' for older workers in ***Chapter 15***. Again, they make the important point that these transitions have become less synchronized, definitive, and standardized—departure from paid work no longer implies retirement. The authors begin from the finding that the level of participation in adult education for those aged 65 and older is lower than for other groups, and seek to identify and examine some of the factors that contribute to this participation, based on survey and interview data. Some of the key factors that they focus on include the individual's state of health, prior education and work biographies, and access to education and training including time and money. They note generational differences in the meaning of education and training with later generations with higher average educational attainment being more likely to integrate education into their lives. Authors attribute participation levels more to prior learning biographies and current provision of learning opportunities than with the effects of aging per se. They therefore challenge some of the negative perceptions around the lack of interest in learning of older workers and retirees.

Consistent with a critical vocational approach, authors' work suggests that exclusion from formal and informal learning opportunities continues to impact people's educational biographies. Those with low levels of education and whose opportunities for learning at work were limited are more likely to make passive transitions, while those who had greater levels of participation in formal and informal learning were more likely to be actively involved in their transitions. The focus on transitions to retirement also draws attention to the danger in conceiving of learning in very instrumental ways (e.g., only for employability) as opposed to encouraging a more holistic vision of learning for life.

The final chapter of this section (***Chapter 16***) focuses on the multiple transitions of persons with disabilities. These transitions may include becoming 'persons with disabilities' (which is analogous to the transition to 'labour market undesirables' for professional immigrants to Canada, as per Slade and Schugurensky) as well as inter- and intra-institutional transitions involving social agencies, educational institutions, and workplaces. Wallace and Fenwick point to the multiple barriers and exclusions faced by people with disabilities because of the expectation of 'ableism' and the focus on particular norms of labour market engagement and practice. As with other marginalized groups, people with disabilities tend to be confronted with models of learning and work which reproduce assumptions about the social distribution of knowledge and the legitimacy of this distribution and associated rewards. Within these models, what people with disabilities offer is frequently construed in terms of deficits rather than strengths and their 'human capital' is devalued. This chapter directs readers to consider similarities as well as differences in the labour market experiences of different 'marginalized' groups.

While several of the chapters in this section explore the barriers facing some of these groups, others emphasize agency and possibilities for resistance both at institutional and individual levels. For example, Mirchandani et al. note that immigrant women did resist exploitative relations at work although this resistance tended to be individual. This brings us back to Sawchuk's comment about possibilities for worker resistance through the collectivization of knowledge.

Together, the chapters in this section effectively explore factors that affect transitions of workers in all their diversity and point to contradictions and tensions within knowledge economy discourse. They thereby begin the process of collectivizing the kind of knowledge that can hopefully lead to resistance and democratic change in learning and work.

PETER H. SAWCHUK

10. OCCUPATIONAL TRANSITIONS WITHIN WORKPLACES UNDERGOING CHANGE: A CASE FROM THE PUBLIC SECTOR

INTRODUCTION

While it is increasingly recognized that learning and transitions do not stop once people gain entry into the labour market, this chapter orients to the transitions that continue to occur within occupational and organizational life. The addition of research on this dimension is essential for putting flesh on the observation that learning/work transitions are not only non-linear but variegated, complicated and deeply interwoven with the nature of work and economy as well. Indeed, neither vocational, education-to-work, nor career transitions research has adequately developed detailed empirical assessments of these intra-institutional instances of transitions. And in an era in which organizational restructuring is increasingly the norm, virtually no research has sought to illuminate the multiple layers of transitions that take place within workplaces as individuals, work processes, technologies and, in the case of the research reported in this chapter, whole occupational categories undergo change.

What we'll see in this chapter is that under such conditions workers undertake extended and differentiated career transitions in the course of training and particularly on-the-job informal learning. The analysis is based on research detailing changes that have occurred in public sector welfare benefits delivery work in Ontario (Canada) since 2002, and how different aspects of these changes can be understood in terms of learning-work transitions. The changes that commenced in 2002 were part of a large-scale work process and technological initiative that changed the nature of welfare work in this province undertaken by an aggressive conservative government seeking to find cost-savings.[1] The research is based on 75 in depth interviews across three, representative regional office clusters as well as a province-wide survey of workers experiences (n = 336). In this chapter, I focus on the occupational/organizational learning-work transitions with special attention to the distinct experiences and patterns of learning of veteran and new benefits workers. In both cases, we see learning-work transitions shaped by the negotiation of treacherous waters of both a new job for some, and new learning for all affecting over 7,000 workers (and over 650,000 welfare recipients).

What emerges in the analysis is the inseparability of work and learning relations for attempts to understand the fullness of occupation transitions. Specifically, I show that multiple layers of transitions are rooted, in this case, in primarily informal

P. Sawchuk and A. Taylor (eds.), Challenging Transitions in Learning and Work: Reflections on Policy and Practice, 189–207.

negotiation over the nature of work and the skills necessary to work effectively. In light of the difficulties with a new computer system and re-organization of the work system, this results in what in other project publications has been termed the emergent 'workaround culture' in welfare benefit delivery offices.

Amidst the occupational/organizational change process we see how veteran workers coped with the transitions. This group entered the occupation in an era in which 'home visits' and genuine 'people-based' social work dimensions of the job were central; an era in which work was managed by more experienced welfare benefits social workers who moved into supervisory roles and who could speak from experience on how to actually do the work effectively. Indeed, this was an era in which entry requirements for the job typically demanded post-secondary social work qualifications, and the need for computer literacy was negligible. Above all, this veteran group of workers appears to struggle to reconcile the transitions that now shape their occupation; a situation, as we'll see, in which extensive occupational knowledge of the past becomes a burden to dealing with the present and future. To cope with these challenges they turn toward and actively construct informal learning networks to share and develop 'workarounds' that allow the system to function. The unique features of this learning-work transition come most clearly into view when compared to the experiences of newcomers to the occupation. Lacking the lived experience of a people-oriented form of welfare social work, newcomers carried few if any of these burdens of institutional memory. With little basis for comparison, we see these workers, quite reasonably, embracing the new work/technological system. These workers are ambivalent about the current workload expectations which have grown. They are equally ambivalent about new supervisor arrangements in which those who manage must do so in traditional ways that focus less on occupational problem solving and more on performance output, given their lack of working knowledge of the new work and technological systems. Moreover, generational difference has granted the younger newcomers higher levels of computer literacy – a new addition to the entry requirements of the occupation. These are entry requirements which have also been progressively down-graded to secondary school since the implementation of the new work/technological system. However, it's important to note that the informal learning networks that the veteran workers have come to rely on so heavily are not always equally available to the newcomers. The under-belly of informal learning structures, of course, is that they depend largely on past relationships, friendships, shared outlooks – what I refer to in Sawchuk (2003) as the dynamics of 'membership'. In turn, the emerging isolation of newcomers from veterans plays a role in solidifying their differences in terms of an overall vision of the nature of the work they perform. In sum, I argue that the learning-work transitions that take place following occupational entry are complex and diverse, and that the nature of work cannot be separate from analyses of learning-work transitions – least of all when those transitions occur within an occupational/work system undergoing transformation itself.

This chapter addresses the 'new world' of welfare benefits work in Ontario demonstrating how employees and employers bargain, formally and most frequently in this context informally, over entry requirements, conditions of work, and the distribution of rewards including career progression. We will see the unique distribution of vulnerabilities across new and more established workers alike, and draw some broader suggestions on the importance of recognizing work/technological labour processes in assessing notions of transition. Below, I begin with a brief review of the literature on learning-work transitions in which I show the gap in considerations of intra-occupational/organizational transitions generally. I indicate that only a small clusters of studies have meaningfully registered the types of dynamics I focus on here. Following this, I turn our attention to the welfare benefits workers in which interview data are presented across several analytic themes which expose the differentiated and differentiating experiences of transitions in a workplace undergoing change. Here I deal with entry level requirements, the practices of veteran and newcomers to the occupation including their distinct visions of the purpose of the work itself, and finally I highlight the dynamics of informal learning networks. I then both test and extend the qualitative findings through a brief analysis of a province-wide survey which contextualizes the comments made by individual workers in terms of aggregate findings. Here we see emphasized a startling paradox of the new economy the implementation of an advanced web-based computer technology, that when paired with a new Taylorized[2] division of labour, makes knowing more about one's work a barrier to coping.

SITUATING ORGANIZATIONAL/OCCUPATIONAL TRANSITIONS WITHIN THE LITERATURE

Of the fairly massive youth oriented school-to-work Canadian and international literature[3], only a small proportion can be said to inform the issue of entry-level workers' experiences upon arriving in the workplace. In this regard, scholars have increasingly recognized that the linear notion of transitions bears little relation to reality (e.g., Wyn and Dwyer, 2000; Anisef, Axelrod, Baichman-Anisef, James and Turrittin, 2000; Heinz, 1998, 2002; Staff and Mortimer, 2003). In this chapter, however, this arrival in an occupation/organization is not the end of the story. Rather learning – indeed as most of the literature indicates rhetorically, an extremely important part of occupational learning – occurs post-entry as the person engages in forms of career development within a sector or organization.

In general terms, mainstream literature that has oriented to occupational transitions has argued that narrow, occupational specific knowledge and skill sets have become less important. Replacing them are abilities related to independence, critical evaluation, conflict resolution and team-work (see discussion by Lehmann, 2000). Herein lies a key theme in what has been called the 'new vocationalism' perspective that largely dominates the learning-work transitions literature; centred as it is on compliant adaptation to the needs of capital vis-à-vis the individual development of 'human capital'.[4] These perspectives have their intellectual roots in the rise of post-industrialism thinking in the of the early 1970s forward in which there has been a consistent presumption that of the need for increasingly high levels of formal, post-secondary education for occupational and life course success in a post-industrial or knowledge economy (e.g., Touraine, 1971; Bell, 1973; Zuboff,

1988; Frenkel, Korczynski, Shire and Tam, 1999). From this perspective, changing skill requirements in the workplace caused by new technologies and different organizational structures are said to emphasize individuality, problem-solving skills, and promote the idea that all workers need to be symbolic analysts or knowledge workers (e.g., Reich, 1991; Grubb, 1996). The contradiction that underlie the comparison of post-industrial thinking, human capital approaches and the 'new vocationalism', on the one hand, and a 'critical vocationalism' on the other is pronounced; and this contradiction includes the experiences of and structures of work and economy specifically as Lehmann and Taylor (2003) point out:

> The reality behind this rhetoric, however, reveals a couple of problems. First, while such a knowledge worker would be characterised by initiative, flexibility and the ability and courage to question the status quo, most vocational education, according to Kincheloe (1999), is still designed to 'instill compliance and facilitate social control' (p. 148). Second, the majority of workplaces continues to be organized around Taylorist principles of control, or are engaged in various forms of re-Taylorisation in response to market deregulation (Bosch, 2000). Therefore, the extent to which students' new-found skills are likely to be actually utilised in the workplace is questionable. (p. 63)

Thus far, then, we've seen a gap in understandings of transitions. This gap revolves around what, exactly, it is that happens upon entry to a job which we can extend to include the relations of learning, intra-occupational/organizational transitions and career development. In this context, the new vocationalism perspective suggests the importance of a range of new social/knowledge work skills that are replacing older, narrower more specialized ones while the critical vocationalism perspective opens up a discussion of the structures of work itself in order to understand the learning-work transition with an emphasis on the conflictual nature of the labour process and economic relations more broadly. However, what happens when the workplace, indeed, the entire occupation, is undergoing transition? In the era of regular organizational re-structuring, this cannot be seen as simply a side-line issue. Rather, now, it must be seen as a *de facto* feature of work life as well as learning-work transition processes.

In this chapter I focus on such periods of change. However, in addition, what we see is an instance which runs counter to the post-industrial, human capital and new vocationalist perspectives. That is, a case in which – despite the introduction of an advanced, web-based computer system (*sine qua non* of the knowledge economy) – in the course of rationalizing the labour process what is sacrificed is not simply the opportunity for workers to use knowledge and skill they've developed in their occupational training (in this case Social Work)[5] but that, as incredible as it might seem, educational requirements are actually lowered because work has shifted from professional or semi-professional to clerical. While the skills of independence, critical evaluation, conflict resolution and team-work are clearly in play, they are just a clearly not in play in the way that mainstream perspectives presume. That is, these skills are far more likely than not are developed in the course of working against rather than in harmony with the existing work/technological system.

Analyses from either new vocationalist or critical vocationalist perspectives are not, however, the only bodies of research that bear on the topic at hand. There is also some scholarship focused on career theory and career transitions which should be registered. Career theory and its related areas of empirical investigation have been a staple in Human Resource Development and Organizational Behaviour literature going back at least 50 years where Wilensky (1961, 1964) summarizes the state-of-the-art at that time, rooted deeply in the economic optimism, cooperation and highly structural organizational conditions that characterize much of the first quarter century following the World War Two. Since Wilensky, however, the field has become increasingly organized by psychological orientation paired with a relatively unquestioned alignment with the needs of management for cooperation and control. A review of contributions to the several handbook-style collections in the area that have emerged over the last two decades or so (Arthur, Hall and Lawrence, 1989; Kummerow, 2000; Feldman, 2002) confirms that, since Wilensky's analysis, a great deal has changed. We can note for example a general split between more optimistic accounts of 'boundary-less' careers unencumbered by restrictive organizational structures (e.g. Arthur and Rousseau 1996), and others which illuminate negative changes based on the degradation of occupational laddering (Osterman 1996).

For our purposes here, however, there is a need to take a closer look at career theory's contribution to understanding the learning/work transition within process of occupational/organizational change. Baruch (2006) offers a recent, extended review of the career theory literature with attention to both individual responses and organizational contexts. Though rooted firmly in the post-industrial and new vocationalism school, Baruch indicates that the nature of organizational change is central to how people construct and understand their occupational careers and work.

> Among the changes that have shaped contemporary career systems are developments in the social and economical [*sic*] realms, as well as in individual identities. Global *macro-economic and social forces* provided impetus for a growing number of global careers, for introduction of females and minorities to the full range of roles (albeit discrimination still clearly prevails), for major *restructuring of organizations, and generally a less stable business environment*. At the micro-level, they are coupled by a development in *norms, values and attitudes to life and work*, which are manifested in new behaviors of individuals… On the one hand, the career is the *'property' of the individual*, who may be inspired by new social norms, but on the other hand, for employed people, it is *planned and managed to a large extent by their organizations*. (p. 126; emphasis added)

Baruch (2006) then points us in the direction of the linkages between macro-economics and socio-political change, the role of restructuring which has become prevalent, as well as the dialectic between individual careers and their management vis-à-vis organizations. All these are crucial elements to recognize in the intra-occupational/organizational learning-work transitions at issue here. The bulk of Baruch's review goes on to challenge confirmed dichotomies that characterize the field as a whole: organizational order vs. chaos; boundaryless vs. traditionally structured careers; organizational vs. individual origins of development; and, external vs. internal sources of meaning and occupational success. Indeed, as the author shows, there simply are no clean, dichotomous lines to be drawn between such factors. Clearly, the elements that Baruch (2006) directs our attention to will be relevant to the analysis below as newer and more experienced workers struggle to make sense of their own emerging occupational life and their relations with others.

Analyses emerging from either the new vocationalism perspective or career theory have not, to date, effectively grappled with conditions through which organizational change leads the reconstruction of occupational trajectories. The critical vocationalism approach, however, has raised such questions consistently, though detailed studies of the type offered here have not been forthcoming. In the context of the research presented below I ask several key questions beginning with the following: How does organizational restructuring, impose by macro-economic and socio-political forces shape the individual/organizational management of occupational change? I argue that answers to this other important questions begin to emerge in the qualitative analysis below.

QUALITATIVE ANALYSIS AND DISCUSSION: THE TENSIONS OF TRANSITIONS WITHIN WELFARE BENEFITS WORK

Changes to Initial Qualification for Entry

It seems sensible to begin our analysis at the entry point to the welfare benefits occupation, and as I've noted earlier, things have changed in this regard with the implementation of the new work/technological system. In fact, the formal entry qualifications for welfare work in Ontario have fluctuated significantly over the last 30 years. While some variation remains, in the past there was even greater variation in the way that local municipal units established and put into practice entry requirements for new welfare workers. In fact, in earlier times both formal and informal entry requirements responded much more closely to internal and local labour markets supply. That is, where higher qualifications were more abundant in the local labour market (typically, though not exclusively in large urban areas) entry requirement qualification tended to be higher. In addition, it was not uncommon to find welfare work taking in workers within municipal government who were either downsized in other departments or those who were simply wishing to move into different types of work but who also had the advantage of being an internal candidate in hiring practices governed by collective agreements.

In general terms, however, mirroring the lower educational achievement in the province generally, it can be said that from late 1960s to the late 1980s the minimal qualifications were most likely a secondary school diploma, an orientation to working with people and a good attitude. And, from the late 1980s up until the 2002, welfare work showed a marked heightening of minimal qualifications to begin to include professional social work and related social science credentials (university-based or college-based with some additional work experience). In addition, further background in related social services (child care, corrections, counseling, etc.) seemed to become more important were important.

Since 2002 with the implementation of the new work/technology system, another distinct shift has taken place. While vestiges of local municipal control still accounted for some persistent differences across office clusters, in the first phase of implementation minimal functional qualifications continued to include relevant university and college credentials, but our interview data suggest that emphasis on related social services experience and social work related credentials began to decline. In their place, in keeping the overall occupational changes, computer literacy and specifically 'data processing' experience or related credentials have grown in importance. In fact, we see that for new workers admitted under these different conditions of qualification, transitions into these reconfigured job sets has, on the surface, been relatively smooth in terms of the formal work requirements. That is, they can adequately use the software quite quickly.

This study's interviews inquired into this issues directly.[6] Veteran workers such as the one below who has 10 years seniority contextualize the changes in entry requirements and described things this way.

> **I:** Okay. When you first received the job or when you first applied, what were the formal qualifications that they asked for?
> **S:** You had to have a college or university degree or diploma. Preferably in college they would accept a Social Service Worker Diploma; otherwise it had to be a university degree in Social Work. That was, I think, the primary one, preferably a background in social services but…They've since changed the qualifications and that's what they emphasize more.
> **I:** They emphasize the interpersonal?
> **S:** More the administrative, interpersonal and certainly technical… [in terms of my own background] other than the fact that I was pretty comfortable using a computer, I had taken key – about that time it was called "Typing" in high school, that kind of thing. That definitely was a benefit. And the fact that I was fairly comfortable with computers, they didn't scare me. And I had a computer at home. So I was able – even, like, there were some people who had never literally never touched a mouse before. So the fact that I knew my way around a computer and was comfortable, that was probably one of the biggest things. And the fact that I had really good interviewing skills. It wasn't like I had to learn, like, in the case of some of the new people, they're learning how to interview, especially because they've changed the requirements. They have people who are, like, right now are clerks becoming workers. They don't have the background necessarily in interviewing, and in case management and in all that kind of – in case fields and writing up summaries and that kind of thing that I did. So – you see, I have a BSW [Bachelors of Social Work]. So I had a lot of that training. It was just the technology that I had to learn versus the whole job…. Right now, like I said, mostly it's feeding the information into the computer. I have a social work degree. I don't need social work to be doing overpayment work, right? So

> even as a case manager, all of these – and you can see it in the notes of the newer workers, it's – putting the information on the computer, clients say they haven't worked in eight years. That's it. (HMLAT0303)

In this context, many established workers noted feelings of anger in connection to the changes in entry requirements linking this inherently to the change in the work process as a whole. These workers (both 13 years seniority and post-secondary credentials in social work) commented as follows:

> The qualification of our job description, it is now I guess grade 12 minimum. And I'm very angry about that...People in the office, they've gone through college and university courses and they've had to take out OSAP loans because it was a requirement and I myself think that you need some sort of professional training in order to do the job. What's been happening is they've been taking clerical staff and making them into workers and I'm very angry about that. (HIMAT0404)

> **I:** So these practical skills, is it fair to say they stressed more of a social work type more than the technical thing back then?
> **S:** Yes because you would be going out and seeing them and they would be in crisis or whatever. This seems more data entry, just the facts.
> **I:** They stress more now when they hire people than the social work?
> **S:** Oh yes, they do have the computer skills; I mean that was never asked when we started. (HKMAT0404)

Amongst the things implicated here is a divide between veteran workers and newcomers, firmly established through a combination of work process change, a new technological system which, in turn, encouraged a re-structuring of entry level requirements.

Veteran and Newcomer Experiences

Learning-work transitions within occupational groups and organizations undergoing change are shaped by the entry requirements, but this is only one factor shaping how occupational development takes place. For newcomers, transitions from novice to experienced worker in an organization are deeply shaped by informal learning on-the-job. Just as important for all workers – new and experienced – informal learning networks are also an important factor in describing the overall transition process of the occupation as a whole. The differentiated experiences of newcomers and veterans matters in this regard. Having heard from veteran workers in the previous section on entry requirements, it make sense to hear now from newcomers who describe an uneven, though still clearly detectable divide that has emerged in terms of on-the-job learning.

This worker has only two years seniority and contrasts his experience with veterans. He begins with an elementary point shared by all workers, that management no longer has the capacity to manage based on their knowledge and experience, and later we get a clear sense of the divide that exists in many offices that, ultimately, shapes the career trajectories of newer workers. By the close of the excerpt, however, we also get a glimpse at the specific vision of this reconfigured welfare benefits work from a newcomer's standpoint.

> **S:** Quite frankly many of the managers, not to even slag them, but many of the managers haven't done a Case Manager role in I don't know how many years. Way beyond 10 years, if not, some of them have never done the Case Manager's role with the advent of SDMT.[7] They all done it, quote-unquote, 'on the road' when you know it was easy to do 6 applications a day and get everything done. You could get all your work done and you physically have the cheques here, so and so forth. It's a whole new world since then… I'm not going to belabor the point because I'm sure from the interviews you've had before and 99% what I would think, there's probably a pro and con with SDMT. I like some aspects and because as I said it's the only one I know. I can't compare it to CIMS or CWT, I haven't utilized those formats but I like certain things with SDMT. I like the way it's laid out. I can see everything at a glance with the flick of a button. It's easy to read. I have seen CIMS and CWT and just the way that they formatted it, I find it unclear to read. Everything is the same. There is no highlighted drop downs. With the access buttons and what not [with SDMT], I think that's great. They didn't have that in the previous two but apparently the people who have utilized that say it was more user-friendly. As I said, I can't speak to that but I find that SDMT is quite easy to get around so I find it easy in that respect… Seeing 60 people in a month for example is not an issue for me… Now they lowered [the educational requirements for the job to] grade 12 as I mentioned earlier. You'll get a divided response on how many people think it's a bad thing versus a good thing. Some people think that if you only have grade 12 you can't do this job—that's not true.
> **I:** Just a couple of questions I want to ask you on the previous section. So you feel your job is more oriented, toward a social work kind of feel rather than a clerical office worker?
> **S:** No that's not what I'm stating at all—actually quite the opposite. I reinforce to my participants that I am not a social worker. I work in a Social Service job. I am not a social worker I am an administrator, it says on my stamp Administrator of Ontario Works, that I would agree with. I administer things in a more of a clerical function than actually being a social worker.
> **I:** And is that something for you that there is a little bit of disappointment when you first worked, you thought it would be a little closer to more of social work type thing?
> **S:** Heck no, that's what I wanted… I was ready for a straight desk jockey, administering funds, that was not problem… I wanted it to be more administrative than hands on, hands on, that's a social work job…I like this. (HGWAT0404)

A significant of number of newcomers expressed this level of comfort with the technology. Many others expressed a comfort, if not a preference, for the administrative and data-processing dimensions of the job over the 'social work' aspects.

But, it would be a mistake to paint either newcomers or veterans with the same brush. In fact, some divisions amongst newcomers revolved around the degree to which they saw the 'people side' and the 'social work' aspect of the work necessary, despite little or no first-hand experience in doing it.

Veteran workers were equally likely in our interview samples to speak directly to the differences between them and newcomers, though there are some important differences. Many felt that their experience empowered them in the face of newcomers who are overly reliant on the technology in order to not only understand the job but to do it. Below, in our look at some quantitative data, we'll test the degree to which these and other views are shared, but for now we can examine the comments of this veteran worker.

> It's different now because if this goes down, we're in trouble, we're in big trouble. I'm okay because I know how to do everything manually but it's double the work and you're finished because you have all the manual information but now you have to input it yourself onto the computer. I think we're too dependent on the technology myself. I think we got a lot more done when it was hands on and you just wrote everything out which is wonky but… (HIMAT0404)

Many other veterans, however, noted challenges to their occupational knowledge with the new system; challenges that, for workers such as this one (22 years seniority) who is nearing retirement, held only moderate interest.

> **I:** How have the changes affected professional relations in terms of communication with clients?
> **S:** The only sense that's changed is I feel less confident with what I'm telling them and a lot of what I have to discuss with them undermines my confidence with respect to my job because I have to tell them, you know what, you can ignore that letter because the system doesn't know that you're receiving ODSP and because you're receiving OW it automatically sends the letter. Toronto has to change that process—I can't and in 3 years they haven't decided it's critical to change that process so it's a waste my time to them. That undermines my credibility. To tell someone, ignore something the system has done—that's a bit bizarre to me.
> **I:** Since the work changes have been implemented have you taken part in any education or training program or courses related to your work and/or SDMT specifically?
> **S:** No, because I'm like within 18 months of retirement so I'm not really interested. (HJBAT0404)

Indeed, a wide array of interviewees recalled instances in which the implementation of the new work/technological system had been a contributing factor to early retirement. In the interview data, computer literacy was discussed frequently in this regard, though as we'll see from the quantitative analysis, on the aggregate this may not have played as important a role as many seemed to believe. More likely, as a report that emerged within the first year of the implementation of changes focusing on stress and coping under the new work/technological system

(Lewchuk, 2002) indicates, a complex of factors is at play in determining what learning-work transitions emerge, and for whom. This analysis suggests issues of stress and workload are clearly involved, but also matters related to visions that veteran workers in particular hold for the purpose of their work in serving people in crisis as well as, possibly, an even deeper conflict expressing a tension between prior forms of occupational knowledge and restrictive work systems.

In turning towards a comparison of the contrasting visions of the purpose of one's work, we already can reflect back on the young worker we heard from first in this section who preferred (indeed, he only knew of the job in terms of) the data processing and administrative dimensions. However, this job was once and to a limited degree still is oriented by more than simply using the software. A newcomer with only a year of experience prior to the implementation of the new work/technological system comments on the nature of her work this way:

> **I:** Would you say that the current system is more efficient or less efficient [than the previous system you worked with]?
> **S:** I think it's more efficient. I like it… Because I don't have a problem and I pick this up very easy so I was whipping through it pretty good. Maybe a couple of weeks to get comfortable but like I said in the beginning when they were ironing out everything we had to sometimes do like a workaround because it wasn't working the way they expected. Basically you need to be able to know how to get through the screens. You have to know how to navigate through the screens comfortably otherwise it's going to take you longer to do the job.
> **I:** Finally, I'd like you to describe one of the most recent problems you've encountered in doing your work, and how you went about solving it.
> **S:** I had one that I was doing for somebody else and we were trying to grant him something and he was ongoing with Ontario Disability but he was supposed to be removed but there wasn't anything that I could do. I ended up being a ticket that had to go to Toronto. I didn't learn anything from it.
> **I:** In your personal view, should the new work system be: kept as it is, removed altogether and return to the previous work system, adjusted based on managerial/consultant control; adjusted through new forms of worker involvement in design, or create a new system based on forms of ongoing worker participation?
> **S:** Kept as it is. (HKDAT040)

This type of account was common for newcomers who understood their job frequently as 'getting through the screens'. The downside for this is hinted at in the close of the excerpt however, where the problem of a disabled client in need barely registers with the worker who concludes not only that there was simply 'wasn't anything that [she] could do' but that in addition little was to be learned from the problem. The type of comment lies in distinct contrast to the accounts provided commonly across the more veteran workers. The one immediately below, for example, who like many others consistently ask uncomfortable questions of the new changes.

> **S:** Who's going to suffer? The client is going to suffer and none of us went into this work on the grounds that we wanted to work with some cumbersome piece of technology. We went into this work because of what's behind the technology and it's the individuals that we deal with and our desire to help people.
> **I:** And that is going to be one of the key points of your work—that everybody that goes into this line of work—you're a Social Worker and it implies social and doesn't imply technology.
> **S:** And I said that to my clients a million times. I'm going to be perfectly honest, I sit there and they say you do an awful lot of typing into that thing and it's like yeah and you know what, I though I went into Social Work because I wanted a people job. I've got a computer job. (NF17DB0304)

What becomes clear in looking across the qualitative data is that there are distinct, though not absolute, differences in the entry process of veteran and newcomers which dove-tails with different visions of work and assessments of its purpose.

Informal Structure of Work and its Role in Occupational Transitions

Extending analyses of learning-work transitions into concerns for the nature of occupations and experiences in organizations undergoing transitions themselves, we see a complex and uneven process. Under the types of 'structured career progression' described by the career theory literature from Wilensky (e.g., 1961) forward we expect to find that organizational conditions matter and that a change in structure impacts the career transitions from newcomer to veteran. That is, with changing organizational conditions we expect to see changing patterns through which career development and transitions occur. In the case of this research on welfare work in Ontario, particularly under the specific conditions of technological failure of the SDMT system, a new 'workaround culture' has clearly emerged. And, under these conditions, informal learning arises as the key structure that dictates forms of occupational knowledge development and occupational transition.

What we heard from veterans as oppose to newcomers was quite different, raising the question of what kind of intra-occupational and intra-organizational transitions could be expected under the current conditions. The picture that emerges in interviews with veteran workers suggested some consistent trends through which the change in the work system encouraged not only a workaround culture but also a culture of expanded informal learning networks for occupational knowledge development. Workers with 12 and 6 years seniority in their positions respectively, explained it this way.

> I can see a lot of the more informal like water cooler talking now, and you know it happens like if I had a case, for example, and I don't know how to do something I would ask somebody: Have you ever had this before? And they'd say: 'Oh yes, this is what I did' I've learned a lot more short cuts, so here I am doing it the long way all this time and then somebody just happens to see me and says, 'What are you doing it that way for? Just press this button'. I've had a lot of those. (SC1DB0303)

> Between each other—we, in our office, we have a buddy system where we kind of cover for each other and take care of each other quite often. Like in my little group there is four of us and we work really well together because we're in our own little huddle over there. (NF17DB0304)

Clearly the changes compelled an informal learning response from the worker. These networks generally developed in isolation from management, as one worker above notes in her comments, in part conditioned by the fact that managers rarely had practical experience and expertise to share given the new-ness of the system.

For newcomers, however, things appeared to be quite different. What we see is that, caught in the tension between differential entry qualification, different educational backgrounds, a relative lack of comparative, occupational experiences, and finally, reflecting all of this, distinctive visions of the purpose of welfare work itself, access to informal networks was, in effect, often restricted for newcomers. Comments from a few workers give us insight into this. Each of these workers had less than 2 and half years on the job.

> **I:** How does the system affect the way that co-workers work/communicate together?
> **S:** My experience – I was hired at the same time as 8 other people and sort of became friends with those other people and all our experiences were very different depending on the team we were assigned to. I was assigned to a team that was very cliquey and very run to the supervisor for everything, a very unfriendly team, which is known through the entire organization. So in terms of team work, I would ask a lot of questions and not get a lot of help. In terms of the software SDMT, most people were so busy it felt like their workload tripled, and they just didn't have the time to help out somebody that was new, never mind fix the problems that I created, which was very easy to do with SDMT, it was easy to issue cheques… So it terms of teamwork its very cliquey and depends on the team. Other co-workers had very helpful and experienced team members. (HAAAT0403)

> **S:** I have to resource myself.
> **I:** What do you mean you have to resource yourself?
> **S:** Well if I have to speak to someone I will go find my information while if you're a younger person and more shy, maybe it might be more difficult… For me it doesn't make any difference. I'm very social and outgoing so I'll go and talk to anybody, whether they're on my team or not. I know that there have been some people that have resentment between a person having this type of work compared to the other work—it seems to have divided some people.
> **I:** When you say resentment toward people that have this kind of work, what do you mean?
> **S:** Well like some people are in Verification so they feel that they, they might feel that their job is not quite as important as Case Managing or a Case Manager might feel that the person doing verification has an easier time with the job. (HJAAT0404)

The interview data reveal a clear, if not absolute, pattern. Many newcomers, as in the excerpt immediately above, found their way into these occupational networks. However, many others appeared to not have.

QUANTITATIVE ANALYSIS AND DISCUSSION: CONTEXTUALIZING QUALITATIVE FINDINGS WITH THE PROVINCIAL SURVEY

Having a sense of the meaning that individual workers made of their situation across several thematic areas, it now makes sense to take some time to test some of the key points against the aggregate data provided by the study's province-wide welfare worker survey (n = 336). This survey sampled worker views through a mail-in questionnaire, distributed to workers with an eye toward representing potentially relevant effects of geographical region and different sized offices in the summer of 2005. Response rate for this was just over 30%. Important in the context of the discussion in this chapter, the survey revealed that approximately 17% of current welfare workers were hired since the new system went live in 2002. Twenty four percent of workers sampled were under 35 years old, with 1% of the sample (3 cases) under 25. Separate but linked to age, 18% of the sample had less than 4 years seniority. Twenty four percent of the sample had completed high-school or less in terms of their educational background. Thirty five percent had completed university (with 3% holding a graduate degree). The rest had some completed college diplomas.

A key dynamic that emerges from our survey is that, in opposition to the rhetoric and common sense views of those proclaiming a 'new' and/or 'knowledge economy' and the persistent linkage of such proclamations with the use of advanced ICT, we see something startling. Workers with more experience and greater occupational knowledge – inclusive of a strong institutional memory and orientation to broader purpose of welfare benefits delivery work – actually found the transition to the new work/technological system harder. This is verified in a number of ways that were statistically significant.

More specifically, our survey gathered information on number of years spent in the position. We get a clear sense of the startling learning/knowledge/experience dynamics that emerged out of the transition. The survey showed that 47% of those with 4.5 years or less in their current positions responded that the system was 'easy to learn' where as just 22.5% of those with over 16 years in their current position responded in this way.[8] We see the pattern reproduced for responses to whether the system was 'hard to learn' [just 24% of the newer workers and almost half (49%) of the senior workers indicated this]. The pattern repeats yet again when we compare ease/hardness of learning across overall seniority in the bargaining unit. Presumably this would indicate a broader level of experience in welfare work, perhaps inclusive of different positions. Here we see 60% of those with less than 4 years seniority indicating the system was easy to use (11% indicating it was difficult), and 24.2% of those with 20 or more years of seniority indicating the system was easy to use (56.8% indicating it was difficult). And again, when we check the pattern on the basis of age (as opposed to years in the same position or seniority) we see that those who are younger are more likely to report that learning the system was easy compared to older workers. Half (50%) of respondents between 25 and 34 reported learning the system as easy (22% indicating it was hard to learn) compared to slightly more than one third (38%) of those between 35 and 44 (34% indicating it was hard to learn) and less than one quarter (23%) of those between the ages of 45 and 54 (40% indicating it was hard to learn). While the differences in terms of years in the same position were not statistically significant, those relating to age ($p < 0.01$) and particularly the difference related to seniority ($p < 0.001$) were.

An immediate question which would reasonably arise – indeed one raised by our interview data – concerns the issue of computer literacy levels as partially or wholly responsible for these differences. In terms of reported computer literacy levels across respondents we saw that those who had lower levels found the new system only marginally easier or harder to learn (though the difference was statistically significant at the 0.001 level). That is, 28% of those with low computer literacy indicated the system was easy to learn versus 31% of those with high levels of computer literacy. Interestingly enough, neither did overall education attainment show any substantive role in explaining who found the system easy or hard to learn.

Perhaps most directly important of our cross-tabulations reported here are the effects of the number of different, prior computer systems used by respondents in benefits delivery work in the past. This was cross-tabulated with both ease/ hardness of learning as well as subjective ratings of flexibility/inflexibility of the system. In the case of the first set of variables we see that, consistently, the more experience you had with different benefit delivery computer system prior to the SDMT the more difficult you found the current system to learn. The number of systems, in this regard, were categorized as follows: no previous systems; one other previous system; two previous systems; and then more than two were categorized as three or more. Half (51%) of those who had not used any other computer system rated the current SDMT system as easy to learn whereas less than one third (31%) of those who had used three or more systems rated the SDMT system as easy to use; a difference which was significant at the 0.05 level. Likewise, those who have worked on other systems in the past are more likely to rate the SDMT system as 'inflexible' compared to those who had not worked on other systems. More specifically, less than one fifth of respondents (17%) who had used only SDMT found it to be inflexible compared to nearly half or more than half of respondents who had used either one, two or three or more systems in the past (47%, 53%, and 51%, respectively; $p < 0.01$ level).

These findings begin to suggest several major dynamics in the occupational career transition process that have not been adequately recognized in the literature to date. At first glance a somewhat elementary observation but one clearly absent from the literature on occupational transitions, that the traditional notions of labour market entry through to initiation, establishment of core occupational expertise and maturing mastery have been in this case markedly affected by the organizational change process. Second and more specifically, what emerges across these findings is a reversal of the common sense logic of career development and transitions in the post-industrial, new vocationalist, and particularly, the human capital perspective.

That is, this analysis suggests that the more skill, knowledge and experience one has on the job (controlling for both computer literacy skills or general educational attainment) the more difficult it was to expand that knowledge base. Younger, less senior and less experienced workers, on the other hand, reported much less difficulty in arrangements against which they had little or no basis of comparison. Third, there emerges a need to more fully understand the forces that shape different experiences and different responses to a specific work system changes and the occupational development and transitions involved where such contexts appear to some as having undergone radical change while appearing to others as simply the state of affairs on the beginning of an occupational trajectory. More specifically, a question which arises is how do more experienced workers orienting to (and, in some sense burdened by) a historical vision of their work find themselves in a contradictory relationships to knowledge and skill forms associated with an alternative labour process? Additionally, how does this relate to the on-the-job, and largely informalized, occupational development process in which veterans and newcomers must interact? Are such informal learning networks affected by new workers, who as we have seen in our discussion of the interview data, may or may not (yet) share a basic orientation to the occupation's past, present or future that is consistent with more veteran workers?

CONCLUSIONS

As the literature on learning-work transitions has recognized, clearly, transitions don't end once people obtain a job, and this may even be the case if they remain in that job. Research on this aspect of transitions, however, has not dealt adequately with the contemporary conditions of organizational change which are so common today.

Drawing on original welfare worker research, I described and analyzed an example of a specific occupational/organizational learning-work transitions process with multiple layers. The specific nature of the work change was contradictory; a situation that is increasingly normal for workers today (see Littler and Innes, 2003) but regularly ignored by post-industrial, new vocationalism and human capital scholars. In this specific case, driven by government austerity influenced by both neo-liberal ideology and global economic realities, this contradiction entailed the combination of advanced web-based computer systems with a traditional Taylorized division of labour. The result was to use advanced technology to, in effect, *vivisect* an occupation into discrete, clerical and data-entry functions. Here workers with the institutional memory lament the transition to a less people-oriented, 'social work' oriented job, and newcomers struggle to gain access to the informal networks essential to their own occupational development amidst a largely accepted, truncated vision of welfare work defined by 'moving through screens' and administering funds. Fueled by differential entry requirements, and differential historical memory, the informal structure of access and opportunity became increasingly important and distinguished a separation between veteran and new workers.

The survey results both challenged and confirmed qualitative findings. The survey revealed that presumptions by both veteran and new workers that low computer literacy levels were to blame for the difficulties that veteran workers experienced did not hold up to scrutiny. Though it does seem that the newer and particularly the younger workers did have greater comfort using the new computer system, computer literacy levels did not, in fact, correlate with difficulty in learning the new system for veteran workers. Nevertheless, the survey did confirm, in other ways, differences in veteran and newcomer responses across our provincial sample. Perhaps startling for those presuming the accumulation of human capital can be tabulated irrespective of labour processes or that the introduction of high tech computer systems necessarily entails entry into the preferred realms of a 'new'/'knowledge' economy were the multiple findings that showed the more prior occupational knowledge a worker had the more likely they were to indicate difficulty and inflexibility in the work system.

As a type of (albeit large) occupational 'case study' the research reported here leaves something to be desired. We have no way of knowing, at this point, how prevalent such forms of transition are either in the public or private sector. Research on career dynamics sheds little light on this question, and traditional research from a critical vocationalism perspective only marginally more. Sociology of work and labour process literature, not discussed in this chapter, may be an option though the conceptualization of both individual and organizational change in this tradition has not typically sought to conceptualize such matters in terms of transitions, and nor have they typically oriented to issues of learning. Future studies of this kind, however, might look toward these traditions for inspiration, though not necessarily guidance in this regard. These matters aside, it becomes increasingly clear that analyses of work and learning relations are as inseparable from each other as they are essential for understanding the future occupational and organization-wide transitions.

NOTES

1. See earlier publications from this research for additional context in Hennessy and Sawchuk (2003), Hennessy (2004), Boutilier (2008) and Sawchuk (2009). For further conceptual development see Sawchuk (2006; 2007).
2. Taylorism refers to the Scientific Management system developed by Fredrick Taylor in the early 20th century which sought to use time-motion studies to break up tasks into smaller component units and separate conception of work processes from their execution. These principles were eventually expanded into industrial production organization commonly referred to as Fordism (after Henry Ford).
3. For Canadian literature see recent reviews in Gaskell and Rubenson (2004), Scheutze and Sweet (2003) and Krahn (1996). For internationally oriented reviews of literature see Shavit and Muller (1998), Stern and Wagner (1999), and especially the collection edited by Heinz (1999) which includes Canadian material.
4. For a recent summary of this 'new vocationalism' and human capital perspective in Canada see in particular the section one contributions to Gaskell and Rubenson (2004). For a grounded critique in the Canadian context see Taylor and Lehmann (2003), and in the US context see a book-length analysis in Kincheloe (1999).
5. See Livingstone (2004), Livingstone and Sawchuk (2004) for a review of the prevalence of this underutilization effect in the Canadian economy.
6. The initial 'I' indicates the interviewer speaking, and 'S' indicates the subject speaking.
7. SDMT (Service Delivery Model Technology) was the name of the web-based software that was used in conjunction with the work system change in Ontario welfare work.
8. Data originally based on five point likert scale question. Question reading "In your opinion, SDMT is [a) very easy to learn; b) easy to learn; c) not particularly easy or hard to learn; d) hard to learn; e) very hard to learn]. These categories were collapsed for this analysis to three: easy, neither; hard.

REFERENCES

Anisef, P., Axelrod, P., Baichman-Anisef, E., James, C., & Turrittin, A. (2000). *Opportunity and uncertainty: Life course experiences of the class of '73*. Toronto: University of Toronto Press.
Arthur, M., & Rousseau, D. (Eds.). (1996). *The boundaryless career*. New York: Oxford University Press.
Arthur, M. B., Hall, D. T., & Lawrence, B. S. (Eds.). (1989). *Handbook of career theory*. Cambridge: Cambridge University Press.
Baruch, Y. (2006). Career development in organizations and beyond: Balancing traditional and contemporary viewpoints. *Human Resource Management Review, 16*, 125–138.
Bell, D. (1973). *The coming of the post-industrial society*. New York: Basic Books.
Boutilier, D. (2008). *Working smarter and harder: An investigation of learning information technology in the Ontario public service sector*. Unpublished Doctoral Thesis, University of Toronto, Canada.
Feldman, D. (Ed.). (2002). *Work careers: A developmental perspective*. San Francisco: Jossey-Bass.
Frenkel, S., Korczynski, M., Shire, K., & Tam, M. (1999). *On the front live: Organization of work in the information economy*. Ithaca, NY: Cornell University Press.
Gaskell, J., & Rubenson, K. (Eds.). (2004). *Educational outcomes for the Canadian workplace: New frameworks for policy and research*. Toronto: University of Toronto Press.
Grubb, N. (1996). *Learning to work: The case for re-integrating job training and education*. New York: Russell Sage.
Heinz, W. (Ed.). (1999). *From education to work: Cross-national perspectives*. New York: Cambridge University Press.
Heinz, W. (2002). Transition discontinuities and the biographical shaping of early work careers. *Journal of Vocational Behaviour, 60*(2), 220–240.
Hennessy, T. (2004). *From doctor, lawyer to... glorified babysitter? The gendered nature of Ontario's welfare work reform*. Unpublished Masters Thesis, University of Toronto, Canada.
Hennessy, T., & Sawchuk, P. (2003). Worker responses to technological change in the Canadian public sector: Issues of learning and labour process. *Journal of Workplace Learning, 15*(7), 319–325.
Kincheloe, J. (1999). *How do we tell the workers?: The socioeconomic foundations of work and vocational education*. Boulder, CO: Westview Press.
Korczynski, M. (2002). *Human resource management in service work*. London: Palgrave.
Krahn, H. (1996). *School–work transitions: Changing patterns and research needs*. Ottawa: Applied Research Branch, Human Resources Development Canada.
Kummerow, J. (Ed.). (2000). *New directions in career planning and the workplace* (2nd ed.). Palo Alto, CA: Davies-Black Publishing.
Lehmann, W. (2000). Is Germany's dual system still a model for Canadian youth apprenticeship initiatives? *Canadian Public Policy-Analyse de Politiques, 26*(2), 225–240.
Lehmann, W., & Taylor, A. (2003). Giving employers what they want? New vocationalism in Alberta. *Journal of Education and Work, 16*(1), 45–67.
Lewchuk, W. (2002). *Workload, work organization and health outcomes: The Ontario disability support program*. Hamilton: McMaster University.
Littler, C., & Innes, P. (2003). Downsing and De-knowledging the Firm. *Work, Employment and Society, 17*(1), 73–100.
Osterman, P. (1996). *Broken ladders: Managerial careers in the new economy*. New York: Oxford University Press.
Reich, R. (1991). *The work of nations: Preparing ourselves for 21st century capitalism*. New York: Vintage.
Sawchuk, P. (2003). *Adult learning and technology in working-class life*. New York: Cambridge University Press.
Sawchuk, P. (2006). 'Use-Value' and the re-thinking of skills, learning and the labour process. *Journal of Industrial Relations, 48*(5), 593–617.
Sawchuk, P. (2007). Theories and methods for research on informal learning and work: Towards cross-fertilization. *Studies in Continuing Education, 29*(3), 34–48.
Sawchuk, P. (2009). Re-visiting Taylorism: Conceptual implications for lifelong learning, technology and work in the public sector. In D. W. Livingstone (Ed.), *Lifelong, lifewide: Exploring learning for paid and unpaid work*. New York: Routledge.

Schuetze, H., & Sweet, R. (Eds.). (2003). *Integrating school and workplace learning in Canada*. Montreal: McGill-Queens Press.

Shavit, Y., & Muller, W. (1998). *A comparative study of educational qualifications and occupational destinations*. New York: Oxford University Press.

Staff, J., & Mortimer, J. (2003). Diverse transitions from school to work. *Work and Occupations, 30*(3), 361–369.

Stern, D., & Wagner, D. (1999). *International perspectives on the school-towork transition*. Hampton Press.

Touraine, A. (1971). *The post-industrial society: Tomorrow's social history: Classes, conflicts and culture in the programmed society*. New York: Random House.

Wilensky, H. (1961). Careers, lifestyles, and social integration. *International Social Science Journal, 12*, 553–558.

Wilensky, H. (1964). The professionalization of everyone? *American Journal of Sociology, 70*, 137–158.

Wyn, J., & Dwyer, P. (2000). New patterns of youth transition in education. *International Social Science Journal*, *52*(2), 147–165.

Zuboff, S. (1988). *In the age of the smart machine: The future of work and power*. New York: Basic Books.

PAUL BÉLANGER AND STÉPHANE DANIAU

11. AMBIGUITIES IN CONTINUING EDUCATION AND TRAINING IN THE KNOWLEDGE ECONOMY:

The Biopharmaceutical Economic Sector

INTRODUCTION

The activities in the biopharmaceutical sector, which is one of the fastest growing segments of Quebec economy (Montréal International, 2001, 2006), involve "considerable knowledge input and use of highly specialized manpower."[1] Given such high scientific and technological density, this sector is, indeed, particularly heuristic to explore emerging patterns of lifelong learning in knowledge intensive industries.

How do structured and informal learning activities evolve in different work units of these organisations typical of the new economy, and respectively in their manufacturing units and research departments? Could we discern, in these different work contexts, particular learning patterns and logics? How these different adult learning patterns relates to distinct modes of production, including modes of scientific production?

To answer these questions,[2] we shall begin by presenting the enterprises under study and then draw a portrait of adult learning practices in these organisations; we will then be in better position to examine the relations between observed patterns of education and training activities, on one side, and, on the other, modes of production and different organisation of work.[3] If knowledge intensive sectors of the economy could offer a different picture of adult learning participation, what about the situation within each of these "new" firms? Is the knowledge intensity of the overall production engineering and process being translated in intensity and universality of learning opportunities within each organization? Such an examination of the possible differentiated reality of adult learning in new knowledge economy organizations will look not only at volume, content and type of learning activities and on their possible stratification, but also, and more deeply, at the logics running through these different learning practices and policies to be observed.

PORTRAIT OF THE SECTORS

The biopharmaceutical industry in Quebec is growing rapidly. Main international corporations have a presence in the province and many small and medium-sized companies gravitate around them; in fact, a total of about 160 enterprises are active

P. Sawchuk and A. Taylor (eds.), Challenging Transitions in Learning and Work: Reflections on Policy and Practice, 209–230.

in Quebec,[4] of which approximately 80% are located in the Greater Montreal area (Pharmabio Développement, 2004, 2006), and these companies account for a total of some 18,000 jobs (Montréal international, 2006).

Enterprises in the biopharmaceutical sector can be divided into four categories:

1. The large multinationals, which combine the whole process of bringing drugs to market from upstream research to creation and marketing of products;
2. The generic drug companies which produce and sometimes adapt existing drugs (usually grouped with the multinationals);
3. The "small biotechs", located upstream in the RnD process, focusing on developing certain key active products;
4. Contract research centres, which specialize in the later stages of RnD, in clinical tests and research on industrial processes.

Because of impact of such products on health of individuals, this sector is especially sensitive to the results of medical monitoring (measuring harmlessness)[5] and to changes in public opinion (number of trials).[6] It is also highly regulated since companies must meet very strict national and international quality control standards before bringing their products on the market.

PRESENTATION OF ORGANISATIONS

Company **A** is part of a multinational corporation involved in the research and development, manufacture and distribution of drugs. This major pharmaceutical company has more than tens of thousands of employees around the world and employs about a thousand people in Montreal.

Company **B**, a medium-sized "biotech", specializes in research and development of new "active products" and new molecules for the pharmaceutical industry. Most of their staff of about one hundred employees has a Ph.D. in one of the involved sciences (biology, biophysics, chemistry, pharmaceutical research, etc.). This R&D company finances its activities by means of risk capital based on the possibility that profitable discoveries may eventually be made that can lead to increased investment.

Company **C** is a local company bought out in 2004 by a multinational eager to gain a foothold on the North American continent. It manufactures generic drugs or drugs developed by other companies that hold the patent rights. It employs several hundred people and specializes in products that require special equipment and high levels of quality control.

Company **D** is a subsidiary of a multinational that is active in drug research and development, manufacture and distribution. This major pharmaceutical company employs more than a thousand people around Montreal and several tens of thousands around the world.[7]

PORTRAIT OF CONTINUING EDUCATION AND TRAINING IN COMPANIES IN THE BIOPHARMACEUTICAL SECTOR

Education and training plays an important part in the biopharmaceutical industry. Companies in this sector of industry spend close to 2.5% of their total wage bill on providing structured learning opportunities for their employees (Pharmabio

Développement, 2001, 2006). Within these companies, at least the larger ones, there are three kinds of education and training:

1. Education and training of operators, including training of employees as internal trainers;
2. Education and training of supervisory staff;
3. Education and training of research and development staff.

Here, we shall consider only the education and training of operators and of researchers.

EDUCATION AND TRAINING OF OPERATORS

Technical education and training of operators usually includes several basic types of learning: the company's rules, the operations of the various departments, health and safety measures, how to dress and move around, hygiene codes and awareness of Good Manufacturing Practices (GMPs). Subsequent training covers the manufacturing process in particular, including specific details of the tasks to be performed at a specific work post, handling of equipment, strict application of quality standards and mastering GMPs.[8] With a few exceptions, such as the case of a supplier of new equipment, for example, technical training for operators is given internally.

These enterprises have to obtain and conserve their « Hazard Analysis Critical Control Point » (HACCP) accreditation in order to keep and expand their market; this condition, consequently, obliges them to ensure a strict observance of GMP by their operators. And, because of constant changes in quality standards, production employees are then required to take part again and again in short courses to refresh and update their knowledge of GMPs.[9] Large companies may also agree, on individual basis, to reimburse education fees to formal pre-authorized participation in formal adult learning.

Company A. Previously given on site and without any particular supervision, education and training for a new position in the production units has gradually become better organized and now follows a process prescribed ahead of time. This education and training is given in accordance with an organized coaching method ("*buddy buddy"*) by certified technical trainers who are company employees. They are required to show the actions and modes of operation that must be taken to ensure compliance with the prescribed procedures. These trainers rely on a "system of reminders" that they monitor with the fellow employees and that contains a detailed description of the procedures (very specific) and principles (more general) of GMPs. Trainers or coaches also use a "check list", which enables them to ensure that they have covered all the subjects to be conveyed concerning procedures and handling of equipment. Besides this first control and because of the requirement of compliance with standards imposed from outside by government authorities and from inside by the quality assurance office, this education and training is also systematically assessed at several levels in order to guarantee that the manufacturing work complies with the quality standards and to correct "deviations", which are systematically checked.[10]

Moreover, the institution organizes each year general education and information activities for all employees. Directed by international senior management, this activity takes the form of a one-day information session given to sub-groups of 150 people; it concerns both the company's values and GMPs.

Company B. Since this is a smaller company specializing in research, there is no specially organized internal education and training service. One person is given the task, as necessary and in addition to his or her other responsibilities, of co-ordinating professional development or continuing education activities and requests. The direct supervisors are responsible for partnering with newcomers about the positions they have been assigned. In this case, mutual informal learning within teams is preferred.

Company C. Education and training, which is given by the senior co-ordinator in the quality department, is focused on the specific workpost occupied by the new employee; this training can last from several days to several months, depending on the position. Moreover, throughout the year, all staff, depending on their tasks, is required to take part in training sessions on SOPs ("standard operating procedures") or "recipes" for new products.[11] Education and training related to an employee's position is either given by an experienced operator or specialist within the organisation or, when impossible otherwise, offered informally as self-training supported by directed reading and/or videos created for this purpose. Education and training in procedures and quality control is given by the person responsible in the appropriate department and/or by the quality department co-ordinator. Overall, the amount of technical education and training is important since more than 40% of staff take part in such activities annually.

Company D. The education and training offered in company **D** is both general in nature, concerning, for example, the concept of sterility or even bacteria, and practical, concerning the application of the rules governing the manufacture or handling of specific products. Practical training is given by a colleague at work using manuals setting out the procedures to be applied. Its duration may vary from one day to several months, depending on the complexity of the procedures to be implemented. In addition to these general courses given to all employees, there are specific interventions focusing on the work position held by each employee:[12] thus a supervisor will have to take ten additional courses, a demonstrator seven courses and operators three, whereas the people involved in packaging products do not require any further education and training. Thus, [OUR TRANSLATION] "there is a course curriculum for every position". Moreover, as changes occur in quality standards, people responsible in the different departments offers internal courses that, as needed, focus either on general or theoretical issues, each lasting from 2 to 3 hours, or on practical issues or new procedures, these lasting from a day to one month. These interventions are recorded and checked [OUR TRANSLATION] "to prove that the staff has indeed been trained".[13]

Large companies have developed an internal network of trainers and/or mentors, but the quality of the training given to these trainers varies greatly. For example, company **A** decided several years ago to select among its most experienced and skilled staff trainers who would be responsible for offering technical training and integrating personnel into a new position. These "shop-floor trainers", before being certified and holding their title, have received specific training by the internal education and training department, with the assistance of external agents. This task entitles them to a 2% increase in salary. In company **D**, the "shop-floor trainers" are selected for their technical skills as well as for their ability to convey the information but they do not yet receive particular training.

INFORMAL LEARNING BY PRODUCTION EMPLOYEES AND MANAGERS

Structured activities are only part of the total reality of learning taking place. Under the visible part of the iceberg (Livingstone, 1999, 2003), we find, at all levels of qualifications, a series of informal learning situations and opportunities for group and individual self-training. The appropriation of knowledge and skills and practical knowhow is also achieved through self and inter-learning. The WALL (Work and Lifelong Learning) and NALL (New Approaches to Lifelong Learning) surveys, done in 1998 and 2004, show (see Graph 11.1) that informal learning, through own independent efforts, is regarded by workers as the most important source of learning at work, nearly three times more than employer education and training, while such inter-learning and informal mentoring is officially considered as a second source of knowledge mobilization. According to the 2004 survey, adults spent on average nearly 5 hours per weeks on such work related informal learning. Similarly, forty-five per cent of workers in the AETS survey (Table 11.1) said that they had undertaken job informal learning in the year prior to the survey.

Graph 11.1. Most important source of job-specific knowledge, Employed workers, 1998–2004

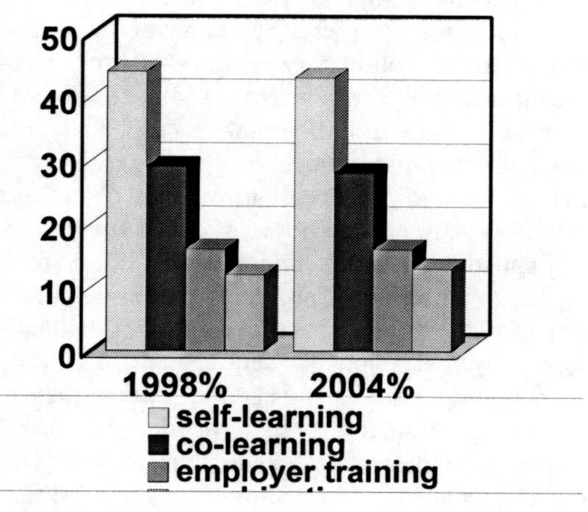

Source: NALL, Survey, 1998, WALL Survey, 2004

Table 11.1. Rate of job-related training in Quebec, 2002 (Total population 25 years of age and older) (Source: Statistics Canada AETS 2003)

Structured job-related learning (%)	Informal job-related learning (%)	Both types of Learning (%)*
22	45	50

* This figure is lower than the total because many individuals were involved in both types of learning activities.

The question is not whether employees in the production units of these pharmaceutical enterprises have also acquire and master advanced knowledge through-informal learning. It is clear, both from quantitative data and qualitative research (Foucher, 2000; Long, 1988, 1991) that workers, at all level of quailfication in enterprises do develop and mobilize their skills and interpretations not only by taking part in organized education and training courses but also through self-learning practices. The question is not only whether the company recognizes this "tacit" reality and whether it takes it into account in its overall continuing professional development strategies and whether such "submerged" learning is recognized and supported. The question, at the end, is whether daily reflexive action of different groups of personnel in their individual and their team work as well as the social and occupational knowledge thus produced have the same space to evolve and be expressed, and, consequently, whether such informal learning can constitute resources, whithin each of these groups, to negotiate and pilote transition into more complex practices and occupational positions.

In the production units of the biopharmaceutical firms, we have observed such overt mention of self-learning in a very limited context, in the cases of workers who could not have attended the prescribed education and training on GMPs and are then giving time for the obligatory reading of procedures. Recognition and organized support for informal learning, as we shall see later, is observed mainly, if not only, among more qualified staff members, especially the scientific staff in Research and Development laboratories.

The education and training practices and policies of production employees are equivocal in this regard. Any outside observer could note the existence of informal and group learning situations in production unit, first of all around health and safety issues and in the daily resolution of problems that arise unexpectedly, especially in the application of GMPs in a specific context (Chatigny, 2004, 2003). One pharmaceutical company, exceptionally, sent a team of employees to observe the handling of new machinery in other plants and then asked them to produce operating manuals that were later given final form by professional writers. It is known that any versatility acquired through experience is then a major asset. Similarly, some studies show that as compared with the prescribed protocol provided for each work position, actual work requires that each individual informally create capacities for readjustment (Chatigny, 2001) and capacities for initiative, especially where mode of production, as it is increasingly the case here, becomes less taylorist oriented.

However, the enormous pressure exerted by quality controls and vertical management of prescribed norms and practices tend very much to force education and learning activities to observe a predominant logic of conformity and consequently to ignore the informal individual and group learning experiences of employees. The crucial gap between prescribed and real work is disregarded; the reflexive and intellectual participation of operators tended to be silenced. The *learning tension and potential for initiative* thus experienced by workers both in their occupational life course and their learning biography is thus ignored, in contrast to other categories of personnel.

CONTINUING EDUCATION AND TRAINING OF SCIENTIFIC PERSONNEL

Let us now look at the continuing professional development of researchers.[14] We should begin by explaining that bringing a new drug to market is a long and costly process consisting of four stages that involve declining levels of scientific complexity:

1. Search for an active product (tests on cells) and selection of dozens of molecules from several thousand products (variable duration);
2. Pre-clinical tests (animal tests) making it possible to select the few most promising molecules that can lead to a patent application (2 to 3 years);
3. Clinical tests[15] (tests on human subjects) at the conclusion of which a single product, which is examined in comparison tests with a placebo, will eventually lead to an application for a notice of compliance (6 to 7 years);
4. After approval by the appropriate authorities (evaluation of tests), industrial engineering research to design the production process and marketing studies for commercialization of the drug (2 to 3 years).

Unlike the education and training undertaken by other groups of personnel and especially workers in production units, the prevalent approach for continuing professional development of researchers is, through various forms, assisted informal learning.

In fact, continuing education of scientific staff tends primarily to be organized on the basis of self-learning activities undertaken with varying degrees of assistance (Carré, 1992). This continuing professional development of researchers through informal learning takes the form of individual documentary research, detailed monitoring of the scientific literature,[16] group learning processes involving peers, including informal discussions around the workbenches (in the laboratory). We should also note the pursuit, which is sometimes encouraged by the company (noticeable in company **B** in particular), of individual research projects ("*side projects*") and of writing of articles for publication in academic journal.

The time devoted to reading is very unequal and its distribution reflects the level of a person's qualifications and responsibility: senior researchers spend twice as much time doing this (up to 20 hours a week), including at home outside regular hours of work, as other professional researchers, who, in turn, read more than research assistants (one or two hours a week).

As far as group learning among peers is concerned, it involves informal exchanges ("*water-cooler meetings*") and much advice given by more experienced people to the other members of the team through support actions (coaching, informal mentoring) that are more or less organized, depending on the size of the organisation. The quality of informal exchanges also depends to a large extent on the personality of those responsible ("some always leave their doors open") and the resources available in the laboratory. These instances of group learning are more closely focused on the research team's task at hand in the companies whereas, in university laboratory, the discussions and informal learning concern both the research program in progress and the academic work (often parallel) of the post-graduate students hired on a part-time basis.

Interviews with scientific staff of the companies enabled us to determine seven different practices used to support and recognize informal learning and to take it into account (cf. Table 11.2):

Table 11.2. Support for informal learning

Support for informal learning practices Indicators	Companies
1. Access to documentary sources	**A, B, C, D**
2. Information, discussion and consultation mechanisms	**B > A & D**
3. Support for participation in peer networks	**B > A, D**
4. Environment facilitating self-learning	**B > A & D > C**
5. Support for innovation creating a continuing demand for informal learning	**B > A > D > C**
6. Reliance on personal initiative to resolve day-to-day problems	**B, D**
7. Personal development plans	**A, D**

Informal learning is clearly the main strategy for continuing professional development and competency structuring and was so in the past (Sirois, 1995). Continuing scientific development of researchers in the companies receives strong support but is still left to personal initiative, except where such learning is required immediately for a current project.

Continuing education of scientific personnel is marked by a predominance of assisted self-learning which is evidenced by the range of organized supports put in place for informal learning. However, reference to Table 11.2 concerning informal learning support, especially indicators 2 to 5, which concern support integrated into the research activity in progress, shows that such organisational support for informal learning varies between organisations; it is more intense, continuous and functional in company **B** than in companies **A** and **D** and more again than in company **C**. As we noted earlier, when we described the companies, this corresponds specifically to the various scientific levels of applied research: the most sophisticated phase 1 research is done only in **B**, whereas **A** and **D** conduct standard pre-test research or drug tests and the research in **C** tends to be more operational and is more focused on techniques for producing drugs or inputs for other companies. In other words, support to informal learning, even within research personnel, tends to differ according to levels of scientific activities.

While continuing scientific professional development in companies primarily takes the form of self-learning, it involves also participation in structured non-formal activities. Such participation varies with level of qualification[17] but has always a direct connection with the work in progress in the laboratory. As a rule, team leaders take part each year, with all expenses paid, in research conferences and seminars lasting from 1 to 3 days on average. They also encourage their senior colleagues to take part in such events at least once in a year, while less qualified researchers participate less frequently. These meetings promote communication with different research networks and make it possible for researchers to learn about the latest trends and discoveries that have not yet been published. We thus observe how these professionals, contrary to personnel in production, received organized support for expressing, evolving and mobilizing informal learning.

Continuing education of scientists includes also, at times, formal education. When the interests of an individual meet those of the company, the firms, especially large ones, may find it advantageous to fund such participation, chiefly where there is a possibility of giving new responsibilities to researchers. It is then primarily to acquire competency related to their management tasks, especially human resources management, that senior researchers make use of formal education in post-secondary institutions (e.g., degrees in administration, like MBA programs).

Some courses too are taken on the initiative of the individuals concerned, while their immediate superiors or team leaders also suggest “refresher” or development activities to meet the needs of current production in the firm.

In larger companies, scientific personnel may obtain reimbursement to cover the cost of academic education for the purpose of completing a degree. As a rule, in pharmaceutical firms involved in pre-testing or testing R and D activities, fees are paid to complete bachelor’s degrees or to attend short college level programs that allow participants to improve their scientific background or master better laboratory practices. In company **D**, continuing education of professionals is supported and managed on the basis of individual plans and “personal projects” recognized by and negotiated with the company, as opposed to the situation of operators where individual monitoring of training tends only to be done as a prerequisite of external quality control policies.

Of course, all laboratory personnel are also required to take part in mandatory training related to safety in laboratory work (chemicals, radiation), learning certain operational techniques relating to the use of new materials (training given by the manufacturer) or learning how to use new software.

RELATIONS BETWEEN MODES OF PRODUCTION AND LOGICS OF LEARNING AND EDUCATION

Are we in the presence of different patterns and logics of education and training? In what way could these models and different intensities of continuing education and training or support to self-learning be explained by the different contexts, levels of qualifications and by diverse work organisations?

Different Models of Adult Learning. The learning demand overtly expressed and the organisation of learning opportunities in these four organisations are marked first by a clear distinction between less qualified staff and qualified staff, a distinction to observed both in the education and training provided and, upstream, in the expression of learning demand.

Different education and training arrangements. Programming the education and training of production employees and, prior to that, formulating systematic diagnosis of the education and training needs of these personnel are well-established activities in large and medium-sized companies. In fact, quality requirements and the need for strict observation of GMPs – a prerequisite in ensuring that these companies obtain and retain their accreditation and thus their permits to export their products – dictate the education demand of operators and of their supervisory staff. Following constant changes of production norms, these demands are frequently altered or updated.

Expression of demand for continuing education of scientific personnel is structured and managed quite differently. The learning demand of scientific personnel tends to be programmed in a less-planned and less vertical manner.

As far as expression of learning demand is concerned, it is difficult to ascertain precisely whether various requests for education and training are made not only on basis of company's requirements (linked to changes in conditions of production) but also on basis of the aspirations, perceptions and constraints of individuals. However, it may be assumed that both the external and the subjective dimensions of the demand for education tend to be taken differently into account between categories of personnel. While, for operators in production sectors, what is "prescribed" predominates and the set conditions of production will determine the learning demand as functional response to production change, there appears to be more room for integrating subjective demand generated by professional and scientific personnel,[18] for taking into account their aspirations, their view of the situation, their experience, their self-learning. Diagnosis of learning demand, in laboratories, is decentralized and is object of formal and informal negotiation; the immediate superior approves organized learning to be taken outside the organization and is entitled to support self-learning initiatives within the firm.

In production sector, forepersons may sometimes, and in a limited way, mediate perceptions and constraints of members of their work teams. Negotiation of learning demand through a mechanism on which employees are represented is generally non-existent, except in a very broad way within unionized companies under the collective agreement (Streeck, 1993) in order, for example, to indicate how participants will be selected and what status and remuneration internal trainers will enjoy.

Evaluation and monitoring tend also to vary according to categories of personnel; while unqualified personnel are evaluated essentially on the basis of what they had to learn and of their compliance with GMP practices,[19] the continuing education of highly qualified staff is at times evaluated and more so at a first level (Kirkpatrick, 1994), taking the form of an assessment of personal satisfaction at the end of learning activities. In short, only prescribed learning linked to compliance by operators with the standards imposed from outside (requirements of good manufacturing practices) tend to be evaluated systematically and this is done primarily in terms of conformity, of the extent to which standards are complied with.[20]

Some companies (**A** and **D**) offer follow-up related to the continuing education of their scientific personnel, in the form of individual plans; the employee's immediate superior or the head of the laboratory takes the time to develop with each member of his or her team a professional development plan with a view to creating a career plan.[21] Such practices are non-existent in the production units, except in the case of records listing the technical training received by each employee, which are sometimes requested by outside quality control public organizations.

Unequal recognition of informal learning. Informal learning at the work place is often misapprehended and, consequently, not supported because of the tendency to restrict the perception of in-house learning activities to structured practices (Livingstone, 2003). In the production sector of the drug industry, this takes a particular form. The arrangement of education and training in the industrial production of drugs focuses, first and foremost, on the application of standards imposed by public regulatory bodies. Consequently, it tends to under-estimate the tension experienced by the employee at his or her workpost between prescribed actions and actual practice (Teiger, 1996).[22] The enormous pressure exerted by and for quality control has a strong tendency to gear the education and training activities of production employees into a predominant logic of conformity. Throughout our interviews with first level management, we did not find any clue on any kind of recognition of the idiosyncratic contribution of employees. The fear of non conformity seems to lead them to ignore or at least pay little attention to the informal learning that is provoked and required by this tension between the prescribed and the real. The fact that little recognition and support are given to self-learning and reflexive practice in production units does not mean, of course, that it does not exist. The inter-learning taking place through mentoring, the unavoidable recourse to floor people when a "bris de machine" takes place, the requirememt of self-training through written documentation for employees who could not attend the group session, are all indirect indicators that the reality, though overlooked, does exist.

Here, the use of the iceberg image (Livingstone, 1999, 2003) is perfect: the discourses of different actors refer only to the visible, formal and organized part of the learning reality. Moreover, this ignoring of informal learning and of autonomous production of knowledge and know-how that we have observed in the work of production employees, is especially significant since we found exactly the opposite situation among R&D personnel.

In this cutting-edge sector, where the need to update the expertise of researchers and professionals, the demand for innovation and the recognized reflexive nature of the work lead companies to support informal learning. As described earlier, the organisational supports for informal learning of research and development staff vary from one company to another as a result of various factors, including work organisation, the pressure of competition on productivity requirements and institutionalized practices of structured learning. Thus, support for self-learning is more intense, constant and functional where the scientific content of research activities is higher, as in company **B**, a small organization which specializes in searching for new molecules.

Learning and participation in structured education in these organisations are clearly hierarchical, however in a peculiar manner. These firms are intensive education and learning organisations through important investments in human ressource development and high rate of participation to learning activities at all levels of qualification or of initial education, a trend contrary to the classic pattern (Bélanger, Doray, Labonté and Levesque, 2004; Bélanger, Doray Levesque, 2007).

What varies is rather the pattern of learning activities. In this economic sector, recognition of informal learning activities and support provided vary drastically according to level of professional activities and sectors of activities. Similarly, structured learning activities tend to be more directly connected to immediate job requirement at lower level of qualification, than at higher level. Hence, the kind of learning opportunities fluctuates with the kinds of professional environments within the organisation (Meignant, 1991) in which the different staff groups work. Consequently, here also (Crossan, Field, Gallacher and Merrill, 2003), the development of self-directed learning as well as type of participation to continuing education depends on the previous educational career of individuals.

Beyond this unbalanced distribution of patterns of learning activities, a more important divide is at work, a divide based on the very logic of learning activities provided or supported.

Logic of conformity and reflexive logic. The continuing education and training activities in which operators in the production sector of the biopharmaceutical industry take part do not seem to differ from those found in other sectors such as the food products industry, where production must also respond to regulated quality control and which is monitored by external public agencies (Bélanger, Larivière and Voyer, 2004). The predominant logic of education and training of production employees, in the companies examined, is one of conformity. Following introduction of good manufacturing practices (GMPs)[23] when people are hired or when they are transfered to other positions, training in prescribed practices are directly bound to immediate production. Observations of a decline in quality lead to an analysis of "deviations" and, subsequently, to remedial training in order to relearn the prescriptions.

Types and modes of production greatly influence the way in which the learning demand of production employees is expressed and defined in these companies. Quality requirements and the need to strictly observe GMPs actually bring about in-depth changes in the expression of learning demand of operators training as well as of front-line supervisory staff, who are also required and even more intensively to take part in training courses on quality control and GMPs. The quality standards imposed from outside, like the protocol provided for each position, are so decisive that responsibility for planning training tends to be shifted from the human resources department to the quality control department.

Here we should note that the gender factor varies with level of qualification and responsibility, but in a rather peculiar and paradoxical way. In production units, education and training, which is required of everyone, does not appear to introduce any bias in this regard, since each and all employees are required to undertake the prescribed training activities. It is in research laboratories above all that problems in reconciling employment, work and intensive self-learning at home[24] (Tremblay 2004) tend to exclude women from positions of responsibility.[25] The important reading time required from senior researchers, outside their normal work schedule, creates an important discriminatory factor for upward mobility, more so, that most maternity leaves tend to happen at a stage, in the researcher professional life course, where her scientific production will be decisive for her future.[26]

Production Methods and Continuing Education and Training

These different models and intensities of continuing education and training or of support to self-learning have to be understood in reference to their related different work contexts and work organisation as well as to the dissimilar modes of production.

The ambiguous nature of the logic of training operators to deal with changes in modes of industrial production. A sword of Damocles in the form of the risk of a failure to observe the quality standards imposed and controlled by external regulatory agencies (the FDA[27] in the US and Health Canada) deeply marks, as we have seen, the training provided in the production sectors of biopharmaceutical companies; it tends to impose a logic of conformity. At the same time, however, modes of production are changing. The digitalization of production equipment requires a higher level of basic skills. Organization of work tends also to become less repetitive as a result of the increasing introduction of new methods of work such as rotating duties or teamwork. Significantly, in two of the studied organisations, such introduction is now proceeding at the request of employees. The expansion of the role of employees asked to become trainers reflects a similar change. More profoundly, organisations are beginning to recognize, as a result of the work done by ergonomists (Teiger and Montreuil, 2001), that an operator's actual work also brings into play an unexpected contribution of the subject in which experiential knowledge, crucial in resolving possible problems, can and does develop.

The existing dominant logic of conformity raises more and more questions and difficulties. Standardized knowledge of prescribed duties is not the only knowledge required by and of operators. Even more, the approach of linear inculcation of such knowledge and the "deviation control" mechanisms that follow may prove to be confusing by creating a certain propensity among employees and first line management to conceal errors, while the risk of such accidental quality defect could be critical for the whole organization. One of the two large organisations studied is indeed changing its approach: while not questioning the quality control, it gives more attention to "esprit d'observation" and to problem-solving capacity of operators.

In contrast with the standardized knowledge that is more manageable in the context of a mechanical type of mass production and organization, the increasingly differentiated production of such industry tends to enlarge the learning demand of both the organization and the workers, leading to more multi-faceted qualifications in order to ensure internal flexibility and job security.

This ambiguity between the prevailing logic of education and training and the changing mode of production has broader implications. First, in order to be precisely functional, a competency must be integrated and mobilized by the subject (Lave and Wenger, 1991) on the basis of his or her experiences and expectations and his or her attempt to integrate the various learning events into his or her particular development and into his or her "educational career" (Crossan, Field, Gallacher and Merrill, 2003). The challenge in the education and training of operators is not only the immediate role they play in production activities, but also, in contrast with the vocationalist trend, the inevitability of a broader and longer-term understanding and implication of a learning strategy formerly confined to short term technical requirement. Hence the issue of redefining the learning demands to encompass not only the short and long term requirement of the organisation, but also the aspiration and experience of their function.

The second challenge in work related education and training is related to the segmentation and flexibilisation of the labour market, hence the growing economic incertitude at both macro and micro levels. The issue is the growing demand by workers, faced by the increasingly precarious nature of their jobs, that their right to work be protected through a broader continuing education and training approach as well as a recognition of their informal and self learning, so as to allow internal flexibility and more mobility within this sector of the economy, and to strengthen individual right to work.

Mode of scientific production and continuing education of researchers. The mode of production in R and D divisions of pharmaceutical industries is much different both from the one in production units and from research undertaken in university context. Research within a biopharmaceutical company is devoted to the discovery of an exclusive drug that, when approved and marketed, will provide a return on the substantial investments required for its development, certification and approval. The mode of scientific production (Gibbons, 1994) of R and D in the drug industry is then focused on problem solving and on mobilizing researchers from various scientific disciplines. These researchers must accept the ever-present risk of a decisive cut in funding by those who invest in the research as a result of their assessment of the future return on research currently under way.[28]

For its part, scientific research at universities in this same field tends to answer to a different logic of scientific productivity, responding to the classic mode of scientific production, primarily in a single discipline, designed in the longer term to advance knowledge in that particular discipline and geared more immediately to academic production. The publication of research reports thus becomes the primary criterion governing the award of research grants.[29]

Both these modes of scientific production are reflected in the methods and contents of continuing education of researchers on both sides. Scientists in the private sector, who are evaluated on the basis of the immediate usefulness of their research activity, tend to participate in learning activities geared to the effectiveness of the laboratory research work in the search for scientific solutions to the problem posed by the organization (for example, a molecule that has a particular therapeutic effect for diabetics). Both structured learning on management and communication and more technical training on procedures or new equipment have to meet functional requirements. Formal education and "*non directly purposeful*" involvement in scientific seminars and conferences thus becomes less common, whereas continuing professional development of a scientist as a scientist, definitely supported by various measures, remains informal and individual in nature. Continuing scientific development will depend on the personal interests of the researcher and will require that he or she devote a substantial amount of time to it outside his or her hours of work. Moreover, while people tend to update their scientific knowledge informally and on an individual basis, they do so because this learning model allows them to take into account the dispersion of the various scientific disciplines mobilized. Recourse to self-learning reflects also the recognition of the intense reflexive nature of the work, a context not only knowledge intensive but also intensive in its requirement for capacity of initiative, a context opposite to the one of employees in industrial production of drugs, where prescribed and standardized required learning are predominant and almost entirely defined externally outside the real life of floor production.

In universities, continuing education, both structured and informal, focuses solely on scientific content; continuing education related to participants' managerial or teaching responsibility is completely absent and not required by any of the "investors" in their research. Scientific congresses, conferences and seminars are practically the only organized activities contributing to their continuing professional development; together with the associated scientific publications, they constitute the space where academic production is justified and validated and where the financial contributions made are justified. These spaces also respond in the longer term to the requirements for promoting knowledge in various disciplines. Participation by university researchers in these academic spaces, where knowledge is updated and disseminated, becomes more intense than with their colleagues in the private sectors and is also distributed hierarchically.

This exploration in the continuing professional education of scientific staff in the biopharmaceutical sector raises two issues that will need to be considered in detail in later studies: the ambivalence of the invisible college and the growing permeability of the two modes of scientific production.

Ambivalence of the invisible college. In Montreal, one of the world centres of pharmaceutical industry, the concentration of enterprises is bound to create an environment conducive to the multi-directional transfer of knowledge among companies, networks of professionals and the many teaching and research institutions located there, as in Finland (Lam, 2002). However, the "patent" exclusivity – which is protected over a long period – of the results of this mode of scientific production, an exclusivity instituted to provide better return on investments, has created a major ambiguity in this environment.[30] The ban on scientists disclosing the fruits of their research tends to reduce their presence in many spaces used for scientific dissemination and exchanges that are characteristic of university research and its mode of scientific production.[31] Confidentiality clauses have the effect of limiting reciprocal transfer of scientific knowledge within this geographically concentrated community of researchers. This context is source of often-vented frustration by the industry's researchers we interviewed.

Furthermore, because of this structural factor inherent in the current capitalist organization of the biopharmaceutical industry, it may be asked whether the potential synergies of this geographic concentration of scientific activity are not being seriously impeded. In fact, the potential synergies promised by this regional conglomeration of research centres relate less to the idea of an invisible college (Crane, 1969) and an informal community of scientific communication (Wenger, 1999) than to a job market with sound communications and organized sectoral consultation (Charest, 2002). The multi-directional transfer of scientific knowledge then tends to occur primarily through university channels and professional networks. What became evident in our research is that large investments made in research by the industry do represent a major input in the development of scientific knowldege, but they have also the insidious effect of leaving the researchers working in the field in a constant state of ambiguity and tension between their scientific interests and the economic interests of their organization.

Permeability of the two modes of scientific production. Gibbons (1991) was able to shed light on this substantial volume of applied research produced in companies outside the universities and their research institutes, namely this second type of production of scientific knowledge, in industry. Since then, some factors seem to indicate a growing permeability between the two modes of scientific production.

Most notably, we are witnessing a rapprochement between pharmaceutical companies and university faculties or institutes linked to this area of applied research. There is, first, the creation of formal education initiatives in companies. Students of chemistry, biology, biopharmaceutical engineering or pharmacology have opportunities to take courses and 'stages' lasting 12 months for credit and for financial reward. The preparation, organization, monitoring and evaluation of these activities, which involve the writing of research protocols or reports on experiments and the development of pharmaceutical formulas or pre-testing or clinical pre-testing work, bring the universities and companies closer together. The company benefits from the contribution of theoretical knowledge; it has the opportunity to assess the student's ability to adapt to an eventual position; it strengthens its links with certain specialists in the field of academic research. The students discover the specific nature of applied research while obtaining experience that will be decisive in their professional future. University institutions, then, tend to increase such networks and contacts, while benefiting from the research expertise indirectly conveyed.[32]

In addition, substantial co-operation is also observed by the solicitation of university research centres as sub-contractors to carry out applied industry related research. Such delegation by companies of part of their research activities certainly provides a new source of funding for university research, but it tends also to introduce in universities the logic of research that governs their own market driven activities. Some professors use their sabbaticals or unpaid leave to also establish their own companies or to bring their discoveries to the testing and production stage.[33] This coming together and the convergence of the research funding criteria that accompanies it help to give priority to the "problem-solving" mode of scientific production over the university mode.

While this permeability remains limited at the present time, the question arises on the future development of relations between universities and biopharmaceutical companies and on the impact this blending of the modes of scientific production will have in the future. In this sense, continuing professional development could very well lose this non-instrumental dimension that the university does or should maintain.

In this changing context, an other complex question of development, diversity and freedom of biopharmaceutical research takes shape. In this area of research "linked to what is human", questions of bioethics and also of social ethics with respect to research priorities and the accessibility of patented drugs and the impact of investment decisions on individual health are multiplying.[34] Continuing professional education of biopharmaceutical researchers, unlike that of doctors (Hudon, 2000), appears, however, to be silent on this social and ethical dimension.

CONCLUSION

In the knowledge-intensive biopharmaceutical sector, education and training as well as support to self-learning have become key factors in the development strategy of this industry. Rates of investment in education and training, participation by different staff groups and the diversity of approaches and forms of support clearly are indication of this new trend.

However, different logics and models of action are cutting across the organization and general orientation of these types of learning activities. While education and training of operators in production unit is intensive, the prevailing logic of these prescribed learning exercises is one of conformity. Yet, this predominance becomes more and more ambiguous because of changes in techniques and modes of industrial production in these new industries, and because of the current impact of rising levels of qualification among the new generation of employees. We have observed that very limited attention is paid to informal and self-learning taking place among production operators. In fact, this less visible and formal part of their continuing professional development is ignored. Such a managerial practice on production floor contrasts with the strong recognition and support expressed for knowledge transfer and informal learning in research units. Here, in the laboratories, continuing professional development in various forms plays a predominant role. In these professional development and knowledge transfer activities, scientific personnel construct or preserve (Dubar, 1989) their professional identity.

Even, among researchers, the learning practices and continuing education patterns show important variations according to levels of qualification; they reflect also substantial ambiguity, if not conflict, between the scientific and economic interests involved in research in this biopharmaceutical industry.

If knowledge economy, that is if knowledge and Research and Development intensive economic sectors foretell the general scheme of tomorrow's *lifelong learning*, our observations raise two major questions. Firstly, beyond the dominance of narrow vocational orientation in production units and beyond the unequal involvement of different categories of personnel in learning activities observed in both production and research, an even more critical question arises on the application of different if not diametrically opposed logics of learning at work according to the different levels of qualification: a logic of conformity in production units and a reflexive logic in applied research. The taylorist request for conforming operators' practices is bound to be confronted through the ambiguous and changing work context of these new industries. The negation or, at the very least, the non-recognition of the complex learning activities of workers, of their real self-learning and problem-solving practices, is bound to become more and more problematic. The ongoing change in the organization of production as well as in the incertitude of the global markets and of the local labour market may generate new individual strategies to protect one's right to work and thus may very well transform the social learning demand. A crucial aspect then will be the way this new learning demand will be expressed, how it will be negotiated and whether significant transformation of the general economy of lifelong learning will then take place. The question is whether the emerging learning cities is not reproducing, however differently and in more subtle forms, the spatial and economic divide of the old industrial cities.

Secondly, we argue that the question of the social distribution of knowledge is about to re-emerge differently. Changes in modes of scientific production and the blending of the academic and industrial scientific production are impacting both on selection of new knowledge to be developed and on the pattern of scientific communication and inter-communications of this scientific production. In that new context, a central question, raised today by these new scientific sectors, is less the distribution of "knowledge" than the risk of market driven convergence in the selection of knowledge to be produced. The risk is to lose, then, the chaotic[35], scientific environment required by the democracy of science, if not by the very development of science itself. A genuine learning society is more than a knowledge intensive society.

NOTES

1 [OUR TRANSLATION] Department of Industry and Commerce, 2001.

2 The data were collected in three series of interviews, the first of which was conducted in 5 enterprises in 2004 with people responsible for training and staff representatives and the second was conducted in 2006 with members of research teams in four major enterprises in the sector. The third series, conducted in 2006–2007 with researchers working in private enterprise and the universities, explored the various modes of scientific production or research and the related models of Continuing Professional Development (Cervero 2001, Centre interprofessionnel du Québec, 2001).

3 This research was funded by the SSHRC as part of the WALL (*Work & Lifelong Learning Research Network*) research program on adult informal learning, directed by David Livingstone at OISE/UofT.

4 Pfizer, Merck Frosst, GlaxoSmithKline, Bristol-Myers Squibb, Johnson & Johnson, Laboratoire Abbott, Aventis Pharma, CTRBBIO-Recherches, DSM Biologies, Methylgene, Novartis, Sandoz, Shering, Shire, Wyeth-Ayerst, etc.

5 This was the case when the drug Viox was banned, which led to a wave of lay-offs in the company (St Onge, 2006, p. 169).

6 [OUR TRANSLATION] "As of August 18, 2006, Merck was facing 14,000 lawsuits involving 30,000 complainants in the US" (St Onge, 2006, p. 174).

7 A fifth company was surveyed only in the first series of interviews in order to obtain a portrait of the training there and thus to confirm our analysis of the training of operators in the production units of this industry.

8 « <in our training> we have to go through the hygiene and local conduct codes. (…). We have to ensure full range of control. For this, we have to make our new employees much aware. We hear telling them: "you will have to work in a special industry, the pharmaceutical industry which is very much controlled by the GMPs that are our guidelines"» <our transation> (supervisor, firm C#2)

9 « *Each time, we introduce or modify a manufacturing procedure, we must train the employees anew* » <our translation> (Manager of a large pharmaceutical firm).

10 "Deviation analysis" is the expression used to refer to the process of identifying, measuring and analysing production errors and to indicate flaws in training.

11 *« There are regular meetings in each of our departments where managers and supervisors discuss the situation (…). In fact, each time an unusual event occurs, an error happens or any activity has not been implemented according to the prescribed process, a written report is done and correcting measures are stipulated »* (Firm C). <our transation>

12 Concerning, for example, the metric system, specific hazardous materials, specific regulations and procedures relating to GMPs, dress, sterilization, filtration, etc.

13 "*When an employee arrives, he or she is automatically given a training record. This is cumulative … there is a central file where the training records of all employees are stored*". (Interview with an employee) <our translation>.

14 Continuing professional education (also called continuing professional development) has become a specific area of expertise: Browell, 2000; Cervero, 2001; Conseil interprofessionnel du Québec, 2000; Daley, 2000; Davis & Fox, 2002; Roscoe, 2001.

15 Products are subjected to three stages of clinical tests (Phase I: several dozen volunteers, 1 year/ Phase II: several hundreds volunteers, 2 years/Phase III: several thousands volunteers, 3 years) and this makes it possible to select the drug, if any, whose harmlessness and effectiveness have been established.

16 Researchers essentially have access through Internet to the same sources of information (scientific journals, university libraries, search engines). The data obtained are then redistributed over the laboratory's Intranet system so that everyone can access them. The total volume of scientific literature that can be accessed is growing exponentially. The tools that can be used to select by key-words are increasingly powerful and the total time devoted to reading tends to remain unchanged, however such process could lead to reduction in the multiplicity and diversity of sources.

17 The time allocated to self-learning through litterature. "*As to the individual activities to keep one up to date, that depends on level <of qualification>. For a technician, this means little. A research subordinate, 5%, a research assistant 20%. Myself, a team leader, it is about 40 to 50% of my time. That implies reading of scientific reviews and newspapers, of internal reports,*" Interview 8, researcher in private firm. <our transation>.

18 Only one company (**C**) encourages its entire staff, including production employees, to continue their education and training on an individual basis.

19 « *A supervisor checks all the procedures that the employee <in training> should have gain knowledge of. This course is then documented and the report which has to be signed by both the trainer and the employee is sent to the quality control department and kept there in our archives to be consulted eventually for further verification either by external agencies in charge of public norms or by our corporate clients. Moreover, we have for each employee a cumulative file <on all the training he has received>* "(Quote from a report of one of the enterprises.) <Our transation>.

[20] « All workposts have been evaluated from that basis <i.e. conformity>. A curriculum is prescribed (…) for each workpost ». (Manager, Firm B). <Our transation>.

[21] « The question of individual professional development is present for all the personnel. (…), however, this is a pressing issue mainly for the management and the professionals.» (Manager, Firm A).

[22] See also the special 2001 issue of *Relations industrielles:* "Ergonomie, formation et transformation des milieux de travail", Vol. 56, No. 3.

[23] Some companies refer to SOPs, *standard operating procedures.*

[24] « I will give you an example. For me it is very frustrating: the morning breakfeast meeting at 7 o'clock. This is for men (…). Myself, I have my children; I cannot, because to be there at 7 h because then, I would have to leave home at 6 o'clock. No school would accept to receive my children that early. So, I never attend these early meetings » (Interview 14, woman researcher in entreprise).

[25] Our survey did not allow us to determine whether a similar tendency exists among middle and higher managers.

[26] *« It is not at all evident for a senior researcher like me when time comes for a maternity leave, to be absent for six months and come back and having missed six month of scientific literature. One feels guilty. Then you have to work three time more to gain the lost time and make sure that nobody will notify that you were absent, that you can operate as if these six months had never existed.*" (Senior woman researcher in private enterprise). <Our transation>.

[27] *Food and Drug Administration.*

[28] *« In the industry, it much more focussed, one has to produce as fast and as efficient as possible, and with the lowest cost. So much so, that, often, when we have at hand some scientific findings that are unrelated <to the specific task>. We are then told: no, no, no, we ask you to do this and nothing else at this moment, because we are investing for that purpose.. (...) So there are people who cannot live in that context, they suffocate »* (Interview 14, researcher in private enterprise). <Our transation>.

[29] « *So, it is a big vicious circle: to bring money to the centre, we need publications that, in turn, require money to be produced. It is a full vicious circle. And I must say that it is a perpetual process without end: when one puts his finger in that cog-wheel, it is very difficult to get out of it* » (Professor in a university).

[30] « The way to produce value is to obtain a biotech process or product protected by intellectual property laws, and then to exploit it. We have to protect what we are doing; this is the way such process or product gains value » (Interview 8: researcher in private enterprise). <Our transation>.

[31] « What interests them most in universites is the fact that they have the freedom to express their ideas, their scientific findings. In the industry, it is always confidential. We cannot share the joy of having done a discovery, before it has been patented and thus protected » (Interview 8: researcher in private enterprise). <Our transation>.

[32] « *Before (...), there was a big separation between university and the industrial milieu. We could say that there were people in fundamental research; they believed that they were doing non profit research people <in university> and that research in industry was always product-oriented. (...) Today, with the availability of information and the pressure to share the same information, there are not big differences. If university labs struggle everywhere to get funds, individuals operating in the firms are showing more and more interest in having their scientific works been disseminated. (...) So, may be, there are less and less differences»* (Interview 8, researcher in enterprise) <our translation>.

[33] From interview 23.

[34] See notes 19 and 20.

[35] I used the term "chaotic" to refer to scientific complexity, cultural diversity and research pluralism as a favorable context for creative and wide-ranging scientific production. This notion can be clarified further when pitted again problematic dimensions such as scientific convergence and "marketisation" of research priorities.

REFERENCES

Bélanger, P., & Federighi, P. (2000). *Analyse transnationale des politiques d'éducation et de formation des adultes*. Paris: L'Harmattan.

Bélanger, P., Doray, P., & Levesque, M. (2007). *La participation à la formation des adultes: une comparaison Québec Canada*. Québec: MESS.

Bélanger, P., Larivière, M., & Voyer, B. (2004). *Les pratiques et l'organisation de la formation en entreprise au Québec*. Montréal: UQAM/CIRDEP, 193 p.

Bélanger, P., Doray, P., Labonté, A., & Lévesque, M. (2004). *La participation à la formation des adultes au Québec*. Québec: MESS.

Browell, S. (2000). Staff development and professional education: A cooperative model. *Journal of workplace learning, 12*(2), 57–65.

Carré, P. (1992). *L'autoformation dans la formation professionnelle*. Paris: La documentation française.

Cervero, R. M. (2001). Continuing professional education in transition, 1981–2000. *International Journal of Lifelong Education, 20*(1–2), 16–30.

Charest, J. (2002). *Évaluation de la politique d'intervention sectorielle d'Emploi Québec. 1995–2001*. Québec: MESS.

Chatigny, C., & Vézina, N. (2004). Polyvalence et formation continue: Des inséparables à réconcilier pour la santé et la sécurité. *Pistes, 6*(1), 15–28.

Chatigny, C., & Montreuil, S. (2003). Apprenticeship in a work setting: the contribution and limits of operational resources constructed by workers. *Safety Science, 41*, 377–391.

Chatigny, C. (2001). *La construction de ressources opératoires. Contribution à la conception des conditions de formation en situation de travail*. Paris: Ministère de l'éducation nationale, de la recherche et de la technologie. Thèse de doctorat en ergonomie/CNAM.

Conseil interprofessionnel du Québec. (2000). *La formation continue et l'amélioration de la compétence*. Montréal: Document issu du colloque du Forum de la formation du C.I.Q.

Crane, D. (1969, June). Social structure in a group of scientists: A test of the "Invisible college" hypothesis. *American Sociological Review, 34*(3), 335–352.

Crossan, B., Field, J., Gallacher, J., & Merrill, B. (2003). Understanding participation in learning for non-traditional adult learners: Learning careers and the construction of learning identities. *British Journal of Sociology of Education, 24*(1), 55–67.

Daley, B. J., & Mott, V. W. (2000). *Charting a course for continuing professional education: Reframing professional practice: New direction for adult and continuing education*. San Francisco: Jossey Bass.

Davis, D. A., Fox, R., & Barnes, B. E. (2002). *The continuing professional development of physicians*. Chicago: AMA Publications.

Dubar, C., & al. (1989). Innovations de formation et transformation de la socialisation professionnelle par et dans l'entreprise. *Production et usage de la formation par et dans l'entreprise. Rapport de recherche*. Villeneuve d'Ascq: Lastree.

Foucher, R. (2000). *L'autoformation reliée au travail*. Montréal: Éditions nouvelles AMS.

Gibbons, M., & al. (1994). *The new production of knowledge*. Thousand Oaks, CA: Sage.

Hudon, G. (2000). Développement professionnel et sociétés commerciales». *Journal de l'Association médicale canadienne, 163*, 668–669.

Kirkpatrick, D. L. (1994). *Evaluating training programs: The four levels*. San Francisco: Berrett-Koehler.

Lam, A. (2002). *Alternative societal model of learning and innovation: The knowledge industry*. Paper given at the DRUID Conference "Industrial Dynamics of the New and Old Economy", Copenhagen, 6-8/6/2002.

Lave, J., & Wenger, E. (1991). *Situated learning. Legitimate peripheral participation*. Cambridge: University Press.

Livingstone, D. W. (2003). *Mapping the iceberg*. Toronto: NALL Working Paper n° 54.

Livingstone, D. W. (1999). Exploring the icebergs of adult learning: Findings of the first Canadian survey of informal learning practices. *Canadian Journal for the Study of Adult Education, 13*(2), 49–72.

Long, H. B. (1991). *Self directed learning: Consensus and conflict*. Norman, OK: Oklahoma Research Centre, University of Oklahoma.

Long, H. B. (1988). *Self directed learning application and theory*. Georgia, GA: University of Georgia.

Meignant, A. (1991). *Manager la formation*. Paris: Éditions Liaison.

Ministère de l'Industrie et du Commerce. (2001). *L'économie du savoir 1984–1999*. Québec. Direction de l'analyse économique. Janvier 2001.

Montréal international. (2006). *Indicateurs de haute technologie et d'innovation du Montréal metropolitain 2006*. Montréal: Montréal international.

Montréal International. (2001). *L'industrie biopharmaceutique du Grand Montréal*. Montréal: Montréal international.

Pharmabio Développement. (2006). *Travaux préliminaires à la mise en place d'un processus de veille concernant l'emploi et la formation dans le secteur des produits pharmaceutiques et biotechnologiques*. Montréal: Pharmabio Développement.

Pharmabio Développement. (2004). *La main-d'oeuvre dans l'industrie des produits pharmaceutiques et biotechnologiques au Québec*. Montréal: Pharmabio Développement.

Pharmabio Développement. (1999). *Portrait sectoriel*. Montréal: Pharmabio.

Roscoe, J. (2002). Continuing professional development in higher education. *Human Resource Development International*, *5*(1), 3–9.

Saint-Onge, J.-C. (2006). *Les dérives de l'industrie de la santé – Petit Abécédaire*. Montréal: Les Éditions Écosociété.

Saint-Onge, J.-C. (2004). *L'envers de la pilule – Les dessous de l'industrie pharmaceutique*. Montréal: Les Éditions Écosociété.

Sirois, N. (1995). *L'autoformation comme stratégie de structuration des compétences professionnelles: une étude de cas dans l'industrie pharmaceutique*. Montréal: HEC. Master's thesis.

Statistique Canada. (2003). *Enquête sur l'éducation et la formation des adultes*. Ottawa: Statistique Canada (EEFA)

Streeck, W. (1993). Training and the new industrial relations. A strategic role for unions. In S. R. Sleigh (Ed.), *Economic restructuring and emerging patterns of industrial relations* (pp. 167–189). Kalamazoo, WE: Upjohn Institute.

Teiger, C., & Montreuil, S. (1996). The foundations and contributions of ergonomics work analysis in training programmes. *Safety Science*, *23*(3), 81–95.

Tremblay, D. G. (2004). *Conciliation emploi, famille et temps sociaux*. Québec et Toulouse: PUQ et Octares.

Wenger, E. (1999). *Communities of practice: Learning, meaning, and identity*. Cambridge: Cambridge Univ. Press.

KIRAN MIRCHANDANI, ROXANA NG, NEL COLOMA-MOYA, SRABANI MAITRA, TRUDY RAWLINGS, HONGXIA SHAN, KHALEDA SIDDIQUI AND BONNIE SLADE

12. TRANSITIONING INTO PRECARIOUS WORK:

Immigrants' Learning and Resistance[1]

INTRODUCTION

There is emerging evidence that immigrant women of colour are systematically channelled into low-paid and dead-end jobs when they arrive in Canada (e.g., Boyd, 1992; Man, 2004; Picot, 2004), and that several industries depend on highly 'flexible', 'disposable' and 'captive' immigrant women workers for their labour supply (de Wolff, 2003; Ng, 2001; Wallace and Vosko, 2003). Few studies, however, have examined the experiences and struggles of immigrant women, many of whom are highly educated, as they transition into precarious jobs. Accordingly, this chapter examines the experiences of immigrant women making their transition into low-end precarious jobs in grocery stores, call centres, and garment factories. We argue that the transition into precarious work involves, first, a material shift where women learn to deal with unstable, poorly paid jobs, and second, an ideological shift where women learn to construct themselves as precarious workers. Much of the literature on transitions focuses on shifts from school to work, or across workplaces. This chapter contributes to expanded notions of work transitions by focusing on the impact of transnational migration. Interviews with women reveal a complex picture where immigrants both learn to function within dehumanizing working contexts (Acker, 1992), and exercise resistance to retain and regain humanity at work.

This chapter is based on interviews conducted in 2003 and 2004 with female precarious workers in the Greater Toronto Area in Canada. Participants in our study included supermarket cashiers, call centre operators and garment sewers who were working on a part-time, seasonal or temporary basis. We conducted fifty semi-structured, in-depth interviews in five languages (Cantonese, English, Hindi, Mandarin and Bengali) with twenty call centre operators, fifteen cashiers and fifteen garment sewers. All but eight of our respondents were immigrants to Canada, and a majority (n = 28) immigrated more than three years before the interviews. Our interviewees were women from China, Hong Kong, Pakistan, India, Tanzania, Philippines, Jamaica, Bangladesh, West Indies, Nigeria, and Sri Lanka. Notably, of these women, twenty-four (1 cashier, 8 sewers and 15 call centre workers) had university degrees from their home countries. With respect to income, 80 per cent of the women earned $20,000 per year or less; 36 per cent of the women earned less than $10,000.

P. Sawchuk and A. Taylor (eds.), Challenging Transitions in Learning and Work: Reflections on Policy and Practice, 231–242.

Regardless of their previous educational and professional backgrounds, these workers shared a common experience at work – the majority did not have experience in the sector in which they were now employed. While for many workers transitions occur across occupationally related sites, for many immigrant women, their transition is characterized by a jarring discontinuity between past education and work, and present occupation. Women noted that precarious jobs were easily accessible and did not require credentials or 'Canadian experience'. Many received depressingly low wages – on average, they made between seven and eight dollars an hour and received no job security or benefits. Several experienced adverse health effects due to the nature of their work. Women also noted that their family lives, educational endeavours, or social and leisure activities were frequently disrupted as a result of constant and unplanned schedule changes in their paid work.

While there has been a growing focus in Canada on the labour market experiences of immigrants, few have documented workers' transitions into the precarious jobs they come to occupy. As noted in our discussion below, women experience a number of social processes, such as professional closure, accessibility of precarious jobs, gendered family dynamics, which channel them into low-end contingent jobs. They then engage in a complex process of informal learning through which they adapt to the new material conditions of their lives, as well as the ideological construction of themselves as precarious workers. With little training support at work, women have to learn to do their jobs through self-initiated and peer learning. Many of the women we interviewed immigrated years ago, and the transitioning process for these women is a long-term endeavour. Part of the transition into precarious work involves evaluating and developing practices of resistance through which they can preserve the little power they hold.

FRAMING THE TRANSITION PROCESS: CLOSURE AND ACCESS

It is well documented that foreign-trained professional immigrants experience downward social mobility after immigrating to Canada despite their significant human capital (Basran and Zong, 1998; Boyd, 1986, 1992; Krahn et al., 2000; Pendakur and Pendakur, 1998; Reitz, 2003). Immigrants, regardless of their educational levels and previous work experience, often serve as a source of cheap labour and tend to be concentrated in low pay, low-status jobs, particularly in the service sector or the garment industry (Sassen, 1998; Teelucksingh and Galabuzi, 2005). Theorists have attempted to explain the underemployment of immigrants in host societies, attributing immigrants' positions in the labour market to education (e.g., Neuwirth et al., 1989), marital status (Fagnan, 1995), occupational training, work experience, and language proficiency (Morawska, 1990; Glenn, 1986). Others see systematic institutional barriers obstructing immigrants' labour market integration process, such as the lack of recognition of immigrants' credentials (Slade, 2004; Cumming et al., 1989), pre-existing ethnic or race relations within the host population, differences in labour markets and related institutional practices, and government policies and programs (Reitz, 2003).

We found that for many immigrant women who are racialized, transition into the Canadian labour market involves entry into jobs in retail, sewing or telemarketing, which are relatively accessible to newcomers, especially to women. These jobs depend on highly 'flexible' and captive workers who have few employment alternatives and who are forced to accept low wages and unstable work schedules. For women trying to acquire English language proficiency or accreditation in Canada, these jobs were their only option to support their spouses and children. Our interview data indicate that women did not plan to work as cashiers, sewers and call centre operators. They turned to these jobs after experiencing exclusion from professional occupations and because of the easy accessibility of jobs in the precarious sectors of the labour market. Some of the people obtained their jobs through answering postings in government offices (employment centres), and advertisements in newspapers and the Internet and through contacting temporary agencies. Most women found work by word of mouth and personal and community networks. Workers comment on the easy accessibility of these jobs:

> That's why I think most immigrants who are coming here in Canada are doing this job, lots of immigrants are in telemarketing and market research, that's for sure, because they don't need very much qualifications, they don't ask you for qualifications. And telemarketing they need a little bit to know how to sell, but market research they [...]only [need] basic computer skills, so it's very good job for them, the newcomers. (Nazia, Call centre worker)

> When I came in January, everybody said that no, it's not possible, that you came here and right away you find your job in your sector because your education is from your country. Even if it is recognized I think so, but they said 'No, it is not recognized over here'. Unless you have some degree from here, then you can get a job in your sector, otherwise even if you a degree and you have experience you cannot [get it]. [S]ituation is not good. This time I made up my mind that whatever job, I will do it. (Sabana, Call centre worker)

A statistician from China recounted her journey into the garment sector:

> At that time, there is a person who speaks Mandarin, and with a master degree, working there. ... do embroidering too. She just came to Canada, cannot find a professional job [and had to work there in the factory]. (Lucy, Garment worker)

For most of the women, professional closure is complicated by language issues, childcare responsibilities, and the need to sustain the household economy:

> I worked as a nurse in Sri Lanka. I did not know what to do [in Canada], because ... different languages and cultures, so everything is different. I came here, ... I had children. That is totally different. I went to a something, support somewhere, asked what to do. She said that I can go for training and spend time and money. We think about it, and at least you have to pass grade 12 English. So .. now I am going to [store], [working as a] cashiers... (Mala, Supermarket cashier)

> I now don't like this job, it's really hard! But I have to do [it], because still my husband [is] not really settled. So we have to...pay our bills and everything. (Nazia, Call centre agent)

Women's participation in the precarious labour force, with unstable employment, shift work and unreliable working hours, has a direct impact on their family lives. Women talked about how their vulnerability is routinely exploited by employers.

> You know we see a lot of mothers, single parents who work where we work and they got to come home, their kids are under 14 or 15, they have to be supervised and they are given shifts like 4 to 10. So they are put in a compromising position. How you are supposed to pick up your job over your child? If you look like the type of person that will be easily taken advantage of you are going to have problems they are going to walk over you with no conscience at all. (Paula, Supermarket cashier)

Women sometimes develop tactics to circumvent the total intrusion of their jobs into their families and to organize their family relations in such a way as to make possible the survival of the household.

> I just told them, because [working on] Sunday[s] is compulsory. I told them that I am taking weekend courses and I cannot make it on Sunday. Because what happened is that my husband gets leave only on Sunday. If I do go on Sunday, we don't meet the whole week. We don't get time to spend together. (Mina, Supermarket cashier)

Another woman who was juggling two jobs while undergoing training as a hair dresser said:

> [T]he schedule is tight. But my husband is going to school, now he is taking a test. But normally he would send me to work and get me from work. If I am too busy, he would cook for me. Worse comes to worse, I will buy a hamburger. (Rose, Call centre agent)

Although both she and her husband were engineers in their home country, at the time of the interview, this woman was the main breadwinner of the household. Her husband was studying full-time to get re-certified as an engineer. This example indicates clearly and unequivocally how gender (sexist and patriarchal) ideology operates in the family: men's careers are considered as primary while women have greater access to precarious jobs and therefore the ability to provide at least some immediate family income. It is precisely the convergence of the financial necessity of maintaining the household, childcare responsibilities, and the 'flexibility' of work in sectors where jobs are increasingly casualized, that hold immigrant women captive in precarious work.

TRANSITIONING INTO PRECARIOUS JOBS

Once locked into jobs in the sectors that make systematic use of precarious workers, the women in our study faced a steep learning curve in terms of the actual work they were required to perform, and the ideological accommodation they had to make. We found that workers across the three sectors we investigated were provided with very little training. Indeed, most learned under the threat of 'getting it or getting fired'. Women spoke of their efforts to learn either by themselves or through relying on their peers to meet the employers' expectations and demands. In other writing (Mirchandani et al., 2008; Maitra and Shan, 2007), we have documented the nature of the learning in which precarious workers engage, and ways in which they draw continually on their prior skill and experience. Here, we focus specifically on the process of transition they undergo to adapt to their material circumstance (low waged, flexible work), and ideological condition (constructions of self as servile and disposable workers).

ADAPTING TO MATERIAL CONDITIONS OF PRECARIOUS WORK

Some of our interviewees mentioned that contingent work had some advantages. For example, Bina, a supermarket cashier related the following:

> Sometimes, my friend call me and we can exchange [shifts], you know, friends … made after the job….I can talk with the supervisor; tell her that we cannot come on Friday. And she will say ok. You can take other time, you [can cancel shift]…

Indeed, call centre and cashier jobs, in particular, may afford immigrants a degree of flexibility, which seems to work for the immigrants who juggle between different work and responsibilities. Nazia, a call centre worker said:

> Right now, when we got job, we tell them...they ask us, 'What days would you like to work, and what time would you like to work?', and we tell them what hours we'd like to work, because there are 3 shifts ... It is very good for the students, who go to school and college, and for people who are doing other jobs.

While some immigrants took advantage of the flexibility some contingent jobs offered, most people complained that they had to deal with a great deal of instability in their work and work times. Indeed, coping with instability is an integral part of their work. For example, Mary, a garment worker was unhappy with her unstable workload. She said: 'You will never know how long you could stay there to work. It all depends on whether they had work to do there'. Mita, a call centre worker complained about the uncertain working hours.

> Oh yes, they cancel many times, and say they don't have enough work, and they don't want that many people schedules, say about 20 people have scheduled and they don't have work for 20 people, then they phone you in the morning and tell you, or sometimes an hour before they tell you. Like the work starts at 5, and we leave the house around 4, so they just call you, maybe 15 minutes before that, and tell you not to come in.

In other cases, women might be asked to leave at short notice. For example, Sun, a call centre worker informed us that her call centre had a target and if the workers could not meet the target, they would be sent home. Mary, a garment worker who was also working as a supermarket cashier faced a similar threat:

> I just did the cashier. But I had to learn how to use the cashier machine. You had to learn how to give change to customers. I might be fired [if] I am not fast enough.

Women in the garment sector reported the most difficult work environments. They reported the lowest wages among the three sectors groups of people. In many cases they worked on piece rate, which masked the real hourly wage:

> One day when I came out and told my husband that I did not want to work there any more. He asked why? I said I only earned about $10 that day. My husband could not believe it, 'really? It can't be true.' I said, 'Yes! I don't want to work here any more!' So, I quit. And then, they fired my husband. They fired him because of me. (Lin, Garment worker)

Observably, precariousness in these sectors also involves discouraging and indeed deterring workers from resisting and fighting back. For example, Lee, a garment worker, told us that at her workplace, workers once tried to fight against their negative work conditions. As a result, she said, '[t]he supervisor asked [one of the workers] to leave... After [witnessing this incidence], we all dared not to fight again, not to get laid off'.

For many workers in our study, transitioning into precarious work means learning to adapt to their new material conditions. For many workers, especially those who held highly paid professional jobs in other countries, the ideological shift was as difficult as adapting to low wages and poor working conditions.

ADAPTING TO IDEOLOGICAL CONSTRUCTIONS OF PRECARIOUS WORKERS

Perhaps the most significant shift which women experience is the attitude of servitude required in many precarious jobs. Many women had skills and knowledge that far exceeded the requirements in their jobs, yet, they had to re-conceptualize their tasks according to the demands of the employer. As one worker pointed out, 'you have to do it [the employers'] way... It's their way or no way' (Carla, Call centre worker). Interviewees from call centres and supermarkets note how they had to learn their place as 'serving' the customer above all else:

> The customers are always right so it doesn't matter what they say even if it's like their fault they are always right... So you are not supposed to say anything back to them, you are not supposed to start yelling or swearing at them. (Razia, Supermarket cashier)

Our study indicates that servility, passivity and docility are seen as integral to these jobs:

> We don't fight with customers. This is our store need.... [Y]ou have to have good manners. If you have customers, first customers first.... We have to serve with customers... We do not want customers getting mad. (Shashi, Supermarket cashier)

> The most important thing is just to sit calm. And you have to be polite, even if some of the people are rude, just don't bother about it. Have a carefree attitude. If you tend to get frustrated, then you will not be able to work. If you take it too hard, if anybody say something and you take it too hard, then I don't think you will be able to work. (Anju, Call centre worker)

Women's transition to precarious work involved learning an attitude of servitude despite their often higher qualifications and experience in professional work. This type of learning also worked to alienate and dehumanize workers.

> But only thing I feel bad is that sometimes if we make minor mistakes customers are rude at me. They use swear words if I am slow. I feel bad but cannot say anything as we have been told not to offend customers. I guess this is stressful. I wish the supervisor would say something to the customer when they are rude. One of my friends told me that this is actually exploitation of workers. But my advice to new workers would be if you in my position that you have to earn money then just work and leave. Don't think about it too much. I never talk about work at home. I just watch TV sometimes when I am too stressed or sad. (Mina, Supermarket cashier)

The culture and attitude of servility is accompanied by the fact that workers in these sectors are made to feel that they are disposable. According to our interviewees, many employers in the garment sector frequently lay off even their best sewers, knowing that they can be easily replaced. The availability of garment workers, especially in the context of a highly unstable and changeable industry, has created a lot of competition amongst workers. The following excerpts from our interviews illustrate our points:

> [I worked there] altogether [for] 3 years. But each year [the employer] lays us off for almost half a year. I was once laid off for one year. ...They wrote a paper for you to go to apply for EI. (Mary, Garment worker)

> The biggest problem was that I had no enough work to do. Or the pay was too low. For example, the current pay is lower. The job market is not so good. There are too many immigrants who came from Mainland China. They do not pick jobs to do. They just take whatever they can get to do. Even when there was not much work to do, they are told to come to work later, but they would even come earlier. When they were told to leave work earlier, they would stay later. As a result, the boss would not necessarily give them extra pay for them working extra hours. And also, the boss would pay even lower because there were people working for him any way. (Nancy, Garment worker)

Instead of feeling valued and rewarded for their efforts, many workers in these sectors feel used and unappreciated. However, women were by no means passive victims of employers' whim. From time to time, they attempted to fight back or negotiate for better conditions for themselves or for others.

PRACTICES OF RESISTANCE

Transitioning into precarious jobs also involved learning practices and strategies that could improve work conditions. While we found little evidence of collective action amongst precarious workers, several workers did engage in individual forms of resistance in order to improve their working conditions. Our data provide stark evidence of the many ways in which precarious employment promotes individualism. Learning and resistance strategies are primarily individualized, with the worker bearing both the risk and the consequences of resistance. For example, the following call centre worker who was treated badly by her supervisor decided to quit her job. She said:

> I said [to the supervisor], 'You make your mouth sweet, instead of saying let me show you the door.' So he felt awkward – he was younger to me, but I used my wisdom, rather than he showing me the door, I knew where the door was, I gave him a candy to keep his mouth a little sweet to the others. (Asha, Call centre worker)

Similarly, a cashier working in a supermarket for three years shared her experience about how she looked directly at her supervisor and returned the gaze of authority when she was treated badly for something that she did not do. She said:

> ...Then the manager's like how do you feel like if I take 20 minutes off your pay check?...I am like just looking at him. He was feeling uncomfortable[.]... I think that just unnerved him, the fact that I was looking at him... To me it was resistance that I looked at him in the eye and not looking away or down. You know I don't have to talk back to him, I can make him uncomfortable by looking at him [now]. (Edna, Supermarket cashier)

Although she knew that she needed this job badly in order to pay her tuition and other expenses, after seeing the very exploitative structure of her job, this worker realized that she had to stand up for her own rights. Subsequently, she decided to take a course on labour issues and law in order to protect herself at work. She not only took the course for her own benefit, but she also informed her colleagues on what she learned from the course. Similarly, a garment sewer decided that she needed a raise. She had to take radical but risky action to make it happen:

> So I told him [the supervisor] I want the increase. I am working hard you know and you have to be fair to me. I am not just working like this only ... [the] trick is if he is not going to give me what I want, I just don't go to work for a day. He is going to be mad. (Yin, Garment worker)

In another case, a call centre worker with extensive experience working in various call centres actually refused to do her surveys as she felt they were badly designed and too long, and that she would not get the right response from her customers. She didn't want her employer to penalize her for not getting the desired number of surveys. She decided to be outspoken at the risk of getting fired.

> I expressed my feelings… that this is a really long survey so…can you please do something…can you please cut down…something or may be then it will help us. (Amina, Call centre worker).

In addition to individual actions that the women took to change their work environments, there were a few examples of cooperative resistance. For example, a garment worker recounted a factory where the workers decided collectively to sew slowly so that the supervisor would meet their demands to correct their adverse working conditions.
She said:

> Yes, we did complain to [the management staff). As the supervisor or the boss comes by, we would yell, 'it's too hot'… Other whites or blacks or other co-workers also went to complain to them. Or we have to sew more slowly. (Mary, Garment worker)

Another garment worker learned to use the law to assert her rights. She and her colleagues were not paid regularly and after surfing the internet and visiting community centres, she launched an appeal at the Ministry of Labour. She then distributed this information to her coworkers, who followed suit and set up cases against the same employer.

Many of the retail workers we interviewed were unionized, although most of the cashiers did not have prior experience with unions, or clearly understood their role. Those who knew about unions generally expressed dissatisfaction with the nature of protection for precarious cashiers and many felt that unions were largely invisible. As one woman notes, unions are 'secret angels, you don't get to see them. We know we have somebody to make complains to but we don't see them. [So] what's the point?' Although some women felt that union presence might give them some protection from getting fired arbitrarily, most of the time they were not sure who to talk to or where to take their grievance. Only a couple of interviewees mentioned hearing about union meetings and receiving monthly newsletters from the union. Even then, they were not sure about the kind of union activities or protection they could get in the workplace. It was telling that most respondents did not even know the name of their union representative and had no idea about union actions in the workplace. Some of the women were not sure if they were unionized. One only found out that she was unionized during the interview when she saw union dues on her pay stub.

CONCLUSIONS

Few studies have examined the experiences and struggles of immigrant women, many of whom are highly educated, as they transition into precarious jobs. This chapter examines the experiences of immigrant women making their transition into low-end precarious sectors in Canada such as grocery stores, call centres, and garment factories. We argue that the transition into precarious work involves, first, a material shift where women are channelled into sectors within which precarious work relationships are prevalent, and second, an ideological shift where women learn to construct themselves as precarious workers.

The transitional phase we focus on is a period of time upon an immigrant's arrival in Canada wherein they have the opportunity to survey the landscape. Regardless of how little or how much money they bring with them, the pressing material needs of shelter, food and clothing begins to delimit the time they have to prepare and compete for professional jobs commensurate with their qualifications. For immigrant women in particular, the gendered dynamic of family life presupposes the primacy of the husband's earning power along with the responsibilities of childcare, food preparation and household management as women's work further constraining opportunities for professional and career development. The perception of the accessibility of service and precarious work presents a choice to provide for the material needs of the family rather than persevering in the pursuit of professional careers, resulting in deprofessionalization and the ensuing professional closure.

Upon entering into precarious work, immigrant women have to construct themselves as workers who are docile, servile and disposable. As part of the survival process, they learn to accept the limitation of their power within these jobs, submitting to exploitation from their supervisors and customers. Some women accept their precariousness but distance themselves from its dehumanizing effects given their needs. Others actively resist while on the job by verbalizing their complaints and negotiating for change.

The analysis in this paper suggests that rather than a universal process describing a movement from school to work, or across workplaces, 'transitions' are highly contextualized social processes that are experienced differently for people occupying various social locations. Women's transitions in learning and work are fundamentally structured by their transnational transition from their countries of origin. Their transitions involve both a material and an ideological dimension, as they learn not only to survive under the pay and structure of precarious employment but simultaneously learn attitudes of servitude and resistance.

Bourgeault states that the experience of deskilling among immigrants 'contradicts immigration policies that strive to seek the 'best and the brightest'' (Bourgeault, 2007: 96). Understanding the experiences of racialized immigrant women and their transition into precarious work within the Canadian labour market provides the opportunity to identify learning opportunities which may enrich transition experiences. First, it is clear that transnational migration requires inordinate effort, skill and learning and this is part of the *work* of transitioning into the Canadian labour market. Indeed, conceptualizing transition as work suggests the need for a much more comprehensive system of transition support for new immigrants, which may include income, education and training support. Second, many immigrant women transition in the midst of childcare and household responsibilities, and without social and financial support for these are forced into jobs in which they do not utilize their education and work experience. Finally, a fundamental shift in employer behaviour is needed to support immigrant transitions. For example, rather than current incentives to provide volunteer or short term jobs for immigrants to gain Canadian work experience, employers should be provided with incentives to create full time permanent jobs for immigrant workers. Such policies and programs, based on understandings of the social differences in the transition process, are likely to provide greater potential for social and economic equality.

NOTES

[1] This paper is based on a research project funded by Social Sciences and Humanities Research Council of Canada. Kiran Mirchandani was the Principal Investigator on this project and Roxana Ng was the Co-Investigator. The remaining authors were collaborators and are listed in alphabetical order. Other group members involved in this project include Jasjit Sangha and (late) Karen Hadley.

REFERENCES

Acker, J. (1992). Gendering organisational theory. In A. J. Mills & P. Tancred (Eds.), *Gendering organisational analysis*. London: Sage.

Basran, G. S., & Zong, L. (1998). Devaluation of foreign credentials as perceived by visible minority professional immigrants. *Canadian Ethnic Studies, 30*(3), 7–23.

Bourgeault, I. L. (2007, Spring). Brain drain, brain gain and brain waste: Programs aimed at integrating and retaining the best and the brightest in health care. *Canadian Issues*, 96–99.

Boyd, M. (1992). Gender, visible minority and immigrant earnings inequality: Reassessing an employment equity premise. In V. Satzewich (Ed.), *Deconstructing a nation: Immigration, multiculturalism and racism in 90s Canada*. Halifax, NS: Fernwood Publishing.

Boyd, M. (1986). Immigrant women in Canada. In C. Brettell & R. J. Simon (Eds.), *International migration: The female experience*. Totowa, NJ: Rowman & Allanheld.

Cumming, P. A., Lee, E., & Dimitrios, G. O. (1989). *Access! task force on access to professions and trades in Ontario*. Toronto: Ontario Ministry of Citizenship.

De Wolff, A. (2003). *Bargaining for work and life*. Unpublished Paper, Feminist Political Economy Network, Graduate Women's Studies Program, York University.

Fagnan, S. (1995). Canadian immigrant earnings, 1971–86. In Don DeVoretz (Ed.), *The economics of Canada's recent immigration policy*. Toronto and Vancouver: C. D. Howe Institute and the Laurier Institution.

Glenn, E. N. (1986). *Issei, Nisei, War Bride: Three generations of Japanese American women in domestic service*. Philadelphis: Temple University Press.

Krahn, H., Derwing, T., Mulder, M., & Wilkinson, L. (2000). Educated and underemployed: Refugee integration into the Canadian labour market. *Journal of International Migration and Integration, 1*(1), 59–84.

Maitra, S., & Shan, H. (2007). Transgressive vs. conformative: immigrant women learning at contingent work. *Journal of Workplace Learning, 19*, 286–295.

Man, G. (2004). Gender, work and migration: Deskilling Chinese immigrant women in Canada. *Women's Studies International Forum, 27*(2), 135–148.

Mirchandani, K., Ng, R., Coloma-Moya, N., Maitra, S., Rawling, T., Shan, H., et al. (2008). The paradox of training and learning in a culture of contingency. In D. W. Livingstone, K. Mirchandani, & P. Sawchuk (Eds.), *The future of lifelong learning and work: Critical perspectives* (pp. 171–184). Rotterdam: Sense Publishers.

Morawska, E. (1990). The sociology and historiography of immigration. In V. Yans-McLaughlin (Ed.), *Immigration reconsidered: History, sociology, and politics*. New York: Oxford University Press.

Neuwirth, G., Jones, S., & Eyton, J. (1989). *Immigrant settlement indicators: A feasibility study Ottawa-Hull: Policy analysis directorate*. Immigration Policy Branch, Employment and Immigration Canada.

Ng, R. (2001). Training for whom? for what? Reflections on the meaning of training for garment workers. *Employment-related training for immigrant women* (Community perspective series). Toronto: Toronto Training Board.

Pendakur, K., & Pendakur, R. (1998). The colour of money: Earnings differentials among ethnic groups in Canada. *Canadian Journal of Economics, 31*(3), 518–548.

Picot, G. (2004). The deteriorating economic welfare of Canadian immigrants. *Canadian Journal of Urban Research, 13*(1), 25–45.

Reitz, J. G. (2003). Immigration and Canadian nation-building in the transition to a knowledge economy. In W. A. Cornelius, P. L. Martin, J. F. Hollifield, & T. Tsuda (Eds.), *Controlling immigration: A global perspective* (2nd ed.). Stanford, CA: Stanford University Press.

Sassen, S. (1998). *Globalization and its discontents. Essays on the new mobility of people and money.* New York: New Press.

Slade, B. (2004). Highly skilled and under-theorized: Women migrant professionals. In R. Baaba Folson (Ed.), *Calculated kindness: Global economic restructuring and Canadian immigration & settlement policy.* Halifax, NS: Fernwood Publishing.

Teelucksingh, C., & Galabuzi, G. E. (2005). *Working precariously: The impact of race and immigrants status on employment opportunities and outcomes in Canada.* Toronto: The Canadian Race Relations Foundation. Retrieved January 15, 2008, from http://www.amillionreasons.ca/WorkingPrecariously.pdf

Wallace, C., & Vosko, L. F. (2003). *Changing Canada: The political economy of transformation.* Montreal: McGill-Queen's.

Kiran Mirchandani
University of Toronto

Roxana Ng
University of Toronto

Nel Coloma-Moya
York University

Srabani Maitra
University of Toronto

Trudy Rawlings
University of Toronto

Hongxia Shan
University of Toronto

Khaleda Siddiqui
Independent Researcher

Bonnie Slade
York University

SHIBAO GUO

13. FALSE PROMISES IN THE NEW ECONOMY

Barriers facing the Transition of Recent Chinese Immigrants in Edmonton

INTRODUCTION

Canada promotes itself as an immigrant country and a land of opportunities with a vast territory and rich resources. Currently it faces an aging population and declining fertility rates. Hence, immigration has been promoted as a solution to help Canada ameliorate its labour shortages in a booming economy, particularly in the province of Alberta. Furthermore, Canada's multiculturalism policies present the country as a culturally tolerant nation, and its favourable integration policies guarantee a smooth settlement and transition for new immigrants. All these promises have been testified as false hopes by recent immigrants from the People's Republic of China (PRC). Since 1998 PRC has become the top source country of immigration with an annual intake of more than 30,000. However, little is known about their settlement and integration experiences.

This chapter explores the transition of recent Chinese immigrants in Canada. It reveals that Chinese immigrants face serious barriers in their transition process. Despite the fact that the majority came with post-secondary education, a large number of them face unemployment or underemployment in Canada. Many cannot find jobs in their original professions because their Chinese qualifications and work experiences are not recognized. Furthermore, lack of social networks, lack of Canadian work experience, and language difficulties are additional barriers facing Chinese immigrants in their new transitions. The findings of this study raise many important questions about barriers facing newcomers to Canada and the changing nature of work and learning in Canada's new economy.

The chapter is organized into four parts. It starts with a review of context and literature, followed by a discussion of the research design. The third part focuses on research findings and the paper ends with discussion and a conclusion.

CANADA'S CHANGING IMMIGRATION POLICY IN THE NEW ECONOMY

The driving forces behind immigration are social, political, economic and demographic. In the 19th century massive immigration was used as a strategy to develop Western Canada and served the economic and demographic interests of the country. In addition, immigration has functioned as a means of social and ideological control. In deciding who is most desirable and admissible, the state

P. Sawchuk and A. Taylor (eds.), Challenging Transitions in Learning and Work: Reflections on Policy and Practice, 243–260.

sets parameters for the social, cultural and symbolic boundaries of the nation, as manifested in historically racist Canadian immigration policies. From the Confederation of Canada in 1867 to the 1960s, the selection of immigrants was based on their racial background. British and Western Europeans were the most 'desirable' citizens, Asians and Africans the 'unassimilable' and, therefore, 'undesirable.' After the Second World War, Canadian immigration policy continued to be 'highly restrictive' despite external and internal pressures for an open-door policy (Knowles, 1997).

In the mid-1960s, Canada was experiencing 'the greatest postwar boom' (Whitaker, 1991, p. 18). Skilled labour was required to help Canada build its expansionary economy, but Europe as the traditional source of immigrants was not able to meet the needs of Canada because of the economic recovery there. Thus, the Canadian government turned its recruitment efforts to such traditionally restricted areas as Asia. In 1967 a 'point system' was introduced by the Liberal government, which based the selection of immigrants on their 'education, skills and resources' rather than racial and religious backgrounds (Ibid., p. 19). According to Whitaker, this new system represented 'an historic watershed,' and 'it did establish at the level of formal principle that Canadian immigration policy is 'colour blind'' (Ibid., p. 19). However, the new selection method was criticized by Matas (1996, p. 100) for being 'in favour of some racial groups and against others'. Despite the criticism, the 'point system' was successful in reversing the pattern of immigration to Canada away from Europe toward Asia and other Third World regions. By the mid-1970s, Canada accepted more immigrants from the Third World than from the developed world, the largest number coming from Asia, followed by the Caribbean, Latin America, and Africa.

Since the mid-1990s, under Canada's knowledge-based economy, immigrant selection practices have given more weight to education and skills, favouring economic immigrants over family-class immigrants and refugees. As Li (2003a) notes, this new shift was based on the assumption that economic immigrants brought more human capital than family-class immigrants and refugees and therefore were more valuable and desirable. According to Li, economic-class immigrants made up more than half of all immigrants admitted throughout the late 1990s. Among them, a considerable number are highly educated professionals, particularly scientists and engineers. In the year 2000, of the total 227,209 immigrants and refugees admitted, 23 per cent (52,000 individuals) were admitted as skilled workers (Couton, 2002).

THE CHANGING PATTERN OF CHINESE EMIGRATION TO CANADA

The history of Chinese emigration mirrored Canada's immigration past. The first group of Chinese immigrants arrived on Canada's west coast in 1858 in search of gold. They came predominantly from the southern Chinese coastal provinces of Guangdong and Fujian as coolie workers and chain migrants. Chinese immigrants were used extensively during the construction of the Canadian Pacific Railway (CPR) (Li, 1998; Tan and Roy, 1985). With the completion of the CPR, the Chinese were no longer welcome. In 1885, the government of Canada imposed a $50 head tax on all incoming Chinese to control their entry, which was increased to $100 in 1900 and to $500 in 1903. When the head tax was found not effective enough to keep the Chinese out of Canada, the federal government passed the restrictive Chinese Immigration Act in 1923, which virtually prohibited all Chinese immigration into Canada until its repeal in 1947. Besides the head tax and the 1923 Chinese Immigration Act, Chinese in Canada also faced other kinds of discrimination. Since they were not allowed to vote, they were prohibited from entering certain professions such as law, medicine, or accounting (Li, 1998; Tan and Roy, 1985).

With the introduction of the point immigration system in 1967, an increasing number of Chinese immigrants arrived in Canada, primarily from Hong Kong. In fact Hong Kong had been the primary source of Chinese emigration to Canada since the Second World War (Li, 1998). According to Li, Canada admitted 30,546 Chinese immigrants between 1956 and 1967, increasing to 90,118 between 1968 and 1976 with the introduction of the point system. These immigrants came predominantly from Hong Kong, accounting for two-thirds of the total emigration from Hong Kong, Taiwan, and mainland China. This trend continued until the mid-1990s, when Hong Kong gave way to the People's Republic of China as the major source of Chinese emigration to Canada (Guo and DeVoretz, 2006a).

China had been isolated from the rest of the world since the People's Republic of China was founded in 1949. However, two historic events that took place during the 1970s paved the way for substantial emigration from the PRC in the 1990s. The first was the establishment of formal diplomatic relations between Canada and China in 1970, which did not set off an immediate upsurge of emigration from China, although it set the political stage for the movement of people between the two nations thereafter. The other, the death of Mao Zedong in 1976, marked the end of the Cultural Revolution. With Deng Xiaoping's rise to power in 1978, a number of reforms were introduced, generally characterized by an open-door policy that shifted the nation's focus from political struggle to economic reconstruction. The open-door policy created the economic conditions for the mobility of Chinese people.

In the early 1980s, direct emigration from China to Canada was relatively small (Guo and DeVoretz, 2006a; Li, 1998). The pro-democracy student movement in 1989 became a catalyst as well as a hindrance for the emigration of Chinese people. On the one hand, the event prompted the Canadian government to issue permanent resident status to many Chinese students and scholars who were studying in Canada at that time. On the other hand, the Chinese government tightened the rules to further restrict people's mobility. However, this restriction did not last long. The 1990s witnessed substantial emigration from China to Canada. China's 'open door' policy and economic development resulted in an economic boom in China and a new middle-income class. Combined with relaxed passport restrictions by the Chinese government, China entered the 'emigration phase' (Wallis, 1998). Furthermore, Canada opened an immigration office in Beijing in 1995, which processed immigration applications directly from China. Given these developments, PRC emigrants outnumbered Hong Kong's and Taiwan's emigrants in 1998, as the PRC became the top source region for immigrants to Canada after 1998 (Citizenship and Immigration Canada, 1999; Guo and DeVoretz, 2006a).

RESEARCH ON IMMIGRANT TRANSITION

In general, immigrants come to Canada under three major categories: economic class, family class, and refugees. The economic class comprises skilled workers and business immigrants. Skilled workers are admitted under a point system using prescribed selection criteria based on education, occupation, language skills, and work experience. Canada has three classes of business immigrants: investors, entrepreneurs, and self-employed persons, each with separate eligibility criteria. Family class immigration reunites close family members of an adult resident or citizen of the hosting country, such as children, parents, spouse, and common-law partner. Refugee protection is usually offered to those who fear returning to their country of nationality or habitual residence because of war, and fear of persecution, torture or cruel and unusual treatment or punishment.

At the centre of this analysis are immigrants themselves. It is important to review what this term means. According to Li (2003a), the notion of 'immigrant' is socially constructed. He argues that it is often associated with people of non-white origin. In the context of Canada, early settlers came mainly from Europe. Only since the immigrant point system was introduced in 1967 has Canada attracted an increasing number of immigrants from Third World countries, notably Asia and Africa. Descendants of early European settlers, now long-established Canadians, do not think of themselves as immigrants. As Li puts it, the term 'immigrant' has become a codified word for people of colour who come from a different racial and cultural background, who do not speak fluent English, and who work in lower position jobs. Li maintains that the social construction of 'immigrant' uses skin colour as the basis for social marking. These individuals' real and alleged differences are claimed to be incompatible with the cultural and social fabric of 'traditional' Canada, and they are therefore deemed undesirable. Immigrants are also often blamed for creating urban social problems and racial and cultural tensions in the receiving society. The social construction of immigrant places uneven expectations on immigrants to conform over time to the norms, values, and traditions of the receiving society.

A shift has occurred in the discourse concerning immigrant settlement and transition. Hiebert and Ley (2001) identify two models related to immigrants' settlement: (i) assimilation, and (ii) integration. While the former signifies the expectation that immigrants abandon their previous cultures and adapt to their new society, the latter is regarded as a two-way adjustment process whereby immigrants and the host society together create a new culture. According to Hiebert and Ley, these two terms are often portrayed as opposites. However, they continue, since the principle of assimilation became increasingly obsolete, integration has become a more acceptable substitute for assimilation. Critics of the discourse of immigrant integration such as Li (2003b) argue that integration endorses a conformity model in assessing immigrants and a monolithic cultural framework that preaches tolerance in the abstract but remains intolerant towards cultural specificities deemed outside the mainstream.

The current immigration policies in Canada's new economy have primarily focused on Canada's labour force shortages and the interests of the state. They ignore the barriers facing the transition process of immigrant individuals. Immigrants moving to a new country are likely to encounter barriers in the process of adapting to a new society. They need assistance with language, employment, housing, daycare, education, health, counselling, legal and social services. A number of studies have identified one such barrier as lack of access to social services in the mainstream (Bergin, 1988; Leung, 2000; Nguyen, 1991; Reitz, 1995). Reitz (1995) concluded from a review of nearly 400 international publications that recent immigrants very often experience low rates of utilization of many important social and health services, despite evidence of significant need and the fact that immigrants contribute more to the economy through taxation than they use in services. The low utilization can be attributed to a number of barriers, including language and cultural difficulties. Others, such as Henry et al. (2006), argue that the persistence of racial inequality in immigrant settlement and adaptation can be attributed to the existing ideologies of democratic racism. While Canadians were committed to democratic principles such as justice, equality, and fairness, people still retain their negative attitudes and behaviours towards minority groups or any differential treatment which is aimed at ameliorating the low status of these groups. The ideology in which these two sets of conflicting values coexist is referred to by Henry et al. as 'democratic racism.'

Other more recent studies identify employment barriers, including the devaluation and denigration of foreign credentials and prior work experience, as new challenges facing immigrants. Despite Canada's preference for highly skilled immigrants, and despite the fact that immigrant professionals bring significant human capital resources to the Canadian labour force, a number of studies have shown that many highly educated immigrant professionals experience deskilling and devaluation of their prior learning and work experience after immigrating to Canada (Basran and Zong, 1998; Henry et al., 2006; Krahn et al., 2000; Leung 2000; Ma, 1996; Mojab, 1999). As Henry et al. (2006) note, there is little re-cognition in Canada of the professional qualifications, credentials, and experiences of immigrants. Some immigrants experience major shifts from prior occupations in sciences, engineering, business, and management to occupations in sales, services, and manufacturing. As a result, they suffer from wage loss and downward social mobility. Highly educated refugees also encounter similar barriers in Canada (Krahn et al., 2000). The situation for immigrant women is even worse. Many argue that in the labour force, the category of 'immigrant women' has served to commodify them to employers, reinforcing their class position in providing cheap, docile labour to the state in exploitive conditions, often permeated with racism and sexism (Mojab, 1999; Ng, 1999). As a result, both immigrants themselves and Canadian society suffer severe economic impacts (Li, 2001; Reitz, 2001).

RESEARCH METHODOLOGY

Two research methods were employed in this study: questionnaire survey and personal interviewing. The questionnaire requested basic demographic information, motivations for immigrating to Canada, and integration experience of Chinese immigrants. It was made available in both English and Chinese and records in the Landed Immigrant Data System (LIDS) were used as a guide to help select respondents. Participants were recruited through immigrant service organizations and churches where Chinese immigrants were more likely to congregate and a total of 124 completed questionnaires were received.

To further probe responses, personal interviews were conducted with willing participants from the survey. Interviewing emphasized personal and lived experiences of participants in the city of Edmonton, Alberta and it allowed me to talk to immigrants in detail about the barriers they faced in their transition. Edmonton was chosen as a research site mainly because of the lack of attention to the experience of immigrants in such second-tier cities despite a growing Chinese population.

Fourteen semi-structured interviews were conducted with participants of different age, gender, educational background, length of stay, employment, and citizenship status. Most were at their prime work age of 25–60 and there was a gender balance. The majority were relatively new to Canada having resided in Edmonton for less than three years; only four had obtained their Canadian citizenship having lived in Edmonton six to seventeen years. Nine skilled workers previously held jobs in China as scientists, engineers, and teachers. At the time of interview, eight were studying for a college diploma or graduate degree while working at a labour job. Each interview lasted between 1 and 1.5 hours. Since not everyone felt comfortable to be interviewed in English, participants were offered a choice between English and Chinese. Data were collected between October 2004 and June 2005 and were analyzed throughout the process. From these data, three compelling cases are presented here to provide a holistic account of immigrant experience in Canada. Furthermore, these three cases represented the transition of many Chinese immigrants interviewed.

REPORT OF FINDINGS

Demographic Information

Among all responses received in the questionnaire, 57% were female and 43% male. Most were married. The age of the participants ranged from 20 to 60, with the majority (63%) between 26 and 40 and a mean age of 34. Clearly the sample represents a younger group, which Canada tries to recruit. They came from more than 40 cities in China with the two largest groups from Beijing and Shanghai. The third largest group came from Harbin, Edmonton's sister city in China. The majority came to Canada as skilled workers (57%) and only one third (32%) came under family reunion, which reflects a recent trend in Canada's immigrant selection practices with an emphasis on economic immigrants (Li, 2003a). They were predominantly recent arrivals to Canada, half having resided in Edmonton for less than 3 years, 18% 3–5 years, 13% 5–10 years, and 19% more than 10 years. The length of stay was reflected in their citizenship status, with only 32% Canadian citizens and the rest permanent residents.

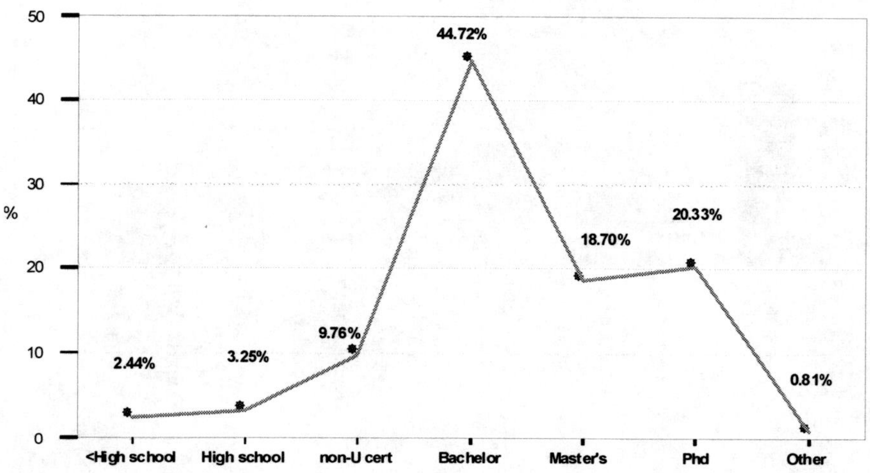

Figure 13.1. The highest level of education

In terms of their educational background, the majority (84%) arrived in Canada with a university degree or higher, including 45% with bachelors, 19% masters and 20% doctorates (See Figure 13.1). Clearly, this was a highly educated group, which also reflects the characteristics of recent Chinese immigrants to Canada (Guo and DeVoretz, 2006a; Lindsay, 2007). Most received their highest education from institutions in China (67%) and a smaller portion from Canada (23%). Regarding their level of English, nearly 80% of those surveyed stated that they had intermediate or advanced English skills.

Motivations for Moving to Canada

People moved to Canada for a number of reasons. Unlike their early counterparts who were here for economic reasons (Li, 1998; Tan and Roy, 1985), the most frequently cited motivations for the recent arrivals were their children's education (44%) and Canada's natural environment (43%), followed by furthering their own education (31%) and obtaining Canadian citizenship or permanent residency (27%). This finding is significant because it differs from the traditional economic motivations for immigrants to Canada. When asked if they had achieved their main goals, less than half (47%) indicated that they had. Of those who said they had not achieved their goals, they were less optimistic about the possibility of achieving their main goals (30%). The major factors that had prevented them from achieving their goals were: language difficulties (81%), lack of social network (55%), lack of Canadian work experience (45%), Chinese work experience not recognized (39%), and Chinese qualifications not recognized (39%) (See Figure 13.2).

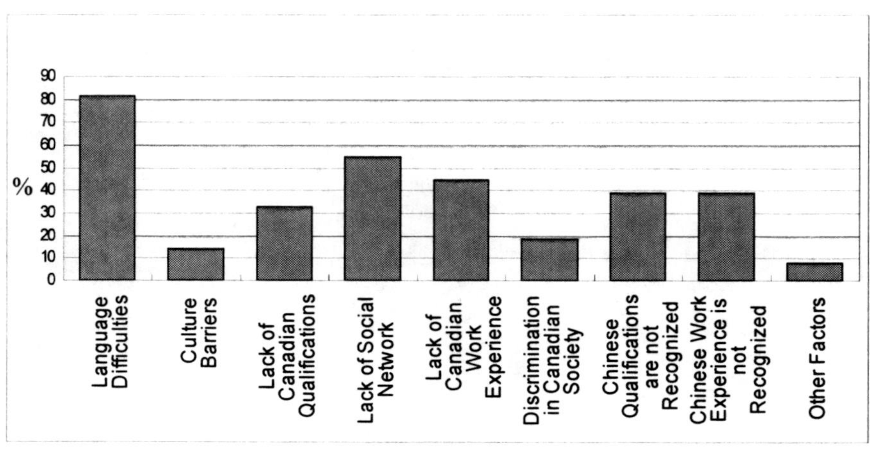

Figure 13.2. Obstacles for achieving main goals

Transition Experience with Multiple Barriers

This section explores the transition experience of Chinese immigrants. Respondents were asked about their employment experience, social life, and their level of satisfaction with Canada. When asked if they had encountered any major difficulties since arriving in Canada, a majority of them indicated they had, including language (85%), employment (56%), lack of social network (45%), cultural adjustment (37%), and being a foreigner (27%). The result supports findings from a number of other studies concerning the experience of immigrant professionals (Basran and Zong, 1998; Henry et al., 2006; Mojab, 1999). While some had only one major difficulty (26%), this study reveals that many encountered multiple ones. The language difficulty was a puzzling one. As reported earlier, nearly 80% of the respondents indicated that they arrived with intermediate or advanced English skills. It is not clear if their original assessment was too high, or some elements of language (such as accent) might not be accepted by the host society. Regarding their level of satisfaction, a large proportion (60%) felt Canada was worse or much worse than expected. One area of disappointment was their social life, with only 40% believing their social life in Canada was better than in China. However, employment was by far the most serious issue for most respondents. When asked to compare their employment situation in Canada with China, half of them reported deterioration, and only 29% indicated improvement (See Figure 13.3). In fact, these barriers are not unique to Edmonton Chinese immigrants. Research shows that recent Chinese immigrants in Vancouver also experienced similar difficulties with their Chinese credentials and work experience (Guo and DeVoretz, 2006b).

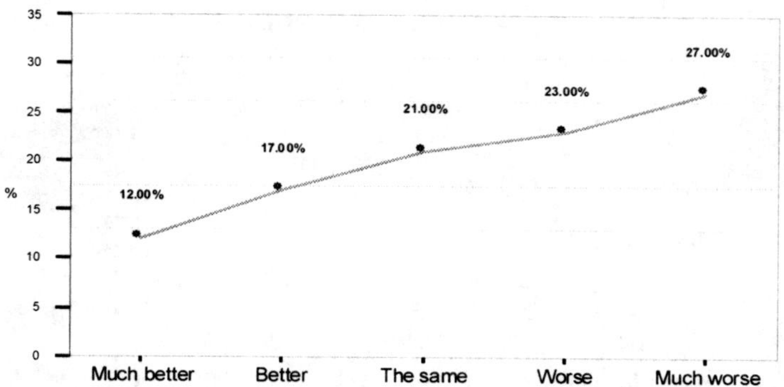

Figure 13.3. Employment situation in Canada

I conducted a comparative analysis to further examine the changes in employment between pre and post arrival in Edmonton. The findings reveal that prior to moving to Canada, one third (34%) held jobs in natural and applied sciences, forming the biggest occupation group among the surveyed. Next were professionals in social science and education (24%), followed by those in finance, business and administration (16%) and managerial positions (7%). After arriving in Edmonton, their employment situation took a downturn. The group with the most dramatic changes was social scientists, teachers and professors with a dramatic decline of 17%. From the change of other occupations, it seems clear that many of them might have gone to construction, trades, and labour work (14%), or some simply did not have a job (18%) (See Table 13.1).

The pre- and post-immigration occupational changes confirm the findings of a number of studies, including the government-sponsored Longitudinal Survey of Immigrants to Canada (Statistics Canada, 2003), which reveal that many immigrant professionals experienced major shifts from prior occupations in natural and applied sciences and management (for men) and business, finance and administration (for women) to occupations in sales and services, and processing and manufacturing. The most mysterious group was students, which dramatically increased from 5% to 18%. It is not clear what motivated them to return to school, what level of studies they were participating in, and if they went back to school voluntarily. But one thing is certain. The change of employment directly affected their annual household income, with more than one third (36%) reporting less than $20,000 which means they lived in poverty. This rate is significantly higher than the 16% low-income cut-off rate for the overall Canadian population and 26% for the Chinese population in Canada (Lindsay, 2007). At the national level, the loss totals $2.4 billion annually for Canada (Reitz, 2001). This raises particular concerns because it happened at a time when the unemployment rate reached its lowest in 33 years both nationally and in the province of Alberta. We need to ask: Who is benefiting from the current economic boom? What will the situation be like without the economic boom?

Table 13.1. Change of occupation before and after immigration

	Occupation Before Immigration		*Occupation After Immigration*	
Occupational Categories	Frequency	Valid Percentage	Frequency	Valid Percentage
Occupation in natural and applied sciences	38	33.9	28	26.9
Professional occupation in social science, education and government services	27	24.1	7	6.7
Professional occupation in finance, business and administration	18	16.1	11	10.6
Middle and other management	8	7.1	2	1.9
Professional occupation in health, registered nurse and supervisors	6	5.4	1	1.0
Students	6	5.4	19	18.3
Construction, trades, and labourers	5	4.5	14	13.5
Unemployed	2	1.6	19	18.3
Occupations in art, culture, recreation and sport	2	1.8	0	0
Food and services	0	0	1	1.0
Total	112	100	103	100

THREE CASE STUDIES

The following three cases are presented to help better understand the survey data. They were selected because they enabled us to focus on the particularities as well as the complexities of each single case (Stake, 1995). All three cases reveal the multiple barriers facing newcomers to Canada in the process of transition.

Case One

Shaoguang Wang[1] immigrated to Canada in August 2001 with his wife. He received his bachelor's degree from Beijing Chemical University in 1993 and subsequently worked for Sino-Pec (China Petroleum and Chemical Corporation) Beijing Design Institute as an engineer until his departure for Canada. He was in his early 30s, young, well-educated, and experienced – the ideal person that Canada tries to recruit for the new economy. He chose Edmonton because of its oil and gas industry. Prior to moving to Canada, he heard of barriers facing immigrants in their transition process. Having landed in Canada, he had a reality shock! He did not realize the barriers were multiple and severe, involving employment, credential recognition, language and culture. He gave himself three months to look for a job. If unsuccessful, he would go back to China. Meanwhile, his wife started her master's degree in agricultural science at the University of Alberta. Once he arrived in Edmonton, he tried his best to look for a job in his field. He sent out numerous resumes which resulted in few interviews. No one offered him a job, either because his English was not good enough or he did not have Canadian work experience (Basran and Zong, 1998). Before Christmas 2001, he decided to return to China to reunite with his son in Beijing, who they left behind with his parents.

Shaoguang and his family lived in an astronaut life for two years before he returned to Edmonton in December 2003. The astronaut life is a special phenomenon for immigrants, which usually involves the man of the household returning to the source country shortly after immigration to work in order to support the family, leaving his spouse and children to undergo the often-difficult process of settlement in Canada in his absence (Waters, 2003). When he returned to Edmonton, he found things were not much better. So he decided to take what he called 'a step-by-step approach' in realizing his professional goal, which was actually a lengthy and painful process. In this process, he changed jobs three times. He started his first job with a food factory which produced Italian sausages and bacon. He described it as 'very heavy labour work.' He was positioned to feed the sausage machine with meat. He said, 'You know, when I was in China, I never did labour work.' He managed the first two days. On day three, he was tired. Then he was placed at the end of the production line, 'surrounded by a group of women,' he said. 'They just put the sticker on the sausages. And they use the little knife to cut the line between the sausages and in fact, it is not light work, I can see that.' Shaoguang worked there for three months and quit after he got his first local reference. Lack of Canadian references is another barrier to immigrant's employment in addition to the devaluation of their foreign credentials and work experiences (Krahn et al., 2000).

Shaoguang's second job was a van driver. He said he had a romantic idea of being a truck driver so that he could visit different places and meet different people. It was also one way to learn more about Canadian society. First, he needed a truck driving license. He spent $3,000 out of his savings to take driving lessons for three months. After that, he started to look for a job as a truck driver. He said he sent out or delivered his resume to many transportation companies, but had difficulty finding a job. He asked, 'Do you know why?' I replied, 'Why?' He said, 'Because I didn't look like a truck drier. People think I look more like an engineer.' In the end, he found a job as a van driver to deliver goods for a rehabilitation centre at $9 per hour. It appears evident that the politics of difference does not only involve phenotypical differences attached to one's skin colour, but also relate to certain physical differences associated with specific professions.

Having worked there for another three months and gaining more experience, he found his third job with a food distribution centre, but this time as a truck driver. He delivered food to pizza and other restaurants. In talking about his experience as a truck driver, he said, 'the most difficult part of driving is back up the semi-truck. You have to drive straight to the door, the loading dock, straight and open your door, so they can unload or load something from the backdoor. If you can not back up straight, it's a lot of trouble there.' Since he did not know the city well, it usually took him longer to finish his work assignment. He said his boss and colleagues really liked him. They told him: 'This Chinese is not so strong but really, really excellent trucker.' After working there for more than one year he quit the job because he did not like the customers he worked with. He told me that sometimes food got lost in the process of moving from the truck to the restaurant. Once he lost a box of cheese. The boss asked him to pay, but he said it was not his fault. So he said, 'I quit.'

Having worked at three different jobs and gained some Canadian work experience, Shaoguang felt more confident than before. He wanted to find a professional job. At the time of the interview in May 2005, Shaoguang was attending a job search program at the ASSIST Community Services Centre, learning to prepare his resume and interviews. He was also attending a refresher program for immigrant engineers at the Edmonton Mennonite Centre for Newcomers, which would prepare him to return his professional field as a technologist. His next goal in this 'step-by-step approach' was to get into a master's program in engineering which would eventually help him become a certified engineer. The question is: How long will that take? Will it take him another five years? Shaoguang's story is not idiosyncratic. I believe it is shared by many immigrant professionals as previously discussed (Basran and Zong, 1998; Henry et al., 2006; Mojab, 1999).

Case Two

Lixia Wu was a journalist, editor, and producer for an English TV station in China before moving to Canada in 2004. Upon her arrival, she spent her first month touring five big cities to explore the country. After one month exploration, she decided to settle down in Edmonton because she liked the city and she also had relatives there. Lixia told me she had had a very comfortable job in China. She was once the number one news anchor in an English TV station in one of the largest cities in Central China. She had travelled to many countries, including Egypt, Israel, France, Italy, and many other European countries. 'And every time we had overseas assignment, I was the only one to go there,' she said. She held a BA in English and a postgraduate diploma in teaching English as a second language. She taught English in a university as her first job. I asked her why she decided to immigrate to Canada. She said, 'Coming to think of it, my original reason for moving to Canada was a naïve one.' She felt there was not much space for her to grow after becoming a producer in the TV station. She wanted a change. She added, 'My life has been full of challenge.' Furthermore, she liked to travel. She decided to immigrate to Canada. At that time, she was single.

The whole application process took more than two years. Lixia said Canada had given the priority to the high-tech applicants. During this period of time, she got married. She said her husband was supportive of her new endeavours. He told her she should come and see if she liked the country. So she did, but came alone. Her husband did not want her to wait for another two years for his application to come through, let alone the landing process did not allow such a long time to land. Upon arriving in Edmonton after her one-month 'honey moon' period in Canada, she started to look for a new job. She sent her resume to the CBC Television, the Global, CTV, and there was no response. She heard from many immigrants that employers were looking for Canadian work experience. She knew without a job, she would not get Canadian work experience. Like many new immigrants, she turned to volunteering for local work experience (Guo, 2006; Slade, Luo and Schugurensky, 2005). First she went to visit a local multilingual radio station because she did radio broadcasting before. She was interested in working for the Chinese program. She was surprised to find that there was a long waiting list, even for volunteering. She said, 'It is a little bit hard to believe' that even if you wanted to be a volunteer, you had to queue up. She even wrote a nice proposal about her ideas for the Chinese program. Although she described the director of the Chinese program as kind and professional, she did not get any volunteer work. She did not want labour work. Like Shaoguang, she decided to return to China. Before she left, she had applied to the MA program in Communication and Technology at the University of Alberta. She felt if she got a local degree, it would be easy for her to get a job. It becomes apparent that Lixia had no choice, but had been forced back to university which differed from the notion of adult learning as voluntary participation (Selman et al., 1998).

At the time of this interview, Lixia had completed one third of the MA course work. I asked her how she liked it. She said it was a nice program, but she was not sure whether it was for her. I asked why. She told me that she should have gone to something more practical. She said, 'I'm nobody here. It's good for me if I'm in China. It can help me move up.' She worried the MA would not guarantee her a job. She added, 'If I choose again, I would go to NAIT to get something practical and go to the job market. Maybe something like administrative assistant.' Lixia's comments made me think of Foucault's notion of 'governmentality' and how learning has been used as a technology of power which governs immigrants through a possible but invisible surveillance of the self (Andersson and Guo, 2009).

Lixia also discussed other challenges facing her transition in Edmonton, including lack of social network resulting from the relocation and disjunction out of immigration (Campbell et al., 2006). She said, 'When I was in China I never realized how important it was to have so many friends. Especially with my work in the TV station, I just needed to call someone and the information came. You didn't even need to buy coffee or dinner.' She was hoping through her MA study, she would get to know many people in her field. I could almost hear her sobbing voice when she talked about how much she missed her husband and other family members. Luckily she got to know many people through an online community which provided information and support for Chinese immigrants in Edmonton. She had also volunteered to help them organize a Chinese New Year party. She said, 'They needed a host for the party. What I could offer was my professional skill.' The volunteer experience helped her get her confidence back. She even started to think about her MA project to investigate the online community for immigrants. Like she stated, this recent development of online community for immigrants also pointed to a new direction for providing accessible social services and support for immigrants. Lixia's experience does not only reveal the employment barriers, but also social isolation facing immigrants.

Case Three

Jiazhi Li moved to Canada from China in November 2002 with his wife and daughter. He held a bachelor's degree in computer science and was a computer programmer in China for 10 years before moving to Canada. He was in his late 30s. Like Shaoguang and Lixia, he was young, well-educated, and experienced. Initially he settled in Toronto, and then moved to Edmonton where he had friends. Prior to moving to Canada, he imagined that the country would promise him a brighter future because Canada needed people like himself. He was disappointed at how things turned out. After arriving in Edmonton, first he needed a job. Wasting no time, he found a job as a kitchen helper in a Japanese restaurant, cutting vegetables, cleaning kitchen, etc. When I probed him naively about how he liked the job, he replied: 'What do you think? Do you think I like it? Of course not. It's very busy and dirty. But you know, as a stranger here, at the beginning, you have no other choice to do what you want to do.' While working at the restaurant, he continued to look for a computer job. He sent out numerous resumes, but only received two telephone interviews. He was told there were plenty of jobs in his area in the United States, but he wanted to stay in Canada. After three months, he knew he would not find anything in his profession in the near future. Hence, he decided to go back to school to get a college diploma. He did not anticipate that he had to go through so many hurdles to enter a college diploma program, even with a bachelor's degree already.

Jiazhi learned from Lixia's mistake. He wanted to get into a practical program. He was interested in the Instrumentation Engineering Technology Program at the Northern Alberta Institute of Technology (NAIT) because he was told there were many jobs in this area. To apply for the program, he first presented NAIT with his university transcripts from China, but the college did not know how to evaluate them. They asked him to send his records to the International Qualification Assessment Services (IQAS) for assessment. IQAS is the provincial foreign credential assessment agency which determines the Canadian equivalency of foreign qualifications for the purpose of entering academic studies, general employment, and professional certification. Since this was for a college admission, IQAS also asked him to submit his school records, which luckily he brought with him to Canada. Two months later, he received the assessment results from IQAS. He got 50 for Pure Math, 65 for Grade 12 Math, and 75 for Physics. I asked him whether he was satisfied with the result, and he said 'No.' He said he was not sure what criteria they used in the assessment. He told me that his high school marks were in the 80s and 90s. Furthermore, he received a bachelor's degree in Computer Science, which required advanced math and physics. He believed that IQAS took the lowest from his high school or university grades for each subject. Based on the assessment, NAIT issued him a 'conditional acceptance,' which asked him to upgrade his English, math, physics, and chemistry. The college told him if he could get good marks in these subjects, he would be admitted. Jiazhi's experience challenges the claim that Prior Learning Assessment and Recognition (PLAR) acts as a transformative social mechanism and a means of social inclusion, particularly for non-traditional learners from marginalised groups (e.g., women, minority groups, older learners, and learners with a disability) (Thomas, 1998; Whittaker et al., 2002). Instead, it reveals that PLAR has become an assessment tool and a technical exercise with the 'R' (recognition) often missing from this process. Rather than facilitating adult learning, it has become a serious barrier and a means of exclusion and governing (Andersson and Guo, 2009).

Suggested by friends, he turned to Alberta College for upgrading. First the college needed to give him a placement test. It turned out that he needed more than just level 30 courses. He had to start from English 20, even after he had taken a 3-month ESL program. The upgrading took him one year while also working in the restaurant to support his family. He never imagined going back to high school again. When I asked him how helpful these courses were, he said they were very easy. In particular, the math courses were a waste of his time. He told me the math and physics courses he had taken even in high school in China were more difficult. He said proudly that he received 90s on average for all his upgrading courses. He was expecting to start the Instrumentation Engineering Technology Program in Fall 2005, which would take two years and thousands of dollars to complete. Jiazhi's learning experience confirms the argument that lifelong learning has become a mode of social control and a new mechanism of self-surveillance, which acts as a new disciplinary technology to make people more compliant and adaptable in the era of flexible capitalism (Crowther, 2004).

All three cases have clearly shown that the transition for immigrant is not a linear process, but instead lengthy, costly, and painful. Despite the fact that all three immigrants came to Canada with rich knowledge and experience, they encountered difficulties in having them recognized. As a result, they suffered underemployment, poor economic performance, and downward social mobility. The cases have demonstrated the politics of work and learning by revealing that they have become vehicles to control and assimilate immigrants. Through the denigration and Canadianization of immigrant's work and learning experience, immigrants were forced to conform to Canadian norms and values.

DISCUSSION AND CONCLUSION

This study set out to explore the transition experience of recent Chinese immigrants from the People's Republic of China. The findings reveal that many recent Chinese immigrants to Canada were young, well-educated, and experienced professionals, many of whom held master's and doctoral degrees. The majority came as skilled workers, which reflected a major shift in Canada's changing immigration policy since the mid-1990s in meeting the needs of Canada's knowledge-based economy. Unlike their early counterparts who were motivated to immigrate for economic reasons, for the recent arrivals non-economic reasons such as Canada's natural environment, educational system, and citizenship form the primary motivations to move. In the process of transition from China to Canada, many of them encountered major difficulties, with language and employment as the most frequently cited barriers. Coupled with the devaluation and denigration of their Chinese educational qualifications and prior work experience, recent immigrants suffered unemployment and underemployment, poor economic performance, lack of social mobility, and negative effects on families. Many lived in poverty. A large number felt disillusionment and despair. Their experiences have testified that Canada's promises regarding jobs, prosperity, and smooth transition were false and misleading. They have also demonstrated the non-linear transition of work and learning for immigrants. It seems safe to say that work and learning have become vehicles to assimilate immigrants to Canada's dominant norms and values, in particular through the process of deskilling and reskilling.

At this stage, it is important to ask: Why do such inequities occur in a democratic society like Canada where democratic principles are upheld and where immigrants are 'welcome'? Since numerous studies reported the issue of foreign credential recognition a number of years ago, the situation has not improved much. What prevents us from moving forward? Drawing on perspectives from critical theory and postmodernism, I have attributed the devaluation and denigration of foreign credentials and prior work experience to the following causes (Guo, 2009): First and foremost, our epistemological misperceptions of difference and knowledge can be blamed. The deficit model of difference leads us to believe that differences are deficiencies, that the knowledge of immigrant professionals, particularly for those from Third World countries, is incompatible and inferior, and hence is invalid. It appears safe to claim that knowledge has been racialized and materialized on the basis of ethnic and national origins. Furthermore, our ontological commitment to objectivisim and liberal universalism exacerbates the complexity of this process. This study demonstrates that by applying a one-size-fits-all criterion to measure immigrants' credentials and experience, liberal universalism denies immigrants opportunities to be successful in a new society. It also reveals that professional standard and excellence has been used as a cloak to restrict competition and legitimize existing power relations. The juxtaposition of the misperceptions of difference and knowledge with objectivism and liberal universalism forms a new head tax to exclude the 'undesirable,' and to perpetuate oppression in Canada.

The findings of this study have important implications for researchers, educators and policymakers. The experience of recent Chinese immigrants requires researchers to redefine transitions of work and learning, as noted in the critical expansive approach to transitions by Sawchuk and Taylor in the Introduction. In particular, we need to examine the non-linear transition of work and learning for immigrants, the multiple barriers facing immigrants in the process of transition, and how socio-cultural differences have been used to entrench social inequality in immigrant's transition. As educators, we need to educate ourselves and the public about the politics of difference and recognition by embracing all knowledge as valid and valuable expressions of human experience. However, we have to acknowledge that the issues facing immigrants are much broader social issues which require political will. It is time for federal and provincial governments to exercise their legislative roles to introduce bills that will make professional associations and employers accountable for how they treat immigrants.

ACKNOWLEDGMENT

The author wishes to thank Jie Xiong in the Department of Educational Policy Studies at the University of Alberta for her capable research assistance.

NOTES

[1] All names are pseudonyms.

REFERENCES

Andersson, P., & Guo, S. (2009). Governing through non/recognition: The missing 'R' in the PLAR for immigrant professionals in Canada and Sweden. *International Journal of Lifelong Education, 28*(4), 423–437.

Basran, G., & Zong, L. (1998). Devaluation of foreign credentials as perceived by visible minority professional immigrants. *Canadian Ethnic Studies, 30*(3), 6–18.

Bergin, B. (1988). *Equality is the issue: A study of minority ethnic group access to health and social services in Ottawa-Carleton*. Ottawa: Social Planning Council of Ottawa-Carleton.

Campbell, K., Fenwick, T., Gibb, T., Guo, S., Guo, Y., Hamdon, E., & Jamal, Z. (2006). Formal and informal processes of learning essential skills: A study of immigrant service organizations. *Proceedings of the essential skills workshop: Looking back, moving forward* (pp. 31–39). Montreal: Université du Québec à Montréal.

Citizenship and Immigration Canada. (1999). *The economic performance of immigrants: Immigration category perspective. IMDB profile series*. Ottawa: Citizenship and Immigration Canada.

Couton, P. (2002). Highly skilled immigrants: Recent trends and issues. *Canadian Journal of Policy Research, 3*(2), 114–123.

Crowther, J. (2004). 'In and against' lifelong learning: Flexibility and the corrosion of character. *International Journal of Lifelong Education, 23*(2), 125–136.

Guo, S. (2006). Mapping the iceberg of informal learning: Exploring the experience of Chinese volunteers in Vancouver. *Proceedings of the 25th Canadian Association for the Study of Adult Education (CASAE) Conference* (pp. 108–113). Toronto: York University.

Guo, S. (2009). Difference, deficiency, and devaluation: Tracing the roots of non/recognition of foreign credentials for immigrant professionals in Canada. *Canadian Journal for the Study of Adult Education, 22*(1), 37–52.

Guo, S., & DeVoretz, D. (2006a). The changing face of Chinese immigrants in Canada. *Journal of International Migration and Integration, 7*(3), 275–300.

Guo, S., & DeVoretz, D. (2006b). Chinese immigrants in Vancouver: Quo vadis? *Journal of International Migration and Integration, 7*(4), 425–447.

Henry, F., Tator, C., Mattis, W., & Rees, T. (2006). *The colour of democracy: Racism in Canadian society*. Toronto: Thompson Nelson.

Hiebert, D., & Ley, D. (2001). *Assimilation, cultural pluralism and social exclusion among ethnocultural groups in Vancouver*. Vancouver: Centre for Research on Immigration and Integration in the Metropolis, Working Paper #01-08.

Knowles, V. (1997). *Strangers at our gates: Canadian immigration and immigration policy, 1540–1997*. Toronto: Dundurn Press.

Krahn, H., Derwing, T., Mulder, M., & Wilkinson, L. (2000). Educated and underemployed: Refugee integration into the Canadian labour market. *Journal of International Migration and Integration, 1*(1), 59–84.

Leung, H. H. (2000). *Settlement services for the Chinese Canadians in Toronto: The challenges toward an integrated planning*. Toronto: Ontario Administration of Settlement and Integration Services.

Li, P. S. (1998). *The Chinese in Canada*. Don Mills: Oxford University Press.

Li, P. S. (2001). The market worth of immigrants' educational credentials. *Canadian Public Policy, 27*(1), 23–38.

Li, P. S. (2003a). *Destination Canada: Immigration debates and issues.* Don Mills: Oxford University Press.

Li, P. S. (2003b). Deconstructing Canada's discourse of immigrant integration. *Journal of International Migration and Integration, 4*(3), 315–333.

Lindsay, C. (2007). *Profiles of ethnic communities in Canada: The Chinese community in Canada.* Ottawa: Statistics Canada.

Ma, A. (1996). *The Chinese perception of community and social services: A survey report.* Toronto: The Taskforce on Sustenance and Transformation of Agencies Serving the Chinese Canadian Community.

Matas, D. (1996). Racism in Canadian immigration policy. In C. E. James (Ed.), *Perspectives on racism and the human services sector: A case for change.* Toronto: University of Toronto.

Mojab, S. (1999). De-skilling immigrant women. *Canadian Woman Studies, 19*(3), 123–128.

Ng, R. (1999). Homeworking: Dream realized or freedom constrained? The globalized reality of immigrant garment workers. *Canadian Woman Studies, 19*(3), 110–114.

Nguyen, T. C. (1991). *Report on the Vietnamese community in the City of York.* New York: York Community Services.

Reitz, J. G. (1995). *A review of the literature on aspects of ethno-racial access, utilization and delivery of social services.* Retrieved from http://www.ceris.metropolis.net/Virtual%20Library/other/reitz1.html

Reitz, J. G. (2001). Immigrant skill utilization in the Canadian labour market: Implications of human capital research. *Journal of International Migration and Integration, 2*(3), 347–378.

Selman, G., Cooke, M., Selman, M., & Dampier, P. (1998). *The foundations of adult education in Canada* (2nd edn.). Toronto: Thompson Educational Publishing.

Slade, B., Luo, Y., & Schugurensky, D. (2005). Seeking 'Canadian experience': The informal learning of new immigrants as volunteer workers. In *Proceedings of the 24th Canadian Association for the Study of Adult Education (CASAE) Conference* (pp. 229–235). London, ON: University of Western Ontario.

Stake, R. E. (1995). *The art of case study research.* Thousand Oaks CA: Sage Publications.

Statistics Canada. (2003). *Longitudinal survey of immigrants to Canada: Process, progress and prospects.* Ottawa: Statistics Canada.

Tan, J., & Roy, P. E. (1985). *The Chinese in Canada.* Ottawa: Canadian Historical Association.

Wallis, D. (1998). Beijing makes it happen. *Vis-à-Vis* , Fall, 4–8.

Waters, J. (2003). Flexible citizens? Transnationalism and citizenship amongst economic immigrants in Vancouver. *The Canadian Geographer, 47*(3), 219–234.

Whitaker, R. (1991). *Canadian immigration policy since confederation.* Ottawa: Canadian Historical Association.

Whittaker, R., Cleary, P., & Gallacher, J. (2002). Accreditation of prior experiential learning: An altered state of learning? In *Proceedings of the 32nd Standing Conference on University Teaching and Research in the Education of Adults (SCUTREA)* (pp. 299–304). Stirling, Scotland: University of Stirling.

Shibao Guo
Faculty of Education
University of Calgary

BONNIE SLADE AND DANIEL SCHUGURENSKY

14. 'STARTING FROM ANOTHER SIDE, THE BOTTOM':

Volunteer Work as a Transition into the Labour Market for Immigrant Professionals

INTRODUCTION

Yana, an engineer in her mid-forties, immigrated to Canada from Russia. She hoped to find work in an engineering firm, continuing in her profession. After qualifying for immigration to Canada as a skilled worker, she was shocked at how difficult it was for her to get an engineering job in Ontario. Frustrated in her engineering job search, she took on survival jobs, such as housecleaning and clerical work, to make ends meet. Her friends advised her to volunteer so that she could get "Canadian work experience". With the goal of improving her English, she volunteered at a seniors' home helping elderly residents in their daily activities. Her second volunteer experience was an unpaid placement with the Ontario government doing data entry. This volunteer work was part of a Coop program offered through the local school board. Most of her learning at this work placement was about the computer software she was working on and was done mostly on her own. During her four months of volunteering full-time at the ministry, she received minimal training and no feedback on her work. This volunteer work was not only completely unrelated to her education and work experience but it was also an isolating experience, although she was happy to learn more about Oracle database systems. After her volunteer work she took on a short-term paid contract doing accounting work. At the time of the interview, she was unemployed and was still waiting for a reference letter, what could be called her "certificate of Canadian experience", from the ministry for her volunteer work. So far, volunteering has not helped her move forward in establishing herself as an engineer in Ontario.

Yana's story is not unique. Together with Australia, Canada has the highest immigration rate in the world. Today, 20 per cent of Canadian residents were born abroad (in Toronto the figure is 50 per cent). Since 1995, approximately 3 million people from all over the world undertook major life transitions by migrating to Canada. Immigration targets aim for an intake of about between 250,000 people annually (CIC, 2007a)[1]. These high immigration rates are underpinned by both demographic and economic imperatives. Due to the combination of low fertility rates, an aging workforce, changes in technology and the growing importance of a knowledge-based economy, there has been an increased

P. Sawchuk and A. Taylor (eds.), Challenging Transitions in Learning and Work: Reflections on Policy and Practice, 261–281.

reliance on immigration as the means for labour force growth. Statistics Canada (2003a) has estimated that in the near future all labour force growth will be the result of immigration. Canada is not the only country facing these demographic and economic challenges; indeed, most Western industrialized countries are competing for skilled migrants. The vast majority of these migrants come to Canada from "non-traditional" countries in South and Southeast Asia. Since 1967, economic migrants have had to qualify for immigration to Canada through an assessment tool (known as the Point System) that measures a migrant's human capital. The Point System assigns points for English and French language proficiency, education levels of the principal applicant and their spouse, work experience, age, adaptability[2] and arranged employment in Canada. To qualify as a skilled worker, an applicant must have "one continuous year of full-time, paid work experience or the equivalent in part-time continuous employment" within the last 10 years in management, a professional job or technical and skilled trades[3] (CIC, 2007b, para. 5). The federal government gives priority to economic migrants over those seeking family reunification; in recent years the government has set the level for skilled workers at approximately sixty per cent of the total[4]. As a result of the stringent assessment process for economic migrants and the high immigration levels, Canada receives many highly educated and experienced professionals every year, the majority of whom are people of colour[5].

Throughout the history of Canada, integrating immigrants into the labour market has been one of the most important transitions for both the individual immigrant and the Canadian economy as a whole. The federal immigration selection system is geared to select people based on their "ability to contribute to Canada's economy" (CIC, 2005). The system has been criticized for not being responsive to shifts in the labour market and for prioritizing university education over skilled trades; skilled labour shortages in various sectors ranging from doctors to auto mechanics have been a reality in many regions in Canada for the past several years and more are predicted (Zakaluzny, 2007). Researchers have shown that over time, it has become more difficult for racialized professional to integrate into their professions. The links between immigration status, unemployment, poverty, gender and race have been researched and it has been shown that there is a racialized and gendered labour market where people of colour, particularly women, are over-represented in low income sectors (Bannerji, 2000; Galabuzi, 2006; Jackson, 2002; Kunz et al., 2000; Shan, 2006; Slade, 2004). There are also critiques of how the federal immigration selection system is disconnected from provincial and municipal immigrant settlement programs and policies; this disconnection is often cited as a major contributor to the deprofessionalization of many highly skilled immigrants, who experience significant difficulties integrating into their professions, especially in regulated professions (PROMPT, 2004; Shan, 2006; Slade, 2004).

In this chapter, we draw on empirical data from the study "The Informal Learning of Volunteer Workers", which focused on the connections between informal learning and volunteer work among immigrants who volunteered to improve their access to the labour market. Elsewhere we have written about volunteerism, informal learning and immigration[6]. In this paper we discuss two transitions experienced by immigrants in their settlement process. The first transition is from qualified and established professionals in their home country to "labour market undesirables" in Canada. The second transition is from "labour market undesirables" to volunteer workers. Regarding the first transition, although 43 of the 45 participants in our study had at least one post secondary degree and years of relevant work experience, they experienced great difficulty in securing meaningful employment. This raises questions about education as a direct, linear route to the labour market, and suggests that social constructions of skill are shaped by gender, race and nationality. Regarding the second transition, participants reported that, in order to access a job in their professional field, they were expected to have "Canadian work experience", and volunteer work was the main avenue to gain such experience.

The volunteer work that the participants undertake deviates from common understandings of volunteer work in three ways: motivation, experience, and sector. First, the main motivation for volunteering was not based on altruistic purposes or on learning basic skills (typical of young volunteers), but on re-entering the labour market in a different society. Second, they were not assisting the work done by regular staff; rather, they worked side by side with paid workers, performing similar activities, but without pay. Third, the volunteer experience included not only community settings and non-profit agencies (typical sectors for volunteerism) but also the public sector and the for-profit sector.

Overall, if measured by obtaining meaningful paid work as a result of the volunteer placement, the strategy of volunteering for "Canadian work experience" was not very successful: several months after their volunteer work, 44 per cent of the participants were underemployed, 42 per cent were unemployed, and only 13 per cent were successful in finding work that matched their experience and education. While the participants reported that they had increased their confidence, self-esteem, social and cultural capital through their volunteer placements, their experiences raise questions about labour market exploitation and the impact of gender, race and nationality on an individual's perceived skill level. For instance, we could ask: why are these highly skilled immigrant professionals, many of them people of colour, deemed undesirable as paid professionals but acceptable as unpaid workers?

THE INFORMAL LEARNING OF VOLUNTEER WORKERS STUDY

This study is one of thirteen projects in the "Changing Working Conditions and Lifelong Learning in the New Economy" research network, coordinated by the Centre for the Study of Education and Work of the Ontario Institute for Studies in Education, University of Toronto. The main concern of the national network is an exploration of the current forms, contents, and outcomes of organized educational, training and informal learning activities in Canada's 'new economy' (Livingstone, Myles, Doray, Hubich and Collins, 2004). Our study was conducted in partnership with A Commitment to Training and Employment for Women (ACTEW), a "provincial charitable, non-profit network of supporters, trainers, agencies, and organizations delivering employment and training services to women" (ACTEW, 2007). ACTEW was responsible for recruiting the study participants, conducting the interviews and transcribing the audiotapes. Most interviews were conducted by an ACTEW's research assistant who at that time was also a graduate student at OISE. Both ACTEW's executive director and the research assistant served on the research project's Community Advisory Board, a group of 15 representatives from community-based agencies and advocacy groups who provided guidance on the project design and implementation. The interview guide was reviewed in detail by the Community Advisory group, and revised according to their feedback. After the individual interviews were analyzed, we held a focus group with Chinese immigrant volunteers to deepen our understanding of certain issues, such as the relationship between the volunteer placements and subsequent employment. We focused on Chinese immigrants because, demographically, they are the largest immigrant group in Canada. Participants for this focus group were recruited through a posting on a Chinese language listserve.

In total, we interviewed 45 volunteers: 30 women and 15 men. Although they came from 17 different countries, almost 47 per cent of the participants were from China. They entered Canada as members of all immigration categories, economic, humanitarian and family class; the vast majority, however, were skilled workers. Forty-three participants (96%) had completed at least one university degree and, on average, the participants had 10 years of professional work experience prior to immigrating to Canada. Professions included medicine, engineering, business administration, teaching (in school systems as well as universities), psychology and information technology. Most participants had been in Canada for five years or less. Forty out of the forty-five participants (89%) were people of colour. With respect to age, 20 per cent of the group were under 29 years of age and 18 per cent were older than 40 years old. Most participants (62 per cent) were between 30 and 39 years of age. Overall, participants embodied the intended outcome of immigra-tion policy: they were well educated, had years of work experience in a professional field, and were the right age for the labour market.

TRANSITION 1: FROM QUALIFIED AND ESTABLISHED PROFESSIONALS TO "LABOUR MARKET UNDESIRABLES"

In recent years, there has been growing concern and attention paid to the deskilling and deprofessionalization of highly skilled immigrants (Bauder, 2003; Li, 2005; Mojab, 2000; Reitz, 2005, 2001). These and other studies confirm that the transition from highly skilled and sought-after immigrant to established Canadian professional is a difficult one. Ideally, this transition should be facilitated by government agencies, employers, professional associations and educational institutions, but this is not always the case. The unemployment rate among recent immigrants (landed in past five years) is twice of their Canadian-born counterparts: 12.1% and 6.4% respectively. Moreover, although immigrants have higher educational levels than people born in Canada, a significantly higher portion of recent immigrants are employed in jobs with lower skill requirements than their Canadian-born counterparts. (Statistics Canada, 2003a). Lochhead (2003:2) refers to the high levels of poverty and unemployment experienced by immigrant families as a "transition penalty". Some participants understood this penalty as the price to be paid by the so-called sacrificial generation:

> New immigrants have lots of skills and we have to fight, because there is less opportunity for us. There was one teacher in one of the programs I was in and she told us, "why do you guys come here, it's so hard, if I was somebody who did hiring, I would choose someone who graduated from a university in Canada, not another country". So, it's depressing for those people who have to go to university again, who have to start over, but that's the truth. Everybody's doing that. As a first generation, you have to sacrifice a lot to achieve, to really get into society.

It is pertinent to note that immigrants do not experience unemployment and poverty in a homogenous manner (Jackson, 2002; Kunz, Milan and Schetagne, 2000; Ornstien, 2000; Teo, 2004). The extent to which immigrants experience marginalization varies according to their social location. Li (2001) analyzed the 1996 Census data for university educated people by gender, race, place of birth and place of education, and concluded that not only immigrants' credentials carry a penalty compared to those of native-born Canadians, but also that "a foreign degree affects visible minority immigrant women and men more adversely than white Canadians" (p. 118). Li notes that it is not possible to separate the international credentials from the person who holds them; the recognition of international degrees occurs in a context of a society that privileges men over women and white people over people of colour.

Our data confirms the findings from other research studies that show that immigrant professionals experience deskilling (Alboim and The Maytree Foundation, 2002; Boyd and Thomas, 2002; Brouwer, 1995; Couton, 2002). The Longitudinal Survey of Immigrants to Canada (LSIC) found that 70 per cent of immigrants experienced barriers in gaining access to the Canadian labour market at an appropriate level (Statistics Canada, 2003b). Barriers included recognition of international educational credentials and work experience, lack of networks and language barriers. The devaluation of international work experience and educational credentials heavily contribute to the "occupational skidding" (Kofman, 1999) that many participants in our study also experienced. In the LSIC survey, six out of ten immigrants who were employed at the time of the survey were not working in the profession or occupation in which they were educated and experienced (Statistics Canada, 2003b). According to Bannerji (2000):

> By locking immigrant workers into zones of menial labour and low wages, the state has brought down the wage structure of the country as a whole. It has actively de-skilled and marginalized Third World immigrants by decertifying them and forcing them into the working class ...this device had created a reserve army of labour consisting of both males and females. As any study of homeworkers, piece-workers, cleaners of public spaces, or domestics will show, non-white or "immigrant" women occupy the worst position among these marginalized labour groups. (pp. 76–77)

The LSIC survey revealed that the biggest barrier to finding appropriate employment for immigrant professionals was the lack of "Canadian work experience" (Statistics Canada, 2003b). This emphasis on "Canadian work experience" in hiring practices is particularly relevant to our study, and explains why so many immigrants choose volunteer work as a strategy to re-enter the labour market. According to Picot and Sweetman (2005), "immigrants from non-traditional source countries receive close to zero economic benefits from pre-Canadian potential labour market experience" (p. 19). Alboim, Finnie and Meng (2007) agree that international work experience is devalued but estimate that one year of foreign work experience is "worth only about one-third of what Canadian-based experience is worth" (p. 13).

Canada's current immigration strategy rests largely on human capital theory, which assumes a positive correlation between years of education and earnings. However, as Reitz (2005) notes, this theory is weak when applied to immigrants. In his own words:

> Whereas human capital theory suggests that workers' earnings reflect the productive value of their skills – particularly skills based on formal education and work experience – immigrants' recent labour market outcomes contradict that expectation. Immigrants' skills have risen to unprecedented levels yet their earnings have fallen in both relative and absolute terms. Of immigrants arriving in 2000, for example, about 45 percent had university degrees yet their earnings after a year in Canada were less than those of previous comparable cohorts of immigrants going back to 1980. (p. 5)

Before coming to Canada, most participants in our study enjoyed high levels of social status as professionals, as well as a high level of cultural capital and social capital (in Bourdieu's sense) in their home countries. Upon arrival in Canada, they experienced a sudden drop in status and capital. Their social status largely vanished, significantly affecting their self-esteem. Certain elements of cultural capital, like mastering linguistic and cultural codes, holding a university degree, or having expertise and experience in a professional field, could not be taken for granted anymore. Likewise, most of their social and professional networks remained in their home countries, ineffective to make any difference in the Canadian labour market. Hence, it is not surprising that several participants reported experiencing low levels of cultural literacy and professional isolation in Canada. Upon arrival in Canada, after going through a stringent selection process, many immigrants encountered unexpected difficulties in getting a job. One participant reported:

> I was shocked to learn that there were such unfair employer practices in Canada. The government is not telling the truth about this country. I got high points for education and experience and I can't get a good job. Immigration should tell people that they should expect troubles finding jobs in their fields.

Indeed, in a survey of 2,091 employers conducted by Public Policy Forum (2004), researchers found that employers "overlook immigrants in their human resource planning, do not hire immigrants at the level at which they were trained, and face challenges integrating recent [less than 10 years in Canada] into their workforce"

(p. i). While 39 per cent of employers believed that "work experience from other countries was equal to Canadian work", on average 50 per cent of the public, crown corporations, non-profit and private companies surveyed indicated that "Canadian work experience was required" and that "work experience from other countries was accepted but not necessarily considered equal to Canadian work" (p. 4).

Researchers have identified other barriers to a smooth, successful transition into the Canadian labour market such as the non-recognition of foreign credentials, inaccessible licensing processes of professional regulatory bodies, unfamiliarity with Canadian culture, English or French language proficiency and racism (Guo, 2007; Krahn, Derwing, Mulder and Wilkinson, 2000; Li, 2001; Slade, 2004). Given current and impending skill shortages in the Canadian labour market, it is puzzling why it is so difficult for internationally educated and experienced professionals to find work in their professions. Many immigrants, when faced with labour market exclusion, undertake volunteer work as a strategy to re-establish themselves in their professions. Volunteer work provides a means by which they can gain access to Canadian workplaces, get exposure to "Canadian culture" and increase their chances of finding suitable employment.

TRANSITION 2: FROM "LABOUR MARKET UNDESIRABLE" TO VOLUNTEER WORKER

Volunteerism is a significant activity in Canada. According to *Caring Canadians, Involved Canadians: Highlights from the 2004 Canada Survey of Giving, Volunteering and Participating*, almost 12 million Canadians (45% of the population aged 15 or older) volunteered almost 2 billion hours of their time during a one-year period (Hall, Lasby, Gumulka and Tryon, 2006). This has been estimated as the equivalent of one million full time jobs. Volunteering in this survey, is defined as "perform(ing) a service without pay, on behalf of a charitable or other non-profit organization" (p. 68). While the motivation for volunteering is most often expressed as wanting to help one's community or use their skills, studies such as the national Survey of Work and Lifelong Learning[7] (Livingstone and Scholtz, 2006) have showed that many people, especially new immigrants, volunteer to improve job opportunities. While 24.5 per cent of Canadian born respondents indicated that they volunteered to improve their job opportunities, the number was much higher for immigrants: 44.7 per cent for immigrants who had been in Canada five years or less and 57.9 per cent for immigrants in Canada for six to ten years. This suggests that many immigrants have accepted volunteering as one solution to integrating themselves into the labour market. Indeed, all participants in this study volunteered to improve access to the labour market. As one participant put it:

> For us new immigrants, you have to go into employment in this way [volunteering] because no one will accept you, no one will believe you can do the job.

For participants in this study, the main reason for volunteering was to gain "Canadian work experience" (47%). Other reasons mentioned were to improve understanding and use of English, especially work-related language (36%), to learn about "Canadian culture" (22%), to get a job (20%), to network (18%), to be in a "real" Canadian workplace (16%), to meet people (11%), to have something to do (9%) and to get involved in Canadian society (7%). Participants recounted that after they had an unsuccessful job search, they received advice from friends, relatives, teachers and state representatives that they should volunteer to get "Canadian work experience". Many immigrants felt that volunteer work was a necessary route to paid employment:

> I was told by a social worker that was the only way to get exposure into the Canadian way of life and meet the people was to volunteer. I thought that by volunteering that I would be in a position to get a job because of the networking.
>
> The reason I started volunteering was I needed to learn more about the labour market here, to adjust to being in this work environment, to know it, to have a knack for it, you know, and just to feel better about myself.

Volunteering as a way to get into the labour market was also promoted by other immigrants who had been successful in finding paid work through the volunteering route:

> I always thought of myself as a lucky one because I volunteered there and then I got a position in the same organization. I have some friends they came from China too. And because I did it successfully, I always kept telling them you should volunteer first and then you do the network and then you try to find a position.
>
> I was told by a friend, "if you can have a chance to volunteer in Canada, the volunteer experience is very, very important. Someday, it will be very useful to you." That is why I decided to do it.

The ability to volunteer is enabled by immigration policy requirements for skilled workers to have enough money to support themselves and their dependents after arrival.[8] For a single applicant, this amount is $10,168. For a family of four, the amount is $18,895[9] (CIC, 2007c).[10] The participants were able to volunteer and live off their savings, but only for a limited amount of time.

> I don't mind to volunteer in certain places at certain times, but after, I like to work, not just volunteer anymore. Now there are no jobs were you can work there for a length of time. There are contracts. So to work I volunteer in different places, because that's where I gain my experience, my different knowledge.... I can't volunteer all the time, I need something to live off of.

The volunteer work placements were brokered through community-based agencies (usually through an employment assistance program) or negotiated independently by the individual. The site of volunteer work included the non-profit (82%), for-profit (16%) and public sectors (2%). Some of the volunteer placements were part of Coop programs delivered by community organizations and local school boards. The length of time for the volunteer placements varied widely. Some participants volunteered two or three hours per week; others worked close to full-time hours for a fixed period of time, usually three months but one participant worked for five months, full-time hours. Volunteer tasks varied from placement to placement – network administration, website development (for those with computer skills), looking after kids (summer camp) arts and crafts for kids, teaching computer software classes, setting up and maintaining computer networks, general office support, accounting, filing tax returns, interpreting for people who had limited English and wrapping gifts. Some of the tasks required only general and basic skills, such as gift-wrapping at a shop, while the others needed more professional skills and knowledge, such as computer network setup and writing computer software code.

Many people reported working alongside paid employees as a member of the team in a for-profit setting. For example, John, an electrical engineer with nine years professional experience in both China and Japan, found a volunteer position for a high profile technology company posted on an internet newsgroup in Toronto. After a competition with six other candidates, he was selected for the position. In his three-months volunteer work, he worked in a project team developing software for a specific client. He worked forty hours a week plus overtime and because he did not have a computer at home, he did all his overtime at the office. He performed the same work as the other team members, the exception being that they were paid employees. Not only was he not paid anything for his three months of work, but he had to pay his own workplace insurance while he was working/ volunteering. He acknowledged that he accepted these conditions:

> They were clear with me that they were not going to give me anything. This was the price I had to pay to work there. I also had to buy a car, since the location was far from my home, but this allowed me to spend more time on my work, and it contributed to the good relationship I built with my boss. My boss did try to have the position turned into a paid contract after the first month, but higher management said "no".

After he left that volunteer work, he applied for jobs without getting responses from companies. He also approached job agencies who, at first, were interested in the experience he had with the company, but when they learned that it was a three month volunteer job, they told him that it was not real experience. They asked him why he did not get a full-time job if he had worked out so well.

Other participants who volunteered in the for-profit sector noted that they would have liked to be able to use all their talents and not just some of them, as well as to be involved in different stages of a process and not just in some of them. Consider the story of Ana, a psychologist from Brazil with ten years experience working in corporate human resources who volunteered at a major Canadian bank. Her placement was part of a two months mentoring program out of a community-based organization. She was the first volunteer in this human resources department, and negotiated this placement through her own contacts. In designing the volunteer work for her, community organizations and the bank recognized her experience and skills in human resources by having her work on a campaign to prescreen people from two employment equity groups: people with disabilities and Aboriginal people. She worked for 15 hours a week doing tasks that were related to her expertise, but could not use all of her skills and experience as all of her time was spent contacting clients over the phone. Moreover, she was involved only in the contacting phase, but was not asked to be part of the selection process.

OUTCOMES OF VOLUNTEER WORK PLACEMENTS

Unfortunately, the case of John was not an exception. Indeed, the strategy of volunteering to gain appropriate work was only successful for a slim minority of the participants. At time of the interviews, only 13 per cent of participants were in a job that matched their skills and experience. Almost half of the participants were either unemployed (42%) or underemployed (44%).[11]

The largest group of participants were those who were unemployed after their volunteer placements. Table 14.1 includes the 20 people who regardless of their international education and work experience, and Canadian volunteer experience, were unsuccessful in even getting even a minimum wage survival job. In this group of participants, there were two immigrants with backgrounds in science who volunteered at for-profit companies writing software code. While John, whose story is described above, was working as "part of the team", part of Alfred's volunteer work was to debug software codes at his home on his own. Other participants who had expertise in accounting also reported volunteering doing people's tax returns for a for-profit company from home. More than half of the men (53%) and 40 per cent of the women were in this category.

Table 14.1 Demographics of participants who were unemployed

Sex	*Country of Birth*	*Age*	*Profession*	*Site of Volunteer Work*	*Volunteer Placement*	*Work in Canada*
Female	Kenya	35–39	Teacher (B.Ed.)	Non-profit	Administration, research, orientating people	Unemployed
Female	Kenya	under 29	high school graduate	Non-profit	administration work	Unemployed
Female	Ukraine	35–39	Counsellor	Non-profit	Helping newcomers fill in forms, courtroom interpretation	Unemployed
Female	Russia	45–49	Engineer	Public	Data entry	Unemployed
Female	USA	30–34	Non-profit Administration	Non-profit	Gift wrapping, fundraising	Unemployed
Female	Columbia	35–39	Business Administration	Non-profit	Community outreach	Unemployed

(Continued)

Sex	*Country of Birth*	*Age*	*Profession*	*Site of Volunteer Work*	*Volunteer Placement*	*Work in Canada*
Female	Bangladesh	30–34	Doctor	Non-profit	Administrative work	Unemployed
Female	China	30–34	IT	Non-profit	IT work, network maintenance, software training	Unemployed
Female	China	30–34	BA (sociology), Broadcaster	Non-profit	Daycare, reading stories to children	Unemployed
Female	China	35–39	Accountant	Non-profit and For-profit	Administrative work, Internet research	Unemployed
Female	Indonesia	45–49	Teacher's Assistant	Non-profit	Daycare	Unemployed
Female	China	under 29	Teacher	Non-profit	Administrative work, interpreting, counselling	Unemployed
Male	Zimbabwe	35–39	Bachelor of Social Work	Non-profit	Facilitating workshops for children	Unemployed
Male	Congo	35–39	Journalist	Non-profit	Helping newcomers fill in forms and do resumes	Unemployed
Male	China	30–34	Engineer	Non-profit and For-profit	Teaching computer class and Market Research	Unemployed
Male	China	30–34	Engineer	For-profit	Software development	Unemployed
Male	China	30–34	Engineer	Non-profit	Teaching children crafts	Unemployed
Male	China	40–44	Professor	For-profit	Developing software	Unemployed
Male	Indonesia	under 29	Accountant	Non-profit	Computer support	Unemployed
Male	China	under 29	Information Technology	Non-profit	Computer support	Unemployed

Table 14.2 summarizes the situation of those participants who were underemployed after their volunteer work. Underemployed includes those who were working in their own fields but at a much lower level (and pay) then their qualifications, as well as those in unrelated "survival" jobs characterized by low pay and irregular hours. Underemployed skilled immigrants experience a double jeopardy when trying to find an appropriate job in their profession. Not only do their skills become outdated in light of changes in their fields, but they also suffer a deskilling process with respect to their original capacities. Half of the women (50%) and slightly more than one quarter (27%) of the men were considered underemployed.

Only 13 per cent of the participants in this study were able to secure employment in their professions after volunteering for "Canadian work experience". While there were three women and three men in this category, the men were more successful overall as these numbers represent 20 per cent of the men but only 10 per cent of the women. The six participants who were able to secure work matched to their education and work experience had two things in common (see Table 14.3). The first was that the work they performed in their volunteer placement was closely connected to their educational backgrounds and work experience. The second common element to their experience, related to the first, was that through their volunteer work they were able to develop meaningful social networks. For these participants, the volunteer work acted as a successful stepping stone to paid work, as it allowed them to draw on their prior professional experience from abroad while building social and cultural capital in Canada in their profession.

Table 14.2. Demographics of participants who were underemployed

Sex	*Country of Birth*	*Age*	*Profession*	*Site of Volunteer work*	*Volunteer Placement*	*Work in Canada*
Female	Zimbabwe	30–34	Commerce	Non-profit	Serving food, talking to homeless people, helping with bingo, cashier	Administrative work
Female	Albania	40–44	Teacher (B.Ed.)	Non-profit	Administration work	Telemarketing/ data entry/ administrative work
Female	Iran	30–34	Professor	Non-profit	LINC teacher, outreach worker and translator	Outreach worker/ESL teacher
Female	Columbia	40–44	Engineer	Non-profit	Wrapping presents	Quality testing in a factory

(Continued)

Sex	*Country of Birth*	*Age*	*Profession*	*Site of Volunteer work*	*Volunteer Placement*	*Work in Canada*
Female	Brazil	40–44	Psychologist/ Human Resources	For-profit	Working in a large bank in the HR department recruiting Aboriginal people and people with disabilities for jobs	Waitress, telemarketing, sales
Female	India	35–39	MBA	Non-profit	Conducting a program evaluation/ report writing	Job Developer
Female	India	40–44	BA Economics	Non-profit	Administrative work	Program Assistant
Female	China	30–34	Financial	Non-profit	Administrative work	Program Assistant
Female	Korea	30–34	Engineer	Non-profit	Teaching basic computer skills	Fast Food outlet, retail work
Female	China	30–34	Teacher (B.Ed.)	Non-profit	Daycare	Daycare
Female	China	35–39	MA Computer Science	Non-profit	Computer support	Assistant support analyst
Female	China	35–39	MA Information Science	Non-profit	Computer support and website administration	Technical writing
Female	China	under 29	MBA (France)	For-profit	Accounting work	Office helper, cashier in a cafeteria, assistant accountant
Female	Indonesia	under 29	Accountant	Non-profit	Arranging special events	Temp work doing accounts payable, part time receptionist at Accounting company
Female	China	under 29	International Trade	Non-profit	Data entry, reception work	Reception

(Continued)

Sex	*Country of Birth*	*Age*	*Profession*	*Site of Volunteer work*	*Volunteer Placement*	*Work in Canada*
Male	Bosnia	35–39	Teacher (B.Ed.)	Non-profit	Teaching computer class, coaching soccer team	Landscaping
Male	India	40–44	Marketing	Non-profit	Administrative work	Sales
Male	Sri Lanka	under 29	Professor	Non-profit	Computer support	Sales
Male	China	30–34	Accountant	For-profit	Administrative work, preparing tax returns	Labourer/Fast food restaurant worker

The case of one woman with expertise in marketing can help to illustrate this situation. Initially, she attended an employment program in a community-based organization that had a volunteer placement doing clerical work in a government office. Soon after she started the placement, she realized that the experience was not going to help her find work in marketing. She left the program and started to volunteer in another program that made a special effort to closely match her skills and experience to the volunteer placement. In this program, she was able to get a volunteer position in a marketing department for a large, for-profit company. Through the course of this placement she gained new experiences and made some connections that helped her to be offered a paid job in marketing. She noted that had she remained in the first volunteer placement, the chances to obtain a job in her field would have been very slim.

Table 14.3. Demographics of participants who found appropriate paid work

Sex	*Country of Birth*	*Age*	*Profession*	*Site of Volunteer work*	*Volunteer Placement*	*Work in Canada*
Female	China	30–34	Accountant	Non-profit	Preparing tax returns, helping organize special events	Accountant
Female	China	30–34	Marketing	Non-profit and For-profit	Administrative work; Marketing analysis	Marketing
Female	China	under 29	Engineer	Non-profit	Teaching basic computer software and web design	Computer technician/ web developer

(Continued)

Sex	*Country of Birth*	*Age*	*Profession*	*Site of Volunteer work*	*Volunteer Placement*	*Work in Canada*
Male	Zimbabwe	35–39	high school graduate	Non-profit	Helping students with homework and seniors with tax returns	Accounting clerk
Male	China	30–34	Information Technology	Non-profit	Computer support	Software design assistant
Male	China	30–34	Information Technology	For-profit	Information Technology	Information Technology

RECOMMENDATIONS TO IMPROVE THE VOLUNTEER PLACEMENTS

Participants were asked for their recommendations as to how their placements could have been more valuable. The major recommendation was to match the skills of the volunteer to the work placement. In other words, the aim of volunteer placement should not be just to provide 'Canadian experience" to immigrants, but "relevant Canadian experience". Indeed, many participants commented that it was not possible to get relevant experience if they were not given proper exposure to that experience. Some complained that certain companies took on volunteers to get the work done that no one else wanted to do, especially the monotonous work such as filing or repetitive manual labour that take most of the time and provide very few opportunities to get actual professional work experience. One participant commented:

> Some of them only like to use volunteers for short time and then nothing more. This does not give the volunteer very long to network or gain knowledge. Volunteer placements should be structured more like student internships.

Other participants cautioned immigrants from volunteering for too long, as it was possible to develop social networks in a shorter period of time. This way, they noted, the volunteer was less open to exploitation from the employer. One man shared his experience in this regard:

> Basically, when I look at it now, at the time the company needed someone to do their website, but it was only for a short amount of time, and the employer wants it to be free. That's why they choose us. Of course for us we need the Canadian experience. That's why we do this. I worked very hard and showed my talents, showed my hard working, with the hope that they would keep me afterwards. But eventually I got laid-off because they don't need me anymore. I know volunteering though the Co-op program is a positive way of getting new immigrants into a job, but some employers take advantage of the newcomers.

IMPLICATIONS FOR THE NOTION OF "VOLUNTEER" WORK

> When I started to send my resume, I expected that I had done a good search – 1000 companies in my database. I knew everything in Canada and in Toronto but I didn't get a job. After that I started from another side, from the bottom. I volunteered. I didn't get paid any money but I felt like I worked there and I felt like I was worth something, like you are useful.

Given the range of work these professional immigrants performed under the "volunteer" umbrella, it is important to broaden the notion of volunteerism to include these experiences. This is particularly relevant because the traditional definition of volunteer work (unpaid, freely chosen and benefiting the community) does not easily apply to the case of recent immigrants. Indeed, in many cases, the decision to engage in volunteer work is not the result of free choice but by labour market pressures, and in that sense it is more socially coerced than based on individual freedom. Likewise, the implicit notion that volunteer work should benefit the community–as implied in the traditional definition–is challenged when many immigrants do volunteer work in the for-profit sector. In this case, the boundaries between volunteer work and labour exploitation are not always clear and distinct.

Although in most cases volunteering did not lead to a well-paying professional job, the informal learning from the experience serve as a way for participants to regain social and cultural capital (Bourdieu, 1986) as well as self esteem and confidence. Many participants indicated that the informal learning from the volunteer work placements was far more significant than the formal job-related training they received. Interestingly, forty per cent of the participants identified communication skills, including the ability to practice speaking English, as the most important learning acquired during their volunteer experience. Other key aspects of their informal volunteer learning were the value of networking (36%), knowledge of Canadian workplace practices (25%), adapting to and understanding "Canadian culture" (16%), increased self-confidence (16%) and working in a diverse workforce (13%). The following quotes from two different participants illustrate some of these aspects:

> I think, first, it gave me the chance to know about Canadian working environments or, how you said, cultures. It's hard to come from what we have in China. So it is a great opportunity to know something like that. And of course I also improved my English speaking skills. Sometimes, I spoke to clients and I got feedback from them so they actually give me the confidence that I can actually handle work quite well in a brand-new environment. I feel it [volunteering] is very important when you try to start a new life here.

> I learned about how the Canadian office work, how the coworkers work together, they go out for lunch, and enjoy things together, also I met lots of people. The most important thing I learned was socialization, to be part of the Canadian culture. I could meet people and learn from their culture.

SUMMARY, CONCLUSIONS AND RECOMMENDATIONS

Immigrants to Canada often face the "Canadian work experience" catch-22: many employers require one year of Canadian work experience, but it is close to impossible to acquire such work experience because few employers would hire someone without Canadian work experience. This can become a very frustrating experience for professional immigrants who come to Canada wih specialized skills, university degrees and high expectations. Volunteering is one avenue used by immigrants to obtain the "Canadian work experience' (George et al., 2000). This was the context faced by participants in this study. After successfully qualifying through the Canadian immigration selection process, once in Canada the majority of our participants found themselves in a situation in which their former social status declined and they became "labour market undesirables". Integration into the Canadian labour market is not easy, especially taking into account that new immigrants experience a sudden drop in social status, citizenship rights, social capital (e.g., networks) and cultural capital (e.g., language, understanding of informal norms, etc.).

From varied sources, our participants were told that as new immigrants they had to get "Canadian work experience", which would prove to be one of their most formidable employment barriers. They were also told repeatedly that one of the most viable options to gain Canadian work experience was to do volunteer work. Participants raised questions, however, about how much value other employers place on the volunteer work experience. They felt that Canadian employers would not recognize the volunteer work in the same way as paid work experience. One participant said:

> At first I thought that people would value the volunteer work. A lot of people told me, you need the experience, and if you write down the volunteering, they will say, oh look. But even with the volunteer experience, they don't look at my resume. But now, even though I have volunteering, it's not enough, they don't care.

Unfortunately, the experience of this participant was not an exception. The vast majority of the participants in this study (87%) were either unemployed or underemployed even after getting their "Canadian work experience" through volunteering. The experience of the few who managed to find a job in their field suggests that volunteering for "Canadian experience" is more likely to be a successful strategy to access a relevant job in the Canadian labour market if certain circumstances are present. A particularly important condition is to ensure a close relation between a) immigrants' past experience, b) the nature of the volunteer work, c) their job expectations and c) the realities of the Canadian labour market.

Some participants called for an increased partnership between community-based agencies and for-profit companies to increase the availability of volunteer placements outside the non-profit sector. This recommendation reflects the fact that while only 16 per cent of the participants had a background in social services, 69 per cent of the volunteer placements took place in community organizations. Due to this situation, 71 per cent of the participants did volunteer work that was completely unrelated to their professions. Because the match between the education, work experience and volunteer placement is a critical success factor for immigrant volunteers to access the paid labour market, the participants' call for enhanced volunteer opportunities in the for-profit sector is reasonable and merits consideration.

Our study raises three interesting challenges that have theoretical and practical implications. First, the study challenges the notion of education, training and skill enhancement as a direct, linear route to the labour market. Despite the fact that almost all of our participants had at least one university degree and many had taken additional training courses in Canada, 42 per cent were unemployed and 44 per cent were underemployed at the time of the interview, after their volunteer placements were completed.

Second, our study challenges a limited understanding of the concept of work that focuses only on paid labour, and argues that volunteer work needs to be considered within the continuum of work. Several participants in our study worked for no pay side-by-side with paid workers performing the same tasks. This indicates that in these situations there is potential for a great deal of exploitation, and more research needs to be done to both highlight the issues and examine the conditions under which highly skilled racialized immigrants are working for free.

Third, our study challenges the traditional understanding of volunteerism as freely chosen and contributing to the community. These professional immigrants did not freely choose to volunteer; that decision was to some extent influenced by labour market pressures, and for this reason we may need to consider the notion of 'coerced volunteerism'. Likewise, these participants do not conform to the profile of the altruistic volunteer, as they volunteered for instrumental reasons: to try to find better, meaningful paid work in a new country. The traditional conceptualization of volunteerism is also challenged by the fact that many participants performed their volunteer work in for-profit companies, a trend that has not yet received enough attention in the research literature on volunteerism.

In closing, both our study and the literature suggest that employers seldom value volunteer work experience as highly as paid work experience. Our study also highlights the importance of non-formal and informal learning in the transition from volunteer work to paid work and the impact of gender, race and class processes in shaping people's access to the labour market. The main practical recommendation emanating from this study relates to the importance of matching volunteer placements more closely to the immigrant's education, experience and occupational orientations. In terms of suggestions for further research and policy debate, we argue that there needs to be more research on the efficacy of volunteering as a strategy for labour market access in order to address the following questions: What are the factors that hinder or enhance the experience of immigrant professionals in accessing the Canadian labour market? What are the roles played by employers, government agencies, educational institutions, professional colleges and immigrant groups in facilitating or delaying this transition? We would also like to pose two questions for debates on policy: Should immigrants be working for free at all, especially when the work is

performed in the for-profit sector? Should there be more paid internships, provincial and federal employment programs developed to encourage employers to hire new immigrants directly?

NOTES

[1] Of this number, between 141,000 and 158,000 are skilled workers. Also, as of March 29, 2007 there were 800,000 applications in a backlog waiting to be processed (CIC, 2007, p. 25).

[2] Adaptability includes points for education level of spouse or common-law partner of principal applicant, previous study or work in Canada, and relatives in Canada. See http://www.cic.gc.ca/english/pdf/kits/guides/EG7.pdf.

[3] Canadian National Occupational Classification (NOC) Skill Type 0, A or B.

[4] Each year since 1995, the proportion of family reunification immigrants has declined. In 1995, 36 percent of all immigrants were family class; in 2005, family class only made up 24 per cent of the total.

[5] As of September 18, 2003, the pass mark is 67/100. To do a self assessment, go to http://www.cic.gc.ca/english/immigrate/skilled/assess/Education.asp.

[6] See Mundel, Duguid, & Schugurensky, 2006; Slade, Yuo & Schugurensky, 2006; Duguid, Slade & Schugurensky; Mundel & Schugurensky, 2005; Slade, Luo, & Schugurensky, 2005)

[7] The survey, conducted in the winter and spring of 2004, is based on interviews with 9,063 Canadian adults.

[8] This requirement is waived if the applicant has arranged employment in Canada.

[9] Also, they have to pass a medical exam, security and criminal checks and language proficiency tests (more money). This is in addition to the processing fee ($550 per person) and the right of permanent residence fee ($490 per adult).

[10] This money must be presented in the form of cash, securities or money orders, bankers' drafts to a Customs Officer at the time of arrival in Canada (see http://www.cic.gc.ca/english/immigrate/skilled/arriving.asp).

[11] The numbers do not add to 100 per cent exactly (unemployed participants 20/45 = 44.444%; underemployed 19/45 = 42.222%; and appropriately employed 6/45 = 13.333%).

REFERENCES

ACTEW. (2007). Retrieved July 17, 2007, from http://www.actew.org/

Alboim, N., & The Maytree Foundation. (2002). *Fulfilling the promise: Integrating immigrant skills into the Canadian economy.* Toronto: Caledon Institute of Social Policy.

Alboim, N., Finnie, R., & Meng, R. (2007). The discounting of immigrants' skills in Canada: Evidence and policy recommendations. *IRPP Choices, 11*(2). Retrieved July 13, 2007, from http://www.irpp.org/choices/archive/vol11no2.pdf

Bannerji, H. (2000). *The dark side of the nation: Essays on multiculturalism, nationalism and gender.* Toronto: Canadian Scholars' Press.

Bauder, H. (2003). Brain abuse or the devaluation of immigrant labour in Canada. *Antipode, 35*(4), 699–717.

Bourdieu, P. (1986). The forms of capital. In J. G. Richardson (Ed.), *Handbook of theory and research for the sociology of education* (pp. 241–258). New York: Greenwood Press.

Boyd, M., & Thomas, D. (2002). Skilled immigrant labour: Country of origin and the occupational locations of male engineers. *Canadian Studies in Population, 29*(1), 71–99.

Brouwer, A. (1999). *Immigrants need not apply.* Toronto: Caledon Institute of Social Policy.

Citizenship and Immigration Canada. (2007a). *2007–2008 report of plans and priorities for citizenship and immigration Canada.* Retrieved July 13, 2007, from http://www.tbs-sct.gc.ca/rpp/0708/ci-ci/ci-ci_e.asp

Citizenship and Immigration Canada. (2007b). *Skilled workers and professionals.* Retrieved July 18, 2007, from http://www.cic.gc.ca/english/immigrate/skilled/index.asp

Citizenship and Immigration Canada. (2007c). *Skilled workers and professionals: Who can apply-proof of funds*. Retrieved July 13, 2007, from http://www.cic.gc.ca/english/immigrate/skilled/funds.asp.

Citizenship and Immigration Canada. (2006). *Facts and figures 2005 immigration overview: Permanent and temporary residents*. Retrieved July 1, 2007, from http://www.cic.gc.ca/english/resources/statistics/facts2005/index.asp

Citizenship and Immigration Canada. (2005). *Annual Report to Parliament on Immigration*. Retrieved July 17, 2007, from http://www.cic.gc.ca/english/resources/publications/annual-report2005/annex.asp

Couton, P. (2002). Highly skilled immigrants: Recent trends and issues. *ISUMA: Canadian Journal of Policy Research, 3*(2), 114–123.

Duguid, F., Slade, B., & Schugurensky, D. (2006). *Significant yet Unrecognized: The informal learning of volunteers in two settings*. Retrieved July 12, 2007, from http://www.wallnetwork.ca/resources/Schugurensky_CASAE_2006.pdf

Galabuzi, G. (2006). *Canada's creeping economic apartheid: The social exclusion of racialized groups in the new century*. Toronto: Canadian Scholar's Press.

George, U., Tsang, K. T., Man, G., & Da, W. W. (2000). *Needs assessment of mandarin-speaking newcomers*. Toronto: South East Asian Service Centre.

Guo, S. (2007). Immigrants as active citizens: Learning in social action. In L. Servage & T. Fenwick (Eds.), *Learning in community. Proceedings of the joint international conference of the adult education research conference (AERC) and the Canadian association for the study of adult education (CASAE)* (pp. 265–270). Toronto: CASAE.

Hall, M., Lasby, D., Gumulka, G., & Tryon, C. (2006). *Caring Canadians, involved Canadians: Highlights from the 2004 Canada survey of giving, volunteering and participating*. Ottawa: Statistics Canada. Retrieved July 12, 2007, from http://www.givingandvolunteering.ca/pdf/CSGVP_Highlights_2004_en.pdf

Jackson, A. (2002). *Is work working for workers of colour?* Ottawa: Canadian Labour Congress.

Kofman, E. (1999). Female birds of passage a decade later: Gender and immigration in the European union. *International Migration Review, 33*(2), 269–299.

Krahn, H., Derwing, T., Mulder, M., & Wilkinson, L. (2000). Educated and underemployed: Refugee integration into the Canadian labour market. *Journal of International Migration and Integration, 1*(1), 59–84.

Kunz, J., Milan, A., & Schetagne, S. (2000). *Unequal access: A Canadian profile of racial differences in education, employment and income*. Toronto: Canadian Race Relations Foundation.

Li, P. (2005). *Destination Canada: Immigration debates and issues*. Oxford: Oxford University Press.

Li, P. (2001). The market worth of immigrants' educational credentials. *Canadian Public Policy, 27*(1), 23–38.

Livingstone, D. W., & Scholtz, A. (2006). *Work and lifelong learning in Canada: Basic findings of the 2004 WALL survey*. Retrieved June 18, 2007, from http://www.wallnetwork.ca/resources/WALLSurveyReportFINALMarch2007.pdf

Livingstone, D. W., Myles, J., Doray, P., Hubich, L., & Collins, M. (2004). *National survey of learning and work*. Retrieved May 25, 2007, from http://wall.oise.utoronto.ca/research/research_teams.htm

Lochhead, C. (2003, July). *The transition penalty: Unemployment among recent immigrants to Canada: Canadian labour and business centre commentary*. Retrieved July 3, 2007 from http://www.clbc.ca/files/Reports/Fitting_In/Transition_Penalty_e-CLBC.pdf.

Mojab, S. (2000). The power of economic globalization: Deskilling immigrant women through training. In R. M. Cerver, A. L. Wilson, & Associates (Eds.), *Power in practice: Adult education and the struggle for knowledge and power in society* (pp. 23–41). San Francisco: Jossey-Bass.

Ornstien, M. (2000). *Ethno-racial inequality in Toronto: Analysis of the 1996 census*. Toronto: City of Toronto.

Picot, G., & Sweetman, A. (2005). *The deteriorating economic welfare of immigrants and possible causes: Update 2005*. Ottawa: Statistics Canada. Retrieved July 12, 2007, from http://www.statcan.ca/english/research/11F0019MIE/11F0019MIE2005262.pdf

Policy Roundtable Mobilizing Professions and Trades (PROMPT). (2004). *In the public interest: Immigrant access to regulated professions in today's Ontario*. Toronto: PROMPT.

Public Policy Forum. (2004). *Bringing employers into the immigration debate: Survey and conference*. Retrieved June 22, 2007, from http://www.ppforum.com/common/assets/publications/en/bringing_employers_into_the_immigration_debate.pdf

Reitz, J. (2005). Tapping immigrants' skills: New directions for Canadian immigration policy in the knowledge economy. *Institute for Research on Public Policy Choices, 11*(2). Retrieved June 29, 2007, from http://www.irpp.org/choices/archive/vol11no1.pdf

Reitz, J. (2001). Immigrant success in the knowledge economy: Institutional change and the immigrant experience in Canada, 1970–1995. *Journal of Social Issues, 57*(3), 579–613.

Schugurensky, D., & Mündel, K. (2005). The 'accidental learning' of volunteers: The case of community-based organizations in Ontario. In K. Künzel (Ed.), *International yearbook of Adult education 31/32* (pp. 183–206). Cologne: Böhlau-Verlag.

Schugurensky, D., Mündel, K., & Duguid, F. (2006). Learning from each other: Housing cooperative members' acquisition of skills, knowledge, attitudes and values. *Cooperative Housing Journal*, Fall, 2–15.

Schugurensky, D., Slade, B., & Yuo, L. (2005). *"Can volunteer work help me get a job in my field?": On learning, immigration and labour markets.* Retrieved July 15, 2007, from http://wall.oise.utoronto.ca/inequity/LL&W2005/SchugurenskyPaper.pdf

Shan, H. (2006). *Learning on the periphery: Chinese immigrants coping with the regulatory practices of the medical profession in Canada.* Paper presented at the 25th Conference of the Canadian Association for the Study of Adult Education (CASAE). Retrieved June 13, 2007, from http://www.oise.utoronto.ca/CASAE/cnf2006/2006onlineProceedings/CAS2006Hongxia%20Shan.pdf

Slade, B. (2004). Highly skilled and under-theorized: Women migrant professionals. In R. Baaba Folson (Ed.), *Calculated kindness: Global economic restructuring and Canadian immigration & settlement policy* (pp. 102–116). Halifax, NS: Fernwood Publishers.

Slade, B., Yuo, L., & Schugurensky, D. (2006). *Seeking 'Canadian experience': The informal learning of new immigrants.* Retrieved July 10, 2007, from http://www.oise.utoronto.ca/CASAE/cnf2005/2005onlineProceedings/CAS2005Pro-Slade2-Luo-Schug.pdf

Statistics Canada. (2003a). *Census of population: Labour force activity, occupation, industry, class of worker, place of work, mode of transportation, language of work and unpaid work.* Retrieved July 18, 2007, from http://www.statcan.ca/Daily/English/030211/d030211a.htm

Statistics Canada. (2003b). *Longitudinal survey of immigrants to Canada.* Retrieved June 10, 2007, from http://www.statcan.ca/Daily/English/030904/d030904a.htm

Teo, S. Y. (2004). Between imagination and reality: Tales of skilled immigrants from China. *Canadian Diversity, 3*(2), 21–31.

Zakaluzny, R. (2007). Industry facing technologist, technician shortages. *Ottawa Business Journal.* Retrieved July 18, 2007, from http://www.ottawabusinessjournal.com/312729634731591.php

Bonnie Slade
Post-Doctoral Fellow
York University

Daniel Schugurensky
Department of Adult Education
University of Toronto

PIERRE DORAY, ELAINE BIRON, PAUL BÉLANGER,
SIMON CLOUTIER AND OLIVIER MEYER

15. ADULT EDUCATION AND THE TRANSITION TO RETIREMENT[1]

INTRODUCTION

This paper is part of a research project designed to give us a better understanding of the relations between life transitions and participation in adult learning. Throughout their lives, individuals are bound to encounter forks in the road. The passage from childhood to adolescence, then to adulthood, and finally to retirement, are transitions that punctuate the lives of individuals. People may change jobs or experience changes in their state of health or upheavals in their personal lives as a result of marriage or divorce. Our research was designed to gain an understanding of the relationship between these times of transition and participation in adult education and training and to elucidate the meaning or meanings given to adult learning by those involved.

This analysis will focus on one particular transition: the passage to retirement. The greying of the population has become a dominant feature of advanced industrial societies; the number of elderly workers and retirees is growing in relation to the overall population. In fact, it is estimated that in Canada in 2041, more than one person in four, or 23%, will be 65 years of age or older.[2] This trend is certain to raise a number of questions in terms of access to education and training such as that provided for the older adult population.

Earlier quantitative analyses of participation on the basis of age show a decline in such participation. Older workers and retirees participate less in formal activities (Sylva, 1998; Courtney, 1992). Studies in 11 industrialized countries show that *young adults between 25 and 34 are twice as likely to participate in adult education and training as people between 55 and 64* (OECD, 2000, p. 24). This tendency can also be seen in the WALL survey, as Figure 15.1 shows. An initial decline is observed among individuals 45 years of age or older. Later, retirement is another time when the level of participation declines with the result that the level of participation among people 65 and older is quite low.

Obviously, retirement is a critical moment in the history of individuals' participation in these activities. We might assume that following retirement, involvement with education would be of secondary importance in the daily lives of individuals and could even just disappear altogether. However, this view of things would be only partial because the "loss of interest" in education and formal training makes itself felt much earlier as the decline in participation begins earlier in peoples' lives. This chapter will explore this transition to retirement in order to determine

P. Sawchuk and A. Taylor (eds.), Challenging Transitions in Learning and Work: Reflections on Policy and Practice, 283–308.

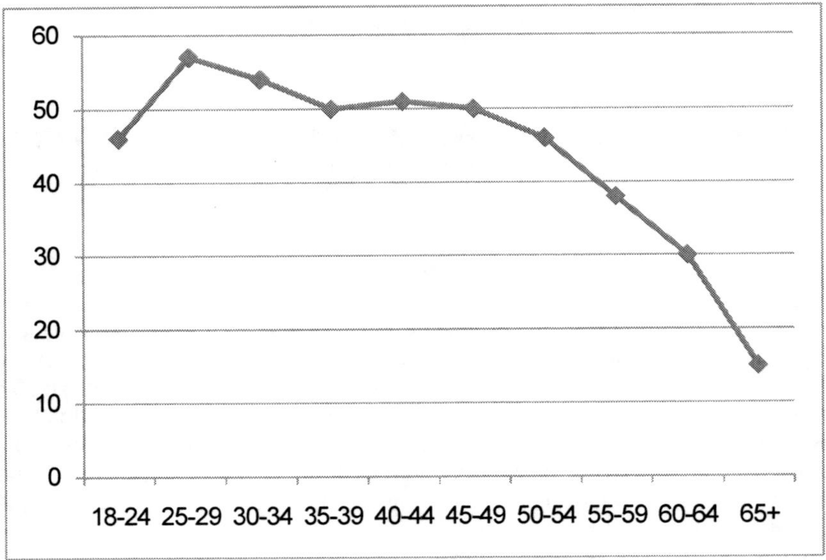

Figure 15.1 Rate of adult education participation Canada, WALL, 2002

the conditions and situations that lead retirees, despite the general trend, to take part in education and training activities. We shall attempt to determine which retirees take part in such activities and the significance of this participation in the context of their daily lives.

THE INCREASE IN AGE AND EDUCATION: REAL SOCIAL CHALLENGES

In recent decades, the average retirement age has declined substantially in most industrialized countries, and the possibility of early retirement has generally been used as a tool for managing the labour force through external flexibility. Thus, a rapid decline has been observed in rates of formal and informal professional activities *among workers over 55* (Guillemard, 1994, p. 2). *The thresholds at which activity transitions into inactivity are occurring at increasingly young ages* (Guillemard 1989, p. 3). It seems that the capacity and desire of older workers to continue working depend both on the conditions in the labour market and on the state of their health, their working conditions and their motivation.

More recently, irrespective of expectation related to the new knowledge economy, the reorganization of the Fordist model of development has given way to "desynchronization" of transition periods and of precarious situations arising between the time when people stop work and when they retire: "*Over the last fifteen years we have witnessed a sudden upheaval in these chronological markers that punctuated the end of one's career and determined the identities and symbolic horizons of individuals located at each stage in the life cycle*" (Guillemard 1994, p. 177).

Thus, the final departure from the world of work no longer automatically implies that the individual will enter the retirement system. This departure is not only shifted in time but it also becomes less and less definitive. The last stage of the life cycle set aside for retirement is substantially remodelled "*in that the right to inactivity at the end of one's life, which is conditioned by a contribution to the productive effort during one's life, is blurred*" (Guillemard, 1994, p. 5). This tendency has apparently been accentuated by the greying of the population, which has also led to greater use being made of older manpower.

Against a backdrop of increased use of older manpower, new measures emerge. The validation of informal training and knowledge derived from experience appears to be an effective way to strengthen the capacity for action of older retired workers as a result of the recognition of their skills in various areas of activity, and thus to facilitate their participation in further training. Informal training and continuing professional development are essential in helping older workers to adjust to fluctuations in demand and employment prospects and to avoid undesired retirement (ILO, 2001).

However, participation in education and training activities may meet other demands than the simple goal of increasing employability, whether these are aspirations linked to social inclusion or a search for independence; educational biographies do not necessarily stop when people end their working lives. Thus, progress in technological resources makes it necessary to update and permanently renew skills, specifically in order to ensure the social and political inclusion of individuals. *The integration of older people into the information society is a major challenge. If there is a risk to which these people are exposed, it is the risk of isolation and thus of marginalization* (OECD, 2000, p. 46). Carlton and Soulsby (1999) also state that the decline in educational activities involves an acceleration of the aging process, especially among older people whose financial situation is precarious or whose health is poor. It is with this diversity in educational demand and the predictable participation in structured activity according to previous educational experience and background in mind, considering as well the possible active or passive piloting of that life transition, that we must attempt to understand the meaning of participation in education and training in greying populations.

THEORETICAL MARKERS

Global Markers

An analysis of participation in adult education is often used to understand the overall development of adult education in a society. Participation in activities and supply of structured learning opportunities are frequent indicators of institutionalizion of adult education. Recent work by the OECD (2003; 2001) provides examples of this. A second possible analytical approach offers a better understanding of the factors that affect individual participation in education and training activities. The goal is something more than a mere description of the demographic and social characteristics of participants. In fact, it is an understanding of the processes and mechanisms that lead individuals to participate in organized learning activities which in turn illuminates important aspects of the transitions associated with older workers' lives.

Inequality in adult education participation could be explained by the social position of individuals and by actual developments in this field, which itself is subject to social and economic changes. In reference to Bourdieu's theory of social reproduction (Bourdieu and Passeron, 1970), some analyses of adult education participation highlight the presence of similar logics of reproduction within this field (Schubert, 1973 and 1977; Dubar, 1981).

Another tradition has also sought to determine why individuals do not participate by identifying explicit obstacles to participation. Cross (1981), who was followed by several researchers (Scanlan and Darkenwald, 1984; Darkenwald et al., 1985) includes transitions as appropriate times to register for education and training in her model. This then becomes a resource for a more active undertaking for the transition.

Researchers have also proposed explanatory models of participation that combine social context, personality traits, personal situation and participation (Cookson, 1986; Rubenson, 1977). For example, Blair, McPake and Munn (1995) suggested that participation be defined as the result of the interaction of objectives and the conditions governing participation. The goals often take root in people's life conditions and they also carry the project forward. While this perspective underlines the dynamic between people's projects or aspirations and the conditions they face in trying to implement their educational projects, it tends to ignore the immediate context and the different ways of forming learning objectives, one element of which is undoubtedly the subjective relationship that individuals maintain with education and training.

We, however, prefer to define participation in adult education as a product of the dynamic established between a demand for an activity and an organization of the education and training field, both aspects being social constructs. This view of participation highlights primarily the fact that participation is a product of both personal "decisions" and an institutional framework that organizes the field of adult education and learning, and consequently steers the demands of members of society.

Considering demand sociologically leads to a questioning of the social forces that motivate people to participate in an activity and of the decision-making methods of those involved. One of these forces is the cultural constructs and the skills that make up the individuals and shape the ways in which situations and practices are represented, perceived and anticipated. These arrangements and skills are mobilized to judge situations and to choose among various possible courses of action. The importance of these constructs relating to educational choices no longer needs to be established. Structural approaches have widely shown the impact of social origin, gender and membership in a particular ethnocultural group on educational careers both in initial education and in continuing education and training. Psychosocial approaches also recognize the importance of cultural capital in participation in adult education. This is due to the role cultural capital plays in how individuals decide to participate to adult education, both in terms of the interest in a specific type of adult learning (valence) and the "chances" of success (expectancy) (Rubenson, 1977). Cultural capital modulates methods of judgment and appreciation, leading to different evaluations and different commitments. Variation of life contexts and conditions is reflected the unequal nature of learning/work transitions.

Considering demand sociologically also leads to reconstructing it from both the perspective of personal decisions made by the subjects and the structuration of the field and the organizations in question. In the case of company-provided education and training, for example, participation depends not only on an individual desire of workers but also on decisions of the hierarchical leadership and the policies of companies (Méhaut, 1978; Dubar 1995; Doray, 1999). In this sense, the social logics at work with respect to education and training for retirees may vary, depending on social development, health policies, needs of the informal economy, etc.

Work on on participation in adult education stress the fact that the most significant factor is the level of earlier education, which suggests that educational experience and the relationship with schools structures attitudes to education generally and has an effect throughout an individual's life. Moreover, the difference in participation between men and women is closely linked to this factor; the level of former education has a greater impact on the participation of women, for whom the likelihood of participating combined with their earlier educational status is greater (Doray, Bélanger, Levesque, 2005). Earlier education also impacts on their tendency to indicate that one's learning demand has not been met (Doray, Bélanger and Labonté, 2005; Doray and Livingstone, 2002). However, the effect of cultural capital is greater than the relationship with formal education. For example, participation increases with the level of literacy and reading habits while it declines with the amount of time a person spends watching television. It may be assumed that the connection with written culture influences participation.

It is possible to make a distinction between conditions of life in the home and those at work. The former determine access to two resources: time and money. The question of time revolves, among other things, around the reconciliation of work, family and studies, and this is not resolved in the same way by men and women as a result of the division of domestic work along gender lines. The financial issue is as important because many training activities require the payment of fees. It is as true in the private training market as in universities (access to which is not guaranteed in many countries).

Conditions of employment have an impact on participation in the form of access to educational resources in companies (Gagnon, 2004; Gagnon, Doray and Bélanger, 2004). Inequalities are declining in various occupations, although managers and professionals show a high rate of participation while workers clearly participate less. They are also linked to characteristics of companies such as their size, which sector of industry they belong to, the presence of innovation, etc. The planning of activities involves several factors such as economic conditions and strategies, manpower-management policies, the degree of internal organization of the company and of training as well as the industrial relations system.

The adult learning supply variable, however, must be designed broadly to indicate first the availability of education and training, as well as the educational or socio-economic conditions and related public policies that may influence physical and social access to education and training activities. Finally, supply is also defined by the make-up of the different public and private providers of training, whose operating conditions and development strategies differ very greatly. In short, supply is conditioned not only by macro-social actions but also by local or micro-social involvement.

A look at transitions and life cycles allows us to understand both the cumulative processes throughout people's lives and the educational momentum created by life's transitions. While a subject in the process of a transition tends to make use of adult learning opportunities to increase his or her capacity for action and thus to better steer this change, his or her participation is still affected by the dynamic between the learning demand and educational supplys. On the one hand, the way in which the transition is experienced socially may be broadly influenced by the nature of the cultural capital and the evaluation and perception systems of those involved. On the other hand, transitions may lead to changes in an individual's life conditions, which may, in turn affect the resources available to him or her, as well as his access to activities. Finally, the organization of the supply may structure participation by offering activities that are more or less relevant to the transitions. Retirement is a heuristic moment in life course to analyse this relationship between the learning demand and the supply of education and training beyond the predominant logic of work related learning.

Around Participation at the Age of Retirement

Biological age in itself is of little use in explaining participation. That said, it can serve as a useful marker for detecting the factors and situations that affect participation. For example, the state of a person's health may decline and impose an obstacle to participation in formal activities or, paradoxically, it may provide an incentive because of the need to check a diagnosis made by a professional. Thus, it is necessary to stress social age rather than chronological age. Retirement obviously reduces the possibilities of participation offered by employers. To what extent, then, are the possibilities of participation for retirees reduced as a result of a supply of adult training that is largely designed to provide occupational qualifications?

Participation in adult learning activities declines with age. Many reasons are given for this. An initial interpretation, which may be associated with the cultural constructs, representations and models, is linked to a representation of aging that is widely associated with retirement, which is itself linked to the creation of an image of life cycles that structures the institutionalized relationships between training, work and leisure time (Bélanger, 1992, p. 344) at no fewer than three stages: childhood and adolescence are associated with a person's schooling; adulthood with work and old age with retirement. The organization of the cycle of life that has emerged with industrialized society might tend to remove individuals from education and training activities even though they have the time to become involved.

Again in terms of cultural and social representations, prejudices about one's ability to learn based on age are always tenacious, even though experience shows that the vast majority of preconceived notions concerning the educational ability of older workers are not justified. Persons aged 50 and over[3] (Carlton and Soulsby, 1999) have recognized capacities for learning to which may usually be added some relevant experiential knowledge. According to another study, *the average difference in effectiveness at work between age groups is usually much less substantial than differences among the workers in a single age group* (ILO, World Employment Report, 1999, p. 10). What is more, the hiring and retention of employees of all ages by companies has the advantage of providing those workers with a wide range of skills and ensures that they do not lose the knowledge accumulated and the collective memory they bring with them; paradoxically, this allows them to adjust more easily to new realities (ILO, 2005).

The cultural attitudes towards adult learning are constructed through earlier educational experiences and in particular through the personal experience of education, which may account for the strong connection between adult education participation and initial education. Thus, individuals who have had difficult experiences of education or grew up in a social context where education and graduation did not have the strategic value it tends to have today may have created a distant relationship with continuing training. The work of Antikainem, Jarmo and Juha (1995, 1998, 1999 and 2002) reinforces this idea. These authors suggest that education be understood in its cultural dimension by establishing the significance that education has for individuals. In this regard, they have identified three educational cohorts, that is three generations for whom education and training have different meanings. The first generation includes people born in 1935 or earlier. Their educational experience was brief although it was an ideal. The members of the second generation were born between 1936 and 1955 and experienced increased access to educational resources, which they viewed as a useful tool throughout their professional careers. The members of the third generation, who were born after 1956, integrate education into their lives and view it as an activity in its own right. These representations, which build a relationship with education, may play a role in the decision to participate in adult education.

In regards to cultural constructs, one final interpretation involves declining participation as a result of lower expectations for economic benefits due to aging. For example, older workers would be less interested in education and training because the expected economic benefits such as increased salaries would be less substantial since they cover a shorter period. In other words, participation would depend on a cost/benefit analysis showing that increasing age reduces the benefits.

The validity of the above-mentioned interpretation, however, is limited. First of all, we may disregard the cost of not investing in the continuing professional development of older workers and secondly, we might consider the interplay of other factors influencing participation, namely, the conditions of people's lives, cultural constructs and the availability of training. Thus, while it is possible for a cost/benefit analysis to be carried out by individuals as part of their decision to take courses for professional purposes, can the same reasoning possibly be applied to activities that do not serve professional purposes or have economic spin-offs?

In this sense, the nature of the activities may bring different types of decision-making into play that does not depend solely on instrumental rationality, especially an instrumentality linked exclusively to the formal economy.

Several studies (Méhaut, 1978, Dubar, 1995; Bélanger, Doray, Labonté and Lévesque, 2005) have identified a series of organizational factors that reduce participation by older workers. Employers often believe that older workers are less productive and find it more difficult to adjust to new technologies. Consequently, they tend to give younger employees more opportunity to participate in activities associated with technological change. Furthermore, some employers assume that older workers will retire before the cost of their education and training can be absorbed (Carlton and Soulsby, 1999).

In employment, therefore, older workers are less likely to access the education and training resources of companies in the decade preceding their retirement and their subsequent educational career is accordingly hampered, *since age has been held up as a primary cause of discrimination in distributing work* (Bélanger, 1992). However, access to high-quality education and training plays a key role in preventing and overcoming social exclusion and discrimination, especially in the labour force. Emphasis is also placed on "*the importance of training as a tool that, when combined with other measures, can overcome the challenges posed by the informal sector, which includes a large number of older workers*" (OECD, 2000, p. 41).

Retirees are not a uniform category; social and professional differences that have led to social and cultural distinctions over time continue to exist. "*Quality of life on retirement and the chances of participating in continuing training to improve that quality of life will be marked by the conditions of employment and the conditions in the lives of those involved and the impetus to learn and participate creatively that they have received*" (Bélanger 1992, p. 350). Thus, participation in training by older workers tends to be influenced by their professional past and, consequently, by the alternation of training and work they may have experienced throughout their lives. The pursuit of educational opportunities is closely linked with social and economic conditions, the level of initial training and the most immediate training they have received rather than with aging in the narrow sense.

Access to two resources related to people's life conditions can also influence participation: time and money. Retirement closes off access to all educational resources linked to work and companies. However, it does offer an increase in free time. Studies of participation have repeatedly found a paradoxical tendency in the situation of retirees: the increase in free time does not generally translate into increased participation in training. Given this situation, it seems clear that if free time is a precondition for participation, it does not become a sufficient condition for it. The economic and cultural conditions of a person's life also impact on access, and in this regard retirees find themselves in the same situation as people generally, but the general decline in the participation rate, regardless of social and economic status, also needs to be explained.

There may be many reasons for not participating: a participant's lack of financial resources, lack of supervision, lack of human resources to plan and manage availability, geographic constraints and a lack of mobility, which is itself closely related to the economic and also the health conditions governing a person's life. These are some of the factors that may combine to reduce demand (Bélanger, 1992). It would be enlightening in this regard to examine participation in the retirement-preparation courses that have been developed in many companies and the growth of learning-in-retirement courses at universities to determine whether and to what extent this availability is reflected in greater participation by the older cohorts.

In light of these studies, the transition to retirement may also very well be seen as a transition that tends overall to reduce participation merely as a new cycle where the individual continues his or her educational career, only differently. Analysis of the context and conditions in which these retirees live and of their representation of training will make it possible to clarify atypical forms of participation.

METHODOLOGY

This study is part of the *Work and Lifelong Learning* (WALL) project, a wide-ranging national research endeavour focussing on work and learning throughout people's lives. Based in Canada, the university research teams involved in this project have looked at various aspects of learning in the context of the ongoing reengineering of work.

A survey by questionnaire collected quantitative data from a large number of respondents (N = 9,600) across Canada and provided the core material for an analysis by the different work teams. The quantitative section of our analysis, which is based on this survey, is designed to determine the effect of the retiree's situation on his or her participation (see Table 15.1). The main variable distinguishes three categories: people who have not retired, young retirees (respondents who were 64 or younger) and retirees who were 65 or older. We also wanted to examine the situation in light of two other variables that impact on participation, namely the sex of individuals and their earlier education. We also sought to verify the relationship between retirement and participation, adjusting for state of health, which could become an obstacle. Finally, three aspects of participation in adult education and training were selected: actual participation in formal activities, recognition of informal learning and identification of unmet demand.

To supplement the quantitative survey, we completed a qualitative survey of the impact of the transition to retirement. We held 83 semi-conducted interviews with respondents from the national questionnaire, based in Toronto or Montreal. Out of 83 individuals, 14 had already retired. Postulating that transitions in life are heuristic points for understanding the significance that the subjects ascribe to training, the respondents were selected on the basis of whether they reported recently experiencing an important personal or professional transition. This qualitative survey, based on what the respondents said, was designed to gather their representations of adult learning and the strategies they implement in managing or piloting their transitions, which could well include the use of different forms of learning, both formal and informal. The passages, earlier educational and school experiences and the different methods of learning they used at a time of transition are the subject of our analysis.

Table 15.1. Variables in quantitative analysis

Name	*Definition*	*Categories*
Relationship on retirement	Differentiation of respondents on basis of whether or not they are retired on the basis of their age	• Non-retired population • Young retirees (people 64 and younger) • Retirees (people 65 and older)
Participation in education and training	Participation in formal activities	• Participating in a formal activity • Not participating in a formal activity
Identification of informal learning	Informal work-related training (people at work only)	• Yes • no
	Informal training related to volunteer activity (volunteers only)	• yes • no
	Informal training in domestic life	• yes • no
	Informal general-interest training	• yes • no
Unmet demand	Identification of unmet demand	• yes • no
	Obstacles to training	• Inconvenient timing • The training was too expensive • The program was not offered • Lack of need for formal training • Lack of qualifications or pre-requisites • Lack of time • Other family responsibilities • Lack of support from employer • Child-care problems • Health reasons • Physical or mental disability • Language problem • The courses are too boring • The school or training location was not welcoming
	Self-assessment of state of health	• poor health • reasonable or excellent health

Name	*Definition*	*Categories*
	Decline in state of health	• yes • no
	Existence of physical or mental disability	• yes • no
Cultural capital	Level of earlier education	• Elementary school • Less than secondary school graduation • Secondary school graduation • Post-secondary education • College graduation • Bachelor's degree • University or professional diploma

PRESENTATION OF DATA

A Portrait with Figures

The goal of the quantitative analysis was to determine whether there is an association between the fact that a person reported him- or herself as retired and eventual participation in adult learning activities during the years preceding the administration of the survey. The first finding was the fact that being retired tends to reduce participation in formal education and training activities, regardless of the age at which the person retires.

According to the survey data, while 43% of all Canadian adults took part in a formal education and training activity[4] (Figure 15.2), this rate declined to 25% among young retirees under 65 and to 14% among older retirees. The difference between men and women is minimal (less than 3 percentage points) among those who are retired and not retired and are 64 or younger but the participation rate for retired women who are 65 and older is higher (6 percentage points) than is true of men in the same age group.

An initial explanation of the decline in participation by retirees might focus on a decline in their state of health, a resource that can be essential for involvement in an education and training activity. Of the three reasons given, in fact, one was retirees' declining state of health. Thus, of retirees 64 or younger, 6% stated that their health is fragile. This figure grows to 11% for retirees 65 or older. The proportion of retirees claiming that their health has deteriorated varies from 27% to 38%, depending on the age group of retirees, while the percentage claiming a disability increases from 14% to 19%. Our survey shows a certain relationship (Figure 15.3) in the health indicators of retirees and participation in training by retirees who have turned 65. These differences are not significant for younger retirees among whom the trend is reduced, as a slight increase in participation could be detected. In fact, these results suggest that changes in health might provide a reason to seek education and training but it must be noted that here too the difference is small.

	Women[1]	Men[1]	Total
Not retired	50.4	46.8	48.6 N = 7,084
Retired and 64 or younger	25.2	23.7	24.6 N = 427
Retired and 65 or older	16.5	11.0	14.2 N = 1,225
Total	43.6	41.5	42.6 N = 8,736
Significant chi squared			

Figure 15.2. Rate of participation in formal training by sex and retirement status, Canada, WALL, 2002

	Not retired	Retired and 64 or younger	Retired and 65 or older	Total
Poor health[1]	25.2	20.0	8.0	19.2
Reasonable or excellent health[1]	49.5	24.7	15.1	43.8
Decline in state of health				
yes[1]	43.8	24.8	16.3	35.9
no[1]	49.7	24.5	13.0	44.4
Persons with disability				
yes[1]	35.7	31.1	8.9	28.1
no[1]	49.8	23.6	15.5	44.3

[1] Significant chi squared of input table

Figure 15.3. Rate of participation by relation with retirement and state of health, Canada, WALL, 2002

The effect of cultural capital, specifically educational capital, is still present and participation by level of earlier education fluctuates (see Figure 15.4). Retirees who already tend to participate less than non-retirees also show a significant variation in their level of participation depending on the level attained in their earlier education.

If we shift our attention to informal forms of learning, we see that the vast majority of individuals in employment report involvement in informal learning, which means, by definition, that retirees are excluded (Figure 15.5). Forms of learning associated with volunteer activities do not vary at the time of retirement although older retirees claim less frequently to participate in such learning. Overall, more than three retirees in four who engage in volunteer work report that they are involved in informal forms of learning in connection with that work. Recognition of informal learning associated with domestic life or areas of general interest is reported by at least four individuals out of five, regardless of retirement status, although older people are always less prepared to recognize such forms of learning.

In the overall non-retired adult population, 46% said that they wanted to participate in adult learning activities but had not been able to do so. This proportion of people reporting unmet demand declines among retirees: the figure for young retirees is 23% and that for the oldest cohort 15%. Reference to unmet demand also varies according to other individual characteristics. It is less marked among men than among women (Figure 15.6) and also varies by level of education: it is particularly low (less than 10% of retirees) among people who have completed only elementary school but increases to one person in five among retirees who have completed secondary school and is generally even higher among retired respondents who had completed post-secondary education (Figure 15.7). Overall, recognition of unmet demand varies with a person's status with regard to retirement, sex and level of education. These data reflect a well-known cultural phenomenon indicating that individuals who are better educated tend to value structured education and training and consequently are more likely to report unmet demand. The fact remains, however, that one young retiree in four and one older retiree in six wished to obtain education and training and was unable to do so.

	Not retired	Retired and 64 or younger	Retired and 65 or older	Total
Elementary school	7.8	12.7	4.8	6.5
Less than secondary school graduation[1]	33.6	10.9	13.3	28.9
Secondary school graduation[1]	38.3	21.7	14.7	34.8
Post-secondary education[1]	52.1	32.3	27.3	49.7
College graduation[1]	54.6	30.4	22.9	51.0
Bachelor's degree[1]	64.9	47.4	30.9	62.3
University or professional diploma[1]	66.1	50.0	28.6	62.7
Total	48.6	24.6	14.2	42.6

[1] Significant chi squared of input table

Figure 15.4. Rate of participation in formal activities by status on retirement and highest level of education completed, Canada, 2002, WALL

	Not retired	Retired and 64 or younger	Retired and 65 or older
Informal work-related training (people at work only)	91.2	-	-
Informal training related to volunteer work (volunteers only)	83.5[1]	81.6[1]	75.0[1]
Informal training in domestic life	88.6[1]	87.8[1]	81.1[1]
Informal general-interest training	89.9[1]	85.4[1]	81.3[1]

[1] Significant chi squared of input table

Figure 15.5. Informal forms of learning in Canada and status on retirement, 2002, WALL

	Not retired	Retired and 64 or younger	Retired and 65 or older	Total
Women	50.0	26.5	16.7	43.5
Men	42.7	18.5	12.1	38.0
Total	46.4	23.0	14.8	40.8

Figure 15.6. Unmet demand by sex and retirement status, Canada, 2002, WALL

	Not retired	Retired and 64 or younger	Retired and 65 or older
Elementary school	13.6	8.6	9.0
Less than secondary-school graduation	35.8	22.0	13.3
Secondary-school graduation	41.2	18.6	14.7
Post-secondary education	49.7	45.2	32.3
College graduation	51.3	25.0	17.4
Bachelor's degree	55.8	27.0	32.4
University or professional diploma	49.2	35.7	23.8
Total	46.4	22.7	15.1
Significant chi squared of table			

Figure 15.7. Unmet demand by level of earlier education and retirement status, Canada, 2002, WALL

One final aspect concerns the identification of the explicit obstacles to participation (Figure 15.8). Generally speaking, these do not have the same importance for retirees as for the public at large. The obstacle most frequently mentioned by the cohort of non-retirees was lack of time. However, retirees, especially those 65 and over, most commonly cited health reasons or disabilityas the cause of lack of participation. More than one-quarter of retirees 64 and under referred to health problems; this factor was clearly more common among older retirees. The disability factor followed the same patterns.

Institutional obstacles (the timing of the education and training was inconvenient and, to a lesser extent, cost) were mentioned most frequently. For retirees, the fact that the timing was not convenient is the most important obstacle because one retiree in two said so. For retirees 64 and under, the other two obstacles were, in order of importance, lack of time and the cost of the training. For older retirees, the lack of a need for formal adult learning was given as the reason why they do not participate by close to one-third of respondents, whereas the obstacles of cost and lack of time were cited by more than 20% of these individuals.

In fact, the legitimacy of adult training as an "interesting" retirement activity varies by age and earlier education. Overall, however, the dominant tendency is toward a general decline in participation: while retirement frees up time, the time devoted to training activities does not necessarily increase; on the contrary.

	Not retired	Retired and 64 or younger	Retired and 65 or older	Total
Institutional obstacles				
Inconvenient timing	56.9[1]	49.3[1]	45.5[1]	56.3[1]
The training was too expensive	51.8[1]	37.5[1]	22.3[1]	50.3[1]
The program was not offered	11.9	12.3	14.0	12.0

Continued

Personal obstacles				
No need for formal training	9.6[1]	25.8[1]	31.5[1]	11.2[1]
Lack of qualifications or prerequisites	7.2[1]	0[1]	9.2[1]	7.1[1]
Lack of time	62.7[1]	43.1[1]	26.4[1]	60.9[1]
Other family responsibilities	40.6[1]	25.0[1]	15.6[1]	39.3[1]
No support from the employer	20.5	-	-	20.5
Child-care problems	10.2[1]	0[1]	1.6[1]	9.7[1]
Deterrents				
Health reasons	7.0[1]	22.2[1]	27.5[1]	8.1[1]
Physical or mental disability	5.5[1]	13.9[1]	21.3[1]	6.3[1]
Language problem	2.8	0	3.3	2.7
The courses were too boring	5.0	2.8	0.8	4.8
The school or training location was not welcoming	1,5	2,8	1,7	1,5

[1] Significant chi squared of input table

Figure 15.8. Reasons for not participating by retirement status, Canada, 2002, WALL

Qualitative Analysis

In order to understand what significance older individuals attribute to participation in education and training, we analysed the transition to retirement of fourteen (14) individuals by grouping them on the basis of the amount of formal education they had received earlier in their life course. The statistical correlations found between the level of education received by individuals and the participation rate in educational activities now allows us to better understand the meaning of these relationships within the different groups of retirees.

Retirees with little earlier education. This first sub-group consists of five retired respondents with little earlier training (less than high school graduation). None of these retirees reports participation in formal adult learning. Only one respondent said that she reads regularly and her reading selections include esoteric subjects. In the absence of greater cultural capital, everyone seems to rely greatly on their family and social network to deal with the problems they encounter, without this social capital becoming, as can be seen in other social groups, a decisive factor in learning.

Salvatore develops few strategies and adjusts passively to his new situation; he allows those around him to perform many domestic tasks: "*I put it [the laundry] in a bag and I go to my sister-in-law's; she says, put it in the washing machine; do that for me, please*". **Odetta** counts on the assistance of her children, who have registered her at a cultural centre for seniors: "*I didn't, my daughter kept phoning. She said what am I going to do with this mother of mine? Somebody sent her there* *from the phonebook, they said join the community and you'll be alright. I'm there five years now*". **Océana**, whose family lives in the United States, feels that nothing has changed in her life since she got cancer and her husband died: "*... no, no, I did everything that I had always done with him*". Her informal learning can be summarized as consisting of solving crossword puzzles, which was recommended to her by her doctor. After the death of her spouse, she became involved in volunteer activities in an attempt to distract herself. However, this involvement did not seem to be associated with a desire for learning: "*But I wanted to be busy, and that's one of the things that helped me is being busy. And I would work so hard that I would come home and go to bed!*".

As noted in the quantitative survey in Figure 15.4, participation in adult education depends on the level of education received. The more education an individual has received, the greater his or her demand for education and training will be. Indeed, of the five retired respondents who had received little initial training, none said that he or she was significantly involved in organized training activities.

For **Merv**, the significance of adult learning relates essentially to work. In fact, all formal training activities in which he was involved in the past were designed to develop his professional knowledge: "*I took only specific courses available in my work, which was more like seminars, informative meeting like for example ... there was a lecture from Kodak about how to handle this new film ...*". In the absence of a more diversified image of his educational demands, participation becomes associated with the stage of his life spent in the work force.

As for **Madeline**, she rejects the culture of education by claiming to be above any learning system: "*I have always been a person that knows as knowledge of ... like you ... university. Knowledge that I have knowing. I do not know how come*".

The response was slightly different to the question concerning informal learning. It should be noted that indicators of informal learning were not defined prior to the interviews and the interpretation therefore varied with each respondent. For most of them, informal learning meant activities that took place outside an institutional framework. Thus, **Madeline** likes to read and **Odetta** is involved in activities organized by her seniors' club; **Merv** regularly devotes himself to building his DVD collection. **Océana** solves crossword puzzles. In all these cases, these cultural or social activities are identified as voluntary informal learning moments that are recreational in nature.

The transition to retirement occurred **passively** for three of the five respondents. In most cases, this transition is marked above all by important changes in their health and/or that of a relative: "*I'm a recovered cancer patient. I had ovarian cancer and I had chemotherapy for six months*".

We also observed that in these cases involving little initial education, the transition gave rise to little or no positive involvement with structured education and training. Factors that may explain their non-participation include little initial education, age and the state of their health. The health indicator was an important deterrent for three of the four respondents in this category, unlike the situation disclosed by the statistics in Figure 15.8, where the health reasons deterring people from participating in training are not often referred to by non-retirees and are fairly insignificant for retirees.

Retirees with substantial earlier training. Among those retirees who received substantial earlier education, we find two sub-groups: a first group of individuals who participate primarily in informal learning and a second in which the respondents report both formal and informal learning activities.

The first category includes four retired persons who received substantial initial education; while they had not participated in any formal educational activity during the last year, they were engaged on an ongoing basis in informal learning activities for purposes of personal development. Although these respondents said that they were not participating at the time of the survey, three of them indicated that, throughout their lives, they had always greatly valued formal adult learning. Only **Socrède** criticized educational institutions: "*at school, they don't learn much at school in the final analysis. It's a big daycare centre, that's all!*" The others have a positive image of education. **Olin** views his classical schooling as an important tool equipping him to better cope with life: "*With the knowledge that I have, I can get by. Over time, the knowledge acquired, the information, the training, the re-education, the philosophy, the supplements to the classical course were a happy experience for me*".

Three of them have a social network that is a source of continuing informal learning, including **Socrède**, whose initial reaction to the unknown was to consult the people in his circle: "*If there is something that is beyond me, there's probably also someone who has the answer somewhere.*" Referring to an earlier discussion, he said: "*I had had a disagreement with her and it took me a few years before I could say: Good Lord, she was damned right; nothing is certain.*" **Serge** wants knowledge to function as a guide for him when he travels abroad: "*I had known someone who spoke Spanish very well and who had also been to Cuba several times, and I became a great friend of his at one point. He worked nearby and I saw him often. And then, he used to go to Cuba so often and I had never set foot in a place like that so at one point I said to him: why don't you show me how to go about travelling.*" He also developed a network of acquaintances on the Internet in order to meet some of his personal and recreational needs: "*... a nice woman I met over the Internet was passing through Montreal. She came from Ohio and her husband owns horses; so I spoke about my method of using the computer to place bets and she absolutely had to have a look at it. Oh, I said, you'll be surprised. Well, I needed her because I am not able to enter the sites of American racetracks; if I want to place bets I can only bet here.*" However, **Olin** complained that he did not have this social capital that favoured informal learning and he felt that he was intellectually isolated from others: "*But in company, I'll talk to them but I must not go too far. When I meet people, if I go too far in the intellectual area, I lose them.*"

Odile explains her past lack of commitment to formal learning by the difficulty of reconciling family, work and study: "*... I had a family, those aren't ideal conditions to go back and study and I didn't have the inclination either ... I would have loved to obtain training to learn something else but to learn more of the same thing with people, you learn it from human contact*". Today, she is considering the possibility of registering for a course for recreational purposes: "*... I do not understand how people get bored in retirement; you know, I cannot understand that because there are so many things. Courses are given, well, in September at the* *university, there is a campus near me that offers courses of all kinds, on memory, on the arts ...*" ... "*Certainly I think that training can help but the ideal would be to have training and experience as well ...*". These examples corroborate the data in Figure 15.8, which show that unmet demand is more likely to come from educated people, whether or not they have retired.

The second category includes the five individuals who have retired, received extensive initial education and participate in formal types of adult learning. The approach to training has changed, however, from one involving a professional logic to a situation involving different kinds of logic (personal development, development of social involvement, recreation, etc.).

Of the five respondents who participate, two strongly criticized formal adult learning and did so for rather similar reasons. **Sofia** felt that the oriental cooking course in which she registered did not offer the same level of knowledge as she had acquired from Japanese students she had hosted as part of an exchange program. The same was true of the photography course she took and that was probably not geared to her needs: "*But there again, I was not satisfied. The courses were based on Canon equipment and I have a Minolta. So I didn't think it was fun because I constantly had to adapt and it was extremely difficult.*" **Nelson** was also dissatisfied with the content of the advanced guitar course he had been taking for some time. According to him, his level of knowledge is greater than the practical and theoretical concepts he is studying. "*My thoughts were, sit down and write a critique of the course and I should write for the professor why I would not use that terminology, whether it is in general use or not ...*". We note that the reasons for the lack of participation mentioned by the respondents correspond only partially to the data in Figure 15.8. Rather, the statistics indicate lack of time, problems with schedule management and lack of a need for formal adult learning as the decisive factors governing non-participation, whereas the most important obstacles noted in the interviews related more to the inadequacy of the adult learning supply.

Of the other three respondents, **Marvin** and **Kaitlin** said that they were satisfied with the structured adult learning they had participated in: "*I have also taken a course with the University of Toronto monitored a course ... in the history of Toronto. Just because I felt that, hey you know what? I know a lot about it, I just want to know more about it*". In addition, this participation seems to meet a need felt by respondents for personal realization. For this reason, **Sofia** was determined to complete the courses despite the inadequacy of their contents: "*I found that I was pretty good. It's not funny to rediscover yourself with that but ...*".

These respondents expressed a desire to take other courses eventually, always with a view to personal growth: "*I'm not going to seniors' activities (laughs). But I'm going to that in September because I have a bit of osteo-arthritis, like all older women so I am going to go and take swimming*".

The transition to retirement for all these respondents was an active process in which education and training played a significant role. For four of them, participation in formal adult learning activities met a double requirement: it helped distract them and maintained their social network. What **Marvin** said on this subject is important: "*You need a social structure during the day. You can't sit at home and vegetate. I think that is a great way of getting old. So the activities in the* *community, like the church and credit union, the health club are very important*". For **Nelson**, structured learning is a prerequisite for his personal development. His participation in a music course was imposed on him in that this was the only means by which he could access a group of musicians: "*... motivate me to do a bunch of things that I had not done because I didn't think they were necessary if I wasn't gonna play with anybody. And then I felt, if I wanna play with somebody, I'm gonna have to do this and this (classes)*". Interestingly, **Odèle** participates in formal learning activities for the purpose of maintaining her social relations..

While all the cases in this category involve a positive relationship with formal adult learning, the cases of **Marvin** and **Nelson** provided an insight into a tendency that complements the assessment of informal learning: "*I think a lot of people believe that learning has to be strictly academic and it's not. We're learning all the time. And there's a million different things to learn ... like making stained glass and cooking and things like that ... that are very important to an individual*". What is more, for **Odèle**, the relationship to non-structured learning is part of a logic of exchange that brings her closer together with her social circle: "*I've also read the books they read so that I can have discussions with them ... if I discuss with him, I discuss what interests him*". We find that all these respondents experience great cultural and social forces that seem to allow them to initiate actions that take the form, among others, of increased participation in formal and informal learning. **For Kaitlin** and **Odèle**, cultural capital takes the form of travel and attending concerts; for **Sofia** it takes the form of practising piano. Finally, in all five cases, the maintenance of social capital occurs as a result of a systematic integration of courses of all kinds: "*Socialize ... it keeps the wheels going around ... I think that's as important as exercising your body*".

Although one respondent had officially retired, he fitted a different model of participation in that his adult learning activities were professional in nature. **Othello**, who was a partner with his brother in a real estate business, helped his brother as a consultant in his son's company: "*I maintain an office because he (brother in law) and I are partners in a real estate business in the area of Rawdon*", and this leads him to want to keep up to date in his field of work. Note that Othello chooses out of desire and not out of obligation to continue a professional activity part time.

CONCLUSION

During an initial analysis of the relationship between life transitions and participation in adult education, we noted four possible transitions: professional transitions, transitions in an individual's personal life, migration and health-related transitions. We realized that the transition to retirement includes in part professional transitions, health-related transitions and, in some cases, transitions in an individual's personal life. What is more, it can be understood only in light of an individual's entire life trajectory and the transitions that punctuate it.

The analysis allows us first to distinguish between participation in formal activities and informal learning. The first is the act of a minority (one out of five younger retirees) and the second of a large majority, as the quantitative and qualitative data show. Overall, the image of the iceberg offers an appropriate depiction of participation in formal and informal adult learning in that it has a small visible section, formal adult education, and a large invisible section, informal learning. The differences between retirees in the national survey (with different levels of education) and the retirees who agreed to participate in the qualitative analysis is more pronounced in formal learning than in informal learning. Beyond these initial observations, the analysis of the fourteen individual trajectories allows us to understand the significance that various retirees give to formal learning and informal forms of learning. It gives us a better idea of how earlier education, by constituting a precondition for involvement in a later education process, helps not only to determine participation throughout a person's life, including retirement, but also to model the kind of transition that individuals then experience.

At the beginning of this chapter, we defined participation as the result of the meeting between a demand for and the organization of adult learning, both aspects being social constructs. This exploration of the participation of different groups of retirees clearly shows that the relationship between participation and the transitions cannot be understood outside this dynamic of demand and supply.

Through our analysis we detect a dual influence on the demand for participation in formal activities: that of a person's initial education and that of the condition of retirement. Participation during retirement, like participation generally, is affected by the level of education attained: the more educated a person is, the more he or she will participate. There is continuity in educational biographies in terms of the educational and cultural capital accumulated over the years. Individuals with little cultural capital thus tend to have an image of adult learning that is linked exclusively to their life in the work force and at work. As a result,, the transition to retirement does not tend to produce any demand for adult learning. This is case whether for the purposes of better directing their transition or for benefiting from their new situation to take personal initiatives that would involve organized learning activities. The world of multi-purpose lifelong learning has never had much significance for them, especially when structural factors make such participation more difficult. The situation for highly educated retirees is quite different: the intensive educational biography, never exclusively linked to continuing professional development, merely carries on for purposes of both personal development and participation in society.

This effect of cultural and educational capital can also be seen in the recognition of informal forms of learning. Better-educated people recognize more easily the educational ramifications associated with the cultural or social activities in which they are involved, as the qualitative analysis shows. They also use group learning within their network to resolve problems of information or know-how. Among retirees who received less early formal education, informal learning does occur but it often seems to be limited to activities that reflect the logic of "passing time".

The interviews also allowed us to see the contexts in which participation in formal and informal learning is associated with an individual's active assumption of responsibility for his or her transitions. In this regard, the contrast between retirees is striking. The transitions of less educated individuals are endured, and training and education does not seem to them to be a legitimate tool or even relevant. Others live their transitions more actively. Indeed, more educated individuals seem to direct their transitions, making use of various forms of learning in order to mobilize and appropriate the knowledge and know-how they need. This, in turn, makes them more critical of the supply of training. Familiarity with the world of education can thus be seen in the criticisms made of the availability of adult learning. In short, the ways in which people adjust to transitions are marked by the kind of educational experiences they had earlier.

At the same time, continuity in access to educational resources is linked to the ability of the individual to mobilize those resources. In this context, health turns out to be very important. A poor state of health acts as an obstacle, as many retirees expressly point out. It might be assumed that a poor state of health would give rise to new educational demand, either formal or informal. However, as recent literature on the subject of "health literacy" has emphasized (Nielsen-Bohlman et al. 2004), this did not happen.

Perhaps the most significant factor with respect to the differentiated expression of demand and the decline in demand expressed among less educated groups is the effect of how individuals interpret learning. The transition to retirement, the time when a person's link to work is broken, would also be the time for a break with education and training. This is often identified as being the case, especially in adult population who received extensive initial education followed by an active educational career (Crossan et al., 2003). The representations of retirement as a point or stage in life course would exclude education and training, just as the image of aging would exclude any association with active learning. We may well question whether we are facing a similar problem to that observed by Antikainen (1998), namely the existence of interpretation of education that differ by generation.

In terms of the adult learning supply, our analysis of the experience of retirees indicates the great impact the current availability of adult learning activities has on participation. The many criticisms expressed by educated retirees and the frequent references to the obstacles linked to inadequate availability of adult learning activities clearly show the importance of the type of education provided.. For some three decades now, there has been specific supply of activities such as third age universities (Swindell, 1995, 2000), or "retirement-preparation" courses given in companies, unions or public educational institutions. However, our data seem to indicate that these responses affect only a minority of retirees, probably those who belong to the best educated segments of the elderly population.

In the overall economy of lifelong learning in Canada, public measures of regulation designed to correct market rules are confined to work-related education and training and to basic skills education, while supply to meet all other learning demand tends to respond to pure market logic. In this context, it is easy to understand why more educated retirees, seeking continuity in their educational lives, express their frustration at the unmet demand, whereas others do not even succeed in expressing such demands. This relationship between adult learning supply and participation is reflected to some degree in the informal learning practices reported primarily by younger and more educated retirees. Such individuals tend to see informal learning as complementary to other learning practices or even as a substitute.

This research raises two issues, first that of the negative representation of both aging and learning possibilities after leaving the work force. Continuation of educational biographies has more to do with the expression of learning demand, not to mention the supply of educational opportunities and socio-economic conditions, as it does with aging. . In this regard and in light of the extension of the average length of people's post-work life course and the questioning of the "deficit tradition" in the public discourse on aging, more specific research would be required to better determine the dynamic between demand and supply of adult learning, particularly in regards to what we now agree to call the "two generations of seniors".

Certainly, our analysis does not lead, at least at this point in time in this country, to recognition of retirement as a time when participation in learning activities should increase due to more free time. However, given the close relationship that our study highlights between earlier educational experiences and participation in adult learning after a person has left the work force, the growth of an increasingly educated aging population will probably change the demand for learning. It will be necessary to study such transformations in learning demand. Equally important will be the analysis of how the retirees' learning demands change the existing supply of structured adult learning and organizational support

NOTES

1 The preparation of this study has been made possible by a grant from the SSHRC. The authors would also like to thank Nikunja Népal and Karima West, who helped to conduct the qualitative survey.

2 Statistics Canada, 1996, *Canadian Social Trends*, Fall 1996.

3 Although all societies contain seniors, the boundary between what is an adult and what is a senior is a social and cultural construct that leads to the determination of classification criteria or points at which people become seniors. This boundary may seem to be socially and culturally arbitrary.

4 We used the following definition of participation in formal education: a participant is any person who has engaged in a fomal activity with the exception of full-time students who do not receive any support from their employer.

REFERENCES

Alheit, P., Bron-Wojciechowska, A., Brugger, E., & Dominicé, P. (1995). *The biographical approach in European adult education*. Wien: Edition Volkshochschule.

Antikainen, A., Jarmo, H., et al. (1995). In search of the meaning of education: The case of Finland. *Scandinavian Journal of Educational Research, 39*(4), 295–310.

Antikainen, A., Jarmo, H., et al. (1999). Construction of identity and culture through education. *International Journal of Contemporary Sociology, 36*(2), 205–228.

Antikainen, A., & Juha, K. (2002). Educational generations and the futures of adult education: A nordic experience. *International Journal of Lifelong Education, 21*(3), 209–219.

Antikainen A. (1998). Between structure and subjectivity: Life-histories and lifelong learning. *International Review of Education, 44*(2-3), 215–234.

Arrowsmith, S., & Oikawa, C. (2001). Tendances relatives à l'apprentissage des adultes. In *Statistique Canada, a report on adult education and training in Canada: Learning a living* (pp. 35–55). Ottawa: Statistics Canada and Human Resources Development Canada.

I.L.O. (1998). *Employability in the global economy – how training matters, World Employment Report 1998–99*. Geneva: International Labour Organisation.

Barr-Telford, L., Cartwright, F., Prasil, S., & Shimmons, K. (2003). *Access, persistence and financing: First results from the postsecondary education participation survey (PEPS)*. Ottawa: Statistics Canada, Catalogue: 81-595-MIF2003007.

Bélanger, P. (1997). The amplitude and the diversity of organized adult learning. An overview of adult education participation in industrialized countries. In P. Bélanger & S. Valdivielso (Eds.), *The emergence of learning societies: Who participates in adult learning?* (pp. 1–22). London: Pergamon Press.

Bélanger, P., Doray, P., Labonté, A., & Levesque, M. (2005a). *Les adultes en formation: les logiques de participation*. Montréal: CIRDEP-CIRST/UQAM et Québec: MESSF.

Bélanger, P., Doray, P., Labonté, A., & Levesque, M. (2005b). *Les participations atypiques: des exceptions qui indiquent de nouvelles voies*. Note de recherche n°6. Montréal: CIRDEP-CIRST/UQAM et Québec: MESSF.

Bélanger, P., Doray, P., Labonté, A., & Levesque, M. (2005). *Les adultes en formation: les logiques de participation*. Montréal: CIRDEP-CIRST/UQAM et Québec: Emploi Québec.

Bélanger, P. (1992). *L'éducation des adultes et le vieillissement des populations: Tendances et enjeux*. Revue Internationale de Pédagogie.

Béret, P., & Dupray, A. (1998). La formation professionnelle continue: de l'accumulation de compétences à la validation de la performance. *Formation emploi, 63*, 61–80.

Betcherman, G., Leckie, N., & McMullen, K. (1998). *Barriers to employers-sponsored training in Canada*. Ottawa: Canadian Policy Research Network.

ILO. (1999). *World employment report*. Geneva: ILO.

BIT. (1998). *Employability in the global economy – how training matters, World Employment Report 1998-99*. Geneva.

Blair, A., McPake, J., & Munn, P. (1995). A new conceptualisation of adult participation in education. *British Educational Research Journal, 21*(5), 629–644.

Bourdieu, P., & Passeron, J.-C. (1970). *La reproduction*. Paris: Éditions de Minuit.

Bowl, M. (2001). Experiencing the barriers: Non-traditional students entering higher education. *Research Papers in Education, 16*(2), 141–160.

Carlton, S., & Soulsby, J. (1999). *Learning to grow older and bolder*. Leicester, UK: National Institute of Adult Continuing Education (NIACE).

Chicha, M.-T. (1994). *La participation des travailleuses à la formation en entreprise et l'accès à l'égalité: une jonction intéressante mais peu explorée*. Montréal: École de relations industrielles, Université de Montréal. Document de recherche no 94-01.

Conseil supérieur de l'égalité professionnelle. (2002). *L'accès des femmes salariées à la formation continue et ses effets sur leurs carrières*. Paris: la Documentation française.

Cookson, P. (1986). A framework for theory and research on adult education participation. *Adult Education Quaterly, 36*(3), 130–141.

Couppié, T., Epiphane, D., & et Fournier, C. (1997, Octobre). Insertion et débuts de carrières: les inégalités résistent-elles au diplôme? *BREF, 135*, 4 p.

Courtney, S. (1992). *Why adults learn? Towards a theory of participation in adult education*. London: Routledge.

Cross, K. P. (1982). *Adults as learners*. San Francisco: Jossey-Bass Publishers.

Crossan, B., Field, J., Gallacher, J., & Merrill, B. (2003). Understanding participation in learning for non-traditional adult learners: Learning careers and the construction of learning identities. *British Journal of Sociology of Education, 24*(1), 55–67.

Darkenwald, G. D., & Valentine, T. (1985). Factor structure of deterrents to public participation in adult education. *Adult Education Quarterly, 35*(4), 177–193.

de Montlibert, C. (1973). Le public de la formation des adultes. *Revue française de sociologie, XIV*, 529–545.

de Montlibert, C. (1977). L'éducation permanente et la promotion des classes moyennes. *Sociologie du travail, 19*(3), 243–265.

Doray, P., & Livingstone David, W. (2004). Entre la pyramide et l'iceberg les diverses figures de la participa tion à la formation des adultes, article soumis au *Canadian Journal of Adult Education*

Doray, P. (1999). La participation à la formation en entreprise au Canada: quelques éléments d'analyse. *Formation-Emploi, 66*, 21–38.

Doray, P., & Arrowsmith, S. (1997). Patterns of participation in adult education: Cross national comparisons. In P. Bélanger & A. C. Tuijnman (dir.), *New patterns of adult learning: A six-country comparative study* (pp. 39–75). London: Pergamon.

Doray, P., & Rubenson, K. (1998). Canada: The growing economic imperative. In P. Bélanger & S. Valdivielso (dir.), *The emergence of learning societies: Who participates in adult learning?* (pp. 23–42). London: Pergamon.

Doray, P., Bélanger, P., & Labonté, A. (2005). *Les contours de la demande insatisfaite de formation.* Note de recherche n° 5. Montréal: CIRDEP-CIRST/UQAM et Québec: MESSF.

Doray, P., Bélanger, P., & Levesque, M. (2005). *La participation des femmes à la formation des adultes: une situation en changement.* Note de recherche n° 7. Montréal: CIRDEP-CIRST/UQAM et Québec: MESSF.

Doray, P., Bélanger, P., Motte, A., & Labonté, A. (2005). *Les facteurs de variation de la participation des adultes à la formation au Canada en 1997.* Note de recherche n° 3. Montréal: CIRDEP-CIRST/UQAM et Québec: MESSF.

Dubar, C. (1995). *La formation professionnelle continue.* Paris: Éditions La Découverte, collection Repères.

Fletcher, C. (2002). Formation continue à la française et système de laissez-faire britannique: quelles chances pour les femmes. *Formation-Emploi, 78,* 17–33.

Fournier, C. (2001). Hommes et femmes salariés face à la formation continue. *BREF, 179,* 4 p.

Fournier, C. (2003). Développer la formation des «seniors»? Deux questions préliminaires. *Formation Emploi, 81,* 37–49.

Fournier, C. (2006). Les besoins de formation non satisfaits des salariés au prisme des catégories sociales. *Formation-Emploi, 95,* 25–39.

Gagnon, L. (2005). *Une analyse multiniveau des facteurs en présence dans l'accès des employés à la formation en milieu de travail.* Montréal: Département de sociologie, UQAM, mémoire de maîtrise.

Gagnon, L., Doray, P., & Bélanger, P. (2004). En entreprise, quel sera le scénario de développement? *Possibles, 28*(3–4), 134–153.

Gorard, S.-R.-G., Renold, E., & Fevre, R. (1998). *Family influences on participation in life long learning.* Working paper 15. Cardiff: School of Education, Cardiff University.

Guillemard, A.-M. (1983). *Politique de désemploi des travailleurs vieillissants et remodelage du parcours des âges.* Gérontologie et Société – Cahier no 24. pp. 6–21.

Guillemard, A.-M. (1989). *Les transformations de la sortie d'activité au niveau international. Ver un réexamen du rôle de la retraite* ? Université de la Sorbonne et CEMS. Paris. pp. 1–35.

Guillemard, A.-M. (1995). *Penser le sujet autour d'Alain Touraine.* Paris: Colloque de Cerisy.

Hédoux, J. (1982). Des publics et des «non-publics» de la formation des adultes. *Revue française de sociologie, XXIII*(2), 253–274.

Henry, G. T., & Basile, K. C. (1994). Understanding the decision to participate in formal adult education. *Adult Education Quarterly, 44*(2), 64–82.

Houle, C. O. (1961). *The inquiring mind.* Madison, WI: University of Wisconsin Press.

Institut de la Statistique du Québec. (2006). *Développer nos compétences en littératie: un défi porteur d'avenir.* Québec: Institut de la Statistique du Québec.

Jacobs, J.-A., Lukens, M., & Useem, M. (1996). Organizational, job and individual determinants of workplace training: Evidence form the national organizations survey. *Social Science Quaterly, 77*(1), 159–176.

Johnstone, J. W., & Rivera, R. J. (1965). *Volunteers for learning.* Chicago: Aldine Publishing Co.

Kennedy, S., Drago, R., & Sloan, J.-M. (1994). The effect of trade-unions on the supply of training: Australian evidence. *British Journal of Industrial Relations, 32*(4), 565–580.

Knoke, D., & Kalleberg, A. L. (1994). Job training in U.S. organizations. *American Sociological Review, 59*(4), 537–546.

Labonté, A., Doray, P., Bélanger, P., & et Motte, A. (2005). *Une analyse comparative Québec-Canada de la participation à la formation des adultes.* Note de recherche n° 2. Montréal: CIRDEP-CIRST/UQAM et Québec: MESSF.

Livingstone, D. W. (1999). *The education-job gap: Underemployment or economic democracy.* Toronto: Garamond Press.

Livingstone, D. W. (2001). *Working and learning in the information age: A profile of Canadians.* Ottawa: Canadian Research Networks.

Méhaut, P., et al. (1978). *Formation continue, gestion du personnel et marché de la formation.* Paris: Éditions du CNRS.

Merril, B. (1999). *Gender, change and identity: Mature women students in universities.* Aldershot: Ashgate.

Nielsen-Bohlman, L. T., Panzer, A. M., Hamlin, B., & Kindig, D. A. (Eds.). (2004). *Health literacy, A prescription to end confusion*. Washington, DC: National Academies Press.

OECD. (2005). *Promoting adult learning*. Paris: Organisation for Economic Cooperation and Development.

OECD. (2000). *Des réformes pour une société vieillissante*. Questions socials, Paris: OCDE.

Organisation International du travail (OIT). (2002). *Une société sans exclusion pour une population vieillissante: La question de l'emploi et de la protection sociale*. Document presented by the ILO to the Second World Assembly on Aging, Madrid.

Painchaud, L., Doray, P., & Mayrand, P. (2000). La formation sur mesure au Québec: qu'en disent les participants. In D. D.-G. Tremblay & P. Doray (Eds.), *Vers de nouveaux modes de formation professionnelle. Rôle des acteurs et des collaborations*. Sainte-Foy: Presses de l'Université du Québec.

Peters, V. (2004). *Working and training: First results of the 2003 adult education and training survey*. Ottawa: Statistics Canada.

Quigley, A. B., & Arrowsmith, S. (1997). The non-participation of undereducated adults. In P. Bélanger & A. Tuijnman (dir.), *New patterns of adult learning: A six country comparative study* (pp. 101–130). London: Pergamon Press.

Reay, D., Ball, S. J., & al. (2002). It's taking a long time but I'll get there in the end: Mature students on access courses and higher education service. *British Educational Research Journal, 28*(1), 5–19.

Rubenson, K. (1977). *Participation in recurrent education*. Paris: Organisation for Economic Cooperation and Development, Center for Educational Research and Innovations.

Rubenson, K., & Schuetze, H. G. (2000). Lifelong learning for the knowledge society: Demand, supply and policy dilemma. In K. Rubenson & H. G. Schuetze (Eds.), *Transition to the knowledge society* (pp. 355–376). Vancouver: University of British-Columbia, Institute for European Studies.

Rubenson, K., & Xu, G. (1997). Barriers to participation in adult education and training: Towards a new understanding. In P. Bélanger & A. C. Tuijnman (dir.) (Eds.), *New patterns for adult learning: A six-country comparative study* (pp. 77–100). London: Pergamon Press.

Scanlan, C. S., & Darkenwald, G.-D. (1984). Identifying deterrents to participation in continuing education. *Adult Education Quarterly, 34*(3), 155–166.

Service Canada. (2005). *Mythes et réalités au sujet du vieillissement de la main-d'œuvre*. Government of Canada. Retrieved from http://www.servicecanada.gc.ca/

Silva, T., Cahalan, M., & Lacireno-Paquet, N. (1998). *Adult education participation decisions and barriers: Review of conceptual frameworks and empirical studies*. Washington, DC: US Department of Education, Office of Educational Research and Improvement, National Center for Education Statistics, Working Paper No. 98-10.

Statistique Canada. (2003). *Adult education and training survey: User guide 2003*. Ottawa: Statistics Canada.

Statistics Canada & OECD. (2005). *Learning a living: First results of the adult literacy and life skills survey*. Ottawa: Statistics Canada and Paris: Organisation for Economic Co-operation and Development.

Swindell, R. (2000). A U3A without walls: Using the internet to reach out to isolated older people. In *Education and Ageing, 5*(2), 251–263.

Swindell, R., Thompson, J. (1995, July-August). An international perspective on the University of the third age. *Educational Gerontology, 21*(5), 429–447.

Tuijnman, A., & Boudard, E. (2001). *Adult education participation in North America: International perspectives*. Ottawa: Statistics Canada and HRDC; Washington: U.S. Department of Education.

Wikelund, K. R., Reder, S., & Hart-Landsberg, S. (1992). *Expanding theories of adult literacy participation: A literature review*. Philadelphia: University of Pennsylvania, National Center on Adult Literacy, Technical Report TR 92-1.

Elaine Biron
Professor
College Saint-Laurent
Centre interuniversitaire de recherche sur la science et la technologie

Dr. Pierre Doray
Professor of sociology,
Centre interuniversitaire de recherche sur la science et la technologie
Université du Québec á Montréal.

Dr. Paul Bélanger
Professor of Education
Director of the Centre for Interdisciplinary Research and Development and Advanced Studies in Lifelong Learning
Université du Québec á Montréal.

Simon Cloutier
Centre interuniversitaire de recherche sur la science et la technologie
Université du Québec á Montréal.

Olivier Meyer
Centre interuniversitaire de recherche sur la science et la technologie
Université du Québec á Montréal

JANICE WALLACE AND TARA FENWICK

16. TRANSITIONS IN WORKING DIS/ABILITY:

Able-ing Environments and Disabling Policies

INTRODUCTION

In this chapter, we explore the experience of persons with dis/abilities who experience particular challenges in a 'knowledge economy' because of uneven access to and mobility across learning/work opportunities that are constructed around notions of the able body. In particular, we attend to the difficult transitions experienced by disabled persons over their life course both within and between institutional settings as they attempt to engage their skills fully in educational institutions and Canadian workplaces. We argue that the difficulties of these transitions have been exacerbated within the regulatory regimes of the new economy. In addition, as workers increasingly experience age-related changes to their abilities and mobility, particularly with the removal of mandatory retirement policies in most Canadian provinces, issues of disability in the workplace will inevitably increase and thus the need for more critical attention to disability issues in the workplace is required.

Persons with disabilities, despite Canadian employers' 'duty to accommodate', face discrimination in the workplace including informal stigma, marginalization, insufficient provision of necessary support, and stress-producing expectations that they conform to narrow norms defining the 'good employee' and the 'acceptable body' (Church, Frazee, Luciani, Panitch and Seeley, 2007). Even in educational organizations, where we might anticipate greater understanding of difference and provisions for equity, individual tenured professors report that they are being refused accommodation and forced onto medical leave (Disabled Faculty Network, October 2006).

Moments of transition intersect disability issues on many levels. Persons with disabilities struggle with the loss of assistive technologies and learning supports when they transition from formal education to the workplace (Houghton, 2006). In fact, individuals often encounter a series of inter-institutional transitions between agencies and workplaces, finding themselves and their 'disability' reinscribed at each passage. Persons with physical disabilities report difficult transitions negotiating spaces between home and work. More broadly, most workers can expect to experience transition into or out of various levels of disabling conditions that affect their well-being throughout their working lives, including invisible disabilities such as mental illness produced by workplace stress. Current definitions of disability

P. Sawchuk and A. Taylor (eds.), Challenging Transitions in Learning and Work: Reflections on Policy and Practice, 309–324.

tend to be so rigid and medicalized that these transitioning states are not often recognized nor accommodated in formal workplace practices. Informally, such transitions open identity struggles for individuals finding themselves avoided and marginalized by former colleagues, or lacking basic supports that enable them to function in the workplace.

In the discussion that follows, we will explore transitions related to dis/ability in the workplace, situating them within an argument for holistic able-ing environments and basic improvements to workplace policy. The chapter draws upon findings of a recently completed study involving activists, community organizations and employers. The study was exploratory, designed to identify key issues and approaches for further research.

DISABILITY IN THE WORKPLACE: OVERVIEW

To consider disability in the workplace is to immediately encounter a range of definitional, epistemological and ethical issues. What conditions does the term 'disability' represent, and according to whose categories? Who has the right to know and name who is disabled? Can different forms of disability be collapsed to consider general issues affecting persons with disability?

In this chapter we adopt the argument of Hester Parr and Ruth Butler (1999) that, while it is important to recognize and differentiate specific mind/body differences and the responses they incur or require, there are dangers in partitioning these as totally divorced from each other and from other concerns about ableism and disability. Parr and Butler suggest that mind-body differences can be conceptualized as different states-of being on a continuum of human mind-body characteristics: as biomedical categorisation (illness), as functional limitation (impairment), or as disability (experiences of inequality due to physical and social barriers within society). As such, disability can affect individuals' functioning, mobility and/or physical appearance, in ways that in the workplace can invoke discrimination. Legislation has been adopted in the US (Americans with Disabilities Act 1990), UK (Disability Discrimination Act 1995) and in Ontario[1] (Ontarians with Disabilities Act 2001) to make such discrimination illegal. However as Agocs (2002) has argued, there is little monitoring of the implementation of such policies, and little recognition of the important role that workplace culture – the attitudes and behaviours of co-workers – plays in promoting discriminatory practices regardless of existing policies.

The current situation in Canada is that involuntary unemployment rates among persons with disabilities in Canada are more than 50%.[2] Many workers with disabilities who actually manage to obtain paid employment tend to be ghettoized into low status, low paid jobs. England (2003) draws from several empirical studies to show that 61.2% of Canadians with moderate and severe disabilities believe that they have been denied jobs because of their disability. But gaining entry to employment is only the beginning of a long struggle for persons with disability. Most analysts agree that contemporary work organizations are characterized by 'ableism': the unacknowledged imaginings of shared communities of able-bodied/ableminded people which results in an othering of people whose bodies and minds do not meet with a mystical 'norm'. Chouinard (1997) is credited with first recognizing and defining ableism: ' ideas, practices, institutions and social relations that presume ablebodiedness, and by so doing, construct persons with disabilities as marginalised, oppressed, and largely invisible 'other'' (p. 380).

In practical terms, ableism functions through physical and social barriers to the participation of disabled persons in the everyday activities of a work environment. Work structures, including production quotas, time schedules, new technologies and standardization of tasks, have all been designed for the able-bodied person. Much of the research and advocacy on behalf of disabled persons has focused upon improving accommodation in the workplace (accessible spaces, personal mobility aids, communication in various modes) and enabling freer access of disabled persons with assistive technologies, both physical technologies and human assistance and processes. Some employers balk at providing accommodation believing it to be expensive and unfair by favouring one individual, although in fact workplace accommodations have been demonstrated to be far less expensive and inconvenient than many assume.

But to focus only on physical barriers is to assume that technology and other accommodations will fix the problem of improving disabled persons' autonomy and inclusion in workplace communities. As Gleeson (1999) shows, the larger problem is how work is valued. Regimes of production, the current hyper global competition, individualist notions of merit and productivity, and institutions such as professional hierarchies result in a general de-valuing of disabled persons as an expensive burden, as bodies 'out-of-place' within accepted notions of embodied employment. From a Marxian perspective, Hall (1999) traces this devaluation of disabled persons in the workplace to capitalist economic structures that emphasize industrial production, separate home from work, and person from knowledge; these structures produce the disabled as object in a binary of abled/disabled, and exclude them, socially and spatially, from valued work activity. The very question of what counts as skill in a job has been shaped according to ableist norms, to the point where the tasks required to achieve specific goals required by a work organization are mostly conceived as activities to be performed by able-bodied people. Johanna Johnson (2007), a young elementary school teacher in Vancouver, British Columbia who happens to be quadriplegic, says she is often confronted by the assumption that she must be unable to teach children because she is confined to a wheelchair: yet teaching is knowledge work that can be performed in many ways.

ISSUES OF DISABLED PERSONS IN THE CANADIAN WORKPLACE: RESULTS OF A STUDY

In our own exploratory study, we interviewed eight people: mostly researchers in workplace disability issues and leaders in agencies devoted to employability of disabled persons. We asked them two main questions: What, in your opinion and experience, are the key issues faced by persons with disabilities in the workplace? What suggestions have you as we consider an approach to research questions and research methods exploring issues in the workplace for persons with disabilities?

The findings of these interviews were then presented to a full-day symposium of 31 persons that included, besides the original interviewees, activists in workplace disability issues, representatives from government and industry expressing interest in disability issues, and additional university-based researchers. About half of these participants had disabilities including blindness, muscular dystrophy, mental illness, paraplegia, and multiple sclerosis. The symposium discussions examined and expanded the interview findings to determine what were the continuing issues and priorities in the workplace for persons with disabilities.

Among these interviewees and symposium participants, the major issues in the workplace encountered by persons with disability were generally agreed to include fear and stigma; increased performance pressures; inappropriate job fit; insufficient accommodation and assistance; inappropriate expectations; negative consequences of disclosure; and limited definitions of disability. Threaded throughout these issues were problematic passages of transition, which will be discussed in the next section.

Fear and Stigma

The primary problem appears to be fear and stigma attached to persons with disabilities by some able-bodied colleagues and managers. This may be linked to discomfort or awkwardness at different physical appearances, misinformation and stereotypes about disability, or lack of provision for voice of persons with disabilities. Disabled individuals report being treated as troublesome because of their 'special'[3] needs for equipment and accommodation. They also report being marginalized: overlooked in promotion and excluded from informal social gatherings. Sometimes they encountered outright hostility from colleagues or even employers. Most concurred that stigma and fear in work organizations was especially pronounced in relation to mental health issues (persons with psychiatric or emotional disorders).

High Performance Pressure

The pressure to 'keep up' in the high performance environments typifying contemporary organizations causes stress, sometimes exacerbating or even creating conditions of disability. Employers have fears about meeting expectations for productivity that can be projected onto the disabled person who is viewed as falling short, and persons with disabilities can be perceived to be a liability on a team by fellow employees. High performance expectations affect hiring practices as well, in several ways. Those participants who worked in advocacy organizations that were attempting to find employment for disabled persons reported many incidents where clients were either denied an interview outright, despite obvious qualifications, or encountered strong evidence of the fear and stigma described above when they met employers for an interview. More pertinent to the effects of high performance pressure, however, is the increasing devolvement of human resources hiring processes to recruiting agencies, who are under pressure to put forward only those persons with disabilities who will be most successful. Indeed, individuals, themselves, disabled or not, can be complicit in increased workload and performance expectations, internalizing these expectations and driving themselves ever harder with deleterious effects on their health; this can be especially true of disabled persons trying to prove that they are not a burden for their team or organization.

Inappropriate Fit of Job and Person

Participants in our symposium emphasized that the desired goal was not to ensure access for all persons with disabilities to whatever occupation they desired. Some stated that individuals, including individuals with disabilities, can over-estimate what they can accomplish and can be unaware of the best fit of career, industry, and type of organization where their skills will be an asset. Some individuals, we were told, have not identified or do not want to identify their disabilities for themselves (this is different than the issue of choosing not to disclose a disability to someone else, such as an employer). Some know what type of vocation they want and need but can't find it. Any of these situations can lead to a mismatch of job to person. When a person has disabilities, the result of a mismatch may result in serious problems in activity processes and staff relations, such as other employees becoming frustrated, that can stigmatize the person with disabilities rather than addressing the systemic issue of fit. Conversely, said our participants, a 'good fit' in vocation and organization can be a trap over time; an individual with disabilities can become stuck and afraid to leave.

Inadequate Supports and Assistive Technologies

Despite legislation that guarantees disabled persons the right to the necessary accommodation to ensure their participation, they continue to experience lack of workplace supports. Why is this? Our participants suggested a variety of reasons. Chief among them is lack of information. Employers continue to be unaware of challenges faced by persons with disability, their need for supports like personal assistance, flex time, office accessories, etc., and the legal requirement to provide such supports. Some employers are fearful of how assistance, such as working dogs in the workplace or accommodating severe allergies, might affect the whole working environment,. There is often minimal to no support available for persons with invisible disabilities, or with 'minor' disabilities. Accommodation, when it is provided, can be resented by fellow employees, who wonder why assistive aids are provided to a colleague that they also would find useful. Further, persons with disability don't always know the resources and assistive supports available to them, and may not understand their legal right to obtain such accommodations. When they are identified and obtained, some assistive technologies may not translate easily to the workplace. Another set of issues identified by participants included the difficult transition between educational institutions where assistive devices may be available and workplaces where they most often are not. For example, postsecondary counsellors who enabled the provision of appropriate services for students with disabilities reported that there was no coherent guidance system available for students and their potential employers to enable both to access the support and technologies that might be required once the student moved into the workplace: e.g., tutoring, assistance with coping strategies, etc., for persons with learning disabilities. Furthermore, the tasks for which accommodation was required in a postsecondary institution were often different than those tasks for which accommodation might be required in the workplace, but there was no follow-through guidance available. As a result, the student and/or the employer were left to identify and locate assistive devices and funding to procure them – if, indeed, both the student and the employer persisted to this point. In some cases, the required accommodation reaches beyond the employers' purview: e.g., transport issues getting to and from work, or housing issues. Finally, what is required may not be technological assistance so much as the reconfiguration of task processes and productivity expectations.

Inappropriate Expectations

Our participants emphasized that everyone in a work organization should expect the same recognition, benefits, and pay as everyone else, and demonstrate commitment to good work and to the organization – within their own capacity. While it could happen that an individual with a disability expects better work than what is on offer, and an individual could use a disability to claim special exceptions from expectations, it is more likely that persons with disability will encounter unrealistic performance expectations by employers. For example, some participants reported that, once 'special' needs are accommodated, employers may expect disabled persons to strive for 'normalcy' in producing the same volume of work and scope of mobility as other employees. However, while such norms disadvantage every worker, given that employee functionality and productivity varies considerably with the individual and over the life course, they are particularly pernicious for disabled persons who often feel much more vulnerable to such expectations, particularly in an increasingly competitive and entrepreneurial workplace.[4]

Negative Consequences of Disclosure

Disclosure of one's disability is a deeply complex and contested issue (Houghton, 2006; Valle, Solis, Volpitta and Connor, 2004). On the one hand, to not disclose is to be refused access to legally-guaranteed accommodations for one's disability. But to disclose can entail labelling oneself using categories of disability enshrined in company policy, which may be inappropriate for one's unique condition, and can risk stigma and marginalizing. According to our participants, many disabled individuals not only do not disclose, but go to dramatic lengths to hide their disability. Hiding strategies can include taking work home, using cheat sheets to 'keep up' with the pace of work, arranging required medical care outside work hours, disguising physical changes and physical differences, and generally hiding one's personal strategies of physical and mental accommodation for one's disability. Persons with mental health issues tend not to disclose these at work and, therefore, take on much of this hiding work in addition to the strain of their disability. Even among those who disclose their disability, such individuals often self-limit their personal career aspirations. They may undertake to educate their employers and co-workers about what they need and what their disability means to the workplace, and often will use humour to reassure co-workers. In other words, the person with the disability becomes responsible for managing the issue through coping strategies, often hidden and unrecognized, which has two main effects: first, this individualization limits employers' sense of responsibility to provide accommodation and second, it continues to reproduce worker health and disability as an individual's problem rather than a systemic issue.

Limited Definitions of 'Disability'

At the root of many of these issues are the distinctions of ability/disability. Current definitions tend to pathologize disability as a deviancy rather than recognizing a range of mind-body differences. In measuring and classifying disability, important questions need to be raised about who does the measuring and based upon what criteria. These questions become critical when what counts as 'real' disability determines employer-supported accommodation and insurance.

Misunderstandings abound. For example, 'disabled' persons are often associated with visibly evident wheelchairs or developmental disabilities, and employers may focus on hiring persons with visible disabilities as 'window dressing' for public relations: that is, being 'seen' as accommodating of disabled persons (Wooten and James, 2005).

Persons with visible disabilities, however, are in the minority. Invisible disabilities are far more prevalent, including mental illness and emotional disorders, as well as chronic medical conditions such as diabetes, emphysema, rheumatoid arthritis, and fibro-myalgia. Persons with 'invisible' disabilities may be excluded from any support, and may be treated suspiciously as seeking unwarranted personal exemptions in work organizations. Indeed, some temporary medical conditions function as disability – that is, they require special accommodation and even produce stigma and marginalization in the workplace – but are not often recognized as such within the limited informal and formal definitions of disability available. Further, individuals with the same condition can have very different needs, characteristics, and expectations because they are individuals with different histories, experiences, circumstances, interacting conditions, and so on. Overall, our participants emphasized that different types of disability, and the existence of multiple disabilities, need to be recognized: physical, auditory, developmental, mental, health-related (e.g., heart disease), and cognitive disabilities. Further, they pointed out that disability can be treated differently depending on one's professional status and education: classism in disability needs stronger analysis.

Overall, there is nothing new about these broad issues encountered by persons with disabilities in work organizations. But, sadly, while they continue to persist, they continue to receive little attention in the broader workplace literature outside of disability agencies and studies. Taken as a whole, all of these issues hold implications for workplace learning, from the most obvious need to educate employers to raise awareness and understanding of disability issues, to educating persons with disabilities about their workplace rights and the resources available to them. Further complicating these issues and the learning that is embedded in them is the fact that disability is a dynamic, not a static phenomenon; its issues and people affected by them are in continuous transition.

TRANSITIONS AND PERSONS WITH DISABILITY IN THE WORKPLACE

Disability in workplace policy still functions, in the main, to label disability using rather rigid medicalized definitions in order to prescribe necessary accommodation, thus producing disability as a static condition that is present or absent. Yet people with disabilities describe their everyday work lives as a series of passages, transitioning from one state to another, which are navigated with difficulty. These transitions affect identity, security, positionality, and even personal and vocational capacity. Yet these transitioning states are not often recognized or accommodated in formal workplace practices. In the discussion that follows, we will explore the meaning of anecdotes shared by our participants that typify the difficult transitions embedded in the daily lives of disabled persons seeking or engaged in employment. We have chosen these anecdotes because they are representative of many other stories that were shared with us during our exploratory study.

Transitions from Formal Education to the Workplace

During our interviews with counsellors specifically responsible for accommodation of disabled students in post-secondary institutions, they pointed to several dilemmas for students making the transition from the formal education sector to the workplace. First, as mentioned earlier, disabled students who were close to completing their program and potential employers were often not aware of the kinds of accommodations that might be necessary in order to ensure success in the workplace. Therefore, while these students had been able to achieve success with the support of technical equipment and/or accommodations provided during their studies, they and their potential employers were thrust into a labyrinth of agencies that might help identify what was needed to ensure success in the workplace and who might fund the accommodations, if necessary, with little guidance.

Second, conditions in the economy were often more responsible for the changing fortunes of disabled persons seeking employment than the enactment of or conformity to policies and practices seeking to increase their opportunities. For example, career counsellors we spoke to in Alberta championed the optimum conditions in Alberta's heated economy for disabled students to find employment. Indeed, job opportunities are abundant in all levels of the province's economic sector, however, the inference was that in most cases, the able-bodied would occupy their preferred jobs first, but, because there are not enough workers to occupy all of the positions available, the full employment of preferable employees would leave room for those employees who were less desirable, such as immigrants, visible minorities, and disabled persons, to take what was left. While there is an indisputable logic in this assumption, it does nothing to disrupt the ableist positioning of disabled workers as less desirable than those perceived to be 'normal', thus leaving them vulnerable to the whims of economic shifts. Indeed, with the current economic downturn that is sweeping across globalized economies, the displacement of disabled workers is a predictable outcome.

Third, those students making the transition into the workplace with invisible disabilities were thrust into the 'to come out or not to come out' dilemma once again. Houghton's (2006) study of disabled students at a postsecondary institution in England reveals the tensions many disabled students feel when making the transition from education to the workplace. She writes:

> In talking to a number of students with hidden disabilities gaining information about job related support is likely to be hindered due to their decision not to disclose. There was a sense in which they assumed that once they left university they would be on their own and were surprised and uncertain about the likelihood of employers acknowledging and addressing their support needs. As extracts from Dave's story indicates: [He wonders] 'If I tell them I'm dyslexic I can't see what they could do ...I hadn't planned on saying anything, but I didn't know about the support you might get so I'm thinking it might be an advantage ... I would like to know though, you probably can't answer, but does it impact on discrimination?' (p. 7)

Dave's story is a common one for those we talked to in postsecondary institutions who faced similar questions and were all too familiar with the discrimination that would indeed be faced in the workplace. While some counsellors take on the responsibility to help students prepare for not only the role demands of the workplace but also the social stigma that may be encountered, most students face these questions and tensions alone and with little information to enable them to act strategically, in the absence of systemic change, in their own interests.

Transitions between Agencies and Workplaces

While the transition from school to the workplace is challenging, many participants reported that most institutions, such as schools, health providers, and employment agencies, while often believing that they were acting on behalf of disabled persons, were often complicit in first inscribing and then reinscribing medicalized notions of 'disability' through their practices. In doing so, ableism becomes entrenched in the expectations and consciousness of not only employers but even disabled persons themselves, unless resisted. Thus participants in the study reported that transitioning from one institutional setting to the next – e.g., moving from secondary school to a postsecondary institution, or from hospital to an employment agency – meant having to fill out similar forms and submit to the same questions seeking information about the person's disability yet again. Doing so had the effect of reinscribing the experience of pathologizing one's body and mind over and over again to the exclusion of more holistic revelations of identity that included disability as part of a complex lived experience.

Jane[5], a participant with a chronic medical condition, described feeling more and more disempowered as she moved from doctor to government employment agency to employment agencies specifically focused on placing disabled persons. At each stage of the process, she became increasingly conscious of being defined as 'less than' the 'norm', especially as her 'weaknesses' became the focus of initial interviews and compulsory 'training'. The narrow focus of these intake interviews, generic workshops, and available courses, although required by government policy in order to trigger funding mechanisms for the employment agency, did not address her specific needs or enable her to draw on skills she already had. In fact, it was as though those skills had disappeared and she became a *tabula rasa* when labelled as disabled.

Jane's experience demonstrates two things. First, many agencies set up to enhance employment opportunities for persons with disabilities are, themselves, caught by policies that are premised on medicalized and ableist assumptions about disabled persons. For example, their funding is often tied to the provision of workshops and courses that are then required of their clients before they can access other services, whether they are necessary or not. In addition, counsellors may bring an ableist consciousness to their work, despite their best intentions. One participant exemplified this when describing in detail the 'unreasonable' demands of a student who wished to be housed on the same floor as her friends, despite the fact that this meant carrying her up some stairs, rather than choosing a flat that was more accessible but distant from her social circle. Rather than commenting on the fundamental unfairness of the lack of universal access that caused this student to have to make this difficult choice, she went on to describe how these same 'unreasonable' expectations were characteristic of this student's job expectations. The inference was that this client should be satisfied with what was available with little need for employers to accommodate her physical needs in order to fulfil both the ends of the organization and her desire for intellectual, emotional, and social expression in the workplace.

The second issue that is demonstrated in Jane's employment dilemma is the stereotyped presumptions that persons with disabilities encounter when they find themselves negotiating the transition between their own self conception and the one that seems to be held by employment agencies and employers. The imposition of processes that reinscribe at every transition a stereotypical notion of what it means to be disabled often means the loss of a sense of oneself as a fully realised person who has varying degrees of strengths and weaknesses depending on temporal, social, economic, and geographic context. As Jane described her experience with various government and employment agencies, she said, 'I feel like I have become my disability.' Of course, her disability is an important part of her identity as are her artistic skills, empathy, strong people skills and work ethic, and a struggle to remain organized – all of which she brings to her current workplace. Her point was, however, that her workplace identity was truncated by the very processes required by company and provincial policies, as a result of her disabling condition, in order to 'help' her realise her full potential.

Transitions Negotiating Spaces between Home, Work, and Extra-Workplace Activities

While accommodations in the workplace were an important area of discussion in both our initial interviews as well as the symposium, an equally but often overlooked issue was also raised by several participants: transitions between home and work and between work and social and informal spaces with colleagues. One participant, a high ranking government employee who required a wheelchair, told about his difficulties in making the transition out of his 'safety bubble' – his description of his long-time office – to a new office required by government restructuring. He had developed a routine that enabled him to move from home to his car to a parking garage and then to his office with relative ease. The building in which his office was located as well as his office were organized in a way that accommodated his mobility needs, and the employees in his office building were aware of his needs and had the knowledge necessary to assist him as necessary. There were also locations for socializing nearby that were accessible for him and his colleagues. The move to his new office required creating a whole new 'safety bubble' that necessitated considerable workplace learning – most of it organized and supplied by him – to create the knowledge base required for his physical, social, and work-related needs to be accommodated. Social spaces were not as close in his new work location and so he had to give up socializing with his colleagues or find various locations that were desirable for his colleagues and accessible for him.

In narrating his story – one that was echoed by many other participants – it became clear that organizational transitions require a great deal of time to plan for not only workplace accommodations but also the enabling conditions for persons with disabilities to get to and from the workplace, yet these needs are ignored or detached from workplace requirements for accommodation. Transportation needs are often difficult to arrange and are frequently unreliable. For those who are able to drive their own vehicles, parking arrangements are often difficult to arrange because of highly prescriptive conditions for providing disabled parking or are distant from the workplace. For example, organizational parking rules at one of the researchers' universities state that a person who is not able to walk without assistance for a certain distance is eligible for disabled parking but, because the parking building requires negotiating stairs in order to access most university buildings, applicants with severe arthritis may not qualify because they can walk the required distance unaided; the fact that they may have extreme difficulty with stairs is unaccounted for in the university's parking policies. Building accessibility getting to and from one's place of work may be problematic as well. For example, those with limited vision may find signs in new workspaces difficult to read because of low contrast between the letter and background colours thus making it difficult to find washrooms, cafeterias and the like.

Equally important in making the transition to full participation in workplaces was the significance of accessible social spaces for activities that build work relations and are often the space in which valuable workplace knowledge is shared informally. A quick lunch out at noon, a coffee before work, a drink on Fridays on the way home from work require an inordinate amount of planning for disabled persons with, for example, mobility or vision issues. Arranging transportation is often unreliable and limited for workplace requirements and even more problematic for impromptu social activity. Participants described feelings of frustration in having to continually educate their colleagues about what was necessary to accommodate their needs in social and other extra-workplace activities, such as professional development. Thus, even in workplaces where direct work needs are accommodated rather well, other enabling conditions for getting to and from work as well as fully participating in the informal activities related to work are often limited or require a great deal of extra work for the disabled person to ensure accessibility.

Workplace transitions frequently require transitions in accommodation as well – a significantly more difficult change for many disabled persons than for their colleagues. Suitable accessible accommodation is often very difficult to find because of its scarcity and, in some cases, its vulnerability to marketplace pressures.[6] Some participants reported having to give up on employment opportunities that they wished to pursue because suitable accommodation within reasonable distance from the workplace could not be found. Others related their struggles in taking on new jobs and staying in their current residence because a closer one could not be found, and then having to accommodate long, exhausting commutes while working through the new demands precipitated by their employment transition.

Transitions Into/Out of Disabling Conditions

All of the challenges for disabled persons that we have described so far are ones that many non-disabled persons may experience at some point. Of the four identified groups in Canada whose employment needs are addressed in policy – visible minorities, aboriginal peoples, women, and the disabled – only disability is a discriminatory condition in the workplace that may happen to anyone at any time either temporarily or permanently.[7] In fact, conditions in the workplace are often responsible for the transition experienced by many workers from abled to disabled. Ipsos Canada (2004, 2006 cited in BC Partners for Mental Health and Addictions Information, 2006) reports that increased depression, anxiety, and burnout among 25–54 year olds[8] has led to much higher rates of absenteeism as well as 'presenteeism' – lack of focus and decreased productivity while at work – in increasingly stressful workplaces.

Not surprisingly, disability claims are increasing as a result of workplace stress. 'According to Watson Wyatt, a firm that audits disability claims, psychological conditions like stress, anxiety, and depression are the leading causes of both short term and long term disability costs' (2005, cited in BC Partners for Mental Health and Addictions Information, 2006). Besides the psychic damage that may be inflicted in the workplace, workers may also be injured at work or become ill due to environmental conditions in the workplace, such as toxic chemicals, resulting in physical, psychological, or cognitive distress that leads to short or long-term disability. Workers may also experience illnesses unrelated to the workplace but with disabling effects in the workplace.

These transitions while employed may have detrimental effects on an employee's sense of efficacy, self-worth, and identity. For example, one of our participants related a story shared with her by a senior executive in a large financial institution who was struggling with the physical effects of cancer. The dramatic alteration in his appearance due to medical interventions was read by others as 'disabled' and altered their interactions with him in important ways. He spoke about the painful realization that his friends and colleagues were avoiding him and that he was being cut out of some business decisions, effectively limiting his potential contributions as a friend, colleague, and employee, despite his ability and desire to carry on many of the same functions he had prior to his illness. Like many participants in our exploratory study, difference for this senior executive was reinscribed by medical institutions, applications for accommodation, as well as the averted eyes in corporate hallways, the memos not received, the invitations not extended – that is, the lived experience of transitioning from being read as 'abled' to 'disabled' in the workplace.

CONCLUSION

Inequitable opportunities for work and problematizing notions of linear and comparable transitions across social groups within a 'knowledge economy' have been taken up by researchers in relation to workplace learning, including barriers experienced by new immigrants, Aboriginal workers, unemployed youth and visible minorities. Yet the continued workplace exclusion and struggles of persons with disability in work has not yet established a significant line of research in work-and-learning studies. To that end we initiated our exploratory study of disability issues in workplace learning to determine *with* the community of disabled persons and allies what research of these issues should be explored further. We confirmed with them that research should avoid homogenizing or essentializing populations of persons with disabilities, avoid idealizing a few success stories, avoid a focus solely on visible disability, and learn from and then move beyond personal narratives and single cases – as valuable as they often are. Many of the questions that follow were suggested by the participants in our symposium and confirm many of the themes of this book:

For work organizations, particularly employers: How can employers best assist their employees with disabilities? How can agencies help employers meet their 'duty to accommodate' (e.g., providing information, etc.)? How can businesses be persuaded to get involved in disability issues? How can disability issues be made more a priority with employers? How can productive dialogue between employers and advocates/activists/labour relations be fostered? What are employers' worldviews? What incentives might help employers hire persons with disabilities? What is the business case for hiring persons with disabilities, for small as well as large organizations? How can assistive technologies translate to the workplace (e.g., tutoring services, academic strategies assistance)? What should happen when disability is acquired in the workplace?

For individual persons with disabilities: What is the effect on individuals of having to identify their disabilities/weaknesses over and over as they move through different agencies? How do people with disabilities make the transition to expose their disability without losing a job or a promotion? How do workplace experiences of persons with visible disabilities compare with those of persons with invisible disabilities? How does a person with disabilities become a good advocate for him or herself and who is available to provide assistance?

For policy makers: What incentives would encourage employers to hire persons with disabilities? How can policy better regulate the legal entitlement of persons with disabilities to accommodation? How could policy assist in the transitions encountered by persons with disabilities? How might the policies of various agencies and organizations be harmonized to enable transitions between them for disabled persons?

Clearly, participants in our exploratory study recognize and embody the inequities of learning/work opportunities available to disabled persons in a knowledge economy and their experiences exemplify degrees of biographical agency dependent on the degree of conformity they are able to demonstrate to ableist assumptions. Certainly, their questions draw attention to the difficult transitions that are a part of their life experience as they move within and between institutional settings. For example, those workers who become disabled while employed experienced a kind of identity trauma in negotiating a place within a familiar organization while workers transitioning from school to work found access to appropriate assistive technologies difficult to access or were simply denied access to the workplace altogether. Whatever the disabled workers location, however, it was clear that current regulatory and efficiency discourses premised on ableist assumptions formed a formidable barrier for disabled workers.

Our exploratory study was helpful in locating research nodes where transitions occur in order to identify issues for further study in the context of work-and-learning as well as critical policy studies. Not only are the challenges for moving forward found in the number of questions that need to be explored – some of which are listed above – but also in the demonstrable resistance from some employers for critically analysing their policies and practices. Based on the experience of other researchers, for example, we have decided to move ahead with research in not-for-profit and publicly funded organizations in order to avoid the heavy censorship of findings that sometimes occurs when research occurs in highly competitive corporations who are loath to disrupt a carefully crafted public image. Another challenge is finding appropriate literature to support our work. While a body of literature is growing, some of it cited in this paper, more needs to be done. What has become clear to us in our exploratory research and in the literature reviews that we have undertaken is that current policy and practice is not working well for large numbers of persons with disabilities; this is particularly true when disability intersects with gender, race, and class issues. It is our hope that by identifying the issues in workplace learning that were identified in our study and describing our findings in this chapter, we will motivate more scholars in work-and-learning and critical policy studies to pursue these questions with the vigour and rigor that they deserve.

NOTES

1. In Canada The Employment Equity Act, renewed in 2002, is designed to embrace the needs of Aboriginal, visible minority, and women workers as well as workers with disabilities.
2. The HRDSC report, *Advancing the Inclusion of People with Disabilities* (2006), reports that, while the news is not yet good, it is moderately encouraging. The Report suggests: Overall, the employment situation of people with disabilities has improved over the last six years. The percentage

of people with disabilities who were employed full-time, full-year increased from 42.4% in 1999 to 46.4% in 2004, compared to an increase from 62.8% to 65.3% for people without disabilities in the same period (p. 48).

3 The perception of the needs of disabled persons for equipment and/or accommodation as 'special' was seen as highly problematic by participants at the symposium who noted that able workers are 'accommodated' in workplaces as well, but because doing so is normed, these accommodations become invisible until those whose minds and bodies do not conform to the elusive norm can only be included through 'special' accomodations.

4 See Blackmore & Sachs, 2007; Hennessy & Sawchuk, 2003 for a more general discussion of workplace stress in managerialist work environments characterized by increased high stakes accountability, competitiveness, and entrepreneurialism. The first looks at the effects of managerialism on women administrators in K-12 schooling in Australia and the second looks at the restructuring of work under the watchful gaze of a major management consultant firm in Canada.

5 A pseudonym has been assigned to add to the clarity of the idea being explored and protect the identity of the participant.

6 A recent case in Red Deer, Alberta demonstrates this point. A multiple dwelling building was built that was fully wheelchair accessible as part of an initiative to provide affordable housing to low income and disabled persons. The project was made possible with the support of public funds and managed by a non-profit organization. Some residents received rent assistance and rents were maintained at an affordable level, despite rising rents in the private sector. Claiming a financial loss, the non-profit organization running the building was given permission to sell it for conversion to renovated condos – renovations that would remove accessibility at well over $200,000 each – despite the fact that Red Deer would no longer have affordable accessible accommodation with the loss of this building.

7 I am not discounting the possibility of a sex change but the population percentage who choose to do so is significantly lower than those who may become disabled – seldom a choice for those who experience disability temporarily or permanently.

8 The largest proportion of employed workers fit this demographic, an age range that is often considered the most productive work years.

REFERENCES

Agocs, C. (2002). Canada's employment equity legislation and policy, 1987–2000. The gap betweer policy and practice. *International Journal of Manpower*, *23*(2), 256–276. Retrieved from http:/ www.heretohelp.bc.ca/publications/factsheets/workplace.shtml

Blackmore, J., & Sachs, J. (2007). *Performing and reforming leaders: Gender, educational restructu ing, and organizational change*. Albany, NY: SUNY Press.

Chouinard, V. (1997). Making space for disabling differences: Challenging ableist geographies (gu editorial essay). *Environment and Planning D: Society and Space*, *15*(4), 379–386.

Church, K., Frazee, K., Luciani, T., Panitch, M., & Seeley, P. (2007). Dressing corporate subjectivi Learning what to wear to the bank. In S. Billett, T. Fenwick, & M. Somerville (Eds.), *W subjectivity and learning: Understanding learning through working life*. Dordrect, Netherl Springer.

England, K. (2003). Disabilities, gender and employment: Social exclusion, employment equi Canadian banking. *The Canadian Geographer*, *47*(4), 429–450.

Gleeson, B. (1999). Can technology overcome the disabling city? In R. Butler & H. Parr (Eds. *and body spaces: Geographies of illness, impairment and disability*. London and Nev Routledge.

Hall, E. (1999). Workspaces – refiguring the disability-employment debate. In R. Butler & (Eds.), *Mind and body spaces: Geographies of illness, impairment and disability*. London York: Routledge.

Hennessy, T., & Sawchuk, P. (2003). Worker responses to technological change in the Cana sector: Issues of learning and labour process. *Journal of Workplace Learning*, *15*(7/8), 31

Houghton, A. (2006). *Disability effective inclusive policies: Student and staff pers experiences throughout the student lifecycle*. Paper presented at the 36th Annual Conference, 4–6 July 2006, Trinity and All Saints College, Leeds.

Ipsos Canada. (2006). *The 2006 Expedia vacation deprivation survey*. Toronto. Retrieved August 14, 2007, from www.ipsos-na.com/news/pressrelease.cfm?id=3083.

Ipsos Canada. (2004). *Contributors to workplace absenteeism and healthcare benefit costs*. Toronto. Retrieved August 14, from www.ipsos-na.com/news/pressrelease.cfm?id=2089

Johnson, J. (2007, March 2). The full-circle effect – Sharing of education. Keynote address delivered to the *Disabilities and Health Research Network Conference: Participation in the Workplace*.

Parr, H., & Butler, R. (1999). New geographies of illness. In R. Butler & H. Parr (Eds.), *Mind and body spaces: Geographies of illness, impairment and disability*. London and New York: Routledge.

Valle, J., Solis, S., Volpitta, D., & Connor, D. (2004). The disability closet: Teachers with learning disabilities evaluate the risks and benefits of 'coming out'. *Equity & Excellence in Education*, *37*, 4–17.

Watson Wyatt Worldwide. (2005). *Rising mental health claims top list of concerns in 2005 Watson Wyatt Staying@Work survey*. Retrieved August 14, from www.watsonwyatt.com/news/press.asp?ID=15216

Wooten, L., & James, E. (2005). Challenges of organizational learning: Perpetuation of discrimination against employees with disabilities. *Behavioral Sciences and the Law*, *23*, 123–141.

ALISON TAYLOR AND PETER SAWCHUK

17. AFTERWORD

INTRODUCTION

The preceding chapters present a critical and expansive exploration of learning and work transitions. Interwoven throughout the text of the different authors are concerns about the assumptions underlying current education and training practices, policies and the implications of these policy approaches for the transitions of vulnerable groups. Alternative understandings of learning and work transitions are presented through case studies of pathways across institutional settings as well as within institutional settings, many of which offer detail on the lived experiences of immigrants, racialized and working class youth, people with disabilities, women, and Aboriginal youth. Through these analyses we gain an understanding of how academic inquiry can contribute to critical discussion within research and policy communities about transitions. This chapter revisits key themes and discusses directions for future work.

CHALLENGING KNOWLEDGE ECONOMY DISCOURSE

In our introduction, we note that educational and training policies and the practices of individuals and groups reflect contemporary discourses around the 'knowledge' economy. We noted from the beginning that, while recognizing that there is some evidence of a general trend toward more discretion for workers on technical tasks and more delegated authority for workers (Livingstone, 2009; see also Felstead, Gallie, Green and Zhou, 2004), we cannot assume that skill requirements for all workers have increased because of new technologies and more flexible organizational structures. Rather, there are different interpretations of macro-level changes that are rooted in different theoretical perspectives. For example, building on the types of questions we reflected upon throughout the text, does the demand for higher levels of skill in the labour market reflect an increase in actual skill requirements within workplaces (technological functionalist perspective)? Does it indicate competition between status and other social groups (Weberian social closure theory)? Does it suggest fundamental tensions within capitalism and the labour process (Marxist theory)?

Several authors in this book argue that the education and training policies they explore are rooted in a type of technological functionalism, which assumes that the educational requirements of jobs in industrial society constantly increase because of technological change and that formal education can and should provide the

P. Sawchuk and A. Taylor (eds.), Challenging Transitions in Learning and Work: Reflections on Policy and Practice, 325–333.

training necessary for more highly skilled jobs. In this regard, it could be said that formal education is seen as the most appropriate way to disseminate socially important knowledge and skills and to ensure the social placement of individuals based on merit (cf. Wotherspoon 1998). Schools and post-secondary institutions therefore help to sort individuals to fill different positions in the social hierarchy by streaming and credentialing in different 'pathways'. The idea of an educational 'arms race' which is described by some authors in this volume is consistent with human capital theory. This approach suggests that a society with more formally educated workers will be a more productive society and that increasing formal educational attainment will lead to higher earnings at an individual level.

Yet authors challenge these assumptions based on their research. For example, Livingstone suggests that there is an oversupply of post-secondary credentials based on the increasing proportion of workers—including professional and managerial workers—who feel overqualified for their jobs. Lehmann and Tenkorang's study of first generation youth entering university suggests that although they have gained access, important questions remain about whether they will achieve their educational and career goals given the increasing general gap between expectations and achievement and their lack of social capital. In other words, will the promises of the knowledge economy be fulfilled for all youth even if they enter post-secondary education? College credentials tend to yield lower returns on investment than university qualifications and can serve the latent function of 'cooling out' many working class and lower middle class students, according to Tambureno. Despite concerns about shortages in the skilled trades, Watt-Malcolm finds that there is little effort made to attract non-traditional entrants such as women. Therefore, a good case has been made that access to different kinds of formal education and the experience of formal education differs markedly across class groups.

Access to training and the utilization of skills in the workplace also differ across occupational groups. For example, Bélanger's study of firms in the biopharmaceutical sector indicates that highly qualified workers participated in more self-learning, non-formal and informal leaving within a logic of reflexivity, while training for less qualified workers seems to express a logic of conformity focused on immediate job requirements. These findings challenge the idea that all workers have gained more discretion and control over their work. Further, Sawchuk's study of the new computer system introduced to welfare workers supports the idea that technological change can challenge worker autonomy, not necessarily expand it. This work suggests that the effects of changes in the labour process cannot be assumed and that the implementation of change is likely to involve struggles that are rooted in contradictions within the capitalist labour process which, in turn, shapes intra-occupational transitions.

Moving beyond class and occupational groups, several authors suggest that gender, race, and disability form the bases of difference in the utilization of the talents and abilities of workers as well. For example, the evidence from chapters in this volume supports the idea that a 'transition penalty' is experienced by highly qualified immigrants whose credentials and work experience are often not recognized by Canadian employers. And, despite immigration policy that favours skilled workers, many are forced to repeat education, accept less valued work, and/or engage in volunteer work in the hopes of gaining access to appropriately skilled work (Guo; Slade and Schugurensky; Michandani et al.). Similarly, persons with disabilities must contend with institutional processes that emphasize their limitations and de-emphasize their skills. Disability is rendered as an individual problem to be disciplined and a technical problem to be controlled (Michalko and Titchkosky; Wallace and Fenwick). Mainstream institutions and programs that are set up to help vulnerable groups (women in trades; Black youth; First Nations youth) often construct these people as deficient, lack resources, may in some cases be mis-directed, and/or may simply have unrealistic expectations. For example, 'just-in-time' training that fails to acknowledge the needs of vulnerable women entering trades is likely to set them up to fail (Watt-Malcolm) while programs that assume linear transition models are likely to leave poor Black and Aboriginal youth behind (Carter, Taylor and Steinhauer).

Findings of authors regarding the difficult transition faced by vulnerable groups reinforce the idea that skill involves an assessment of value that is rooted in politics: it is socially constructed (Gaskell, 1992). Or, as Fenwick puts it (in Fenwick, Guo, Sawchuk, Valentin and Wheelahan, 2005): '[s]kill' is an illusion that floats according to the prevailing knowledge politics and observer bias' (p. 2). Further, the accumulation of power, resources, and rewards through the monopolization of skills and credentials structures positions within society (Murphy, 1988, p. 50). Therefore, the experiences of immigrants, persons with disabilities and other vulnerable groups can be argued to reflect social closure--a process of subordination whereby one group monopolizes advantages by closing off opportunities to another group of outsiders. The experience of vulnerable groups may additionally be explained, as we suggest in our introduction, in terms of the tensions and contradictions that are inherent within capitalist processes of control, conflict, accommodation, and occasional resistance. That is, the reproduction of social inequality may be actively supported by attempts to appropriate greater value from workers, which foments class antagonism and deepens divisions between different types of workers. From this perspective, as Lloyd and Payne (2002) suggest in the UK context, developing more equitable policies requires locating issues of class, conflict, and power at the centre of the skills debate.

THE NEED FOR A MORE HOLISTIC VIEW OF LIFE TRANSITIONS

Authors' work suggests alternatives to dominant ways of thinking about learning and work transitions. As stated in our introduction, first is the need to understand school-to-work transitions as but one inter-institutional dimension of the full range or dimensions of learning/work transition processes as a whole. Read as a whole in this way, we see that across the chapters school-to-work transitions are informed by transitions *between* school and the workplace, between schools and intermediate organizations (e.g., apprenticeship programs, youth employment initiatives, or agencies meant to support workplace accommodation for people with disabilities), *between* the workplace and the school system, *within* the school systems, and *within* organizations. Informing our understanding of this range of transitions is our call for expanded definitions of learning and work which seeks to recognize informal learning as well as organized or formal learning across instances of work, upaid as well as paid.

Focusing on the multiple, non-linear, and diverse learning and work transitions of different groups produces analyses that challenge the often limited focus of policy in Canada and other OECD countries on the delivery of formal programs by vocational education and training institutions (cf. Lloyd and Payne, 2002; OECD, 1998, 2000). For example, we see that persons with disabilities frequently experience challenging transitions through the various agencies that they are required to deal with as well as once they enter the paid workplace. Taking a holistic and longitudinal view of the experiences of these individuals, it is argued that problematic constructions of disability have made the transition across schools, post-secondary institutions, community agencies, and the workplace such that individuals constructed as 'disabled' begin to feel that they '*are* their disability' (Michalko and Titchkosky; Wallace and Fenwick). From this perspective, it is not sufficient to rely on institutional 'fixes' that focus only on schools or community agencies. Similarly, Guo's discussion of professional immigrants' decisions to return to formal education in the hopes of increasing their labour market prospects suggests that a strict focus on school-to-work transition models does not capture the experiences of their non-linear and challenging transitions. Taylor and Steinhauer's expanded view of transitions that examines institutional constraints within band-operated schools as well as the challenges presented by post-secondary institutions and economic realities in First Nations communities similarly highlights the need to think about transitions within and across institutions, and within the broader social, political, and economic context.

Related to the idea of expanding our ideas about transitions is the need to expand our ideas about work and learning. For example, Carter suggests that community programs for disadvantaged Black youth may contribute to their personal growth and development more effectively than do schools because they explicitly challenge linearity of school-to-work transitions to de-centre the 'lock-step approach to education and training.' They do this by providing a safe space for youth to informally learn work skills that are relevant to their lives without the immediate demand to gain credentials. This is consistent with the more holistic approach recommended to address lifelong learning in First Nations, Métis, and Inuit communities in Canada (Canadian Council on Learning, 2007) and has an important message for policy-makers in Canada and other countries who are fixated on the provision of short term, narrowly focused training for work. It also supports the argument of UK writers that the extent to which learning is emancipatory or oppressive depends partly on the balance and interrelationships between attributes of in/formality (Colley, Hodkinson and Malcom, 2003).

Immigrants' ideas about volunteer work as a necessary step to gain access to Canadian labour markets, further expands our conceptions about the function and value of 'unpaid' work as well as the potential for exploitation by employers. Focusing on the perceived value of informal learning for these voluntary workers compared to the formal training they received also expands our thinking about what workers need to learn, how, and where. At the same time, both Bélanger and

Sawchuk remind us that there is a tendency to ignore the informal individual and group learning experiences of employees within the workplace and that by surfacing this dimension of learning we see how transitions within the workplace are shaped by significant divisions (e.g., occupational group or age). Despite lip service to lifelong learning, the non-recognition of informal learning is therefore problematic.

FUTURE DIRECTIONS FOR RESEARCH

Our volume as a whole sustains a series of recommendations for future research which we summarize explicitly in this short section. Research over the past decade has in several cases begun the long road to rehabilitating the concept of 'transitions' across institutions and practices of learning and work. These efforts should include more international comparative initiatives that explore how particular groups of workers negotiate their transitions within and between formal education and work, and how changes in the institutional and regulatory context, and labour processes within particular firms and sectors affects transitions. Building on the chapters in this volume, we see three key areas where conceptual as well as empirical development needs to take place.

In the first instance, by the very nature of the diversity of entry points and empirical foci contained in this volume we demonstrate the relevance of, and need for more, attention to the non-linear nature of work and learning transitions. As Furlong, Cartmel, Biggart, Sweeting and West (2003) have noted, linearity still describes the 'successful' transitions process for some social groups and individuals despite the growth of employment during formal studies and the explosion of continuous education during periods of employment. However, there has also been a trend toward increasing fragmentation of opportunities and experience such that the processes of transition are 'highly differentiated, reflecting and constructing social divisions in society in complex ways' (Evans and Furlong, 1997). Therefore, what is clear is that non-linearity has become a more appropriate descriptor of learning and work transitions. While a number of writers focusing on school-to-work transitions in other countries have made this observation (cf. Raffe, 2003; Shildrick and MacDonald, 2007; Dwyer and Wyn, 2001), studies of other types of transition are needed. A coherent understanding of the non-linear character of transitions must be built upon the bed-rock of quality particularistic cases, the relative paucity of which currently hampers meaningful theoretical as well as policy-oriented conclusions.

Second, while learning and work transitions feature instances of both linearity and non-linearity, central to understanding either is the rejection of universality and the recognition of social differences and identity (cf. Stokes and Wyn, 2007). The range of social differences dealt with in this volume offer, in part, an explanation of the non-linearity of contemporary transitions as well as the unevenness of outcomes in terms of economic inclusion, exclusion and opportunity. However, the recognition of social differences in the research literature that focuses on learning and work transitions is in its early stages; and moreover, it has fixated primarily on youth and young adults. We expand on this with the inclusion of adults. However, the research herein speaks to social difference and its reproduction at particular 'nodes' in the learning and work transitions web. What is clear is that understanding of each form of social difference explored in this volume requires exploration across the full range of progressive and digressive points of learning and work transition: a task for future research by our authors, ourselves and others.

Third, we recommend further research into the effects of specific sectoral dynamics which in turn shape the functioning of specific labour markets. Clearly the 'demand side' of the learning and work transitions process continues to be under-recognized by many, though not all scholars. An understanding of the dynamics of job entry specific to economic sectors and indeed specific types of firms is required for an adequate understanding of transition processes. Research focused on the organizational responses to globalization has been conducted (cf. Lauder, Brown and Ashton, 2008) as has work focused on the transitions of different groups between formal education and training and work. But there is arguably a need for more Canadian and international research that links institutional, sectoral, and organizational changes with transitions in the lives of individuals. Chapters in this book which explored occupational transitions in the public sector and pharmaceutical industry expand the more narrowly conceived notion of school-to-work transition, and provide insight into participation in activities such as continuing education (e.g., Courtney 1992; Sawchuk 2003). There is therefore potential to bridge disparate but related academic literatures. As we saw, an expansive understanding of learning to include both formal and informal attributes becomes necessary. Likewise, it is at the point of production, within the work process itself, that the skills utilization or 'under-employment' problem comes most clearly into view.

FUTURE DIRECTIONS FOR POLICY

The studies in this book challenge assumptions around the linearity and universality of learning and work transitions that are reflected in policies of the World Bank, International Monetary Fund, OECD, and national and provincial, state or territorial governments. Because many countries are grappling with similar issues related to the political economy of skill and social justice within a globalized economy, we hope this work will contribute to discussions beyond Canada. Other countries are exploring questions about who is able to participate in learning and work and on what terms. As we note in our introduction, current policies generally assume that the problem is with vocational education and training (VET) systems which are not producing skilled labourers in sufficient numbers to ensure competitiveness in the knowledge economy. However, this 'supply side' focus ignores difficulties in gaining access to VET and labour markets, and the lack of utilization of skills of vulnerable groups. Research reported by authors suggests that in addition to thinking about ways to improve high school, continuing education, and post-secondary education programs, there needs to be more discussion within the policy community about the following issues:

First, although hardly a new issue in policy circles across most industrialized countries, access to post-secondary educational programs remains a serious issue that should not be allowed to submerge. For example, there continues to be a strong correlation between university attendance and parents' education and family income. Working-class and lower middle-class students are more likely to attend college programs or enrol in apprenticeships. The educational attainment of Aboriginal youth is much lower than for other Canadian youth. High school streaming in school launches young people on different post-secondary pathways and also needs to be a topic for discussion. Who is included, who is excluded and the mechanisms by which selection occurs are therefore important. Since Canada has one of the highest rates of post-secondary educational participation among OECD countries, we can assume that such questions are even more pressing in other contexts. Such traditional matters, at risk of invisibility in national contexts where overall educational attainment levels are on the rise, remain important policy questions that play a central role in labour market access.

Second, learning and work transitions are not linear and formal educational programs are not the answer for all youth and adults. Therefore, there is a need to look beyond programs that privilege credentials (even those with little labour market value) above all else. Community organizations that provide opportunities for non-formal and informal learning to vulnerable groups must be considered as legitimate players in any well-functioning VET system of the twenty-first century. Bridging programs are important but must go beyond 'quick fixes' by responding to student needs and abilities, and providing sufficient training and support to maximize success. We concur with some of the features that contribute to effective youth transitions that were identified by the OECD (2000) as follows: a healthy economy; bridges between vocational education, apprenticeship, and tertiary education; tightly-knit safety nets for those at risk; and effective institutions and processes. Of course, what constitutes effective institutions and processes is open to interpretation, depending on policy objectives and assumptions. For example, another feature identified by the OECD is 'clearly defined learning pathways and qualifications frameworks,' which potentially narrow the type of learning and learner that is privileged, and the ability of individuals to deviate from established paths.

Third, expanding on this question of development of the VET system, we view it as increasingly important for policy to address 'demand side' issues in a way that recognizes social differences. That is, access and retention issues in the workplace related to the discrimination often faced by persons with disabilities, women in non-traditional occupations, immigrant groups, as well as Aboriginals and other racialized groups tend to be de-emphasized. Rather, this approach places blame on individuals and educational and training institutions for poor labour market and economic performance rather than ensuring that employers also take responsibility. This is a matter of state regulation. A strong role for workers' organizations and regulatory measures is arguably needed to move employers toward more democratic work practices (cf. Lloyd and Payne, 2002). In addition, despite attempts to engage employers in 'transitions' partnerships, more attention needs to be given to ensuring that they are aware of issues related to learning and work transitions and are taking steps to ensure that skills are developed, recognized, and rewarded in the workplace.

Fourth, there is more general matter of which can be termed 'the problem of policy silos'. Our focus on inter-institutional and intra-institutional transitions lends support to the argument that policies that cross traditional boundaries (e.g., compulsory and post-secondary education, training, social services, economic sectors and firms) are needed. While this is recognized by attempts at 'joined-up' policy in Canada and other countries (Riddell and Tett, 2001), studies reported in this book suggest that much work needs to be done. Part of this work involves providing greater public support to develop and sustain partnerships that involve a wider variety of institutional players (cf. Taylor, 2006). In addition, there is a need for different levels of government to address the lack of coherence across policies related to education and training, particularly those directed towards vulnerable groups (cf. Taylor, Friedel and Edge, 2009).

Finally, there is the matter of credentialism. Related to several of the above recommendations, there is a need to investigate the significance of formal educational credentials as job requirement criteria by asking what skills are actually required for certain types of work, what is the relationship between credentials and these skills, who is excluded by 'credential inflation,' and what is the role of formal education beyond credentialing graduates (cf. Livingstone, 2009). These questions suggest the need to question the education 'arms race' not only for its inefficiency, but for its role in practices of social closure. Related to this, policies that treat learning more holistically and that recognize, utilize, and reward workers' capabilities in formal education and work should be explored in order to address the challenging transitions in learning and work that have been well-documented in this book.

REFERENCES

Brooks, R. (2007). Transitions from education to work in the twenty-first century. *International Journal of Lifelong Education, 26*(5), 491–493.

Canadian Council on Learning. (2007). *Redefining how success is measured in First Nations, inuit and métis learning*. Ottawa: Authors.

Colley, H., Hodkinson, P., & Malcom, J. (2003). *Informality and formality in learning. A report for the learning and skills research centre*. London, England.

Courtney, S. (1992). *Why adults learn: Towards a theory of participation in adult education*. New York: Routledge.

Dwyer, P., & Wynn, J. (2001). *Youth, education and risk*. London: Routledge/Falmer.

Evans, K., & Furlong, A. (1997). Metaphors of youth transitions: Niches, pathways, trajectories or navigations. In J. Bynner, L. Chisholm, & A. Furlong (Eds.), *Youth, citizenship and social chance*. Aldershot: Ashgate.

Felstead, A., Gallie, D., Green, F., & Zhou, Y. (2007). *Skills at work 1986–2006*. Oxford/Cardiff, UK: ESRC Centre on Skills Knowledge and Organizational Performance.

Fenwick, T., Guo, S., Sawchuk, P., Valentin, C., & Wheelahan, L. (2005, December). Essential Skills, Globalization and Neo-Liberal Policy: Challenging Skills-Based Agendas for Workplace Learning. In *Proceedings of the fourth international conference on researching work and learning*. Sydney, Australia.

Furlong, A., Cartmel, F., Biggart, A., Sweeting, H., & West, P. (2003). *Youth transitions: Patterns of vulnerability and processes of social inclusion*. Edinburgh: Scottish Executive.

Gaskell, J. (1992). *Gender matters from school to work*. Toronto: OISE Press.

Lauder, H., Brown, P., & Ashton, D. (2008). Globalisation, skill formation and the varieties of capitalism approach. *New Political Economy, 13*(1), 19–35.

Livingstone, D. W. (Ed.). (2009). *Education and jobs: Exploring the gaps*. Toronto: University of Toronto Press.

Murphy, R. (1988). *Social closure: The theory of monopolization and exclusion*. Oxford: Clarendon.

Riddell, S., & Tett, L. (2001). Joined-up or fractured policy? In S. Riddell & L. Tett (Eds.), *Education, social justice and inter-agency working. Joined-up or fractured policy?* London/New York: Routledge.

OECD. (1998). *Pathways and participation in vocational and technical education and training*. Paris: Author.

OECD. (2000). *From initial education to working life: Making transitions work*. Paris: OECD.

Raffe, D. (2003). Pathways linking education & work: A review of concepts, research, and policy debates. *Journal of Youth Studies*, *6*(1), 3–19.

Shildrick, T., & MacDonald, R. (2007). Biographies of exclusion: Poor work and poor transitions. *International Journal of Lifelong Education*, *25*(5), 589–604.

Stokes, H., & Wyn, J. (2007). Constructing identities and making careers: Young people's perspectives on work and learning. *International Journal of Lifelong Education*, *26*(5), 495–511.

Sawchuk, P. H. (2003). The 'unionization effect' amongst adult computer learners. *British Journal of Sociology of Education*, *24*(5), 639–648.

Taylor, A. (2006). The challenges of partnership in school-work transition. *Journal of Vocational Education and Training*, *58*(3), 319–336.

Taylor, A., Friedel, T., & Edge, L. (2009). *Pathways for first nations and métis youth in the oil sands*. Report prepared for Canadian Policy Research Networks, Ottawa.

Wotherspoon, T. (1998). *The sociology of education in Canada: Critical perspectives*. Toronto: Oxford University Press.

CPSIA information can be obtained at www.ICGtesting.com
Printed in the USA
LVOW09s1734210616

493517LV00004B/93/P